INDIA'S ISRAEL POLICY

INDIA'S ISRAEL POLICY

P. R. Kumaraswamy

Columbia University Press New York

Columbia University Press
Publishers Since 1893
New York Chichester, West Sussex

Library of Congress Cataloging-in-Publication Data
Kumaraswamy, P. R.
India's Israel policy / P. R. Kumaraswamy.
p. cm.
Includes bibliographical references and index.
ISBN 978-0-231-15204-4 (cloth : alk. paper)—
ISBN 978-0-231-52548-0 (ebook)
1. India—Foreign relations—Israel. 2. Israel—Foreign relations—India. 3. India—Foreign relations—20th century. 4. Religion and politics—India—History—20th century.
5. Arab-Israeli conflict—Influence. I. Title.

DS450.I7K86 2010
327.5405694—dc22

2009051651

Columbia University Press books are printed on permanent and durable acid-free paper.
This book is printed on paper with recycled content.

Printed in the United States of America
c 10 9 8 7 6 5 4 3 2 1

References to Internet Web sites (URLs) were accurate at the time of writing. Neither the author nor Columbia University Press is responsible for URLs that may have expired or changed since the manuscript was prepared.

To my wife, Lin Qian, for all her love and affection

Contents

Acknowledgments

"I have nothing to lose except my obscurity." That was the only answer of mine that would satisfy Netanel Lorch, Israel's military historian. At a small farewell lunch in the Maiersdorf Faculty Club at the Hebrew University of Jerusalem, Lorch, who had served in Sri Lanka, wondered whether I would be as critical once I returned to India. That promise, which I made in October 1988, kept me going.

It is my guru, Professor M. S. Agwani, who, in his own intimidating style, made me a serious student of the Middle East. It was under his supervision that I completed my doctorate on the subject. Studying under him remains an enduring and memorable experience for me.

I had the good fortune to have had teachers, especially Professors K. R. Singh, Gopalji Malviya, Sadanand Patra, and A. H. H. Abidi, who showered me with great patience, encouragement, and abiding personal interest.

Professor Subramanian Swamy's provocative November 1982 article in *Sunday* kindled my interest in and inspired me to study the prolonged absence of Indo-Israeli relations. He found time in his busy schedule to go over my manuscript and offer critical comments.

A number of leading figures in both India and Israel shared their knowledge and wisdom. They include President Chaim Herzog and Morarji

Desai, the former prime minister. Starting from my first meeting in July 1988, the late Walter Eytan spent hours in clarifying many of my doubts. Ya'acov Shimoni, the former Israeli diplomat, kindly allowed me access to his private papers.

Over the years I have had the fortune of interacting with innumerable scholar-friends, including Ashok Kapur, Avraham Altman, Avraham Sela, Barry Jacobs, Barry Rubin, Ben-Ami Shillony, C. Raja Mohan, Dan and Lihi Laor, David Shulman, Edy Kaufman, Efraim Inbar, Efraim Karsh, Eli Joffee, Gerald Steinberg, Gideon Shimoni, Hamid Ansari, Jasjit Singh, M. L. Sondhi, Mark Heller, Moshe Ma'oz, Moshe Yegar, Naomi Chazan, Nissim Rejwan, Reuven Kahane, Steve Cohen, V. Narayana Rao, Yezid Sayigh, Yitzhak Galnoor, and Yitzhak Shichor. In times of crisis, Sreeradha Datta has always been around and *smilingly* spent long hours going over many of my academic writings.

I had the privilege of meeting a host of Indian diplomats who served in Israel and who shared their knowledge with me. The kindness and generosity of Anita Nayar, N. A. Prasad, Pinak Chakravarthy, Deepak Kaul, P. K. Singh, Ranjan Mathai, Raminder Jassel, Shiv Shankar Menon, Subrata Das, and Virendra Gupta are second only to their professionalism and passion for promoting bilateral ties. Despite his busy schedule, Ambassador Arun Kumar Singh went over my draft and offered valuable comments on post-1992 developments.

Over the years, I have interacted with a number of Israeli diplomats, especially David Danielle, David Granit, David Matnai, Eliyahu Elath, Mark Sofer, Netanel Lorch, Oded Ben-Hur, Reuven Dafni, Ruth Kahanoff, Yossef Hassin, and Zev Sufott. Innumerable persons shared their knowledge and clarified some of the nuances of bilateral relations: Ari Rath, Erza Kolet, Judith Roumani, M. R. Masani, Madhu Limaye, Yoram Mayorek, and Yuhuda Paz. In the late 1980s, I interacted with a number of Palestinian figures, including Hanna Sinora, Lesly Abu-Katar, Manual Hassassain, Mehdi Abdul Hadi, and Nafez Assaily.

I wish to express my sincere thanks to the staff of the following libraries and institutions for their help: in Jerusalem, *Al Fajr* (daily), the Central Zionist Archives, the Israel State Archives, and *The Jerusalem Post* archives. In India: the American Studies Research Center, Hyderabad; the Indian Council of World Affairs; the Institute for Defense Studies and Analyses; Jawaharlal Nehru University; the Lok Sabha Secretariat; the National Archives of India; and the Nehru Memorial Museum and Library, all in New Delhi. The library staff of the Harry S. Truman Research

Institute for the Advancement of Peace at the Hebrew University of Jerusalem, especially Amnon, Avi, Cecil, Riccardo, and Tirza, offered me a good working environment. The acrimonious debates at the Institute for Defense Studies and Analyses, where I briefly worked, influenced my thinking on contemporary developments in the Middle East.

It was my field trip to Israel in 1988, which was generously sponsored by Jawaharlal Nehru University, that opened up my horizon. I am thankful to the Truman Institute for being my academic home during my long stays in Israel.

When I was down and out, numerous friends have provided encouragement and moral support. They include Atul Kumar, Atul Mishra, G. V. C. Naidu, Liat Peretz, Narasaiah, P. Ventakeswaran, Pathaks, Rajesh and Raji, Ranjita Das, Sima Baidya, T. Sreedhar Rao, Uri and Navah Ramon, V. Rajagopal, and V. Ramakrishanan.

Since joining JNU in 1999, my graduate students have given me comfort and stimulation and have often enabled me to sharpen my understanding of the Middle East. Special mention is reserved for Bhupendra Kumar Singh and Khinv Raj, who helped me solve innumerable problems along the way. On numerous occasions, my colleagues, especially Girijesh Pant, Gulshan Dietl, and P. C. Jain, gave me a helping hand.

Since the late 1980s, I have enjoyed stimulating intellectual exchanges with my peers, especially Professor Irene Eber. In between her moving house, proofreading, and organizing conferences, she painstakingly went over my manuscript. Master and Naomi have made many of my weekends a delightful diversion. For nearly two decades, my friend D. Shyam Babu has remained a great source of inspiration, intellectual honesty, and professionalism.

When many others were reluctant, Anne Routon had faith in me and saw this manuscript through its stages of publication. She made working with Columbia University Press a pleasure. Thanks, my friend. My gratitude also goes to my three anonymous reviewers; their inputs have made this a better book. Thanks also to Robert Fellman for his immensely detailed and very thoughtful copyediting.

My parents-in-law and Lin Xiaozhong and Lin Tong have been generous with their kindness and affection.

All my life, I have enjoyed the love and affection of my grandparents, my late mother, Sreedhar, Jayanthi, and Ravi Mama. Appa has been my friend, philosopher, and guide and, despite all my limitations and shortcomings, he has retained his abiding faith in me.

Ever since I first met her in Jerusalem in the summer of 1988, my wife Lin Qian has happily endured my eccentricities and unending demands. To her I dedicate this volume.

I am grateful to all those mentioned here and many more. As the Bhagavat Gita says, *You are your friend and you are your own enemy.* And all errors and omissions are mine.

INDIA'S ISRAEL POLICY

The good things in life are like the birth of a child. Ninety percent waiting.
—James Michener

1 Introduction

When it comes to the Jews, Israel, and the wider Middle East, even Mahatma Gandhi is not infallible. At one level, he appeared to have repudiated any Jewish claims to Palestine. This was evidenced by a widely quoted statement he made in 1939: "Palestine belongs to the Arabs in the same sense that England belongs to the English and France to the French."[1] For many Indians and non-Indians alike, this signaled his unequivocal rejection of a Jewish national home in Palestine. Careful examination of his other statements, including a confidential note he wrote to his old Jewish friend Hermann Kallenbach in July 1937, presents a much complex picture. Moreover, on the eve of the World War II, the Mahatma strongly advocated Jewish nonviolence against Adolf Hitler. This, he hoped, would melt the Fuehrer's heart and force him to abandon his destructive path. At the same time, the Indian leader chose to "understand" the Palestinian Arabs' use of violent tactics against the British authorities. In a similar vein, a decade earlier the Mahatma did not demand that the Indian Muslims practice nonviolence as a precondition for his support for the Khilafat struggle.[2] A very selective use of morality, personified by Mahatma Gandhi himself, has been the most dominant feature of India's Israel policy. Until full relations were established in January 1992, India was cool, unfriendly, and even hostile to the Jewish state. This was so despite India being free of any forms of anti-Semitism and remaining friendly toward the Jewish people since their first known arrival in India, following the destruction of the Second Temple in A.D. 70. Despite being hospitable to the Jews, India's policy toward Israel was long manifested by nonrelations rather than by cordial ties. The prolonged absence of diplomatic ties with Israel is an aberration in India's overall attitude toward the Jewish people.

For decades, Israel remained the most controversial and deeply divisive issue in India's foreign policy. The Indian attitude toward Israel was in sharp contrast to its policies regarding China and Pakistan. Prolonged differences, tensions, and even armed conflicts with these countries did not prevent New Delhi from maintaining normal diplomatic ties with both countries. Israel, with whom it never had any bilateral dispute, remained an outcast. The prolonged nonrelation was justified by moral self-righteousness, and critical issues such as domestic influences rarely received adequate attention. The tremendous progress in bilateral relations since 1992 should be seen against the backdrop of protracted Indian reluctance to come to terms with Jewish history and nationalist aspirations.

Regarding India's foreign policy, Israel occupies a unique, controversial, and unparalleled position. Until full diplomatic relations were established in January 1992, Israel did not fit into any pattern or model that could explain New Delhi's policy toward the world outside its borders. No other issue was as contentious and acrimonious as the absence of formal Indian ties with Israel. It lacked domestic consensus, exposed a hypocritical aspect of India's foreign policy, and dented the moral credentials of India's venerated leaders. For nearly four decades, it was an aberration and, at times, an embarrassment for the mandarins of India's policy.

Unrequited love. This term aptly explains the Indian responses to prolonged Israeli overtures. Since the founding of the Jewish state, India reacted and responded, often negatively, to various Israeli efforts toward recognition and normalization. India was active when violence erupted in the Middle East and did not accommodate Israel's concerns and fears. While Israel eagerly sought close ties, Nehru's India was reluctant and coy. For over four decades, it was India that decided, shaped, and controlled the bilateral developments. In the absence of diplomatic ties between 1948 and 1992, even the term "relations" may not be appropriate. During this phase, nonrelations remained the hallmark of India's Israel policy. It was only after Prime Minister P. V. Narasimha Rao's decision in

January 1992 that one can speak of "relations" and debate the influence of one upon the foreign-policy interests and calculations of the other.

Despite the eventual emergence of widespread support, India's Israel policy never enjoyed unanimous support within the country. The issue was first discussed in the Indian Constituent Assembly in December 1947, more than five months before the establishment of Israel.[3] Since then, the official Indian policy regarding normalization and India's attitude toward Israel has come under close public scrutiny and criticism. Some of the most acrimonious debates in the Indian parliament revolved around Israel. More than any other foreign-policy agenda, the recognition of Israel and, subsequently, the establishment of diplomatic relations with it preoccupied the Indian lawmakers. The absence of relations became a powerful instrument through which the opposition could vent their disapproval and anger, and such a stance should not be dismissed as a political gimmick.

The Indian leaders were equally aware that their position regarding normalization was rather weak and untenable. Over the years, a number of them admitted that relations should have been established immediately after Nehru's decision to recognize Israel in September 1950. During his meeting with the visiting Israeli diplomat Gideon Rafael in 1961, the Indian prime minister conceded that very point.[4] Likewise, his close confidant Krishna Menon told Michael Brecher that if India "had sent an ambassador at that time [that is, soon after recognition] there would have been no difficulties."[5] Morarji Desai, who was prime minister from 1977 to 1979, reflected similar sentiments.[6] In the wake of normalization, Indian intellectuals argued that had relations been normalized in the 1950s, the hype and expectations surrounding the 1992 decision would have been prevented.[7]

The unfriendliness toward Israel contradicted the traditional Indian attitude toward Judaism. Historically, anti-Semitism has been alien in Indian culture. Theologically, Hinduism can and did coexist with Judaism without much difficulty, in part because of their mutual suspicion and opposition to conversion. As a nonproselytizing religion, Judaism does not threaten Hinduism. This is in contrast to the other two Semitic religions, Christianity and Islam, for whom converting others into their faith remains a cardinal theological goal. Furthermore, at the height of the Nazi persecution a number of European Jews took refuge in India, and amid the nationalist struggle against the British, Nehru, as the leader of the Indian National Congress (or Congress Party), was instrumental in securing employment for some of these refugees. At the end of the World War II, India became a safe haven for Jewish refugees from Iraq and Afghanistan until their emigration to the newly formed state of Israel. Official hostility toward Israel but prolonged hospitality toward the Jewish people is another paradoxical element of India's Israel policy.

As the opposition parties argued, Nehru's India remained hostile to Israel even in the absence of any tensions—let alone disputes. If the public postures are an indication, India remained more hostile to Israel than toward its political, territorial, and military adversaries. Between 1947 and 1992, India fought four military conflicts with Pakistan and China. In India's assessment, both these countries are in illegal occupation of vast Indian territories. The 1962 Sino-Indian conflict dealt a crushing blow to Nehru's leadership aspirations in the Third World. In the case of Pakistan, the hostilities often spilled into cross-border terrorism and its support for separatist militants in Kashmir. Despite these conflicts, New Delhi has always maintained formal ties with both Pakistan and China, and even during the military conflicts India did not expel their ambassadors. India decreased its diplomatic presence in Beijing following the Sino-Indian war but did not terminate its relations. Israel remained an exception. A controversial media remark even led to the Israeli consul (the highest Israeli representative in India) being declared *persona non grata* in 1982.

Israel was unique in another sense. India's refusal to maintain formal relations did not inhibit its leaders from seeking help and assistance from the Jewish state. Ironically, this trend began with Prime Minister Nehru. A few months after voting against the UN partition plan, he sought agricultural experts from Israel.[8] A couple years later, despite a stalemate on the diplomatic front, India again sought similar assistance from Israel. This seeking help without normalization was more pronounced in the security arena. During the 1962 Sino-Indian debacle, Nehru sought and obtained limited quantities of military assistance from Ben-Gurion. Likewise, anti-Israeli statements in public did not inhibit his daughter, Prime Minister Indira Gandhi, from establishing closer ties with the Israeli intelligence establishment.[9]

This private sympathy and public hostility was common to a number of Indian personalities. Even those who were friendlier toward Israel had their limits, at least in public. Sardar K. M. Panikkar, India's first ambassador to China, personified this duality. In early 1947, he was confident that after partition India would be free from Muslim influence and would be more sympathetic toward Zionist aspirations in Palestine. A few years later, he even lamented India's belated recognition of Israel. Yet in his autobiography, published in 1955, he sang a different tune and joined the official chorus against the formation of Israel.[10] The same holds true for Rabindranath Tagore, a Nobel laureate, who felt that his sympathies for Jewish nationalist aspirations in Palestine were "private" views that should not be publicized.[11]

This duality continued after India gained independence. The Israeli collaboration with the British and French during the Suez war of 1956 provided an opportunity for Nehru, as the Israeli action had all the hallmarks of an aggression against a fellow member of the emerging Afro-Asian bloc and was a sign of collaboration with the imperial powers. Using the conflict as an excuse, he formally deferred normalization with Israel. But at the same time, he expressed no qualms about seeking closer ties with London and Paris. Indeed, his opposition to the policies of the imperial powers was accompanied by his desire for stronger bilateral ties with them. The British aggression against Nasser did not impede India's continued membership in the British Commonwealth, and the same holds true for Nehru's policy toward France. It is thus not possible to explain away India's Israel policy within the context of its opposition to and disapproval of the policies of the latter or its connections to colonialism. Indeed, with the sole exception of its opposition to apartheid in South Africa, India's opposition to the policies of a country was not accompanied by its refusal to maintain normal relations with it.

Furthermore, Nehru's strong disapproval of Israel's action during the Suez crisis was accompanied by an accommodating and pro-Soviet view during the roughly contemporaneous Hungarian crisis. Even within the Middle East, India has been selective in condemning aggression. The anger and frustration exhibited by India following the Israeli actions against Egypt was conspicuously absent when Saddam Hussein invaded, occupied, and annexed Kuwait in August 1990. Likewise, Indian leaders rarely spoke in support of the national rights or to condemn the statelessness of the Kurdish people.

During the 1950s, securing international acceptance of communist China was a major foreign-policy priority for Nehru. He wanted the outside world, especially the United States, to have normal ties with China, even if the West had strong reservations over the nature of the government in Beijing. He stressed that political differences among nations could never be resolved through exclusion and boycott. He even urged the Arabs to resolve their differences with Israel through negotiation. Nehru and his successors, however, could not internalize these noble ideals and treat Israel as a normal country. Far from treating it as a friend—let alone an ally—for over four decades, India was not prepared to maintain even a modicum of ties with it. As David Ben-Gurion lamented, the high moral principles advocated by Mahatma Gandhi and Nehru were never applied to India's Israel policy.[12]

Israel was an exceptional case even when compared to Pakistan, a country described by some as India's "center of gravity."[13] During the cold war, India's foreign-policy choices were often shaped by the attitude of other countries toward Pakistan. The pro-Pakistan slant of the United States, for example, partly resulted in India moving closer to Moscow. Although India was not in a position to retaliate over Middle Eastern support and sympathy for Pakistan, its unequivocal support for the Arabs over Israel was never reciprocated. If the Arab states (especially Nasser's Egypt) remained neutral during the Sino-Indian war of 1962, most remained sympathetic to Pakistan during the Indo-Pakistan wars of 1965 and 1971. Though the impact of Arab support did not influence the outcome of these conflicts, they pointed to India's limited influence in the Middle East. As King Abdullah remarked during his state visit in January 2006, the Arabs perceived India to be a friend but saw Pakistan as an Islamic brethren. During much of the cold-war era, India's influence in the region vis-à-vis Pakistan was limited, and India never took the Arabs to task for their refusal to accommodate Indian concerns, despite the latter acceding to their demands regarding Israel. It settled for suffering in silence. Avoiding any open discussion on Arab support for Pakistan, New Delhi merely highlighted the Arab "understanding" during conflicts and thereby hoped to minimize any negative fallout.

Whichever way one looks at it, Israel has been a unique, controversial, and at times hypocritical dimension in India's foreign policy.

Contrasts and Convergences

Contrasts with Israel were often used to explain prolonged nonrelations. There is nothing in common, the argument went, and therefore no relations. The contrasts between India and Israel are interesting and colorful. While the Indian nationalists were fighting the British, the mainstream Labor Zionist leadership was compelled to identify itself with the imperial power and its interests. Obviously the Zionists could not have fought the British, the only power that was prepared to endorse and help their political aspirations, and still hope for a Jewish national home in Palestine. Following Israel's and India's independence, the two countries took divergent paths. Anti-imperialism emerged as a cornerstone of India's foreign policy; driven by regional hostility and isolation, Israel was compelled to continue and even strengthen its links with the imperial powers. Such a stand complicated things for Israel, especially when anti-colonialism and anti-imperialism became the theme song for the newly independent countries of the Third World.

Second, the partition of the subcontinent was relatively easy and mutually accepted. Despite their ideological reservations and opposition, the mainstream nationalists accepted the religion-based partition of India. The Congress Party opposed the two-nation theory propounded by Mohammed Ali Jinnah but accepted the communal partition as a price for freedom. Despite the communal riots that followed, both the Congress Party and the Muslim League accepted and implemented the partition of the subcontinent. This was not the case in the Middle East. The Arab majority in Palestine unanimously rejected the UN plan that advocated the partition of the Mandate territory into independent Arab and Jewish states. They were supported by the neighboring Arab countries, who opposed, both politically and militarily, the implementation of the UN plan. Indeed, until the late 1980s, mainstream Palestinian leadership refused to accept the UN resolution of November 29, 1947.[14] As a result, unlike South Asia, the division of Palestine proved to be agonizing, complicated, and protracted. This in turn had negative repercussions for Israel and its political and diplomatic fortunes.

Third, India's identification with the process of decolonization in Asia and Africa was consistent and hence relatively fruitful. Israel, on the other hand, could not take a stand. Preoccupation over its problems with the Arab world forced it to be less enthusiastic about decolonization. The convergence of its interests with France over Algeria, for example, led to both countries forging closer ties in the 1950s and resulted in nuclear cooperation. The same holds true for other former colonies who gained independence from the European powers. As with the *yishuv* over British India, the colonial powers proved to be politically more attractive to Israel than the liberation movements.

Fourth, India was more fortunate than Israel in facing organized hostility. In spite of its best efforts, Pakistan was unable to forge an anti-Indian political bloc. Though at times critical of India over Kashmir and the welfare of Indian Muslims, the Organization of the Islamic Conference (OIC) has not been hostile to New Delhi. India has been far too important politically and economically for the Muslim world to adopt an explicitly hostile stand, especially when India had closer ties with some of the prominent members of the OIC. Israel, however, was less fortunate. The Arab League, formed in 1945, emerged as the principal political forum against the Jewish state, and an anti-Israeli posture soon became a cover for deeply seated inter-Arab quarrels. First, the Arab League tried to prevent the formation of Israel. Once this failed, the Arab League members sought to strangle the newly formed state by invading Israel hours after its establishment. Following the Arab-Israeli war of 1948 (or the war of independence, in Israeli parlance), the Arab League used its powers and clout to enforce a politico-economic embargo against Israel. These efforts led to Israel being excluded from various regional and international organizations, meetings, and groups, thereby institutionalizing its international isolation. This was not the case for India.

Fifth, India had to face serious challenges to its territorial integrity in form of wars with Pakistan and later China. Six decades after independence, it has unresolved border disputes with almost all of its neighbors, both large and small. Yet India's existence was never in question. At worst, its regional adversaries have sought to limit its power and preponderance. Israel, on the contrary, has been less fortunate. Its existence as a sovereign entity has not been accepted by a vast majority of Arab and Islamic countries. It took three decades for an Arab country, Egypt, to formally recognize the Jewish state. Until they were revoked following the Oslo accords, the charter of the Palestine Liberation Organization (PLO) explicitly challenged and denied the existence of the Jewish State. The Hamas charter still does not accept Jewish sovereignty over the "Islamic land" of Palestine. More than sixty years after its formation, Egypt, Jordan, Mauritania, and Turkey are the only countries in the Middle East that formally recognize Israel. Thus recognition and acceptance continues to be the major foreign-policy objective of the Jewish state.

Last, although both countries are formally committed to the principle of secularism, Israel primarily sees and defines itself as a Jewish state. Unlike India, it does not subscribe to separating religion from national-identity formation. Provisions such as the Law of Return, preferential treatments to exclusive Jewish institutions such as the Jewish Agency and Jewish National Fund, and the primacy enjoyed by Judaism in state symbols such as the national anthem, flag, holidays, and dietary laws explicitly preclude non-Jews from easily identifying themselves with the state. In this sense ironically like the other countries of the Middle East, Israel has yet to evolve a territory-based national identity. India is placed slightly better in this regard. Periodic communal tensions and violence against minority groups has challenged India's secular foundations, but mainstream political forces, including the nationalist Bharatiya Janata Party, are formally committed to keeping the country secular. This is evident when Indian leaders recognize and accommodate the views of India's Muslims when dealing with Israel. The Arab minority in Israel, on the contrary, does not influence Israel's policy toward the Arab world.

This is only one side of the story. Any nuanced understanding of India's Israel policy would have to be located in some of the larger similarities shared by both countries. Both countries have more in common than many care to admit. Placing them in a comparative perspective would enable us to appreciate not only the post-1992 developments but also the dilemma faced by Nehru regarding normalization. Both gained freedom around the same time: India in August 1947 and Israel the following May. Despite their recent emergence as sovereign entities, both countries trace their history and civilization to well before the birth of Christianity. As Chaim Weizmann taunted the British during the run up to the Balfour Declaration, both nations were civilizations long before London and Paris became cities. And both countries are immensely proud of their unique traditions, cultures, and civilizations.

As modern political entities, both almost treaded the same path. Their formation not only coincided but also raised similar issues. Their freedom was accompanied by partition along religious lines and a resultant communal bloodbath. They were confronted with hostilities from their immediate neighbors and their state-building efforts were complicated by the influx and absorption of a large number of refugees. Both attained independence around the same time and from the same imperial power, Great Britain. As free nations, they were not willing to entangle themselves in the Eurocentric cold war, and both consciously pursued a policy of nonalignment (or nonidentification, as it was known in Israel). In the early years, both countries had a similar worldview; on a host of international issues such as the Korean crisis, the recognition of communist China, and the larger cold war, both Nehru and Ben-Gurion adopted identical views. In the early years, there was considerable mutual goodwill toward each other.

Despite Nehru's initial reluctance to recognize it, Israel was enamored by the foreign-policy vision of the Indian leader. This approach is vividly apparent in the long letter written by Israel's most senior diplomat, Walter Eytan. Outlining Israel's foreign policy to the head of the Israeli delegation to the Lausanne Conference on August 11, 1949, Eytan observed:

> In the course of a debate on foreign affairs in the Indian parliament on March 8th of this month Pandit Nehru made the following statement:
>
> We are friendly with all countries. We approach the whole world on a friendly basis, and there is no reason why we should put ourselves at a disadvantage by becoming unfriendly to any group. India has a vital role to play in world affairs. There is absolutely no reason why we should be asked to choose between this ideology and that. In the past, India spread her cultural doctrine to other countries, not by force of arms, but by the strength and vitality of her culture. There are no reasons why she should give up her own way of doing things simply because of some particular ideology emanating from Europe. By aligning with any particular group we lose the tremendous vantage ground we have of using the influence that we possess—and that influence is growing—for the sake of the world peace. We do not seek domination over any other country, and do not wish to interfere in any other country's affairs, domestic or other. Our main stake in world affairs is peace; to see that there is racial equality and that people who are subjugated are free. For the rest, we do not seek to interfere, and we do not desire other people to interfere in our affairs. If there is interference, political, military or economic, we shall resist it. The supreme question today is how can we avoid a world war. If there is a World War, it will mean such a catastrophe that for a generation or more the progress and advancement of humanity will be put at an end. This is a terrible thing to contemplate. Everything should be done to avoid the catastrophe. I feel that India can play a big part and may be an effective part in helping the avoidance of war. Therefore, it becomes all the more necessary that India should not be lined up with one group of Powers or other, which for various reasons today are full of the fear of war and are preparing for it. This is the main approach of our foreign policy. It is possible that other countries who are also not happy at the prospect of war may support our attitude and back us in this march. . . .

> In the passage I have just quoted you have only to substitute the name "Israel" for "India" and you have an excellent statement of the principles of Israel's foreign policy. I am convinced that with India thinking this way and Israel thinking on the same lines . . .

Eytan concludes that both India and Israel could join hands and contribute to world peace.[15]

It is unusual and extremely rare to quote the statement of a foreign leader to explain one's own policy, but Eytan did exactly that in 1949. One can also find Nehru's influence in the initial Israeli policy of neutrality during the Korean crisis and in the Israeli recognition of communist China.[16] Israel often used such similarities and convergences of views to highlight and promote its friendship toward India.

Both contrasts and convergences had their utility. Prior to normalization, the former dominated Indian thinking and for many they were useful tools to explain and justify the prolonged absence of relations. Normalization of relations has reversed this trend, and noting points of convergence between the two nations has become more common. That both nations are ancient civilizations and the prolonged absence of Indian anti-Semitism have become prominent in Indian political discourse on Israel. Earlier, such references were politically imprudent, but after 1992 they became essential ingredients of the Indian policy.

India's Israel policy is also unique in another sense: domestic determinants played a pivotal role in some of the critical decisions concerning Israel. Although the Indian nationalists understood the history of Jewish suffering and persecution, it was accompanied by a marked lack of sympathy for Jewish political aspirations in Palestine. The absence of a significant Jewish population in India was compounded by another factor, namely, the Islamic prism.

The Islamic Prism

During the British rule, India had the largest number of Muslims in the world, and currently it has the third largest Muslim community, after Indonesia and Pakistan. This demographic reality was amply reflected in India's policy on Israel. Its unfriendly approach toward Jewish aspirations was partly because its nationalists viewed the problem in Palestine through an Islamic prism. The demand for a Jewish national home in Palestine fundamentally challenged the traditional Islamic attitude toward the Jews. The fulfillment of the Zionist aspirations meant that the erstwhile *Dhimmi*[17] were to become the owners and masters of a land that had been under Islamic rule since the seventh century. If one excludes the Crusades period (1099–1291), Jerusalem and its environs had remained continuously under Islamic rule since the caliph Umar conquered Jerusalem in A.D. 638. Jewish lives and property were protected so long as they were prepared to accept Islamic rule and the conditions imposed by the *Dhimmi* arrangement. The scope of death and destruction rampant in European Christendom thus never visited the Jews of Islam. Zionist aspirations and the demand for a Jewish homeland in Palestine fundamentally altered this historic arrangement. The Zionists now demanded sovereignty, not protection; equality, not toleration; and political rights, not religious privileges.

Only Mahatma Gandhi succinctly captured the essence of this Islamic struggle against Zionism. Disregarding secular arguments, he recognized and accepted the Islamic rationale against Jewish aspirations in Palestine. His familiarity with religious scriptures and his philosophical worldview enabled him to recognize the Islamic nature of the problem and its resonance among the Muslims of India. Unlike the other nationalists, he was prepared to see the traditional claims among Indian Muslims that Palestine was a part of *Jazirat al-Arab* (the Islamic land of Arabia). Interestingly, in the Middle East the expression has been used traditionally only to denote the Arabian Peninsula, but in India it was expanded to include Jerusalem.[18] Mahatma Gandhi was quick to recognize the underlying reason agitating the Indian Muslims regarding the British designs on the crumbling Ottoman Empire. Writing in April 1921, he readily accepted the "injunction" of the Prophet Mohammed regarding *Jazirat al-Arab*. As he rhetorically asked, the Muslims did not fight World War I to hand over Palestine to non-Islamic control. He went on to explicitly rule out non-Muslims seeking sovereign rights in Palestine.[19] Indeed, largely under his influence, in 1922 the Indian National Congress demanded the liberation of *Jazirat al-Arab* "from all non-Muslim control."[20]

This was inevitable. Toward the end of World War I, the Indian Muslims were agitating over the future of the Ottoman Empire, whose sultan was also the caliph. Protection and preservation of the institution that symbolized the unity of the believers preoccupied Indian Muslims and produced widespread public protests known as the Khilafat movement. For the Congress Party and its leaders, this became an opportunity to strengthen bonds with Indian Muslims. Hence, despite the explicitly religious nature of the problem, the Indian nationalists were at the forefront of the Khilafat struggle. Around the same time, the Muslim League, which subsequently championed Pakistani nationalism, began articulating a hardline stand on Palestine. Gradually, the problem of Palestine became an instrument for the Congress Party to further its influence among the Muslims. With the Muslim League clamoring to be the exclusive representative of the Indian Muslims, the Palestine issue became useful to the Congress Party to shore up its pro-Arab and pro-Islamic credentials. Though couched in secular-nationalist expressions, in the early 1930s the Palestine issue became the most prominent foreign-policy concern of the Congress Party.

As time went by, the intensification of Congress Party–Muslim League tension over Muslim support added a new twist to India's attitude toward Jewish nationalist aspirations. Unlike the Muslim League, the Congress Party presented itself as the representative of all Indians, irrespective of their religious, ethnic, linguistic, cultural, and caste divisions. Within this context, the religion-based nationalist argument of the Muslim League became a plot to divide India. The Pakistani nationalism pursued by the Muslim League and the Jewish nationalism in Palestine appeared fractious to the Congress Party. It saw both nationalist arguments as sinister attempts to divide and secede from India and Palestine, respectively. The Congress Party could not accept the Muslim League's argument that the Indian Muslims constituted a distinct nation because they followed a different religion. Likewise, logically, it refused to concede that Jews were a different nation.

For the Congress Party, the endorsement of the right of self-determination did not mean endorsing the Muslims in India and Jews in Palestine as distinct nations. As its representative eloquently argued at the United Nations, "there is no reason why political considerations should be mixed up with religious considerations and why political rights in a state should be confused with religious rights."[21] Its eventual acceptance of the partition of the subcontinent in August 1947 was not an endorsement of the religion-based division propounded by the Muslim League but was the price for India gaining freedom from the British. That a large portion of Muslims opted to stay in India after the creation of Pakistan helped consolidate the Congress Party's opposition to religion being the preeminent determinant of nationhood.[22] At the same time, preoccupied with its rivalry with the Muslim League, the significant historical differences between the Jewish question and the problems of the Muslims of British India did not receive adequate attention among Congress Party circles.

After the partition of the subcontinent, the erstwhile Congress Party–Muslim League rivalry over the support of the Indian Muslims transformed into political competition between India and Pakistan for Arab support. The troubles over Kashmir and Pakistan's attempts to speak on behalf of Muslim citizens of India complicated the matter. Thus, from the very beginning, Pakistan has occupied an important position in India's foreign policy, and this manifested most clearly in its Middle East policy. To counter Pakistan using Islam as its principal foreign-policy instrument, India burnished its secular credentials. Both countries used their respective support for Palestinians as their principal means to establish their pro-Arab credentials. This competition with Pakistan resulted in India making a few controversial decisions, such as its gatecrashing the Rabat Islamic summit in September 1969.

The Islamic influences upon India's Middle East policy were inevitable. Having opted for democracy, both before and after independence, the Indian leaders had to listen to the voices and aspirations of the various segments of the population. A country with extremely diverse religious, ethnic, linguistic, and national groups, democracy was and remains the only option if India is to survive as a political entity. Any other course would have vindicated Churchill's prediction of India being just "a geographic term" and "no more a united nation than the equator." Its leaders, therefore, must respond to diverse pulls and pressures and keep in sync with the aspirations and demands of various ethnic and religious groups, especially on sensitive foreign-policy issues. A wanton disregard of any particular group or segment of the population would have challenged the very idea of India.

Thus various transborder ethnonational links play an important role in shaping India's relations with its immediate neighbors. Its policy toward the ethnic conflict in Sri Lanka, for example, has been heavily influenced by the sentiments of the Tamil population in the southern state of Tamil Nadu. A similar role is played by the Bengali population regarding India's policy toward Bangladesh, Punjabis vis-à-vis Pakistan, and conservative Hindus vis-à-vis Nepal.

The same is true for the Indian Muslims. Their interests in Middle Eastern developments are a function of history, theology, and faith. Even if one presents these through a secular paradigm or Marxist jargons, the sentimental response of the Indian Muslims to the Arab-Israeli conflict is real. As a gentile, *kafir*, infidel, and pagan, a secular Hindu might be indifferent to the contested claims over the Holy Land and might even consider the city of Jerusalem about as relevant as Alaska. This is not possible for a believer. For a Muslim, conservative or otherwise, Jerusalem is not, say, Berlin, which could be divided and then reunified due to political compulsions. Nor is the division of Palestine akin to the Korean Peninsula, which stands divided due to ideological animosity. Whether stated explicitly or camouflaged in secular jargon, religion plays an important role in shaping the views of Indian Muslims toward the Middle East. This is more palpable and pronounced toward Israel and Israel only. For example, the Turkish occupation of Cyprus, the prolonged Syrian presence in Lebanon, or the Iranian occupation of three islands belonging to the United Arab Emirates is largely ignored by Indian Muslims. Even the Iraqi invasion, occupation, and annexation of Kuwait did not receive universal condemnation of the community. The Kurdish struggle for self-determination rarely evokes their interest. Israel's policy toward the Palestinians, in contrast, generates widespread attention, criticism, and condemnation from the Indian Muslims.

Thus no Indian government could ignore the strong Muslim sentiments regarding the Middle East without undermining India's democratic credentials. While the extent to which a particular government is prepared to go varies, Muslim sentiments figure prominently in India's Israel policy. At the same time, political compulsions prevented the Indian leaders from openly admitting to the "Muslim factor" to explain the prolonged absence of diplomatic relations. Such an admission was seen as "communal" and nonsecular. But in their private conversations with Israeli leaders, many, including Prime Minister Nehru, admitted that domestic compulsions over Muslims prevented normalization.

This duality was true for the mainstream Indian intelligentsia. Many have no problem in attributing the pro-Israeli sentiments of the right-wing groups, parties, and individuals to their animosity toward Muslims and Islam. It is widely argued that the Hindu right is pro-Israeli because it is anti-Muslim. The converse argument, however, remains anathema to mainstream scholars. Any suggestion that the Congress Party was unfriendly toward Zionism and Israel because of pro-Muslim political calculations is vehemently denied, dismissed, and even vilified as a conspiracy.

That the Israel policy could be a function of domestic Muslim politics continues to be absent from mainstream political debate within the country. As a result, Maulana Azad became Nehru's adviser on "Arab" and not Muslim affairs, India's gatecrashing at the Rabat Islamic summit in September 1969 had to be given a national-interest slant, and even the Middle East policy of the Hindu nationalists have to be painted in secular colors.

Do the Indian Muslims play a role akin to the Jews of the United States with respect to the Middle East? Such suggestions are generally unpopular in India. Arguments that Indian Muslims influence and shape India's Israel policy remain controversial, "not *kosher,*" and marginal. There are a number of differences between the two communities. U.S. President Harry S. Truman could openly attribute his pro-Israeli policy to the absence of "one hundred thousand Arabs" among his constituency. Indian leaders, on the contrary, are far more cautious in admitting any link between the domestic Muslim population and the nation's Middle East policy. This cautious approach dates back to the immediate aftermath of the Khilafat struggle, when the secularization of the Middle East policy became the prime agenda of the Congress Party. If the Muslim League (later on, Pakistan) used Islam to rationalize its support for the Palestinians, the Congress Party (later on, India) placed its pro-Arab policies within a secular framework. If the driving forces before 1947 were anticolonialism and anti-imperialism, after 1947 it was support for Arab nationalism and righteousness of the Palestinian cause. The Islamic dimension was rarely admitted as a factor in India's prolonged unfriendliness toward Israel.

There are other differences between the political role played by the American Jews and the Indian Muslims. Even though domestic politics led to swift U.S. recognition of Israel, for long the Jewish factor remained dormant. It was only after the spectacular Israeli military victory in the June 1967 war that the ethnonational factor became prominent in U.S. policies and politics. From then onward, for the Democrats and Republicans alike, criticizing Israel is not a sensible political option. Despite occasional differences, mainstream American politicians viewed Israel as pivotal to U.S. interests in the ever-turbulent Middle East. The Indian situation is somewhat different. The domestic Muslim factor has always been a consistent feature of the political scene, though with varying degrees of influence. When they were in power, even the pronouncedly pro-Israeli parties such as the Jan Sangh (later on, the Bharatiya Janata Party) could not ignore the domestic dimension.

Likewise, the emergence of the nascent pro-Arab lobby to counter the perceived pro-Israeli bias in U.S. Middle East policy is a recent phenomenon. In India, however, a powerful segment has been highly critical of the pro-Arab slant of its Middle East policy. Since the days of Nehru, the opposition castigated his unfriendliness toward Israel, depicting the government as the "attorney for the Arab League,"[23] "*chaprasi*,"[24] or the "fourteenth Arab state."[25] While there is a substantial support for India's pro-Arab policy, there has always been a vocal opposition. Until recently, this has not been the case in the United States.

Despite these differences and obvious limitations, it is possible to draw a parallel between the roles played by American Jews and Indian Muslims. In terms of their organization, lobbying skills, and political involvement, they are poles apart. At the same time, both these communities share certain distinct traits that are relevant to the understanding of India's Israel policy. Both have strong ethnonational linkages and attachments to the Middle East, and their foreign-policy involvement is more visible here than toward any other parts of the world. The democratic environment in the United States and India enables both communities to articulate their concerns. For the Jews, a pro-Israeli policy serves U.S. interests, and for the Muslims a pro-Arab policy promotes Indian interests. Both American Jews and Indian Muslims argue that their respective foreign-policy choices are not parochial but are reflective of their respective national ethos and values. If the former harps on the democratic credentials of Israel, the latter highlights the justice of the Palestinian cause. The political influence of both these communities is acutely recognized during elections and other domestic political battles. American leaders do not hesitate to attend important events organized by various Jewish groups; likewise, no Indian politician skips *Iftar* parties,[26] even if they are hosted by bitter political rivals. For U.S. presidents and Indian prime ministers alike, they are high-value political events and not solemn religious occasions.

There is, however, a catch. The role played by the Jews in influencing U.S. Middle East policy is a hotly debated and even contested issue in the United States. Establishing a similar link between the domestic factor and India's Israel policy is a herculean task. India remains the only democratic state that does not declassify official papers. The Right to Information Act introduced in 2005 does not cover the foreign-policy domain, and much of the documentation pertaining to the Nehru era (1947–1964) remains classified. Sifting through the limited archival materials currently available in New Delhi, acrimonious debates in the Indian parliament, and declassified materials in Israel, one can reasonably conclude that the domestic factor played an important role in India's understanding of Jewish history and its policy regarding Israel. Behind the official secular discourse lies a deeply seated domestic, democratic, and demographic rationale: Indian Muslims.

Compulsions

Despite the obvious handicaps, it is possible to reconstruct some of the key developments regarding Israel. The most critical development regarding normalization happened in early 1952. In March of that year, Prime Minister Nehru made a commitment to normalization when Walter Eytan, the senior-most Israeli diplomat, came to New Delhi to expedite the process of establishing formal relations. A vast majority of Indian leaders and diplomats left a favorable impression upon Eytan regarding the establishment of diplomatic relations. Nehru, who was concurrently serving as India's foreign minister, even instructed his officials to prepare the budget for a resident Indian mission in Tel Aviv. The Israeli visitor was informed that a formal decision would be taken by the Indian cabinet "within the next few weeks," following the first Lok Sabha elections. This did not happen—or rather, it only happened four decades later.

By all accounts, both Indian and Israeli ones, the veteran Muslim leader Maulana Abul Kalam Azad stood in the way of normalization. The Congress Party president during World War II, he was a cabinet colleague and close confidant of Prime Minister Nehru. Often portrayed as Nehru's "adviser on Arab affairs," he was held responsible for the absence of relations. Citing opposition from the domestic Muslim population and possible "mischief" by Pakistan in the Middle East, Azad persuaded the prime minister to defer normalization. Nehru, who had unquestionable sway over India's foreign policy both before and after India became independent, bowed to the wishes of the senior-most Muslim leader within the government and Congress Party. Apparently, this policy shift and postponement was not communicated to Israel. An indirect hesitation regarding Israel came in 1955, when India reluctantly bowed to the Arab veto over Israel's participation at the Bandung Afro-Asian Conference. A more pronounced statement regarding normalization came during the

Suez crisis of 1956, when Nehru observed that the time was not ripe for relations with Israel. This subsequently became the standard Indian refrain on normalization.

Interestingly, the two reasons given for Azad's stance—the domestic Muslim factor and Pakistan's diplomatic maneuvers—were actually valid when Prime Minister Narasimha Rao normalized relations with Israel in January 1992. How could a politically weak prime minister such as Rao ignore these compulsions when a more powerful and dominating personality—Nehru—had been unable to? What helped Rao but worked against Nehru? Why was Rao successful? Three closely linked factors worked against normalization during Nehru's time. As discussed earlier, the pro-Arab policy enjoyed strong domestic support from Indian Muslims. Two, both the international climate and India's foreign-policy calculations did not favor a pro-Israeli policy. And finally, despite his towering personality—or because of it—Nehru remained a prisoner of his ideological worldview, which prevented him from understanding the nationalist aspirations of the Jewish people.

During the struggle for Indian freedom, the nationalists identified themselves with other peoples resisting foreign rule. They felt that India's struggle against the British was also a part of the wider struggle against colonialism. This brought them into contact with leaders of various nationalist movements in Asia and Africa and formed the basis for the post-1947 Indian policy toward these countries. Decolonization and anti-imperialism became the hallmark of India's foreign policy. Nehru also visualized a leadership role for India among the newly independent countries. As highlighted by the Asian Relations Conference held in New Delhi a few months before Indian independence, forging closer ties with the decolonizing countries became an important foreign-policy priority. Through the formation of an Afro-Asian bloc of independent countries, Nehru also sought to distance and in the process quarantine India and other countries from cold-war politics. Maintaining political autonomy through a nonaligned foreign policy became the key to maintaining and consolidating the newly won political freedom.

The opposition to imperialism, solidarity with the newly independent countries, and the emergence of nonalignment as its principal foreign-policy instrument naturally affected India's Israel policy. In continuation of the pre-1947 position, India and its leaders took anti-imperialist logic and Afro-Asian solidarity to mean a greater accommodation of Arab views regarding Israel. The growing Arab world weighed heavily in Indian political calculations. As Nehru's friendship with Gamal Abdul Nasser grew, India became less friendly toward Israel. At Bandung, Nehru accepted the Arab veto over Israeli participation and a year later formally ruled out diplomatic ties after witnessing Israel joining hands with the old imperial powers against a fellow member of the Afro-Asian world.

Gradually, India's foreign policy acquired a distinct pro-Soviet bias, and this in turn affected Israel's fortunes. Nehru was vehemently critical of the Suez crisis but treated the Soviet invasion of Hungary a few days later as an "internal" affair of the Eastern European bloc. Indian reactions to the Czech crisis of 1968 and the Soviet invasion of Afghanistan in 1979 were also muted. While such a policy might have served India's vital interests, there was a secondary effect. Before long, the Soviet Union became the "natural ally" of the nonaligned movement, and this in turn contributed to the growing isolation of Israel in the Third World. While the Soviet Union was not a factor in the formulation of India's policy, it offered, especially after the June war, an ideological rationale. For many Third World countries, opposition to Israel became a sign of "progressiveness."

The international situation had an additional dimension: Arab usefulness over Kashmir. Having taken the Kashmir question to the United Nations, Prime Minister Nehru and his successors needed all the international support they could muster. The pro-Pakistani sentiments in some Western capitals and Pakistani membership in the U.S.-sponsored anti-Soviet military blocs complicated the situation for India. Although India's closer friendship with the Soviet Union garnered Soviet veto power in the UN Security Council, Pakistan became India's major concern in the Middle East. It sought to minimize and if possible counter Pakistani influence through its pro-Arab policy.

Third, Nehru's ideological worldview also worked against Israel. From the early 1920s he influenced, guided, and eventually directed the foreign-policy pronouncements of the Indian nationalists and subsequently of the free India. His understanding of Jewish aspirations in Palestine naturally became crucial to the formulation of his Israel policy. At one level, he recognized the Jewish people as an ancient religious group that had endured great suffering and subjugation. At another level, he refused to recognize them as a nation. Nehru's endorsement of the right of subjugated people to freedom was never extended to the Jewish people. If the Jews are not a nation, then he could not endorse their homeland project in the Middle East. Thus ignoring the particular historic circumstances,

Nehru dwelled on the Zionist's reliance on the British for their political goals in Palestine. The marginal improvement following India's recognition of Israel was jolted in 1956, when Israel allied with the imperial powers and attacked Egypt. India's leaders soon reverted to their pre-1947 position and identified Israel with imperialism. So overwhelming was Nehru's influence that even his death in 1964 did not alter these basic tenets.

In 1962, Nehru's utopian worldview crumbled along the Himalayas. His failure to safeguard India's vital interests forced him to settle for a more realistic foreign policy, and he revisited some of the issues over which he had held strong reservations in the past. His seeking of military aid from Israel, however, was only temporary, and the post-Nehru Indian leadership again was unfriendly, critical, and at times hostile toward the Jewish state. What Nehru could not do his successors could not even dream of. The Soviet Union's decision to terminate relations with Israel following the June war added an ideological dimension.

This raises another question. Why did Nehru and his successors fail to distinguish between the normalization of relations and India's differences with Israel over other issues? Why did bilateral relations become hostage to Israel's policy toward the Arabs? Why did India allow third parties to undermine its bilateral relations with Israel when it had no problems or disputes with the Jewish state?

A possible explanation has to be located in India's limited political leverage and economic dependence on the outside world. During much of the cold war, it remained a marginal player. The political and diplomatic clout it enjoyed in the early years came to an abrupt end following the 1962 Sino-Indian war. During the cold war, a strong political stand on various issues remained the principal method by which India could make its presence felt. India's pro-Soviet foreign-policy slant gradually eroded its moral high ground. Its tolerance of the Hungary, Czechoslovakia, and Afghanistan episodes dented the moral component of its foreign policy. Furthermore, the political role India visualized for itself was not accompanied by any corresponding economic component. It had long depended on the outside world for various forms of economic aid, assistance, and even largesse. Its early economic growth rested on massive aid from the United States in the form of PL-480 and support for a green revolution in agriculture. From the mid-1950s, the Soviet Union was a key player in its industrialization, and it provided the backbone of the Indian military. India also was dependent on the Middle East and during the cold war, its economic leverage in the region was negligible. The first oil crisis of 1973 exposed its vulnerability to supply disruptions and price escalations.

Devoid of other avenues, India under Nehru sought to pursue its interests in the Middle East via the Palestinian issue. The problem of Palestine was never a bilateral issue for India, either before or after its independence. It was always part of a larger policy. During the freedom struggle, it was an instrument for the Congress Party to lure Indian Muslims from the Muslim League and its demands for Pakistan. After 1947, the Congress Party's support for the Arabs of British Mandate Palestine and the absence of diplomatic relations with Israel emerged as India's principal foreign-policy instruments in the Middle East. By highlighting its historic support for the Palestinians and trumpeting its anti-Israeli track record, India sought to establish its pro-Arab credentials and further its interests in the Arab world. In the absence of any meaningful economic leverage, support for Palestinians emerged as India's principal political instrument in promoting its interests in the Middle East. Devoid of political or economic leverage commensurate with its leadership aspirations, India failed to make a distinction between normalization as a bilateral agenda and support for the Arabs' cause as a multilateral agenda. The Israel policy was subsumed under support for the Arabs.

Rao was luckier than Nehru. He was able to reverse the four-decade-old policy primarily because the Palestinian factor proved to be a political liability following the 1990–1991 Kuwait crisis. When the Palestinian leader Yasser Arafat identified himself and his people with the Iraqi aggressor, the Palestinian factor was no longer useful. As prominent Arab countries in the Persian Gulf turned against the PLO, India could no longer use its pro-Palestinian credentials to further its interests in the Middle East. The Palestinian factor had to be decoupled from India's bilateral relations with the Middle East. It was the severing of this link that enabled New Delhi to reverse its traditional policy regarding Israel.

The setback suffered by the PLO and the subsequent willingness of the Arab mainstream to endorse a political settlement with the Jewish state had an effect upon India's domestic Muslim population. Given that countries such as Saudi Arabia were prepared to endorse a negotiated settlement with Israel, opposition to India normalizing relations lost steam. Not everyone was satisfied, but opposition to normalization became hollow. In addition, the Madrid conference and the recognition of Israel by the Soviet Union and China influenced the Indian communists.

In discussing this broad picture, this book looks for answers to some widely ranging, critical, and disturbing questions. Why did India pursue a domestically controversial policy toward Israel? What were the roots of India's Israel policy? How relevant has the role played by the domestic Muslim population been? Why did India wait for far-reaching international changes before modifying its policy? Is there a pattern in India's newly found friendship with Israel?

Largely adopting a chronological path, this book traces the Indian policy within four broad timeframes. The first phase coincides with the nationalist struggle, when the Indian leaders were unfavorably disposed toward Jewish political aspirations in Palestine. The second phase spans the formation of Israel in May 1948 and Nehru's assurances in March 1952 in favor of normalization. This phase marked some improvements and was accompanied by an Indian desire to reexamine its earlier stance regarding Israel. This period also witnessed some meaningful interactions between the two sides and raised hopes for a new and productive relationship.

The third phase roughly begins in early 1952, when Education Minister Azad persuaded Nehru to defer normalization. In 1956, India ruled out diplomatic ties, and for the next four decades, the Indian attitude gradually hardened. If relations remained cool during the Nehru years, they rapidly deteriorated and reached their nadir in November 1975, when India joined with the Arab and Islamic countries in denouncing Zionism as racism. Minor improvements in the late 1970s when the opposition Janata Party was in power were nullified when Indira Gandhi returned to power in 1980 and anti-Israeli rhetoric resumed.

The fourth and final phase began in January 1992, when Prime Minister Rao reversed the traditional policy and established full diplomatic relations with Israel. Because of the paucity of discussion, this work primarily focuses on the pre-1992 developments. Indeed, from early 1920, when the roots of the Israeli policy were planted, until relations were established seven decades later, the absence of formal relations remained the hallmark of the Indian policy. This was both unprecedented and deeply divisive. Indeed, the nonrelations were as colorful as the post-normalization developments.

A serious discussion of India's Israel policy would have to begin at the beginning: Mahatma Gandhi. He was not the architect of India's Israel policy, but for a vast majority of Indians he symbolized not only India's struggle for freedom but also its political aspirations. His personal integrity and humility made him one of the most revered figures of the twentieth century. But what exactly were his attitudes toward Jews, Israel, and the Middle East?

No exception can possibly be taken to the natural desire of the Jews to found a home in Palestine. But they must wait for its fulfillment till Arab opinion is ripe for it.

—*Mahatma Gandhi*

2 Mahatma Gandhi and the Jewish National Home

Writing in his *Harijan* weekly in November 1938, Mohandas Karamchand Gandhi (more commonly known as Mahatma Gandhi) observed: "Palestine belongs to the Arabs in the same sense that England belongs to the English and France to the French."[1] This supposedly unequivocal endorsement of the Palestinians and repudiation of the Zionist demand for a Jewish national home figures prominently in Indian discourses on the Arab-Israeli conflict.[2] It is almost impossible to locate any discussion on the Middle East without a reference to this quotation. For example, meeting in Calcutta (now Kolkata) in August 1997, the plenary session of the All-India Congress Committee (AICC) passed a resolution on the international situation. Coming more than five years after the normalization of relations with Israel, it observed: "The Congress recalls that it was Mahatma Gandhi who said Palestine belongs to the Palestinians as England belongs to the English or France to the French."[3] Even the communists, who once accused the Mahatma of being an agent of British imperialism,[4] do not hesitate to rely on him to explain, justify, and rationalize their stance toward Israel.[5] One could go the extent of suggesting that this is the Mahatma's most widely quoted statement on international affairs.

The Mahatma's views are not a guide to India's foreign policy. He is never considered, either by his disciples or by scholars, as a serious thinker on international affairs. Though his views at times provided a moral content, he was not setting the agenda of free India. A number of his positions were quickly, quietly, and forcefully buried by his colleagues and political successors because they were seen as utopian, impractical, unscientific, and even antimodern. From the nonconsumption of alcohol to cottage industries and the village-based economic model, a number of his ideas gradually disappeared from public discourse. One never hears about the Mahatma's friendlier overtures to Pakistan in the immediate aftermath of the partition. It was only after he resorted to a hunger strike that Prime Minister Jawaharlal Nehru accepted his demands for an equitable distribution of assets of British India. His perceived "appeasement" toward Pakistan was the "immediate" reason for his assassination on January 30, 1948.[6]

Why are Gandhi's views on Pakistan irrelevant but what he said about Palestine in 1938 sacrosanct? Was he aware of the historic sufferings of the Jews and their longing for a homeland? Did he consider the rival nationalist claims of the Jews and Arabs over Palestine? Was his opinion colored by his moral commitments to nonviolence and by his wish that Jews realize their aspirations through nonviolence and cooperation? Was he aware of the complexities and predicaments of the problem in Palestine? Was he as categorical as he is commonly portrayed? Are the views of the Mahatma relevant to the understanding of India's foreign policy or only to its Israeli policy? Alternatively, if Mahatma Gandhi's endorsement of the Palestinian claims were unequivocal, how did India square the circle, when it recognized Israel in 1950 and normalized relations four decades later?

In short, is Mahatma Gandhi correct, consistent, or even relevant to the understanding of India's Israel policy?

Empathy but Indifference

The Mahatma was no stranger to Jews or to their historic sufferings. His personal association with Jews dates back to the late nineteenth century, and as he admitted, "I have known [the Jews] intimately in South Africa."[7] Some of them became his lifelong companions, and one can identify the following prominent Jewish personalities who interacted with the Mahatma: Henry S. L. Polak and Hermann Kallenbach knew the Mahatma when the latter was living in and later began his *satyagraha* (nonviolent struggle) in South Africa between 1893 and 1914; the Zionist officials Selig Brodetsky and Nahum Sokolov met the Mahatma on October 15, 1931, in London; the Sanskrit scholar Immanuel Olsvanger visited India in 1936 as the official emissary of the Jewish Agency in Palestine and met the Mahatma; in 1937, Kallenbach came to India and secured a private statement on Zionism and two years later returned and met with his old friend Gandhi; Hayim Greenberg, the editor of the Zionist-socialist periodical *Jewish Frontier*, corresponded with the Mahatma in mid-1939; Joseph Nedivi, the town clerk of Tel Aviv, met him on March 22, 1939;[8] the British MP Sidney Silverman met the Mahatma in March 1946; and the Jewish delegation for the Asian Relations Conference met him in New Delhi in early 1947.

These Jewish associations and contacts fall into two distinct categories. There are those who were drawn to the Mahatma because of their shared interests and admiration for nonviolence, communal living, vegetarianism, natural cures for diseases, or his philosophical worldview. His Jewish friends Kallenbach and Polak come under this category. They lived in his ashram in South Africa, and their friendship continued even after the Mahatma returned to India in 1914 and joined the nationalist struggle. Though prominent, as Gideon Shimoni reminds us, "they were not the only Jews closely associated with him."[9]

In the 1930s, the Mahatma encountered different Jewish figures. They were organized and political in nature. The Jewish Agency sought his endorsement for Jewish nationalist aspirations in Palestine. Toward this end, it enlisted the services of Gandhi's Jewish friends from his South African days. When the Sanskrit scholar Olsvanger met the Mahatma in 1936, he did so not as an individual admirer of the Mahatma but as an official emissary of the Jewish Agency. Soon afterward, upon the request of Moshe Shertok (later Moshe Sharett and Israel's first foreign minister), the head of the political department of the Jewish Agency, Kallenbach sought to influence Gandhi's views on Zionism. In short, if his friends in South Africa happened to be Jews, later on Mahatma Gandhi was courted by those who sought his support and endorsement for Zionist goals in Palestine. This crucial difference is often overlooked by scholars who have dealt with the role and influence of Gandhi's Jewish friends.[10]

As he admitted, through his personal acquaintance in South Africa, Mahatma Gandhi "came to learn much of the long persecution" of the

Jews.[11] He was familiar with the historic sufferings of the Jewish people. Placing their plight within the context of his commitments to the uplifting of India's downtrodden, he saw the Jews as "the untouchables of Christianity." For him, the "parallel between their treatment by Christians and the treatment of untouchables by Hindus is very close. Religious sanction has been invoked in both cases for the justification of the inhuman treatment meted out to them."[12] Their miniscule population in India did not prevent him from frequently referring to Jews along with other religious communities. One can find innumerable references to the Jews in the Mahatma's speeches and writings.

The real problem was not Gandhi's unfamiliarity with Jewish suffering but his failure, if not inability, to see the link between Jewish suffering and their political aspirations for a homeland. The influence of his Jewish friends in South Africa upon his understanding of the Jewish struggle for statehood was minimal, if it existed at all. Lamenting on this, Gideon Shimoni suggests that not only were Polak and Kallenbach not "equipped authentically to interpret Judaism" to Gandhi but that they were "also alienated from normative Jewry, both in the religious and in the communal sense."[13] Moreover, the Mahatma did not suggest any means of resolving the problems facing the "untouchables" of Christianity. In the absence of a link between Jewish suffering and its resolution, Gandhi's position becomes unequivocal as presented by conventional scholarship on the subject. It becomes easier and even inevitable to agree with his statement that "sympathy" for Jews "does not blind me to the requirement of justice."[14]

Long before the Zionists made a concerted effort to win him over, the Mahatma had formulated his position on Palestine. He adopted a pro-Palestinian position in the immediate aftermath of World War I, which generated anti-British sentiments in India, especially among the Muslim population. The dismemberment of the Ottoman Empire resulted in Indian Muslims rallying around the caliph, who was viewed by the believers as their temporal head. The Mahatma perceived the mass agitation among the Muslim community, the Khilafat movement, as an opportunity to forge the necessary but conspicuously absent Hindu-Muslim unity against the British.[15]

In March 1921, the Mahatma categorically defined the Jewish rights in Palestine. Repudiating the Balfour Declaration of November 1917, he observed:

> Britain has made a promise to the Zionists. . . . All I contend is that they cannot possess Palestine through a trick or a moral breach. Palestine was not a stake in the war. The British Government could not dare ask a single Muslim soldier to wrest control of Palestine from fellow Muslims and give it to the Jews. Palestine, as a place of Jewish worship, is a sentiment to be respected, and the Jews would have a just cause of complaint against [Muslim] idealists if they were to prevent Jews from offering worship as freely as themselves.

At the same time, he warned: "By no canons of ethics of war . . . can Palestine be given to Jews as a result of the war."[16] A few weeks later, he went a step further and argued:

> The Muslims claim Palestine as an integral part of *Jazirat al-Arab*. They are bound to retain its custody, as an injunction of the Prophet. But that does not mean that the Jews and Christians cannot freely go to Palestine, or even reside there and own property. What non-Muslims cannot do is acquire sovereign jurisdiction. The Jews cannot receive sovereign rights in a place, which has been held for centuries by Muslim powers by right of religious conquest. The Muslim soldiers did not shed their blood in the late war [World War I] for the purpose of surrendering Palestine out of Muslim control.[17]

Thus Mahatma Gandhi unreservedly endorsed the historical and religious claims of the Muslims and categorically ruled out non-Muslim sovereignty in Palestine.

The Mahatma's remarks about Palestine being an integral part of the *Jazirat al-Arab* came within the context of the Khilafat struggle. As he repeatedly admitted, it became his "duty" to help his Muslim brother "in his hour of peril," and "by helping [the Muslims] of India at a critical moment in their history, I want to buy their friendship." He was honest enough to admit his own predicaments: "I would like my Jewish friends to impartially consider *the position of the seventy million Muslims of India*. As a free nation, can they tolerate what they must regard as a treacherous disposal of their sacred possession?"[18] These statements, which came after the Balfour Declaration (November 2, 1917) but before Palestine was granted to Great Britain as a mandate (July 1922), ruled out Jewish claims to Palestine and their demands for a national home. Palestine, for him, was an Islamic land; Jews had no political claims over it. The Zionists would later regret that these one-sided observations of the Mahatma "went unchallenged."[19]

Following the Khilafat phase, the Mahatma refused to discuss the problem of Palestine and repeatedly admitted his reluctance to express his views on the subject. Despite his meetings with Zionist emissaries in London and in India and the efforts by Kallenbach in 1937, Gandhi made no public statement on the subject. He eventually broke his silence and wrote a long exposition in the November 26, 1938, issue of *Harijan*. Some suggest that his observations were unnecessary and avoidable. Margaret Chatterjee, for example, suggests that the Mahatma could have practiced "noninterference [regarding Jewish] affairs and also refrain[ed] from making judgments about them."[20] But, as the Mahatma admitted at the very beginning of his *Harijan* article, he wrote it because of "several letters" that he received "asking me to declare my views about the Arab-Jew question in Palestine and the persecution of Jews in Germany." Aware of the complexities and controversies surrounding both issues, he confessed that it was "not without hesitation that I venture to offer my views on this very difficult question."[21] He subsequently responded to his critics, saying, "I did not write this article as a critic. I wrote it at the pressing request of Jewish friends and correspondents. As I decided to write, I could not do so in any other manner."[22]

The November 1938 *Harijan* article earned him the wrath of the Zionist leadership and swift responses and rebukes both inside and outside India.[23] The Jewish philosopher Martin Buber joined with Judah Magnes and explained the philosophical underpinnings of the Zionist movement.[24] This was later published as *Two Letters to Gandhi*[25] and at times is described as the "Buber-Gandhi correspondence." Some suggested that "Buber and Gandhi were involved in a *polemical exchange of views* on the Jewish problem."[26] Despite such claims, there is no evidence to suggest that Gandhi read the Buber-Magnes letters, let alone that he replied to them.[27]

Acting on his somewhat neutral stand, which he detailed in his confidential note to Kallenbach in July 1937, the Zionist leadership sought his categorical endorsement for a Jewish homeland in Palestine. The Zionist pressures for a public statement from Mahatma Gandhi boomeranged. Disappointed and outraged by his public endorsement of the Palestinian position, an editorial in *The Jewish Advocate*, based in Bombay (later Mumbai), wrote a "comprehensive and dignified" editorial. It lamented that "we are very sorry that we sought" Gandhi's views.[28] The November 1938 *Harijan* article effectively ended the brief Zionist courtship of the Mahatma.

But why were the Zionists interested in Mahatma Gandhi in the first place?

Zionist Courtship: Too Little, Too Late

Nonviolent struggle against colonial rule was a novelty. Thus the Mahatma's struggle for India's freedom attracted widespread international attention and admiration, and other movements and leaders who were seeking to overthrow imperial and colonial rule looked to Gandhi for inspiration and considered him and his colleagues as friends and comrades-in-arms. Shared interests, whether in his philosophy of nonviolence or political struggle against foreigners, resulted in Gandhi being courted by many different groups, nations, and leaders. Even if material help was limited, shared human concern and the desire to liberate national homes from colonialism resonated with many. Even Westerners, who did not always share his anti-British and anti-imperialist politics, came to appreciate his nonviolence and spartan lifestyle.

The Zionists were drawn to him for a different reason. Their interest was belated, short-lived, and ended in acrimony. According to Shimoni, Gandhi's "unique moral character could not but evoke sympathy and admiration amongst Jews."[29] This explanation is applicable only to Gandhi's Jewish friends in South Africa and not to those who sought his support for Zionism in the 1930s. The Zionist interest in the Mahatma was principally governed by a desire to secure the support of, as Sharett remarked, "the greatest of the living Hindus."[30] G. H. Jansen, a former Indian foreign-service official who wrote for international media from Nicosia, suggested a sinister motive: "the Zionists did not pursue Mahatma Gandhi merely because he was an influence in Asia, [but] rather because he had a large following in the West."[31]

If one examines the timing and substance of the Zionist contacts, a more plausible explanation can be found for the sudden interest in the Mahatma. By the time the first formal but brief contact was made in 1931, Gandhi had emerged and was recognized as the undisputed leader of a country that also had the world's largest Muslim population. This politico-demographic factor compelled the Zionist leadership to pay attention to

India. The Zionists were not alone in looking at India through the Islamic prism. Both the British and Palestinian Arab leaderships were conscious of the role and influence of the Indian Muslims. As will be seen, if the British were afraid of the attitude of Indian Muslims, the Palestinian leadership looked to the same community for political support.

The Islamization of the Palestinian problem by Mufti Hajj Amin al-Husseini raised alarms in Zionist circles. While it was relatively easy for them to overlook British apprehensions regarding the Indian Muslims, the problem posed by al-Husseini was far more serious. Besides being a passionate speaker, he evoked respect and admiration among the faithful because of his official position as the mufti of the third holiest place in Islam. Chaim Weizmann, the president of the World Zionist Organization (WZO), was quick to recognize the consequences of the Palestinian issue spreading to the wider Islamic world. In January 1931, the mufti offered to bury the body of Mohammed Ali, a prominent Indian leader who led the Khilafat struggle, within the precincts of the Harem al-Sharif/Temple Mount in Jerusalem. A few days before Shaukat Ali accompanied his younger brother's body to Jerusalem for burial, Weizmann met the Indian leader in London. This was the first known meeting between the Zionist leadership and an Indian leader. Weizmann's efforts to quarantine the Palestine problem from domestic Indian politics proved ineffective. While Shaukat Ali agreed to Weizmann's pleas in London,[32] once in Jerusalem, he was overwhelmed by the mufti's hospitality. As a result, the Indian leader collaborated with his host in organizing the Jerusalem Islamic Conference later that year.[33]

It was under such circumstances that the Zionists made their first formal contact with Mahatma Gandhi. The meeting took place on October 15, 1931, in London, while Gandhi was attending the Round Table Conference. With a formal letter of introduction from Polak, the Mahatma's old friend in South Africa, the Zionists Selig Brodetsky and Nahum Sokolov met the Indian leader. Brodetsky was a member of the World Zionist Executive and head of its political department in London; Sokolov had just taken over from Weizmann as president of the WZO. Surprisingly, they did not seek the Mahatma's support for a Jewish national home in Palestine. They were aware of failure of the Weizmann–Shaukat Ali encounter a few months earlier and thus hoped that the Mahatma would help keep the Palestinian issue away from Indian politics. They wanted him to assure them that no attempts "to bring the problem of Palestine into the discussion of the Round Table Conference or into the atmosphere surrounding these discussions, would meet with his [the Mahatma's] approval."[34] Preoccupied with India's own problems, the Mahatma was not keen to get involved in the Palestinian issue and accepted their request. Once this limited objective was achieved, Zionist indifference toward the Mahatma and India continued.

Efforts to influence the Mahatma and, if possible, secure his support for Jewish aspirations had to wait until mid-1936. The timing of this attempt once again points to unfolding events in Palestine. Shertok decided to send Olsvanger to India as the special emissary of the Jewish Agency. This happened shortly after the outbreak of a general strike in Palestine that eventually culminated in the Arab Revolt of 1936–1939, which evoked strong responses in the wider Islamic world. Even if they were not converted into concrete actions, one sees clarity and foresightedness in Shertok's thinking. Underlining the need to cultivate Asian leaders, he observed that "once the conflict between us and the Arabs is conceived as one between Asiatics and Westerners or Westernizers it becomes a matter of instinct—not even of political reasoning—for the Hindus to side against the Jews. . . . It will clearly be much more difficult to fight misconceptions after they have hardened and gained currency than to prevent their formation."[35] During his visit, Olsvanger held a brief and uneventful meeting with Gandhi.

The following year, Kallenbach visited India and met the Mahatma after a gap of twenty-three years. By then, the former was a supporter of the Zionist goals in Palestine and brought with him a detailed exposition of the *yishuv* activities prepared by the Jewish Agency. Although the Mahatma "had indicated to Kallenbach his willingness to help Jews and Arabs get together, it is significant that he never made this offer public."[36] To further this endeavor, the Mahatma's close confidant Reverend C. F. Andrews was planning to visit Palestine.[37]

Thus the Zionist approach toward Mahatma Gandhi functioned at three distinct but interrelated levels. First, the leadership traced and enlisted the support of those Jews who were acquainted with him in South Africa. Shertok sought the help of Kallenbach to introduce Olsvanger to the Mahatma and India.[38] Brodetsky and Sokolov met Gandhi in 1931 with a letter of introduction from Polak. Second, a few official Zionist emissaries made direct contacts with the Mahatma. Here one can cite Olsvanger, A. E. Shohet (the editor of the Bombay-based *Jewish Advocate*), and the Jewish delegation to the 1947 Asian Relations Conference as examples. One can also add Kallenbach, who visited India in 1937 and secured a private statement from Gandhi on Palestine. And third, a number of Jewish individuals from Palestine and elsewhere approached him for sympathy and support for the Zionist cause. They include such figures as Margin Buber, Judah Magnes, Sidney Silverman, Hayim Greenberg, and Louis Fischer.[39]

Otherwise, none of the leading lights of Zionism are known to have established any direct and personal contact with the Indian leader. Indeed, in July 1937, Weizmann, who had been marginalized by the rise of David Ben-Gurion, sought the counsel of Kallenbach in writing to Gandhi and Jawaharlal Nehru.[40] This suggestion came more than fifteen years after the Mahatma expressed his opposition to Jewish claims in Palestine. There is no evidence to suggest that the Mahatma had received any letters from Weizmann. Some individuals did approach him, soliciting support for a Jewish national home. But in the aftermath of the *Harijan* article of 1938, the Zionist-Mahatma contacts almost ceased.

Belated attempts to cultivate Mahatma Gandhi were not fruitful, and the disappointment of the Zionist leadership was clear. Olsvanger, who came to India with the explicit purpose of securing the support of the Indian nationalists, quickly dismissed the Mahatma as a "sham saint and simpleton."[41] Within weeks of Olsvanger's arrival, even Shertok developed second thoughts about the Mahatma, remarking:

> Olsvanger writes that Gandhi's position and influence in the Nationalist movement is not what it used to be and that therefore it would be imprudent to try and get a public definition of attitude on his part as this might provoke a repudiation from the official leaders who, while inclined to see our point of view, would be extremely reluctant to do or say anything which might alienate Mohammedan sympathies of which they are much in need.[42]

In a sense, the Zionist leadership wrote the Mahatma's political obituary as early as 1936. As history would have it, even half a century after his assassination, the Mahatma's views on Palestine occupy a prominent place in rationalizing India's Middle East policy.

The Zionists were not alone in expressing skepticism about the Mahatma. A few Indian leaders felt that, given the rigid positions adopted by senior leaders like Gandhi and Nehru, there was a need for an alternate Zionist strategy. One such person was Sardar K. M. Panikkar, then prime minister of the princely state of Bikaner (currently in the western state of Rajasthan) and later India's first ambassador to the People's Republic of China. In 1947, he advised the Jewish delegation for the Asian Relations Conference that the Zionist "efforts should be concentrated not on top leaders like Nehru, Gandhi, [Sardar Vallabhbhai] Patel etc., but on leaders of the second rank, who are free to form, and even to voice, their own unbiased opinion."[43]

On the whole, if Gandhi's 1937 private statement to Kallenbach failed to satisfy the Zionists, the November 1938 *Harijan* article proved to be a disaster and led to widespread disappointment, outrage, and doubts about cultivating Gandhi.[44] The Zionists in India used the pages of *The Jewish Advocate* to rebuke and repudiate his views.[45] In Jerusalem, Eliahu Epstein (later Eliahu Elath), who subsequently became Israel's first ambassador in Washington, was alarmed over the prospect of the Mahatma's views being widely disseminated in the Arab world. He was anxious "to avoid entering into polemic with Ghandi [*sic*] in order not to give unnecessary publicity to his views."[46] Epstein enquired of a Jewish Agency official in London: "Was this article reprinted in the English press and how wide was its circulation?"[47]

Contrary to Olsvanger's assessment, Gandhi was far from a spent force. Recognizing his continued influence over the Indian masses, only months after the *Harijan* article Shohet was pleading with the Jewish Agency officials in Jerusalem: "However cranky his views may appear to the outside world, we should not lose the opportunity of a real and serious attempt to try and convince him."[48] Shohet, who wrote highly critical editorials on the Mahatma following the November 1938 remarks, felt it necessary to accompany Joseph Nevidi, a Zionist emissary from Palestine, in trying to persuade Gandhi.[49] For all practical purposes, however, formal Zionist approaches to Mahatma Gandhi came to a clear halt after the *Harijan* article. Shimoni presents a sober picture when he observed, "if account is taken of his private statements to Kallenbach, his hesitancy to speak out, the double standard by which he judged Jewish self-determination and Moslem self-determination, as well Jewish behavior and Arab behavior, and above all, the realities of the Indian political context in which Gandhi functioned, a more complex pattern of thought suggests itself."[50]

If one examines Gandhi's views on Palestine and Jewish national aspirations, a certain broad—but at times blurred—picture emerges.

Mahatma and the Jewish Cause

The overall views of the Mahatma toward Jewish aspirations exhibited both a degree of consistency and fundamental contradictions. Despite citing him ad nauseam, scholars have only highlighted the former aspect. Though he did say that "Palestine belongs to the Arabs," it was not the Mahatma's central view on the subject.

Let us first look at the consistencies. The Mahatma had argued throughout that the Jewish national home should be realized only with the consent of the Arabs of Palestine. Much to the consternation of his Jewish and Zionist interlocutors, he repeatedly underlined the need for Jewish accommodation with the Arabs. From the very beginning, he was not blind to the Arab character of Palestine, and in so doing, he unequivocally rejected the arguments of Israel Zangwill that Palestine was a "land without people."[51] While gradually diluting his opposition regarding a Jewish homeland, he emphasized the need for the Jews to cooperate with the Arabs.[52] Even in his private statement to Kallenbach, he declared: "No exception can possibly be taken to the natural desire of the Jews to found a home in Palestine. *But they must wait for its fulfillment till Arab opinion is ripe for it.*"[53]

Gandhi periodically repeated this argument, and even in his *Harijan* article, he stressed the need for a cooperative attitude:

> They [the Jews] can settle in Palestine *only by the goodwill of the Arabs.* They could seek to convert the Arab heart. . . . They can offer *satyagraha* in front of the Arabs and offer themselves to be shot or thrown into the Dead Sea without raising a little finger against them. They will find the world opinion in their favor in their religious aspirations. There are hundreds of ways of reasoning with the Arabs, if they will only discard the help of the British bayonet. As it is they are co-sharers with the British in despoiling a people who have done no wrong to them.[54]

In short, Jewish aspirations must be realized in consonance and not in conflict with the Arabs.

This position lines up with the Mahatma's basic belief that liberation could not be realized through a collaboration with imperialism. His attitude toward World War II clearly exhibited this line of thinking. He refused to support the British war effort even in defense of democracy. He was not convinced that the British were fighting tyranny and safeguarding democracy while keeping India under subjugation.[55] Just as he was critical of Zionist dependence upon the British for their political goals, Gandhi also opposed the nationalist leader Subhas Chandra Bose for seeking Japanese help to secure India's freedom.[56] His advocacy for Jewish-Arab cooperation in Palestine was reflective of the prevailing mood in India. In February 1938, the Congress Party urged the Jews "not to seek the shelter of the British Mandate and not to allow themselves to be exploited in the interests of the British imperialism."[57] Likewise, in a personal letter to Olsvanger, Nehru underscored his opposition to any collaboration with imperialism.[58]

Contradictions in the Mahatma's stance are equally interesting. He was the first non-Muslim leader to invoke Islam to justify Arab demands. In his first comments on the subject in 1921, he used religion to dispute Jewish demands. According to him, the injunction of Prophet Mohammed "does not mean that Jews and Christians cannot freely go to Palestine or even reside there and own properties. *What non-Muslims cannot do is to acquire sovereign jurisdiction.*"[59] A few weeks later, he reminded his readers that *Jazirat al-Arab* had been "under Mussalman control" before World War I.[60] Under his influence, the following year, the Indian National Congress demanded that the "effective guardianship of Islam and the *Jazirat al-Arab* [be] free[d] from all non-Muslim control."[61] The introduction of Islamic claims and religious terminology into the political discourse by the Mahatma (and briefly by the Congress Party) came within the Khilafat context. Mahatma Gandhi felt the need to embrace, support, and endorse Muslim religious claims to Palestine.

There is a fundamental problem with Gandhi's approach. If one accepts the injunction in the Qur'an, then it is not possible to overlook the religious claims of the Jews over Palestine. According to the Old Testament, Palestine was "promised" to the Jews centuries before the birth of Islam or the arrival of Prophet Mohammed. Thus, one either accepts the religious claims of both or rejects both Jewish and Islamic injunctions. In the post-Khilafat period, the Mahatma did not use religious terminology to justify Arab claims or negate Jewish demands. This could be interpreted as his realization of the conflicting religious claims over Palestine.

Second, Mahatma Gandhi never questioned the Jewish longing for a homeland or for the city of Jerusalem. He treated it as a religious and not a political question. He gradually modified his November 1938 position and began to recognize the validity of the Jewish claims. The brutality of the Holocaust perhaps compelled him to revisit the whole issue. In June 1946, he told the American journalist Louis Fischer: "The Jews have a good cause. I told [British Zionist MP] Sidney Silverman that the Jews have a good case in Palestine. *If the Arabs have a claim to Palestine, the Jews have a prior claim.*"[62] This is a significant departure from the 1921 statement, when the Mahatma had categorically ruled out Jewish claims over Palestine.

Gandhi repeated this in April 1947, a few days after his brief and uneventful meeting with the Jewish delegation from Palestine. He observed that if the Arabs could "provide refuge for the Jews without the mediation of any nation, it will be in their tradition of generosity."[63] This statement came shortly after Great Britain handed over the problem of Palestine to the newly formed United Nations. A month later, he told a Reuters correspondent: "If I were a Jew, I could tell them: 'Don't be silly as to resort to terrorism, because you simply damage your own case, *which otherwise would be a proper case.*' "[64]

In June, when the UN committee (which also included India) was deliberating the future of Palestine, the Mahatma told an American journalist that the solution to the Palestine problem rested on a total abandonment of "terrorism and other forms of violence" by the Jews.[65] While insisting that their means should be noble, Gandhi did not call for the abandonment of their political demands. These public statements were made long after the 1938 *Harijan* article. Moreover, in his July 1937 confidential statement to Kallenbach, Gandhi was more candid. "No exception can possibly be taken to the natural desire of the Jews to find a home in Palestine," but he added that they should seek this through Arab acquiescence.

In other words, in the years following his "Palestine belongs to the Arabs" statement, the Mahatma had moved away significantly from this position. He was no longer as categorical as he was in 1938. He recognized that the Jews have "a good case," "a prior claim" to Palestine, "a proper case," and was prepared to admit "the natural desire of the Jews to find a home in Palestine." Therefore, to conclude that the Mahatma was opposed to Jewish claims to Palestine or had unequivocally rejected the demand for a Jewish homeland are not substantiated by facts.

If this is the case, then why were these pro-Jewish statements ignored? One could make some inferences. His post-1938 statements indicate that the Mahatma had significantly diluted, if not changed, his opinion on Palestine. Highlighting them would erode the claim that he was consistently opposed to the idea of a Jewish homeland in Palestine. This was not in the interests of the Arabs and Palestinians and would also have worked against India. For a long time, Indian leaders and commentators used Gandhi's 1938 statement to explain, rationalize, and even justify the prolonged absence of relations with Israel and the host of anti-Israeli positions India took since 1947. Any references to post-1938 statements of the Mahatma would have made these claims untenable. Admitting that Gandhi had recognized the "prior claims" of Jews to Palestine would have eroded, if not destroyed, the "moral" content of India's pro-Palestine policy.

But why did the Zionist leaders also ignore these statements? Their interests in the Mahatma, or India for that matter, were belated, limited, and one-sided. Preoccupied with the problem of homeland enterprises, they had little time or interest in non-Western personalities, especially the anti-British Gandhi. Zionist interest and interaction with him came to an abrupt end following the *Harijan* article. They were no longer paying attention to any of Gandhi's subtle shifts; from the Zionist viewpoint, it was too little, too late. In short, not only Palestinians and Indians but also the Zionists choose to ignore the nuanced changes in the Mahatma's post-1938 position.

Third, Gandhi's espousal of nonviolence was not absolute, and this negates his criticism of Jewish violence in Palestine. While deploring the Nazi persecution, in 1938 he urged the Jews to practice nonviolence against Hitler.[66] When his Zionist critics pointed out the plight of Jews in Germany, he replied: "Their nonviolence, if it may be so called, is of the helpless and the weak. . . . I have drawn a distinction between passive resistance of the weak and active nonviolent resistance of the strong."[67] Gandhian nonviolence was effective against the British in India. It is highly debatable whether it could have been replicated in other parts of the world—especially in Nazi Germany. The Mahatma's hope that active Jewish nonviolence would have "melted" Hitler's heart is highly questionable.

Furthermore, the Mahatma demanded Jewish nonviolence against the Nazi dictator in 1938 but took a milder view on Arab violence against the British in Palestine. The *Harijan* article, which appeared during the Arab Revolt in Palestine, deplored the use of force by the Jews in Palestine and their dependence upon the British. At the same time, he declared, "I am not defending the Arab excesses, I wish they had chosen the way of nonviolence in resisting what they rightly regarded as an unwarrantable encroachment upon their country. But according to the accepted canons of right and wrong, nothing can be said against the Arab resistance in the face of overwhelming odds."[68]

In other words, Arab political claims vis-à-vis the British were valid, and the Arabs were outnumbered by a more powerful adversary. Therefore, the Mahatma was prepared to understand if not endorse Arab violence. Ironically, only a few paragraphs earlier, he had implored the Jews to practice nonviolence against Hitler. He chose not to give similar advice to the Arabs of Palestine against the Mandate authorities. Likewise, during the Khilafat struggle, he did not demand nonviolence as a precondition of his support for the Muslims.[69]

Fourth, was the Mahatma realistic when he demanded that the Jews abandon the support and patronage of the British? Was there a possibility that the Zionists could have abandoned the imperial power, sought a compromise with the Arabs, and still secured a homeland? History is not the place to answer such hypothetical questions. But it is obvious that the creation of a Jewish homeland in Palestine meant a massive migration of Jews from the Diaspora to Palestine. At the time of the Balfour Declaration, the Jews were a microscopic minority in Palestine, constituting less than 5 percent of the total population. This objective reality resulted in a number of rather unique international developments, such as the exclusion of Palestine from U.S. President Woodrow Wilson's fourteen principles enumerated at the end of World War I, the British Mandate over Palestine, endorsement of the Balfour Declaration by the League of Nations, Zionist opposition to the Arab exercise of self-determination, and the Zionist linkage between Palestine and the Holocaust. They all emerged from Jews being a small minority in Palestine. The entire Zionist leadership, including binationalists like Martin Buber, who advocated coexistence with the Palestinian Arabs, was unanimous on the question of unrestricted Jewish immigration. Indeed, during the darkest days of World War II, Palestine was a major refuge for the persecuted Jews of Europe.

At the same time, Jewish immigration and the resultant demographic shift in Palestine meant national suicide for the Arabs. Irrespective of their political affiliations, familial loyalties, social status, and religious beliefs, the Palestinians were unanimous in opposing Jewish immigration.[70] Jewish immigration to Palestine, the cornerstone of Zionism, was also the fundamental cause of Arab opposition. Under such circumstances, Arab-Jewish accommodation, as visualized by Mahatma Gandhi, was nothing but a fantasy.

For the very same reasons, expecting the Zionists to give up their support of British imperialism was also unrealistic. The creation of an immigration-based national home in Palestine depended upon the British, the Mandate authorities. Despite all the hurdles and restrictions, during much of the Mandate years, London was their only hope. This dependence upon the British explains the absence of any serious political contacts between the Zionists and the Mahatma or for that matter with the Indian nationalists. The success of the homeland project depended entirely upon the ability of the Zionist to project a convergence of interests with the British. How could they identify with the anti-British Mahatma and still hope to secure the support of the British? In short, realization of a Jewish homeland required the Zionists opting for the Mandate British over the Arabs in Palestine and for imperial Britain over Gandhi in India.

Fifth, Jewish critics of Gandhi at times have accused him of failing to understand Judaism. A harsh editorial in *The Jewish Advocate,* for example, admonished him for his lack of understanding of Jewish history. It accused him of acquiring his knowledge "from Christian missionaries. There is a strong hint of this in your remark that 'indeed, it is a strong stigma against them [the Jews] that their ancestors crucified Jesus'—a remark, if you will forgive us, worthy of a professional missionary or a medieval scholastic."[71] Similarly, the Israeli scholar Shimoni concluded that Mahatma Gandhi "saw Judaism essentially through Christian spectacles," resulting in "a distortion of considerable proportions . . . and Christian-induced misrepresentation of Judaism."[72]

As discussed elsewhere, one can extend this further and argue that Indian nationalists, like their counterparts in many non-Western countries, were unfamiliar or even immune to the Judeo-Christian heritage that prevailed in Europe. Despite religious and cultural proximity to Islam, in the politico-social realm, Judaism found a common cause with Christian Europe.[73] This Judeo-Christian heritage significantly contributed to the emergence and growth of Zionism and the eventual formation of Israel. His student days in Britain and long association with foreigners, however, did not sway Gandhi to these Judeo-Christian sentiments. The concept of divine right and biblical promises were foreign to him. Nor was he consumed by the guilty conscience that dominated mainstream European thinking during his time.

Yet Gandhi was not immune to religious influences. Like his colleagues in the nationalist struggle, he viewed the Palestinian problem through an Islamic prism. His belief that Palestine was an integral part of *Jazirat al-Arab* and his invocation of the injunction of the Prophet bear this out. It would be unfair and even incorrect to accuse him of compromising on truth for the sake of enlisting the support of the Indian Muslims. Nevertheless, the attitude of the Muslim population toward Palestine undoubtedly influenced his thinking. Gandhi was the leader of a nationalist movement, not a sectarian struggle, and thus could not afford to ignore the sentiments of a large segment of the Indian population. The absence of a significant Jewish presence in India also precluded the need for him to seek a compromise between Jewish and Muslim positions on Palestine.

Thus the views of Mahatma Gandhi toward the demand for a Jewish national home in Palestine were not unequivocal and consistent, as they are often presented. On issues such as Jewish violence in Palestine, the need for Arab consent for the realization of the Jewish demands, and Zionist-imperialist connections, he was fairly consistent. On other issues, the picture is more complex. His emphasis on nonviolence was neither universal nor proportionate. During the Khilafat days, he endorsed Islamic sanctions over Palestine but gradually recognized the "prior claims" of the Jews over the same territories. He saw religion as a means of promoting Hindu-Muslim unity in India and thus looked at Palestine through an Islamic prism. Though opposed to religion-based states, both in Palestine and in the Indian subcontinent, he did not reject outright Jewish claims in Palestine. Despite the widespread publicity given to his 1938 statement, as partition became inevitable in India, he began to see the events in Palestine differently. Softening his position, he began to hope that the Zionists could abandon their close links with the British and seek an accommodation with the Arabs. Given the overwhelming odds facing the Zionist leadership, neither was possible.

For their part, the Zionist interest in Gandhi was too little, too late. They sought his endorsement without offering any reciprocal political support for his nationalist struggle. The Zionists were to be partly blamed for "the image of Jews as alien to Asia," because "they avoided an identification with anticolonial nationalist movements."[74] Perhaps this was not possible in light of their need for British support in Palestine. The pro-British Zionist stance had an adverse impact not only on the Mahatma but also upon the Indian nationalist movement. Thus his sympathetic views toward Jewish claims to Palestine, especially after 1938, simply went unnoticed and unrecognized.

The Mahatma's political career spanned over three decades. Yet none of the leading figures in the Zionist movement had met Gandhi in person or established political contacts. His Jewish friends during his South African period had no political or Zionist agenda, although the same cannot be said about other emissaries who were sent to India in the mid-1930 to solicit his support. However, the Zionist emissary who was sent dismissed him as a "simpleton and sham saint." Above all, while demanding his support, the Zionist leadership was unable to reciprocate. It was not able to share or empathize with the Mahatma's struggle against British imperialism.

This asymmetrical situation became even more lopsided as the Indian National Congress formulated its policy toward the problem in Palestine.

If some twenty years ago Zionists would have tried to come into contact with Jawaharlal Nehru, when he studied in Cambridge, we would not see him today taking up such an attitude of lack of understanding towards our cause.

—*Immanuel Olsvanger*

3 The Congress Party and the *Yishuv*

Founded in 1885, the Indian National Congress not only led India's struggle for independence but also showed an active interest in various international developments. The problems faced by Indian laborers in different parts of the world dominated its external interests. It empathized with other national-liberation movements in their fight against imperialism and colonialism. This inevitably drew the INC to the Middle East, a major arena of anti-imperialist struggle since the early twentieth century. In practical terms, it meant the Indian nationalists would get entangled in the struggle for a Jewish national home in Palestine. The Congress Party's positions become pertinent also because it dominated the Indian polity for over a century and for nearly half a century enjoyed a political monopoly in free India. For many Indians and foreigners alike, the Congress Party was synonymous with India's struggle for freedom.

Why were the Indian nationalists drawn into the Middle East? How did they view the Jewish aspirations in Palestine? Did they understand and empathize with the Jewish longing for statehood? Was the Congress Party's stance driven by ideology or the result of domestic compulsions? Can one trace the roots of India's Israel policy to the Congress Party and its stance on Palestine? Finally, how did the Zionists view the Indian nationalist cause and its usefulness for their enterprise in Palestine?

In the early twentieth century, two Middle Eastern developments caught the attention of the Congress Party, namely, the Khilafat struggle and the Palestine question. Toward the closing stages of World War I, the Indian nationalists joined with their Muslim brethren, who were concerned about European powers undermining the office of the caliph. As discussed elsewhere, the Khilafat movement dominated the Indian political atmosphere between 1919 and 1924. In 1922, the Congress Party declared that "effective guardianship of Islam and the *Jazirat al-Arab* [be] free[d] from all non-Muslim control."[1] Capturing the central argument, its president, Mohamed Ali, observed that it would be "a sad day indeed for us when any part of it goes out of the hands of the Muslims, for then we would have betrayed a divine trust. Muslims will never acquiesce in any arrangements that permitted any form of control being exercised by a non-Muslim power over any part of *Jazirat al-Arab*."[2]

As the Khilafat issue faded from political scene, Palestine became the major INC preoccupation in the Middle East.[3] The first direct reference to Palestine came in 1923, when Mohammed Ali, the INC president, urged Indians to make common cause with the Palestinians.[4] In January 1928, the Congress Party adopted its first formal resolution on Palestine. Coming in the wake of the Brussels Congress on Oppressed Nationalities, the party sent its "warm greetings to the people of Egypt, Syria, Palestine, and Iraq and its assurance of full sympathy with them in their struggle for emancipation from the grip of Western Imperialism."[5] For the next eight years, there were no references to Palestine in the deliberations of the Congress Party.

In 1936, the Wardha Session of the Congress Working Committee (CWC) adopted a resolution on Arabs in Palestine. This came in the midst of the disturbances and violence in Palestine commonly known as the Arab Revolt (1936–1939). Without discussing the background, the Congress Party conveyed its greetings and sympathy "to the Arabs of Palestine in their struggle for independence against British Imperialism."[6] This was also the first exclusive INC resolution on Palestine. Subsequently, Palestine became its only concern in the Middle East. As the problem drew more attention from the Muslim League, the Congress Party declared September 27, 1936, as Palestine Day. Meetings were held in different parts of the country to express solidarity with the Arabs.

Nehru, who by then had emerged as the principal spokesperson of the party on foreign policy, attended a mass rally in his native town of Allahabad.

In October 1937, the All-India Congress Committee (AICC) met in Calcutta and registered its protest "against the reign of terror that has been established in Palestine by British Imperialism with a view to coerce the Arabs into accepting the proposed partition of Palestine and assure them of the solidarity of the Indian people with them in their struggle for national freedom."[7] The following February, in his presidential address at the Haripura Session, Subhas Chandra Bose highlighted the contradictory and inconsistent policy of the British in Palestine. Because of the heterogeneous composition of the empire, he observed, the British had to be pro-Arab in India and pro-Jewish elsewhere. Thus, he charged, London "has to please the Jews because she cannot ignore Jewish high finance. On the other hand, the India Office and Foreign Office have to placate the Arabs because of the imperial interests in the Near East and in India."[8] On similar lines, another Congress Party functionary felt that British imperialism had a "clever knack of promising two or more sets of contradictory things. . . . The fact is, and it seems to be quite in keeping with British diplomacy, that Palestine was promised both to the Jews and to the Arabs."[9]

Continuing its earlier policy, the Haripura Congress also condemned "the decision of Great Britain as Mandatory Power to bring about the partition of Palestine and protested against the continued reign of terror." Extending sympathy to the Arabs of Palestine, it felt that the proper resolution of the Arab-Jewish problem would be an amicable settlement between the two parties. It appealed to the Jews "not to seek the shelter of the British Mandatory and not to allow themselves to be exploited in the interests of British Imperialism."[10] Three months later, the INC, for the first time, evoked the right of self-determination for Palestine. Deploring the "unnamable atrocities committed by the British Army and Police," the CWC felt that "the issue of the future government of Palestine should be left to be decided on the principle of Self-determination." On the question of the Jews, it declared in unequivocal terms: "While sympathizing with the plight of the Jews in Europe and elsewhere, the Committee deplore[s] that in Palestine the Jews have relied on British armed forces to advance their special claims and thus aligned themselves on the side of British Imperialism." Demanding direct Arab-Jewish cooperation, it visualized the establishment of a "free democratic State in Palestine with adequate protection of Jewish rights."[11] The fifty-second INC session, which met in Tripuri in March 1939, reiterated this idea.[12]

A month before the Tripuri session, in February 1939, the Congress Party managed to pass a nonbinding resolution in the Legislative Assembly demanding India's withdrawal from the League of Nations.[13] The supplementary motion, moved by Abdul Qaiyum Khan (a lawmaker from the North West Frontier Province, currently a part of Pakistan), cited British policy in Palestine as one of the reasons for the demand.[14] Subsequently, Palestine drew little attention. The INC and its leaders were preoccupied with World War II and the political restrictions that followed. With most of its leaders incarcerated during the war, the Congress Party could not function normally and was unable to focus on external issues.

However, any understanding of the Congress Party's policies toward Palestine would be incomplete without underlining certain crucial omissions: (1) There was no reference to the Balfour Declaration in the INC resolutions.[15] This was in contrast to the Muslim League, which consistently demanded the abrogation of the British promise for a Jewish national home in Palestine. (2) The Congress Party did not take any formal position on the Jewish problem or propose a possible solution for it.[16] (3) The Congress Party never repudiated Jewish claims over Palestine and its criticisms were directed only at the *modus operandi* of the *yishuv*. (4) While maintaining that the British gave contradictory promises to the Arabs and Jews, the Congress Party did not suggest a compromise between these conflicting promises. And (5) even though it demanded a democratic state in Palestine with "adequate protection of Jewish rights," the Congress Party was not clear whether these rights were political and national or religious and social.

Nehru and the Palestine Question

As Bandyopadhyaya reminds us, since the Madras (now Chennai) session in December 1927, Nehru became the "recognized spokesman of the Congress on foreign affairs." After the formation of the Foreign Department of the Congress Party in 1925, "practically every resolution of the Congress on foreign affairs was inspired, drafted, and piloted by Nehru."[17] What were Nehru's opinions on Palestine and Jewish nationalist aspirations?

At one level, Nehru had a sympathetic understanding of the plight of Jews. In May 1933, he wrote:

> They [that is, the Jews] had no home or nation, and everywhere they went they were treated as unwelcome and undesirable strangers. . . . They were humiliated, reviled, tortured and massacred; the very word "Jew" became a word of abuse, a synonym for miser and a grasping moneylender. And yet, these amazing people not only survived all this, but managed to keep their racial and cultural characteristics, and prospered and produced a host of great men. . . . Most of them, of course, are far from prosperous; they crowd in the cities of Eastern Europe and, from time to time, suffer "pogroms" or massacres. These people without home or country . . . have never ceased to dream of old Jerusalem, which appear to their imaginations greater and more magnificent than it ever was in fact.[18]

Like the Mahatma, he was also unsympathetic toward Jewish political aspirations in Palestine. The creation of a Jewish national home in Palestine was unacceptable because "Palestine was not a wilderness, or an empty, uninhabited place. It was already somebody else's home . . . this generous gesture of the British government [the Balfour Declaration] was really at the expense of the people who already lived in Palestine."[19] Regarding Zionist aspirations in Palestine, he remarked: "The Arabs tried to gain their [Jewish] cooperation in the struggle for national freedom and democratic government[20] but . . . [the Jews] rejected these advances. They have preferred to take sides with the foreign ruling power, and have thus helped it to keep back freedom from the majority of the people."[21]

On another occasion, Nehru highlighted the inability of Palestine to absorb new immigrants from abroad.[22] Describing the Palestinian problem as a nationalist struggle against the British, he drew a parallel with India's freedom movement.[23] Speaking in Allahabad on Palestine Day in September 1936, he reminded his audience of the British policy of playing one community off another to further imperialist interests.[24] Writing to the editor of *The Jewish Advocate* in August 1937, Nehru argued that a real solution to the Palestine question should consider the following factors: (1) independence of Palestine, (2) recognition of the fact that Palestine was an Arab country and therefore Arabs must have a predominant voice in it, and (3) recognition of the fact that the Jews in Palestine are an integral factor and their rights should be protected.[25] A few weeks later, in his message to the mufti of Jerusalem, he hoped for an undivided and free Palestine.[26] In October 1938, he declared in unambiguous terms: "Palestine is essentially an Arab country and must remain so, and the Arabs must not be crushed and suppressed in their own homelands."[27] He frequently reiterated this as late as April 1947, at the New Delhi Asian Relations Conference.[28] This eventually became India's policy after independence.

Like Mahatma Gandhi, Nehru's views are also problematic. Speaking in Allahabad in 1936, he ruled out Palestine being a religious issue.[29] Both the Arabs and Jews invoked religious injunctions to buttress their respective claims and positions. The resolutions and pronouncements of various Indian leaders clearly testify to this and, in 1922, the Congress Party itself declared that *Jazirat al-Arab* should remain under Islamic control. Second, despite his prolonged exposure to Western education and culture, Nehru was unable to understand or appreciate the Jewish yearning for a national home. He was not ready to comprehend their nationalist aspirations and their desire to be a free nation. He was primarily preoccupied not with the Jewish national aspirations but their attempts to achieve this with the help of the British. Without ever repudiating Jewish nationalist aspirations, he confined his attention to their "collaboration" with the imperial power.

Moreover, while endorsing Jewish rights in Palestine, Nehru was unable to define them. Were the Jews entitled to any political rights? If so, what were the limits? He reiterated the Arab character of Palestine without ever clarifying Jewish rights. As reflected by the Indian Plan at the UN Committee, he was not prepared to grant any political rights to the Jews but merely settled for civic and religious rights. Above all, Nehru looked at the prevailing international situation through an anticolonial lens. Writing to the Zionist emissary Immanuel Olsvanger in September 1936, he remarked: "I cannot tolerate this imperialism in India or Palestine and the question I ask everyone is whether he stands for this imperialism or against it."[30] His predisposition toward the Arabs made him view Zionism not as a genuine national liberation struggle but merely as a collaborator with British imperial designs in the Middle East and elsewhere. The close ties that the Zionists forged with Great Britain were a result of the harsh political realities of the time. The ability of the Zionists to seek a national home for Jews scattered to the four corners of the world depended entirely upon their success in securing the support and backing of a great power. Nehru was not prepared to appreciate the Zionist predicament.

However, on the central issue of the Holocaust and Jewish suffering, Nehru was more forthcoming and helpful. On this front, the track record of the Congress Party was mixed. It adopted no formal resolution on the Jewish problem that plagued Europe or on the Holocaust. In December 1938, the Congress Party referred to "the plights of Jews in Europe." The CWC resolution on Palestine, declared, *inter alia*: "While sympathizing with the plight of Jews in Europe and elsewhere, the Committee deplore[s] that in Palestine the Jews have relied on British armed forces to advance their special claims and thus aligned themselves on the side of British Imperialism."[31] The primary focus was on Jewish "collaboration" with imperialism and not their persecution in Europe. The foreign-policy resolution adopted in the INC's 1939 annual session made a passing reference to the situation in Europe, lamenting:

> International morality has sunk so low in Central and South Western Europe that the World has witnessed with horror, the organized terrorism of the Nazi government against the people of the Jewish race. . . . The Congress disassociates itself entirely from British policy which has consistently aided the Fascist powers and helped in the destruction of the democratic countries. The Congress is opposed to imperialism and fascism alike and is convinced that world peace and progress required the ending of both of these.[32]

Both these resolutions were adopted well before the formal Nazi decision to annihilate the Jews through mass murder and gas chambers.

Nehru was far more forthcoming and unsuccessfully tried to declare the party's support for Jewish refugees. Keeping in mind "the terrible pogrom in Germany against the Jews," he favored inviting Jewish refugees who could contribute to India's progress. In response to a letter from a Jewish person in Prague, he noted that inviting Jewish experts would be also be beneficial to India.[33] In the early 1930s, many Jewish refugees from Europe approached the AICC seeking employment in India.[34] Even though he was not holding any public office, Nehru

> played a notable role in getting the Government of India to take in Jews. . . . He also succeeded in persuading the reluctant Indian Medical Council to recognize Continental European medical qualifications which enabled many highly skilled refugee doctors to practice in India. . . . Between 1933 and the outbreak of the war, Nehru was instrumental in obtaining entry for several German Jewish refugees into India.[35]

Due to opposition from various quarters, however, "a large-scale emigration of the Jews to India could not be achieved."[36]

The British policy of declaring German Jewish refugees as "enemy aliens" infuriated Nehru, who bitterly remarked, "it will become more and more difficult for [Jewish refugees] to come, as the difficulties placed in their way by the British government are very great."[37] Some argue that the pro-Palestinian policy of the Congress Party "encouraged the British to insist that each Jewish refugee have a guaranteed job before being allowed entry into India."[38] Despite the hurdles and difficulties, a number of refugees came to India, and Nehru pleaded for and facilitated their absorption into various provincial governments. Some prominent personalities, such as the communist leader M. N. Roy and the future diplomats B. Shiva Rao and R. K. Nehru (also a distant cousin of Jawaharlal Nehru), were married to Jewish refugees from Europe.[39]

Nehru, however, faced a serious challenge from the Congress Party. Keeping the unfolding Jewish tragedy in mind, he sponsored a resolution in the CWC. This most likely happened at the Wardha session in December 1938, following his return from Europe. The draft resolution read: "The Committee sees no objection to the employment in India of such Jewish refugees as are experts and specialists and who can fit in with the new order in India and accept Indian standards."[40] This was not acceptable to the CWC and especially to Subhas Bose, the INC president, and was rejected. Commenting on his failure, Nehru felt that Bose "did not approve of any step being taken by the Congress which was anti-Japanese or anti-German or anti-Italian. And yet such was the feeling in Congress and the country that he did not oppose this or many other manifestations of Congress sympathy for China and the victims of Fascist and Nazi aggression."[41]

Nehru had just returned from a European tour, where he had received first-hand experience on the plight of Jews. What motivated him to seek such a resolution? In his April 1939 letter to Bose, Nehru clarified his stance:

> I felt that we must express our opinion in regard to it [that is, the pogrom]. You say that you were "astounded when I produced a resolution seeking to make India an asylum for the Jews." I am surprised to learn that you felt so strongly about this as, so far as I remember, you did not express yourself definitely at the time. But is it fair to characterize my resolution as one seeking to establish an asylum for

> the Jews in India? . . . *It was not from the point of view of helping Jews that I considered this question,* though such help was desirable where possible without detriment to our country, *but from the point of view of helping ourselves by getting first-rate men of science, industry, etc., on very moderate payment.* Quite a number of countries sent special commissions to Vienna, after the Nazi occupation, to pick out good men. Turkey has profited greatly from such specialists. It seemed to me an ideal chance to get the right type of technicians and specialists. Their coming here on low salaries would have helped us also to bring down other salaries. They would have come for a period and not to settle down for ever. And only a limited number would have come, and only such as were of definite use to us and accepted our standards and political outlook.[42]

Nehru felt that India, on the threshold of freedom, would benefit from the expertise and skills of Jewish refugees, while also offering refuge to the persecuted Jews of Europe. Though appearing selfish, he was not alone in making such calculations and indeed was better than many of his contemporaries in other parts of the world.[43]

However, the central issue of the Holocaust still remains. Nehru's desire to host Jewish refugees fleeing Nazi Germany was accompanied by an indifferent attitude of the Congress Party toward the Holocaust. The end of World War II revealed the magnitude of the problem and provided some opportunities for the party to articulate its stance. Indian leaders were not ready to admit any link between the Holocaust in Europe and Jewish aspirations in Palestine. When the Special Session of the UN General Assembly met in April 1947 to deliberate the future of Palestine, India vehemently opposed the proposed UN Special Committee on Palestine (UNSCOP) visit to the Displaced Persons camps in Europe. Even the UNSCOP, of which India was a member, rejected such a linkage, and the majority of the members recommended that "any solution for Palestine cannot be considered as a solution of the Jewish problem in general."[44] This line of argument is more poignantly reflected in post-1947 Indian writings. Whenever Indian scholars discuss the Holocaust, it is invariably linked to Israeli policies regarding the Palestinians. In the words of one: "Close to a million Palestinian Arabs were evicted from their ancestral homelands just as Hitler's tyranny had uprooted many Jews from theirs."[45] Palestinians being asked to pay for Hitler's sins remains their theme song.

In short, the Indian leadership, comprising the Congress Party and its two stalwarts, Mahatma Gandhi and Jawaharlal Nehru, were not in favor of Jewish national aspirations in Palestine. While some of their arguments could be challenged, it is undeniable that they were not ready to endorse the Zionist enterprise in Palestine.

How can one explain and rationalize this pro-Arab and anti-Zionist stand?

Rationale

Asia in general was indifferent to the Jewish longing for a historic home. According to one school of thought, this apathy was due to the absence of the Judeo-Christian heritage in the continent. The history of the Jewish people and their claims to the Holy Land were alien to the predominantly non-Christian Asian masses. Even their Western-educated leaders were less than familiar with Jewish history. In the words of Michael Brecher, Theodore Herzl "did not succeed in his efforts to enlist diplomatic support from Zionist aspirations, but Christian leaders did not question the propriety of his actions or doubt the unique Jewish link to Palestine. . . . Such sympathy, let alone active support, was unthinkable among Asian leaders, because historic Israel, Jewry, and Judaism are little known east of the Arab world."[46] Others, however, attribute the Asian reluctance to its suspicion and disapproval of the goals and objectives of Zionism. For them, serious differences with Jewish aspirations in Palestine made the Asian leaders wary of Zionism's colonial desires. The Asian reluctance to endorse the Zionist aspiration has to be located within the context of the "incompatibility between the anticolonial upsurge in Asia and the methods and goals of the Zionist movement." Furthermore, as M. S. Agwani points out, the European Judeo-Christian heritage "did not prevent the sustained persecution of Jews, a circumstance to which Asian history affords no parallel."[47]

Both arguments are strong but incomplete. The Judeo-Christian heritage significantly facilitated the formation of the Jewish state. A host of "gentile Zionists" actively contributed to the Jewish-homeland project in Palestine.[48] Reasons for their support differed. For some Christians, a Jewish homeland was the fulfillment of the prophecy; for others, it was an atonement for their prolonged persecution of the "chosen people." Support for Zionism was also seen as an "honorable" solution to the age-old

Jewish problem in the non-European and non-Christian Palestine. Thus, predominantly Christian Latin America played a crucial role at the United Nations, and Christian or Christian-majority countries contributed the bulk of the thirty-three votes in favor of the partition plan. In short, the Judeo-Christian heritage contributed significantly to the popularity and international support for Zionism.

Similarly, Islamic countries or countries with a large or sizable Muslim population viewed the Jewish claims in Palestine through an Islamic prism. Persecution of the Jews was alien to Islamic civilization, and there are no Islamic parallels to the Holocaust, blood libel, or pogroms. Under the rubric of *Dhimmi*, the Jews were considered as a protected people with a revealed sacred text. So long as they accepted Islamic rule, their lives and properties were protected. At the same time, the concept of political equality between Muslims and non-Muslims was singularly absent. As Bernard Lewis pertinently asks: "How could one accord the same treatment to those who follow the true faith and those who willfully reject it?"[49] Seen in this Islamic tradition, the demand for a Jewish homeland in Palestine, among others, challenged the traditional Islamic paradigm of *Dhimmi*. As a result, not only Islamic countries but also countries with sizable Muslim populations, such as India, opposed the partition plan in 1947.

In short, countries with large Muslim or small Christian populations were unfamiliar with the historic links that the Zionists sought to establish with their ancient home. Even though most of the Indian nationalists, including the Mahatma and Nehru, were Western educated, they did not understand or comprehend the prolonged Jewish suffering that culminated in the Jewish nationalist aspiration. Like most Arab and Islamic peoples, they traced the problem primarily to the Balfour Declaration. Prolonged Jewish statelessness and their longing for political rights were unfamiliar to them. As a result, Indian nationalists never viewed Zionism as a genuine liberation movement. As an official Indian narrative puts it, "the seeds of the present tension" in the region were "sown at the beginning of [the twentieth] century, when the proposal to create a 'Jewish National Home' in Palestine received the sanction of the British Government."[50] The world was born yesterday.

Second, the imperialist connections of the Zionists figured prominently in Indian thinking. The compulsions that made Herzl highlight "international guarantees" as a precondition for the success of Zionism was never part of the Indian thinking. The Indian nationalists settled for a simple explanation of a complex reality. While the Arab nationalists were fighting the British in Palestine, they felt that the Zionists were cooperating with and benefiting from the Mandate authorities. This imperialist connection dominated Nehru's thinking and his refusal to endorse Zionist aspirations in Palestine. Commenting on this, Ariel Glucklich stated: "instead of identifying Zionism with modern liberation movements, Indian intellectuals identify Zionism with its countries of origin—as English, Russian, and American colonialism."[51] While the Mahatma advised the *yishuv* to abandon relying on "British bayonets," Nehru demanded that Zionists prove their credentials by siding with the anti-imperialist struggle of the Arabs.

Three, as will be discussed below, religious considerations played a critical role in India's unfriendly and indifferent attitude toward Zionism. Commenting on the role played by the Jews in shaping the U.S. policies, one U.S. congressman observed: "Israel succeeds in the Congress for the simple reason. Two or three per cent of the voters care intensely about it and the rest are uninformed and don't care."[52] This logic is equally applicable to India's Middle East policy. The Arab viewpoint on Palestine was strongly articulated by the Muslim leadership both within and outside the Congress Party. Declarations and resolutions on Palestine adopted by various Muslim organizations such as the Muslim League, the All-India Khilafat Committee, and *Jamaa't ulema-e-Hind* testify to the attitude of the Muslims of the Raj.[53]

During the Khilafat period, Mahatma Gandhi and the Congress Party did not hesitate to endorse Islamic claims over Palestine and the need to preserve it under Islamic rule. But they were not ready to accept Jewish religious claims to the same territory. As manifested by the Mahatma, the Indian attitude was conditioned by the need for Hindu-Muslim unity against the British. This became acute in the 1930s when the Muslim League began presenting itself as the authentic voice of the Muslims of the subcontinent. As the Muslim League was demanding the abrogation of the Balfour Declaration,[54] the Congress Party felt compelled to be more supportive of the Arabs of Palestine. Endorsing the Arab cause alone would not have ensured Muslim support for the Congress Party. But it is reasonably certain that a contrary position on Palestine would have alienated the Muslim minority from the Congress Party and pushed it closer to the Muslim League. Though couched in anti-imperialism, the pro-Arab stand of the Congress Party was primarily a political move driven by domestic calculations.

Finally, unlike the Arabs, the Zionists lacked an effective and influential constituency within India. Even individuals who were sympathetic toward their cause, such as K. M. Panikkar and Rabindranath Tagore,[55] were not prepared to come out in the open. The Mahatma's more sympathetic statement to Kallenbach written in 1937 was not made public while he was alive. Panikkar's memo visualizing post-1947 "Hindu-Zionist cooperation" long remained secret and confidential. Thus, well before the question of Palestine came before the United Nations in April 1947, the Indian position was known and well publicized. As far back as in 1938, Nehru visualized the formation of "a large Arab federation with a Jewish autonomous enclave."[56] The following year, the Tripuri Session of the Congress Party proposed an "independent democratic state in Palestine with adequate protection of Jewish rights."[57] This subsequently became the official position on Palestine when India was elected to the UN committee.

However, the Zionists and *yishuv* leadership also share some responsibility for the pro-Arab disposition of the Indian nationalists.

Yishuv and Indian Nationalists

The non-Western world in general and Asia in particular did not figure prominently in the political calculations of the *yishuv*. At one level, with foresight and long-term calculations, the *yishuv* systematically cultivated major powers but paid little attention to the rest of the world. As David Ben-Gurion aptly put it on the eve of the formation of the state, "When we say the whole world it is an exaggeration. We never think of India or China or similar countries, but rather about the countries in which Jews have lived or are living."[58] This indifference was reciprocated by the Asian apathy toward Zionist aspirations in Palestine. Out of the eight non-Arab Asian members, only the Philippines, a former American colony, voted for partition. Five countries, Afghanistan, Iran, Pakistan, and Turkey—all Muslim states—and India opposed partition; nationalist China abstained and Thailand was absent.[59] Real support for partition came from distant Latin America, which overwhelmingly endorsed Jewish aspirations in Palestine.[60] This Asian indifference and isolation was never fully overcome. Even though Israel later on was eager to befriend countries such as Burma (now Myanmar), the overall indifference continued. It was only in 1956, ironically coinciding with the Suez crisis, that

Israeli leaders began to pay serious and concerted attention to Asia in the form of a twelve-nation Asian tour undertaken by Moshe Sharett, the former prime minister.[61]

However, before examining the *yishuv* contacts with the Indian nationalists, one has to examine the obstacles before the *yishuv* leadership. Unlike other territorial nationalist movements in Asia, Africa, and Latin America, Zionism was not just about a nation becoming a homeland—it was about creating a homeland for a dispersed nation. Bringing the Diaspora to their ancestral home was the central pillar of Zionism. Even if Zionism could provide the necessary ideological zeal for Jewish emigration to Palestine or *aliya*, operationalizing such an ambitious plan was truly herculean.

Herzl was clear that without an international guarantee Zionism would have remained a messianic cult without a messiah. The Zionists, who were soliciting the support of all the major powers in Europe, found in Great Britain their principal benefactor. The Balfour Declaration of 1917 and the granting of a Mandate for Palestine made Great Britain the main partner in the Zionist enterprise in Palestine. Since the Jewish national-home project depended heavily upon the cooperation and support of the imperial power, the Zionists could not even dream of being anti-British. Rather than perceiving this as a collaboration with imperialism, one has to see the Zionist alignment with the British as a tactical move toward the realization of their larger political aspirations. As the Revisionist tactics highlighted, the Zionist-British cooperation was not written in stone. Simply put, at least in the initial years the Zionists could not have fought the British and still hoped for a Jewish homeland. The Zionist demands for political support from Indian nationalists, therefore, could not be accompanied by any reciprocal gesture.

Even without the imperial dimension, India was less attractive for the Zionist struggle. Zionist interests were focused on countries that enjoyed significant clout internationally, and their political activities were focused on these centers of international economic or political power. Though London was more forthcoming than the rest, during the run up to the Balfour Declaration, the Zionists worked with other powers, including France, Germany, Russia, and even the Ottoman Empire.[62] During the interwar period, the United States emerged from its self-imposed isolation and began playing an active role in international politics. This resulted in the gradual shift of the nerve center of Zionist diplomacy from Europe to the United States. This is not to suggest that they ultimately ignored Europe but simply that over time the Zionists became more U.S.-centric. India did not fit into any of these categories. It was a colony of the British Empire, and if its economic clout was small, its political influence was even less. It was not in a position to promote and further Zionist interests internationally.

Moreover, countries with significant Jewish populations drew the considerable interest and attention of the Zionist leadership. Their success in Palestine depended heavily upon the solidarity and support of the Jews in the Diaspora and their identification with Zionist goals and tactics. The solidarity of the Jewish community with their goals in Palestine resulted in the Zionist leadership paying attention to larger communities in different parts of the world. Even on that account, India was not an important player. Its tiny Jewish population meant that the Zionists had little interest in India.[63]

Finally, the Jews in India were historically free from the persecution and ill treatment that had plagued them in Europe for centuries. The tolerant and assimilationist nature of Hinduism meant that there were fewer reasons for Jews to mark and maintain their distinct religious identity. Hinduism is apprehensive of proselytizing religions such as Christianity and Islam, but Judaism has never posed that type of threat. Historically, Hinduism and the Hindu-dominated Indian society have been extremely accommodating of Judaism and Jews. Anti-Semitism as it is universally understood has not existed in India.[64] On the other hand, this tolerant environment meant that India was not a crisis area that required the utmost attention of the Zionist leadership. Indian Jews were not a beleaguered community. Ironic as it sounds, Zionism often thrived on anti-Semitism. The rise of anti-Semitism led to an increase in Zionist consciousness among Jews and vice versa. In the absence of anti-Semitism, Zionism never took hold in India.

These facts lead us to an inevitable counterquestion. If India lacked any economic, political, or demographic incentives, why did the Zionists make any efforts at all in courting India?

Why Was India Important?

Israel has long been critical of its "unrequited love affair" with India.[65] The indifference and unfriendliness of the Indian nationalists figure prominently in its discourse. India's "unsympathetic and hostile stand" toward the Jewish state has come under severe criticism, both in Israel and elsewhere.[66] Idealism is the most common explanation for the Zionist interest in India. The familiarity of and admiration for Indian leaders such as Mahatma Gandhi and Nehru by the *yishuv* illustrate this aspect. Long before he became a leading figure in the nationalist struggle, Nehru's *Autobiography* was translated into Hebrew,[67] and so were the poems of the Nobel laureate Rabindranath Tagore. For a language revived after being dormant for centuries, these translations were no mean achievements.

Idealism, ironically, plays only a marginal role in international relations. Hard-nosed and realistic calculations are justified through moral considerations and ethical arguments. While one cannot go to the extent of suggesting that international relations are immoral by nature, one should not attribute the behaviors of groups and states merely to moral and ethical calculations. Zionism was no exception to this trend, and thus one must look for other reasons for the Zionist interest in India. As India was slowly moving toward independence, the Zionists realized that they could not ignore such a big country. Since the end of World War II, it was clear that Britain would relinquish its "jewel in the crown." The formation of the interim government in September 1946 under the leadership of Nehru was a major step in this direction. Meanwhile, India joined the United Nations as a founding member and was slowly making its presence felt as an independent player in a number of international bodies. Its election to the eleven-member UNSCOP in May 1947 pointed to its burgeoning relevance and importance.

There was also a larger political consideration: India's Muslim population. Its unique position as the center of world's largest Muslim population enhanced the importance of British India. As the largest community outside the entire *dar ul-Islam* (House of Islam), the Indian Muslims received considerable attention world over, and the *yishuv* was not an exception. The Zionists were aware of the Muslim factor at the time of the Balfour Declaration. The perceived opposition from Indian Muslims considerably delayed the British decision to endorse the demand for a Jewish national home. Senior officials in the India Office were opposed to Jews being given special privileges in Palestine. Such a move, they feared, would result in widespread opposition from the Indian Muslims and would lead to unexpected consequences. The fears about the negative influences of British officials serving in India weighed heavily upon the Zionist leaders, Weizmann in particular.[68] For the Indian Muslims, Palestine was an integral part of the *Jazirat al-Arab* and could not be handed over to non-Muslims. This became a dominant issue during the final days of the Ottoman Empire, when European powers were seeking to place its Arab areas under an Anglo-French mandate. The Zionist political aspirations in Palestine came into conflict with the Indian Muslim struggle for the preservation of the caliph. The formation of Indian opinion critical of Zionist aspirations in Palestine occurred during this period, when the Indian nationalists, including Mahatma Gandhi, were making common cause with the Muslims on a religious issue.

Furthermore, the potential of Indian Muslims to impede Jewish aspirations in Palestine was exacerbated by another player: Hajj Amin al-Husseini, the grand mufti of Jerusalem. Ever since his appointment to that position in May 1921, al-Husseini was quick to recognize the Islamic nature of the problem in Palestine. He faced a twin challenge—strong internal opposition from other powerful Arab families such as the Nashashibis and growing Zionist activities in Palestine, especially immigration. The British administration was a new and unknown phenomenon, and he was not sure of gaining its confidence, let alone support. The mufti realized that his ability to confront the threats posed by Jewish immigration rested on the expansion of his support base beyond Palestine. Islam could be an effective instrument, and expanding the problem into a larger Arab and Islamic agenda was tempting. Instead of seeing Jewish immigration as an assault on the Palestinians, the mufti projected it as a threat to the Islamic world.[69] Such a worldview naturally drew him to India. In the early 1920s, he sent a three-member delegation to raise funds for the restoration of the dilapidated al-Aqsa mosque.[70] The delegation managed to persuade rich and philanthropic Muslim rulers of India to contribute generously and raised £22,000; the nizam of the princely state of Hyderabad in southern India alone contributed £7,000.[71]

Unlike the Zionists, the mufti had one distinct advantage: the ability to reciprocate. While seeking India's support, he projected the prevailing political climate in Palestine as an anticolonial struggle; the British were the enemies of Indians as well as the Arabs. For a staunch anti-imperialist like Nehru, the mufti, who was despised by the Zionists, emerged as a genuine nationalist fighting for the liberation of the Arabs of Palestine.[72] This ideological convergence overshadowed all the other contradictions between the mufti's brand of Arab nationalism and Gandhian nonviolence. The mufti's reliance on violence, Islamic orientation, and his Nazi connections during World War II became secondary to the Indian nationalists. Much to the chagrin of the Jews, the mufti's personal meeting with Hitler in November 1941 rarely figures in Indian discourses on the Middle East. Besides the leaders of the Congress Party, the mufti succeeded in establishing personal contacts with important Muslim leaders such as Mohammed Ali and Shaukat Ali. He met the Ali brothers, the leaders of the Khilafat movement, in Mecca during the *hajj* pilgrimages of 1924 and 1926.[73] Mohammed Ali visited Palestine in 1928, and in the following year the Indian Muslims sent a delegation to the International Wailing Wall Commission, where Ali delivered "one of the three closing speeches for the Muslim side before the Commission."[74]

The mufti's close association with the Ali brothers bolstered his standing among the Arabs. He could present himself as someone who was courted, consulted, and listened to by Muslim leaders beyond Palestine; this in turn enhanced his prestige among the Palestinians. Through his offer in January 1931 to bury Mohammad Ali's body in *Harem al-Sharif*, in the precincts of the Islam's third-holiest shrine, the mufti received the admiration, appreciation, and gratitude of Indian Muslims. Later that year, Shaukat Ali played a key role in the Jerusalem Islamic Conference organized by the mufti.[75]

India thus provided the mufti with significant political, religious, and even financial support and raised the stakes of the Palestinian gambit. These efforts proved successful when the Muslim League commemorated May 16, 1930, as the first Palestine Day.[76] The popularity of this occasion compelled the Congress Party to adopt this practice: September 27, 1936, was again declared as Palestine Day.[77] The mufti's growing involvement with India's Muslim community rang alarms in Zionist circles. They feared that any active Indian involvement in Palestine would be detrimental to their cause. The Arab opposition to *aliya* was already causing concern in London, and active Indian involvement could only aggravate the situation. Therefore, a denial of Indian support, the Zionists felt, might help curtail the mufti's efforts and his ability to "Islamize" the conflict in Palestine.

With this objective in mind, in the 1930s the Zionists made contacts with Indian leaders.

Zionist Contacts

The Zionists sought and established wide-ranging contacts with the Indian nationalists and various segments of the Indian society. Such contacts were not confined to Gandhi, Nehru, and other senior Congress Party leaders alone but encompassed the leaders of Hindu, Muslim, and Jewish communities in India. They cultivated and befriended academic associations and institutions, Indian officials serving under the British Raj, influential personalities in various princely states, individuals who subsequently became pioneering diplomats of free India, and various other subaltern elements through public meetings and contacts.

Such diverse activities run counter to the popular notion put forth by Indian writers such as Jansen and echoed by Shimoni.[78] The earliest known Zionist contacts with Nehru could probably be traced to the Brussels Conference of Oppressed Nationalities in 1927.[79] In April 1930, Gershon Agronsky visited Bombay on behalf of the Jewish Agency Executive.[80] Olsvanger came to India in 1936, as an official emissary of the Jewish Agency. His mandate was to establish formal links with various Indian leaders and to seek a sympathetic understanding of the Jewish national aspirations in Palestine. Even though he failed to elicit a favorable Indian opinion, he managed to forge personal ties with Nehru that continued long after the formation of Israel.[81] Likewise, Weizmann, who was instrumental in the Balfour Declaration, met Nehru on July 20, 1938, when the INC leader was in London, and subsequently corresponded with him.[82]

During his six-month stay, Olsvanger met and interacted with a host of other Indian leaders, including Sarojini Naidu,[83] Sardar Patel,[84] B. R. Ambedkar,[85] G. B. Pant,[86] Tagore, and C. F. Andrews.[87] While Sarojini Naidu[88] and Ambedkar[89] came out in support of Zionist aspirations in Palestine, others were more cautious. Tagore, for example, was sympathetic to their cause but clarified that his view was "a purely personal one and not meant for newspaper publication."[90] This private warmth and public caution was due to the prevailing pro-Arab position of the Congress Party. The Zionists were successful in convincing many INC leaders to accept their invitation for personal visits to Palestine for a first-hand assessment. Among others, Sarojini Naidu, Andrews,[91] and S. Radhakrishnan[92] agreed to visit Palestine. None of these planned visits materialized. The commencement of World War II and consequent incarceration of Indian nationalists prevented them.

While looking to the Congress Party and its leadership for political support, the Zionists were conscious of the need to cultivate a popular support base in India. This became essential in the light of the indifferent and unsympathetic positions adopted by senior INC leaders, especially Gandhi and Nehru. Both Olsvanger[93] and the Zionist activist Olga Feinberg,[94] who was working for the Women's International Zionist Organization, addressed a number of public meetings in India and spoke about the situation in Palestine and the *yishuv*.

The vocal support for Israel expressed by the Hindu right wing can create the wrong and misleading impression that the Zionists confined their activities to anti-Muslim sections of India. For example, some Indian leaders offered to fight for the Jews.[95] Over the years, the Hindu Mahasabha, Jan Sangh, its later successor the BJP, and similar other groups, organizations, and individuals associated with this segment of the Indian public adopted an overtly pro-Israel stand. This might give the impression that the Zionists approached India within a narrow communal framework. However, the Zionists also invested considerable political capital in India's Muslim community and leadership. As discussed elsewhere, Weizmann's first known political contact was not with the INC leadership but with Muslim leaders. His meeting with Shaukat Ali took place in January 1931, many years before his meeting with Nehru. Likewise, Olsvanger forged personal relations with a number of Muslim leaders of the British Raj, including Khan Abdul Ghaffar Khan,[96] Muhammed Iqbal,[97] and Maulana Abul Kalam Azad.[98] Ghaffar Khan was an influential leader of the Baloch community that eventually became part of Pakistan; Iqbal wrote the song that was adopted as the national anthem of Pakistan. Azad emerged as Nehru's principal adviser on India's Middle East policy and, according to Michael Brecher, sabotaged Nehru's plans to normalize relations with Israel in early 1952.

Olsvanger's interactions with Muslim leaders led to an unusual development. In September 1936, he was asked by the Central Khilafat Committee to speak at its meeting in New Delhi. Declining this unique offer, he argued that in the absence of an Arab speaker from Palestine, "I somehow feel that my addressing the Congress would mean . . . to take advantage of the absence of a possible opponent and that would surely be not fair. If a Palestinian Arab would be present, both he and I could speak and reply to each other before an impartially listening audience."[99] Similarly, in December 1937, another Zionist figure, Richard Freund, met Asaf Ali.[100] A decade later, Asaf Ali represented India at the crucial First Special Session of the UN General Assembly that led to the formation of the UNSCOP.

Another area where the Zionists had a significant edge over the Arab nationalists was their widespread academic interests. This partially explains the pro-Zionist views expressed by a number of Western-educated Indian intellectuals. As early as 1909, Weizmann was offered a senior academic position at the University of Calcutta. The Zionist leader declined the professorial offer on the plea that "this would upset our Palestine plans."[101] Had Weizmann, the key architect of the Balfour Declaration, taken up the offer, the destiny of the Zionist movement most certainly would have been entirely different. During his visit, Olsvanger met a host of Indian academics. Reacting to his suggestion for institutional cooperation between the Banaras Hindu University (BHU) and the Hebrew University of Jerusalem, Pandit Madan Mohan Malviya, the vice chancellor of the BHU, pledged to discuss "the matter with my colleagues when I return to Banaras. But I may say at once that if you wish to send any Jew students to study Sanskrit at the Banaras Hindu University, we shall give him every facility to do so."[102]

In the same year, another academic, B. S. Guha of the Zoological Survey of India, remarked: "It was indeed a very great pleasure to have met you [Olsvanger] and to be able to establish connection with the University of Jerusalem through your good offices."[103] The participation of a ten-member Jewish delegation from Palestine in the first Asian Relations Conference in 1947 brought in more institutional interaction between the Zionists and Indian nationalists.[104] The Zionists also showed a keen interest in those Indians who were representing India in various international forums. The earliest known such contacts date back to 1931, when the Palestinian Zionist leader F. H. Kisch met and befriended Brejendra Mitter and L. K. Hyder, Indian delegates at the Assembly of the League of Nations.[105]

Finally, the Zionists were attracted by the princely states of India and their senior leaders and officials. Among them Shanmukham Chetty, the Diwan (the rank of nobility) of the southern princely state of Cochin (currently part of the state of Kerala), expressed an interest in establishing "trade connections between Cochin and the Jewish Agency for Palestine."[106] In 1938, the princely state of Bikaner (now in Rajasthan) sought technical assistance from the Jewish Agency in dry farming.[107] The Maharaja of Patiala (now in Indian Punjab) along with his foreign minister, K. M. Panikkar, sought cooperation with the *yishuv*. These contacts proved to be useful following the establishment of the state of Israel.

The extensive prestate contacts between the *yishuv* and India lead us to two interesting conclusions. First, if the Zionists failed to elicit favorable and sympathetic responses in India, it was not due to the absence of genuine efforts but despite them. And second, in terms of their sheer number, depth, and diversity, Zionist contacts with and efforts toward India were extensive and far reaching.

There is a catch, however. A comparison between the Zionist efforts in India and in other parts of the world leads us to a different and equally important understanding. A number of figures within the Zionist movement have acknowledged and even lamented that their efforts in cultivating India were too meager. Olsvanger's observation in 1937 clearly highlighted this dilemma. In a candid letter to the British Zionist leader Selig Brodetsky, he observed:

> If some twenty years ago Zionists would have tried to come into contact with Jawaharlal Nehru, when he studied in Cambridge, we would not see him today taking up such an attitude of lack of understanding towards our cause. The same applies to the greater part of those who are today leaders of Indian politics. But the greater part of their intellectuals . . . are at present spending their University years in one or other English towns. That is why the propaganda amongst Indians should be pursued in England. . . . The most dangerous and irresponsible attitude on our part would be to say: "We do not need these Asiatics at this juncture in view of the probable change in the Palestine political status." We cannot take Palestine out of Asia. And whatever the changes may be, friendly connections with big Asiatic communities will always be of paramount importance to us.[108]

A few years earlier, another Zionist emissary had warned: "The time has come for the Zionist Organization to consider without delay what measures can be taken that Zionist may turn its face, so to speak, to the East."[109]

In the absence of any visible progress toward improving contacts with Asia, a couple of years later, Olsvanger suggested:

> Work in India must begin as soon as possible. This would be a three-fold task.
>
> a. Work amongst the Hindus, chiefly in Congress quarters.
>
> b. Work among Moslems.
>
> c. Work amongst the Bene Israel . . .
>
> In addition to this, contact must be kept with the British officials in India, some of whom may one day be transferred to Palestine.

> Our representative in South Africa will have to bear in mind that the Indian community out there can also become either useful or harmful to us.
>
> It would be a grave mistake to rely for our work in India on the Zionists there. The task is too responsible.[110]

Sharing similar sentiments, Panikkar was equally categorical. In a confidential note to the Jewish delegation, the then foreign minister of Bikaner was blunt: "If there is no widespread expression of sympathy even in orthodox Hindu quarters towards Zionist claims, this is due to a large extent to the neglect of India by the Zionists themselves. No attempt has been made in the past to create such an understanding due no doubt to the 'Western' attitude of the Jews in general." How to fix the problem? His advice: "the Jewish Agency should have representation at Delhi."[111]

Taking note of this situation, the Jewish delegation that came to India in 1947 recommended, among other things,

1. a permanent political representative of the Jewish Agency should be immediately sent to India.
2. a desk for India and Asia should be created in the Political Department of the Jewish Agency.
3. regular coverage should be given to India in Palestine press; and
4. the establishment of an economic liaison office in Bombay should be examined.[112]

A year later, Walter Eytan, who subsequently became the first director general of the Ministry of Foreign Affairs, observed: "The KKL [*Karen Kayemet l'Yisrael*, or the Jewish National Fund] has now been looking for sometime for someone to go to India for three purposes: (a) KKL work proper; (b) work among Jewish youth [and] (c) political contacts." He went on to add that as far as he was aware, "they have still not found anyone. I've been trying to help them, but have so far not hit on any bright ideas. . . . *It's perfectly true that we've neglected that country* [India]."[113]

According to Michael Brecher, David Ben-Gurion, "who attached great importance to China in the 1960s, was indifferent to both East and South Asia on the eve of Israel's independence."[114] Indeed, none of the leading figures of Zionism or *yishuv* visited India prior to the formation of Israel.[115] The Weizmann-Nehru meeting of 1938 remained the only high-level meeting between two sides, and by that time, the Zionists had lost India to the Arabs.[116] It is obvious that while their attempts were deeper than has previously been asserted, the Zionists were less interested in India than in other parts of the world. India was not paramount. This indifference came up against a more powerful force that worked against the Zionist interests: India's Muslim population and its involvement in the Palestinian question.

The feeling of Muslim solidarity is greater in India than perhaps anywhere else in the Islamic world, owing primarily to the fact that Islam is a minority in India. In all matters on which Islam feels strongly, Hindu opinion will unconditionally back it in the present political circumstances.

—Historian and diplomat K. M. Panikkar

4 The Islamic Prism

The INC Versus the Muslim League

To understand India's Israel policy, one has to recognize the centrality of Islam and its influences. Overshadowed by generalities, euphemisms, political correctness, and secular rhetoric, this facet has rarely received an informed treatment. Any discussion on the Islamic inputs into India's policy toward the Middle East has become anathema and is often dismissed as an anti-Muslim conspiracy of the Hindu right wing. Numerous writings on the subject have marginalized or ignored the Islamic dimension. Be that as it may, India has always perceived, understood, and articulated its position toward Israel through an Islamic prism. In a sense, this is not different from the U.S. policies regarding the region. As with the United States, for India, Israel is primarily an item on the domestic and not foreign-policy agenda. This was true both before and after India's independence.

To appreciate the Islamic influence during the nationalist phase, we must ask a number of questions. What drew the Congress Party toward the Middle East? How were its interests in the region sustained? How did Islam influence its understanding of the Zionist demand for a Jewish national home? Was there a Hindu view regarding Palestinian developments? As the following narrative indicates, India's interest and involvement in the Middle East, and more particularly Jewish nationalist aspirations, were influenced and at times dominated by the Islamic factor. While its cultural interactions and trade links with the region were centuries old, modern political involvement with the region began when the Muslim world over rallied around the caliph, the title then held by the Ottoman sultan.

The Khilafat Struggle

The Congress Party first became involved in a Middle Eastern issue with the Khilafat question, an issue that dominated India until the mid-1920s.[1] This was the first major occasion when the Indian nationalists showed a direct interest in foreign events.[2] Up until then, their interests were confined to the welfare and conditions of Indians overseas. The treatment of the Ottoman Empire by the Allies during World War I was strongly resented by Indian Muslims. The European campaign was seen not merely as an aggression against the Ottoman Empire but as an attack against Islam, because the sultan of Turkey was also the caliph, the titular head of the Sunni Islamic community.[3] The most vociferous demonstrations in support of the caliph and Islamic solidarity with the Ottoman rulers were to be found among the Indian Muslims.[4] From 1919 to 1924, the Khilafat struggle dominated the Indian political scene, and the Muslim elite discovered in it an issue that could unite the masses against the British. Rallies and other forms of political protests were held throughout the country.

The Indian National Congress and its leaders saw this pan-Islamic solidarity as an opportunity to solidify nationalist feelings among the Muslim masses. For different reasons, both the Hindus and the Muslims resented the British. While nationalist sentiments were slowly growing, the Muslims had an additional grievance: the British had ended Islamic rule in India and deposed the last Mughal ruler. This mutual hatred toward the foreigner, however, was insufficient to overcome their mutual suspicions and fears of one another. Even though Hinduism is not a monolithic religion, for the Muslims it represented a single large homogeneous group of nonbelievers.[5] Many Muslims had misgivings over the motives of the Hindu-dominated Congress Party. Participation in the INC-led struggle, they feared, would undermine and even diminish their distinct Islamic identity. Though latent, these fears were real, as the subsequent partition of the subcontinent demonstrated. In some ways, the fears of Indian Muslims toward the Hindus were not dissimilar to that of the Jews and their struggle in Palestine. Democracy seemed a euphemism for legitimizing majority domination and the resultant loss of their particular identity. Driven by this fear of the other, both the *yishuv* and the Muslim League, which represented this segment of thought in India, found in the British a close and trusted ally. The Congress Party was certainly aware of the misgivings that powerful segments of the Muslim population had regarding the majority Hindus.

It was under these circumstances that the Muslim world witnessed the disintegration and demise of the Ottoman Empire. This radically altered the attitude of the Indian Muslims toward the Raj and brought them into conflict with the British rulers. Their sovereign and temporal loyalties clashed, and they sided with the latter. The Indian Muslims, who had previously been praying for the welfare of their London-based "sovereign ruler," King George V, now offered prayers for their Istanbul-based "temporal ruler," Mehmed VI. This gave birth to a popular struggle among the Indian Muslims known as the Khilafat movement.

The Congress Party viewed Muslim fears over the caliph as a means to forge closer political ties with the community. The participation of Muslims was a precondition for its nationalist credentials, and the Congress Party was aware of the general Muslim mistrust of its legitimacy and objectives. While it had some Muslim leaders among its ranks, its Muslim mass base was small. In December 1923, INC President Mohammed Ali aptly summed up the dilemma facing the nationalists: "the Congress which called itself 'Indian' and 'National' felt the need for Muslim participation, for it could not justify its title without it."[6] Thus its leaders, especially Mahatma Gandhi, saw the Khilafat movement as an opportunity to strengthen Hindu-Muslim unity against the British. Despite obvious religious dogma, the nationalist leaders presented the struggle around the caliph as an integral part of their wider national agenda.

As a result, the INC called for a settlement of the Turkish question "in accordance with the just and legitimate sentiments of Indian Mussalmans and the solemn pledges of the Prime Minister" of Great Britain, failing which, it warned, "there will be no real contentment among the people of India."[7] At a special session in Calcutta in September 1920, the INC went a step further and proclaimed: "it is the duty of every non-Muslim in every legitimate manner to assist his Mussalman brother in his attempt to assist the religious calamity that has overtaken him."[8] The following year, the CWC urged the Indian soldiers who fought in World

War I to not cooperate with the British efforts against Turkey, because such actions were "in direct defiance of Mussalman opinion."[9]

Mahatma Gandhi added the Palestine question to the mix. Writing in *Young India* in April 1921, he elaborated on his earlier position that Palestine could not be given to the Jews as a result of World War I.

> The Muslims claim Palestine as an integral part of *Jazirat al-Arab*. They are bound to retain its custody, as an injunction of the Prophet. . . . The Jews cannot receive sovereign rights in a place which has been held for centuries by Muslim powers by right of religious conquest. The Muslim soldiers did not shed their blood in the late war for the purpose of surrendering Palestine out of Muslim control.[10]

Elsewhere, he observed:

> Whilst every good Muslim must strive to retain the temporal power of Turkey, it is obligatory on him to see that unequivocal Muslim control is retained over *Jazirat al-Arab* which includes Mesopotamia, Syria and Palestine as well and the spiritual sovereignty over them of the *Caliph*, whoever he may be for the time being. No other term can satisfy Muslim opinion. They will not tolerate any non-Muslim influence, direct or indirect, over the holy places of Islam.[11]

Long before the question attracted international attention, Mahatma Gandhi recognized and adopted Islamic sanctions against non-Muslim sovereignty in Palestine. For a brief period, even the Congress Party embraced the Islamic arguments. In June 1922, the Lucknow session of the All-India Congress Committee (AICC) called for the liberation of *Jazirat al-Arab* from all non-Muslim control as a prerequisite for peace and contentment in India.[12] Reflecting similar sentiments later that year, it demanded the "effective guardianship of Islam and the *Jazirat al-Arab* free from all non-Muslim control."[13] In the wake of the abolition of the office of the caliph in 1924, the Khilafat question lost its importance and the Congress Party modified its stance, by demanding "the removal of alien control from the *Jazirat al-Arab*."[14]

By using Islamic claims to justify their support for the Arabs, the Indian nationalists captured the essence of the problem in Palestine. Muslims could not be expected to hand Jerusalem over to non-Muslim control. This reflected the fundamental dilemma facing Muslims regarding the demand for a Jewish national home. More than a dispute over national rights, it was primarily a religious challenge: a former *Dhimmi* group was aspiring to be the owner and master of a land that had continuously remained under Islamic rule since 638, when Caliph Umar captured Jerusalem. If one excludes the period of the Crusades (1095–1291), Jerusalem and its environs had remained under Arab and Ottoman rule for over a millennium. So long as the Jews were prepared to accept Islamic rule and the conditions imposed by the *Dhimmi* arrangement, their lives and properties were protected. The kind of anti-Semitic death and destruction perpetrated by European Christendom never plagued the Jews of Islam.[15] The demand for a Jewish homeland radically challenged this arrangement. The Zionists or "new Jews" now demanded sovereignty, not protection; equality, not toleration; and political rights, not religious privileges.

Even if he did not appreciate the nuanced differences between the old and new Jew, the Mahatma's views on the Palestinian question captured the central arguments of Islam. Unlike other Indian leaders, he had a better grasp of the religious aspects of the issue and was prepared to explain his support for the Arabs using explicit and easily identifiable Islamic motifs. More so than Nehru, he was prepared to see the problem in its true sense: as an Islamic question. Regarding Islamic claims, the Mahatma was less diplomatic and more blunt. As a *wafq* property, he argued, Palestine could not be handed over to non-Muslim sovereignty. In his assessment, the prophet Mohammed had given the holy land to the believers and thus non-Muslims could not aspire for any national home there, as the Balfour Declaration visualized. As discussed earlier, these positions were controversial and not without their share of problems. At the same time, they clearly made Islam a factor in India's understanding of the problem in Palestine.

The intertwining of the protection of the Ottoman Empire and the caliph with the events in Palestine had an overwhelmingly religious flavor. Initially, the Congress Party shared Muslim concerns over Allied war objectives vis-à-vis the Ottoman Empire. It viewed the Allied campaign as a war against an Islamic power whose ruler also functioned as the temporal head of the *ummah* (literally, the community of believers). Once the office of the caliph was abolished by the modern Turkish state, INC leaders shifted their concern to the issue of Islamic holy places not being under Islamic control. Even though nationalism subsequently became the focal point of Indian discourses on Palestine, in the initial years its support for Arabs was wrapped in explicit Islamic claims and rationales.

The long-term consequences of the INC's involvement in the Khilafat struggle were not very favorable. The Hindu-Muslim alliance proved to be as elusive as ever. In the words of the historian B. R. Nanda, the support for the Khilafat issue "really stemmed from the Congress leaders' eagerness to appease Muslim opinion, and somehow to wean the Muslim from unquestioning loyalty to the Raj."[16] Nirad C. Chaudhuri offered a much stronger indictment: "By allying itself with the Khilafat movement the Congress had encouraged the most retrograde form of Islamic group-consciousness."[17] Instead of forging an anti-British nationalist alliance with the Muslims, the Congress Party ended up borrowing Islamic terminology, goals, and demands. As we shall see, even though it could not be outright communal, as was the Muslim League, it could not divorce itself from Islamic influence. Gradually, it began to perceive and present events in the Middle East through an Islamic prism—but it couched its views in secular and nationalistic terms.

The Khilafat episode had some negative repercussions for the Mahatma on a personal level, as well. For a person who later on demanded active Jewish nonviolence even against Hitler, the Khilafat phase was a major aberration. His nonviolent model of defending Khilafat was not shared by many Muslims. Some were uncomfortable with a non-Muslim directing and dictating their religious duty. Even leaders such as Mohammed Ali had reservations over the Mahatma's ethical stand on nonviolence. A tactical and symbolic commitment to Gandhi's nonviolent demands was all that the Khilafat leaders were prepared to give in return for the support of the Congress Party and Hindu masses. Those who viewed the Khilafat struggle as the moment of Hindu-Muslim unity won the day. However, the rapid turn of events in republican Turkey removed the rationale for the Khilafat struggle, and the Hindu-Muslim unity disappeared along with it. Before long, the leaders of the Khilafat struggle parted ways and spearheaded a Muslim nationalist movement based on separatism. This eventually culminated in the partition of the Indian subcontinent and the formation of Pakistan in August 1947.

Before long, the Palestine question became an Islamic agenda item in subcontinental politics and a bone of contention between the Congress Party and the Muslim League. This confirmed the worst fears of the Zionists.

The Congress Party Versus the Muslim League

The Muslim League, formed in 1906, initially had no major antagonisms with the INC. Mahatma Gandhi and other Congress Party leaders took part in the deliberations of the Muslim League, and vice versa. At times, INC and Muslim League sessions were held at the same venue, often one following the other. Gradually, however, relations between the two deteriorated and became tense, especially following the outbreak of World War I and in response to European threats against the Ottoman Empire. As the Muslim League spearheaded the Khilafat struggle, the Congress Party joined the movement with the aim of strengthening and consolidating its support among the Muslims. This ended in a political struggle between the two for the support and loyalty of Indian Muslims. The Muslim League's aspiration to be the exclusive representative of the Indian Muslims conflicted with the INC's desire to represent the entire people of India, without any religious or other social barriers. Such tensions were more palpable vis-à-vis the Palestine question.

While the Congress Party remained unsympathetic toward Jewish nationalism, the Muslim League went a step further and took a hostile position against Zionism. Weeks after Arthur James Balfour promised British support for the creation of a Jewish national home in Palestine, the Muslim League expressed its concern over the "safety and sanctity of Holy Places."[18] Muslim League members talked of the prophet Mohammed's injunction about the need to remove "the Christians, the Jews, and the idolaters from the *Jazirat al-Arab* at all costs." Welcoming the delegates of the eleventh Muslim League session in Delhi in December 1918, Mukhtar Ahmad Ansari (who in 1927 became president of the Congress Party) remarked, "Palestine cannot be handed over to the Zionists, whose sole claim to that land is that centuries before the birth of Christ, the ancestors of the wandering sons of Israel had once lived in it. The achievements of Salahuddin Ayyubi and the blood of *mujahideen* did not flow, in the days of the Crusades, to lose it to a people who cannot put forward any recognizable claim to it."[19] Others argued that if a Muslim country was occupied by non-Muslims, efforts should be made "to get it cleared of them."[20]

Delivering the presidential address in December 1918, A. K. Fazlul Haque underscored the determined support of the Indian Muslims to the preservation and continuation of the caliph. In his view, the Arab

Revolt by Sharif Hussein of Mecca against the Ottoman Empire had "endangered the future of our holy places." In underscoring loyalty to the crown, the Muslim League had its priorities straight:

> We are loyal subjects of the rulers, and are prepared to prove our loyalty in actual practice by making sacrifices. *But this temporal loyalty is subject to the limitation imposed by our undoubted loyalty to our faith . . . we need hardly emphasize that in case there is a conflict between Divine Laws and the mandates of our rulers, every true Mussalman will allow the Divine Commandments to prevail over human laws, even at the risk of laying down his life.*[21]

Disappointed by the British failure to honor its commitments over Khilafat and *Jazirat al-Arab*, the following December the League hardened its position. It warned that "no settlement contemplating the dismemberment of Turkey would ever satisfy the Indian Mussalmans, but keep them in a state of perpetual dissatisfaction and discontent."[22] It declared that the Muslims of India would pursue all "constitutional agitation open to them, including a boycott of the British army, if it is likely to be used outside India for Imperial and anti-Islamic purpose."

Articulating the basic demands of the Muslims in December 1921, Maulana Hasrat Mohani appealed that as per an injunction of the Prophet on his deathbed, *Jazirat al-Arab*, including Palestine, "should be free from all non-Muslim influence and not be under British mandate."[23] Mohani also indirectly rebuked the Ali brothers for cooperating with Mahatma Gandhi over the Khilafat issue and declared that the Muslim community did not need non-Muslim advice or assistance. However, the office of the caliph, which for centuries preoccupied Sunni Muslims, could not keep pace with changing times. The title of "caliph" was insufficient to provide the Ottoman emperor with a human face or guarantee his acceptance by his Arab subjects. Its abolition by Mustafa Kemal Ataturk, a Muslim, made the Khilafat struggle irrelevant.

In subsequent years, domestic concerns temporarily kept the Muslim League from pursuing an external Islamic agenda. It was left to a breakaway faction led by Hafiz Hidayat Husain to return to the Palestine question and make the first formal demand for the withdrawal of the Balfour Declaration. In November 1933, he warned that no Arab would tolerate the "creation of a Jewish National State at his expense, come what may." Demanding an end to Jewish immigration, he felt that imperial interests "require that the Balfour Declaration shall be immediately scrapped."[24] Following the adoption of a resolution to this effect, the Muslim League continuously demanded the abolition of the Balfour Declaration.

By the time the Muslim League held its twenty-fifth session, in Lucknow in October 1937, Mohammed Ali Jinnah had firmly established himself as its undisputed leader. In a passionate speech, he castigated the British for their dishonesty, deception, and betrayal of the Arabs. Speaking in the name of "not only the Mussalmans of India but of the world,"[25] he accused the Mandate authorities of having exploited the Arabs through false and irreconcilable promises. Responding to the Royal Palestine Commission, which had suggested partition as a solution to the Arab-Jewish conflict, Jinnah charged that Britain was hoping to complete the tragedy initiated by the "infamous Balfour Declaration."[26] Following his speech, the League adopted a strongly worded statement stating, *inter alia*: (1) that British policy on Palestine was in conflict with the religious sentiments of Indian Muslims and thus world peace was not possible without "rescission" of that policy; (2) that the Mandate of Palestine was never accepted by the Arabs and must be annulled; (3) that Muslim countries should endeavor to save the holy places "from the sacrilege of non-Muslim domination and . . . from the enslavement of British imperialism backed by Jewish finance"; (4) that the Muslim League endorsed the leadership of the Supreme Muslim Council and the Arab Higher Committee, both headed by the grand mufti of Jerusalem; (5) and that Indian Muslims, in "consonance with the rest of the Islamic world," would treat and respond to the British as an enemy of Islam if it "fails to alter its present pro-Jewish policy in Palestine."[27]

Not surprisingly, expressions such as "Jewish high finance" and other overtly racist or anti-Semitic terms were common in Muslim League deliberations. The twenty-sixth session of the Muslim League, which met at Patna in December 1938, witnessed some unprecedented emotional outbursts. Some members took their cue from Jinnah's warning that the British were stirring up troubles in Palestine "with the ulterior motive of placating the international Jewry which commands the money-bags."[28] In a unanimous resolution, the Muslim League castigated the British for the "unjust" Balfour Declaration and its subsequent policy of repression toward the Arabs. The Muslim League saw it as the problem of the entire Muslim community and that the British failure to modify its support for "Jewish usurpation" would lead to "a state of perpetual unrest and conflict" and provoke an international Islamic coalition against the British.[29]

Prior to the adoption of this resolution, a number of delegates resorted to mouthing familiar anti-Semitic stereotypes about Jews.[30] Coming weeks after *Kristallnacht*, the "night of the broken glass," one Muslim League delegate claimed that "Britain's atrocities against the Arabs were greater than those of Germany against the Jews." Another delegate, who had earlier been knighted by the Crown, claimed that religious scriptures had ruled out any home for the Jews and that "Britain would overrule the will of God in providing a home for the Jews." For another: "both the British and the Hindus were Jews to Muslims, that is, their enemies. In India, Mr. Gandhi was the leader of the Hindu Jews." Calls were made for a *jihad* in defense of Muslims in Palestine, and a delegate named Abdul Khaliq remarked: "The real Jews of the West were the British, and those of the East were the Hindus and *both were the sons of Shylock*."[31] However, this exceeded even the lenient limits of the Muslim League, and, after an admonition from Jinnah, Khaliq withdrew his remark.

The outbreak of World War II significantly altered the political climate in India. Torn between their commitment to fight Nazism and fascism in Europe, the Congress Party leaders were unwilling to support allied war efforts until the fight for freedom included India's independence. Unilaterally committing India to the war, the colonial administration incarcerated the entire INC leadership and throttled its normal functions. The Muslim League, by contrast, was able to conduct its political activities and held five annual sessions during the war. These sessions enabled the Muslim League to articulate the Muslim position on Palestine and to remind the British of its earlier promise to the Indian Muslims over the spoils of the Ottoman Empire in return for Muslim support and assistance during the war.[32]

At its Delhi session in April 1943, the Muslim League expressed its concern and alarm at "Zionist propaganda" and the resultant American pressure on the British to convert Palestine into a Jewish state. Warning the British to desist from harming Arab interests, it expressed sympathy for the Arabs "at a time when the Arab National Higher Committee of Palestine stands disbanded and the Arab nationalists are . . . almost defenseless against organized Jewry and High Finance in the world."[33] In December 1943, the Muslim League demanded an end to all British and French mandates in the Middle East, including Palestine, and called for the establishment of sovereign governments.[34] This was the last annual session of the Muslim League before the subcontinent's partition.

After 1943, the Muslim League's proceedings were confined to council meetings, chaired by Jinnah, that met five times from 1944 to 1947. Its preoccupation with the partition of the Indian subcontinent and creation of Pakistan did not dilute the Muslim League's interest and commitments to the Palestinian cause, however. In April 1946, it demanded that Britain reject the recommendation of the Anglo-American commission, which sought an immediate admission of one hundred thousand Jewish refugees from Europe into Palestine. The Muslim League reminded the British of the commitment it made in the White Paper of 1939, wherein the Mandate power agreed to restrict Jewish immigration into Palestine.[35]

In December 1947, the All-India Muslim League met for the last time in Karachi before transforming into the Muslim League of Pakistan. Meeting about three weeks after the United Nations adopted the partition plan, it expressed its indignation at the manner in which the United Nations had decided the future of Palestine. Claiming to speak also on behalf of Indian Muslims, the Muslim League committed itself to "render every possible help for the achievement of the aspirations of the Arabs in Palestine, and the preservation of its freedom and integrity, which is a matter of concern not only to the Arabs but to the Muslim world as such."[36] In short, since the days of the Balfour Declaration, the Muslim League maintained a consistently hostile and unfriendly stance regarding Jewish nationalism. It often projected itself as a spokesperson for the entire Islamic community, and even following partition it sought to speak on behalf of the Muslims of India.

Such a hard-line position naturally influenced and compelled the Congress Party to accommodate the Muslim sentiments on Palestine. During the Khilafat period, it demanded that *Jazirat al-Arab* remain under exclusive Muslim control. In subsequent years, anticolonialism became its formal platform. At the same time, the not-so-subtle competition with the Muslim League for Muslim support was palpable in its calculation. While not prepared to go as far as did the Muslim League, it was not sympathetic to Jewish nationalism. A pro-Zionist stand would have played into the hands of the Muslim League and alienated a vast majority of the Muslims from the Congress Party. Thus the INC also began organizing Palestine Day celebrations in different parts of the country.

The opposition of the INC to Jewish nationalism in Palestine had another domestic consideration. The Muslim League was presenting Muslims in British India not as a different religious community but as a distinct nation, different from the majority Hindus. This in turn led to the Muslim League projecting itself as the sole representative of the Indian Muslims, and it challenged the right of the other parties, especially the INC, to speak for, let alone represent, Indian Muslims. As Farzana Shaikh aptly summed up, Mohammed Ali Jinnah's "claim for parity developed steadily from simple political parity between League and Congress to communal parity between Muslims and Hindus and culminated finally in the demand for ideological parity between Muslims and non-Muslims."[37]

Endorsing the Muslim League's right to speak exclusively on behalf of Indian Muslims would have harmed the INC and transformed it into a Hindu and not Indian political force. The INC being Hindu-dominated merely reflected the demographic realities of India and was not driven by any religious exclusivist agenda. Accepting the Muslim League's right to speak on behalf of Indian Muslims would have meant recognizing the right of other religious and ethnic groups having separate political representations. That would have been suicidal both for the Congress Party and for the independent India it was seeking. Therefore, much to the annoyance and anger of Jinnah, the INC continued to give prominent positions to Muslims within the party and even elected Maulana Abul Kalam Azad as its president in 1940, a position that he held until 1945.[38]

Having rejected the Muslim League's argument of Muslims being a distinct nation, the INC could not accept similar claims by Jews in Palestine. For "many nationalist Muslims in the . . . Congress, who subscribed to the idea of a secular and undivided Indian state and to whom the idea of religion being the basis of nationality" was undesirable, the two-nation theory of the Muslim League was unacceptable.[39] Any dilution of its opposition to a Jewish national home in Palestine would have exposed the Congress Party and made its stand vis-à-vis the Muslim League vulnerable and untenable. For India and its leaders, especially the Muslim leaders within the INC (such as Azad), Jewish nationalism in Palestine reflected their own trauma over the exclusivist notion represented by the Muslim League. Reflecting this domestic Indian situation, the INC opposed religion-based partition both in India and in Palestine.[40]

Unfortunately, however, the Congress Party advocated two different solutions for the challenges posed by religion-based nationalism. In the Indian context, it was prepared to accept a communal-based partition as the price for freedom from the British. Though not subscribing to the two-nation theory of the Muslim League, the INC leaders, especially Nehru, accepted partition along religious lines, with Muslim-majority areas forming Pakistan.[41] For Palestine, however, Nehru advocated a federal arrangement, something he was not prepared to accept in the Indian subcontinent. Despite past opposition, India eventually accepted Pakistan as an independent state, and for similar reasons it recognized the state of Israel. Continued opposition to the partition of Palestine after a similar religious division of British India would have raised doubts over New Delhi's acceptance of the sovereignty of Pakistan. For the Congress Party, opposition to partition both in India and Palestine was a principled moral stand, and its subsequent recognition of both Pakistan and Israel were signs of political pragmatism.

For its part, the Muslim League faced a different kind of dilemma vis-à-vis Palestine. Its arguments that the Muslims were a separate nation on account of their religion could not be extended to Palestine, where Muslims were in the majority. That would have compelled the Muslim League to recognize the claims of the Jews being a distinct nation on account of their non-Muslim religious affiliation. The arguments of the Muslim League—and later on Pakistan—however, were much narrower, as both adopted a converse position vis-à-vis the Jews of Palestine. Partition was essential for the welfare of the Muslims of India but was an unacceptable proposition in Palestine because it was anti-Muslim. As S. M. Burke aptly put it: "While the device of dividing the country provided the only means of real freedom to the Indian Muslims, the very word partition was anathema to Muslims elsewhere."[42]

This tussle between the INC and the Muslim League for Muslim support partly contributed to the *yishuv's* interest in India. If the Islamic factor influenced the thinking of Indian nationalists toward the problem in Palestine, the *yishuv* leadership was equally worried about the attitude of Indian Muslims in the unfolding problem. On at least four occasions, the Zionist leadership showed concerns about Indian Muslims and their impact upon the Jewish homeland project in Palestine. The first occasion was during the run up to the Balfour Declaration. Due to concerns over Muslim opinion, senior officials in the India Office warned their government against endorsing Zionist aspirations in Palestine.[43] The second occasion arose in January 1931, when the mufti of Jerusalem offered to bury the body of Mohammad Ali in the *Harem al-Sharif.* Alarmed by its political ramifications, Chaim Weizmann, president of the World Zionist Organization, met Mohammad Ali's elder brother, Shaukat Ali, in London. This was the first known contact between the Zionist leadership and an Indian leader. Weizmann hoped to persuade Shaukat, who would be accompanying the body to Jerusalem, to quarantine the Palestine problem from domestic Indian politics.[44] Subsequent developments in India belied Weizmann's expectations. Won over by the mufti's hospitality and warm treatment, the Indian leader became his staunch supporter and played an active role at the General Muslim Congress organized by the mufti later that year.[45]

The third Zionist contact, in October 1931, took place against the background of greater concerns over the attitude of Indian Muslims. This was the first time that the Zionist leadership established formal contacts with Mahatma Gandhi, who was in London to attend the Round Table Conference. Two Zionist emissaries, Seliq Brodetsky and Nahum Sokolov, met the Mahatma, seeking to keep India away from the Palestinian issue.[46] A fourth and somewhat longer campaign aimed at India had to wait until mid-1936, when Immanuel Olsvanger was sent to India as the emissary of the Jewish Agency. During his long stay, he reached out to a large number of Indian nationalists and representatives of other groups. Again his mission was directly linked to events in Palestine and its reverberations in the Islamic world. Olsvanger was sent to India shortly after the outbreak of the Arab general strikes that precipitated the Arab Revolt of 1936–1939. In short, during the prestate years, even the limited Zionist interest in India was primarily motivated by the Muslim factor.

Was there a Hindu perception on Jewish history that could have altered this partisan viewpoint?

Panikkar's Prognosis

The historian and later diplomat K. M. Panikkar recognized and articulated the influence of the domestic Muslim population upon India's Middle East policy. He was one of the few Indians who had long associations with some of the leading personalities of the Zionist movement, including Weizmann, whom he had met in 1926.[47] On the eve of India's independence, he visualized a "Hindu perception" toward a Jewish national home in Palestine. In his assessment, this would be articulated with clarity after the partition of the Indian subcontinent. The Asian Relations Conference, held in New Delhi in March–April 1947, rekindled Panikkar's meetings with the *yishuv*. Hugo Bergmann, a professor of philosophy at the Hebrew University of Jerusalem, led a ten-member delegation that represented the Jews of Palestine. Panikkar, the prime minister of the princely state of Bikaner, was a member of the Indian delegation to the conference. After the conference, when Bergmann visited Bikaner, Panikkar "revealed himself . . . as an ardent friend of our cause and gave important advice as to our future work in India. This advice he wrote down in a memorandum sent by him to Palestine."[48] Panikkar offered meaningful suggestions to the Zionists in a two-page memorandum curiously titled *A Memorandum on Hindu-Zionist Relations*.[49] Written on April 8, 1947, this document throws an interesting light on his overall understanding of the Palestine problem, his evaluation of the Indian political climate on the eve of partition, and its relevance for the post-1947 Indian policy toward the political aspirations of the Jews.

Panikkar began his note with an emphasis on Islam and its role in Indian policy. Because "Islam is a minority in India," he argued, "the feeling of Muslim solidarity is greater in India than perhaps anywhere else in the Islamic world." Due to the prevailing political climate on the eve of partition, the Hindus would unconditionally support "all matters on which Islam feels strongly." Therefore, as far as Palestine was concerned, "official Indian opinion will not be different from that of Islamic countries, though it is unlikely that India will do more than follow the lead of the Arab countries in this matter."[50]

Even though this was the prevailing position, Panikkar argued that "it will be wrong to think that Hindu opinion is solidly in favor of Islamic claims in Palestine." Sympathy for the Jewish cause was inevitable, due to the "stiffening of Hindu opinion generally towards Muslims in the internal politics and . . . because of a genuine and natural sympathy towards the sufferings of the Jews." Once the Muslim League succeeded in creating a separate Islamic state in the subcontinent, "Hindu opinion on the question of Palestine will find its natural and untrammeled expression." He went on to predict that once Pakistan was established, "Hindu leaders and politicians may well take a pro-Zionist line." He blamed the Zionists for their prolonged neglect and indifference toward India, which he felt was responsible for the absence of sympathy "even in orthodox Hindu quarters towards Zionist claims." He was optimistic and visualized "increasing realization on the side of the Zionists that Asia will count a great deal more in world politics, and that *Asia is not* predominantly Islamic, but Hindu and Chinese." He predicted that Hindus would appreciate that "a Zionist Palestine may be an important link in the defense policy of India, that it may, with the support of European nations, be an effective counter-weight to an alliance of Islamic countries in the Middle

East . . . between Hinduism and Judaism there is a great deal in common." Thus the creation of Hindu-Zionist friendship "clearly indicated . . . the interests of both parties."

When the General Assembly deliberated the future of Palestine in 1947, Panikkar became a member of the Indian delegation to the United Nations. Reflecting on that period in his 1955 autobiography, he settled for a sanitized and politically correct version:

> On the question of a Jewish State in Palestine, however, *my sympathies were not all with the Zionists.* The Indian attitude has always been friendly to the Arabs. While sympathizing with the claims of the Jews for a national home in Palestine, I thought that this demand for a State based on religious exclusivism was in the first instance likely to revive Islamic fanaticism and secondly was unjust to the Palestine Arabs.[51]

His appointment to the diplomatic corps and Nehru's cool attitude toward various Israeli overtures partly explain this diluted position. Like others, he was conscious of political correctness.[52]

The real importance of Panikkar's memorandum lay in his willingness to underline the difference between Hindu and Muslim perceptions of the Arab-Israeli problem. He perceived "Hindu" support to the Arabs as a tactical move aimed at forging a Hindu-Muslim unity against foreign rule. Following the formation of a Muslim state in the subcontinent, he was confident that this rationale would disappear and thus visualized a "Hindu" opinion that would be more independent and sympathetic toward Zionism and Israel. Postpartition events, however, took a different course. A large portion of Muslims made a deliberate decision to remain in India, emerging as a powerful and influential minority, and their impact was felt on India's policy toward Israel. Thus, instead of adopting an overtly Hindu-nationalistic position, as Panikkar had expected, the Congress Party came under greater Islamic influence, which shaped Indian perceptions of the Middle East in general and the Arab-Israeli conflict in particular.

Also, the question of the "Hindu opinion on Palestine" is rather debatable. Because of historical and religious reasons, there is an Islamic opinion about and concern regarding Palestine. Like their coreligionists elsewhere, Indian Muslims have a sentimental attachment toward the issue. This is not true for the Hindus. There is neither a need nor a rationale for the evolution of a "Hindu" opinion. Other than adopting the Machiavellian logic of "my enemy's enemy is my friend," there is no compelling reason for a Hindu to be passionate about the holy land or *Jazirat al-Arab*. As a gentile, *kafir*, infidel, and pagan, a Hindu has no sentimental attachment toward Palestine, Israel, or the holy land. The Promised Land—the Jewish, Islamic, or Christian version—is as good, as bad, and as consequential as Alaska. The post-1948 events would disprove Panikkar's optimism.

Thus, during the nationalist phase, the Congress Party and its leaders came under two kinds of pressures. At one level, they had to compete with the Muslim League for the support of the Indian Muslims. A pro-Arab position helped consolidate INC influence among the Indian Muslims. While this alone would have been insufficient, a contrary position would have alienated the party from the Muslims. At another level, INC opposition to religious separatism meant it was unable to endorse Jewish nationalist aspirations in Palestine. It could not support the idea of Jews being a separate nation in Palestine while rejecting similar demands by the Muslim League in India. Thus the Congress Party became pro-Muslim vis-à-vis its domestic constituency and pro-Arab vis-à-vis its external audience. Both positions worked in tandem. At the same time, INC opposition to partitions proved futile. Both India and Palestine were partitioned along religious lines, and India was forced to come to terms with both new realities. This recognition was relatively easier with respect to Pakistan, given the two countries' geographic proximity and shared history. Recognizing the partition of Palestine, however, took longer, as the domestic opinion on Israel still remained contentious. Additionally, there was also the Arab factor to contend with.

The minority report . . . is acceptable neither to Jews nor Arabs. For us to advocate Minority report would please no one and lead us nowhere.
—Vijayalakshmi Pandit, leader of the Indian delegation to the United Nations

5 India, UNSCOP, and the Partition of Palestine

Speaking before the Constituent Assembly of India on December 4, 1947, just days after the UN General Assembly voted for the partition of Palestine, Prime Minister Jawaharlal Nehru declared: "After a great deal of thought we decided that this was not only a fair and equitable solution of the problem, but *the only real solution of the problem.* Any other solution would have meant fighting and conflict."[1] He was referring not to partition but to the ill-fated federal solution that India had advocated as a member of the UN Special Committee on Palestine (UNSCOP). In the wake of decades of violence following the partition of Palestine, many Indian scholars now engage in uncritical adulation of the federal plan and present it as a missed opportunity.[2]

If the Indian proposal was widely hailed within the country, why did it evoke a dismal response elsewhere? Why did both Arabs and Jews refuse to consider Nehru's "only real solution"? Why did the rivals join hands and outright reject the Indian formula? Why is it barely discussed not only by the United Nations but also by scholars of the partition plan?[3] What was this magic Indian solution for Palestine? What about it evoked nearly universal neglect and dismissal? Was the Indian solution a realistic option in 1947, or was Nehru advocating a course that he himself had rejected for the Indian subcontinent?

The UN Special Session

Before examining the Indian proposal, it is essential to remember certain parallel developments in Palestine and India. The period from April to September 1947 was critical for both. As the Palestinian issue came up before the United Nations, India was preparing for independence. Despite being a dominion of the British Empire, it was a founding member of the United Nations, and Nehru had formed an interim government in September 1946. The United Nations began to discuss the Palestine problem in April 1947; India gained independence on August 15, 1947, when the final deliberations of the UNSCOP were underway. The UN report was submitted exactly two weeks later. The developments in the subcontinent shaped and influenced India's position in the United Nations.

By then, the contours of India's position on the Palestine question were firmly in place. Despite internal contradictions and gradual modifications in subsequent years, Mahatma Gandhi's famous statement about Palestine belonging to the Arabs largely reflected the prevailing consensus. At the same time, INC leaders were aware that any solution to the problem should not ignore Jewish interests and aspirations. How could Jewish aspirations be satisfied without diluting the Arab character of Palestine? How does one reconcile the irreconcilable?

As World War II ended, it was obvious that Great Britain was trying to administer an inherently contradictory and unworkable Mandate in Palestine. Its promises to Sharif Hussein of Mecca (enshrined in the Hussein-McMahon correspondence) could not be squared with its pledges to the Zionists under the Balfour Declaration. For over two decades, it unsuccessfully tried to reconcile these two. Even the once-friendly Zionists turned against them. Revisionist groups such as *Irgun*, headed by Menachem Begin, launched a full-fledged terror campaign. The economic cost of winning World War II and its dependence upon the Marshall Plan compelled Britain to reassess its overseas commitments. The decision to withdraw from India further diminished the importance of Palestine to the declining empire. London had to admit failure and cut its losses. But it still needed a face-saving formula.[4]

On April 2, 1947, Clement Attlee, the British prime minister, formally requested that the UN secretary-general "summon as soon as possible" a special session of the General Assembly for the purpose of constituting "a special committee" to decide the "future government in Palestine."[5]

The United Nations sought the views of its member states, and on April 11 the interim Indian government gave its formal consent. Having secured the necessary affirmative response, Secretary-General Trygve Lie summoned the first Special Session of the UN General Assembly, which met in New York City on April 28. The session continued until May 15, when it established the eleven-member UNSCOP. Because of the urgency of the situation, Nehru nominated Asaf Ali, his ambassador in Washington, as India's representative to the First Special Session of the United Nations.

Asaf Ali and the UN Drama

On the eve of the first Special Session, Asaf Ali was given a list of instructions:

> (1) To endeavor to obtain . . . India's membership on the Fact Finding Committee; . . . (2) to be most careful not to commit the Government of India to any views of substance without prior reference; . . . (3) to support the Egyptian proposal for inclusion in the agenda an item relating to the termination of the Mandate and the declaration of Palestine's independence; [and] (4) to avoid raising issues which might affect relations between India and any other country.[6]

It is obvious that India was angling for membership in the proposed committee even before the commencement of the Special Session. Asaf Ali was accordingly advised that it was "for the sponsors of the resolution to make out a case for the termination of the Mandate and to indicate how the vacuum thus created will be filled."[7] Because of the generally pro-Arab postures that the Congress Party had adopted in the past, Nehru did not want Asaf Ali to make statements that would prejudice India's role regarding the future of Palestine. Unfortunately, Nehru's misgivings were not far off the mark.

Asaf Ali played an active role at various stages of the deliberations and in tune with the position of the INC adopted an overtly pro-Arab position.[8] As the United Nations was deliberating the Palestinian problem, India was being partitioned along communal lines. As a leading Muslim member of the Congress Party, Asaf Ali was unable to accept the notion that religion "can convert people into a nation" and strongly repudiated any exclusive linkage between religion and nation.[9] This reflected the prevailing view of the INC regarding the demands of the Muslim League for Pakistan. Of course, even as Asaf Ali was rejecting a religious basis for statehood as "untenable," the subcontinent was being partitioned along those very same lines!

As advised by Nehru, Asaf Ali supported the Arab proposal that called for "termination of the Mandate and proclamation of the independence of Palestine" as the agenda of the proposed UN committee. Overruling suggestions from New Delhi to let the sponsors "make out a case," he argued vehemently in favor of the Arab proposal.[10] Both the General Committee[11] and the UN General Assembly[12] felt that the Arab proposal was incompatible with the original British request that led to the Special Session and rejected the suggestion. Asaf Ali, however, succeeded in inviting the Arab Higher Committee, headed by the mufti of Jerusalem, to testify before the General Committee.[13] Ali felt that if the views of the representatives of the people of Palestine, whether Arab or Jews, were not heeded by the United Nations, then "we shall certainly be prejudicing the entire case."[14]

Asaf Ali supported the Arab countries in rejecting any connection between the Palestine question and the displaced-person (DP) camps in Europe. It should be remembered that the opposition to such a linkage remained a constant theme in India's interventions, both in the Special Session and in subsequent UN deliberations. For example, speaking before the General Assembly shortly after the UNSCOP report was submitted, Vijayalakshmi Pandit, the leader of the Indian delegation, maintained that the problem of the displaced Jews in Europe was

> not the concern of this Committee [the UNSCOP] and should not therefore be mixed up with the issue of Palestine. . . . In fact a great deal of the uneasiness that exists today in the minds of the Arab population in Palestine and in other Arab countries is due to the fact that vigorous attempts have been and are still being made to view the Palestine question as mainly one of finding a home for the large number of displaced Jews. It is a clear duty of this Committee to say unequivocally that while the United Nations have a very grave responsibility in regard to the displaced persons of Central Europe, the Committee feels most strongly that this should not be mixed up with the question of the future government of Palestine.[15]

Naturally, Asaf Ali voted against a Panama-Guatemala resolution that called for a visit by the UNSCOP to the DP camps in Europe.[16] However, a resolution to this effect was adopted by the committee, by an overwhelming majority of thirty-six votes in favor to eight against, with fourteen abstentions.

The second major contribution of the Indian representative pertains to the composition of the proposed committee. Asaf Ali concurred with the U.S. position that permanent members of the Security Council should be excluded from the committee. Much to the annoyance of some, he pointed out that with the sole exception of China, other great powers had strong political and economic interests in the Middle East and would be unable to perform their tasks objectively.[17]

The Indian representative offered explicit support to the Jews when he endorsed the motion for inviting the Jewish Agency for Palestine to testify before the General Committee. He felt that, as with the Arab Higher Committee, the views of the Jews and their representatives should be heard: "we are playing Hamlet without the Prince of Denmark. . . . Where are the great representatives of the Jewish people who are also interested in this problem?"[18] This "Prince of Denmark" remark drew widespread domestic criticism, especially from the Muslim League. In India, the Congress Party and Muslim League were not only fighting over the status of Muslims, in the about-to-be-divided India but also over who would represent Indian Muslims. The Muslim League perceived, projected, and promoted itself as the sole representative of the Muslims of the subcontinent. It was not prepared to accept that the Congress Party could represent the legitimate interests of the Muslims. If they could do so, there would be no rationale for a Muslim League—let alone a separate Muslim state. Nehru once again pushed back against this notion by appointing a Muslim to represent India at this crucial UN debate, which had strong Islamic undercurrents and overtones. Asaf Ali's "Prince of Denmark" remark thus complicated the situation.

In a letter to the Arab Executive Committee in Palestine, a functionary of the Muslim League observed: "Asaf Ali was not representing the Muslims of India. He was selected by Pandit Nehru, the Congress leader, and the Muslim League had no hand in his appointment. The statement of Mr. Asaf Ali runs contrary to the sentiments of 100,000,000 Muslims in India who stand and always will stand by their Arab brethren of the Middle East on the Palestine issue." *The Dawn*, a Karachi-based daily founded by Mohammed Ali Jinnah, reminded its readers that Asaf Ali's remark "should go a long way towards disillusioning those few people in the Arab world who might have set some store by the professions of the Hindu Congress about its support of the Arab cause. . . . Mr. Asaf Ali does not represent Muslim India and is acting contrary to Muslim India's views."[19] In other words, Asaf Ali's invitation to the Jewish Agency to testify before the committee became an anti-Muslim act, even though the Indian envoy had earlier made similar suggestions regarding the Arab Higher Committee!

The Zionists were equally upset over Asaf Ali's overtly pro-Arab stand. Eliahu Epstein, the head of the Jewish Agency office in Washington, offered a scathing assessment.[20] Writing in January 1948, after the UN approval of the partition plan, he commented:

> The [Indian] Ambassador here [in Washington], Mr. Asaf Ali, was the *worst opponent* we had at the Special Session of the United Nations General Assembly in April last year. Besides that, *while the Arabs fight us openly, he has been engaged in intrigues and double crosses,* and has confused many of our people by his hypocrisy and machinations. Although he was not a member of the Indian delegation at the last session, there is no reason to believe that he has made an about face or that his character has improved.[21]

Likewise, Taraknath Das, a U.S.-based academic and active champion of the Zionist cause, felt that Asaf Ali "was so pro-Arab that he earned the title, Indian Attorney for the Arab League."[22]

Normally, one could dismiss these observations as partisan, motivated, and even prejudiced. Unfortunately for Asaf Ali, even Nehru was unhappy with his performance. During the session, Nehru was disappointed at Ali's hostile responses when Britain expressed its hesitation to honor any UN recommendation that went against its imperial interests. Ali's stance violated Nehru's April instructions to avoid controversy. The envoy's rebuke of the empire came when Nehru was pursuing delicate negotiations with London over the transfer of power. Nehru was quick and candid: "I do not have [a] full report of what you [Asaf Ali] said but I would suggest your avoiding raising issues which might affect relations between India and any other country. As we have informed you in our brief, we support [the] Arab cause. *Nevertheless we should avoid as far as possible needless controversy.*"[23]

On May 14, as the Special Session was coming to a close, Nehru complimented Asaf Ali for shouldering additional responsibilities at the United Nations. At the same time, he did not hide his concerns:

> I have a feeling . . . that perhaps fewer commitments might have been made on our behalf in regard to *certain matters*. It pays often enough not to give too frequent expression of our views. Though you balanced your observations, when there are many observations they are apt to irritate one party or the other needlessly *as they appear to have done sometimes*. There have been a few adverse comments here [in New Delhi] on what you have said and a general feeling that it would have been better not to say so much.[24]

According to Nehru's biographer, "certain matters" pertained to Asaf Ali's support for the Arab proposal for granting immediate independence to Palestine.[25]

Others were even more categorical. An official note prepared by the Ministry of External Affairs, also headed by Nehru, was blunt:

> It is clear, both from the telegrams and from press reports, that from the very beginning Mr. Asaf Ali had taken a very active part in the discussions. . . . His part in the proceedings appears, however, *to have gone rather beyond his instructions*, which were [that he] be most careful in the expression of views, as well as to leave it to the sponsors of the resolutions to make out a case for the termination of the Mandate and to indicate how the vacuum thus created will be filled.[26]

In a word, Asaf Ali's overenthusiastic pronouncements and observations at the Special Session were not appreciated by the Indian government.

India was concerned over the possible negative fallout from Asaf Ali's performance. On April 9, days before it had formally communicated its support for convening a Special Session on Palestine, India outlined its priorities: "In view of the Indian interest in this problem, we should presumably try for membership of this committee."[27] Another Indian official was rather cautious: "It is possible that Muslim opinion in India might regard us as taking our duties too lightly if we do not try; on the other hand one's natural inclination would be to avoid being too closely embroiled in a problem of the size and ugliness of Palestine."[28] Thus, the official communication to Asaf Ali regarding his nomination for the Special Session advised him to work toward securing India's membership in the proposed committee.[29] Partly because of this desire, he was counseled to be cautious, lest he jeopardized India's chances.

Unfortunately for India, the pro-Arab stance adopted by Asaf Ali adversely affected its chances. It did not figure in the initial list of seven countries proposed by the United States[30] or in the two more names added by Chile.[31] New Delhi was aware that "without the support of the USA, India will stand little chance of being included in the fact-finding committee."[32] Reacting to India's exclusion from the American list, Asaf Ali cabled New Delhi: "It appears from informal conversations that India was omitted from the United States' . . . list because of statements of Congress and [Muslim] League leaders in India and [because of] the attitude of [the] Indian delegation here [in New York] indicated that *we were not 'neutral' but favored Arabs.*"[33] He repeated this observation a few days later when he sent a detailed report to New Delhi.[34] As they were seen as a party to the Palestinian problem, the Arab countries were excluded from the proposed committee, and thus pro-Arab India was the closest thing that they could have gotten in the UNSCOP.

Fortune favored India, though. To better represent the geographical distribution of UN members, the Political Committee decided to increase the number of nations composing the proposed committee to eleven. This brightened India's chances.[35] Since all nine names proposed by the United States and Chile were unanimously accepted, it was decided that the remaining two members would be elected from the Asian and South Pacific region. India was nominated by Iran, who appeared in the U.S. list. It defeated Siam (now Thailand) by thirty-four votes to seven; Australia narrowly defeated the Philippines by twenty-one to twenty votes, with India voting for the winner. Following the election, Asaf Ali regretted the contest with Siam, "who while hoping for our election did not wish to withdraw. *We remained in the contest at urgent requests of Arabs.*"[36] India thus became a member of the eleven-member UNSCOP. This twist of being "elected" and not "nominated by consensus" rarely figures in Indian discussions concerning the UNSCOP. The drama indicates both the Indian desperation to join the committee and the international reservations over its neutrality on the Palestine issue.

As the committee was expected to begin its deliberations soon, Asaf Ali suggested that a nominee "be chosen immediately."[37] India swiftly nominated Abdur Rahman as its representative to the UNSCOP. Unlike

Asaf Ali, he clashed with Nehru over his "UN personality" and solutions to the Palestine question.

Abdur Rahman and UNSCOP

The selection of Rahman for the important task of UNSCOP representative is both interesting and intriguing. Once again, the Islamic prism through which India viewed the problem of Palestine influenced his candidacy. The Foreign Office was more forthcoming and candid than the political leadership. In its assessment, it was "necessary to find, at a very short notice, *a suitable Indian Muslim with wide legal knowledge*" for the job.[38] Since the problem was primarily political, it is unclear why it preferred someone with "legal knowledge." The other criterion of a "suitable Indian Muslim" was definitely aimed at the unfolding domestic situation and the impending partition. Instead of seeking a suitable person knowledgeable on the Middle East, it sought an "Indian Muslim." Was it because Muslims better understood and could articulate the Palestinian problem? Was it because the problem was Islamic rather than political? Or, by sending a Muslim to the UNSCOP on the eve of India's partition, was Nehru conveying a powerful message to the Muslim constituency of the Congress Party? In the absence of additional records, one can only speculate.

The selection of Sir Abdur Rahman raised an additional problem. He was a judge at the Punjab High Court. Though it was still part of India, Lahore, where the High Court was located, had a Muslim majority and was to eventually become part of Pakistan. India's partition greatly influenced Rahman's views and figured prominently in his interactions with the Indian government, even leading to a mild confrontation with Nehru.

In line with the Indian position at the Special Session, Rahman demanded the participation of Palestinian Arabs in the UNSCOP deliberations. He vehemently argued that the task would be unsatisfactory "unless the Arab case is explained to us by those who have studied the problem and are vitally interested therein." The Arab Higher Committee, whose cooperation India sought at the Special Session, however, chose to boycott the UNSCOP proceedings in Palestine. Rahman still did not give up and suggested that the views of the neighboring Arab countries should be heard before the UNSCOP finalized its recommendations. In a letter to the committee chairman, Emil Sandstorm, he stated: "in all probability, without the help of these countries in the first World War, the question which we are called upon to consider might never have arisen."[39] The committee accepted his suggestion and held a special session in Beirut. There was a notable absentee: Transjordan. Thus, before heading to the Beirut meeting, Rahman proceeded to Amman and lunched with Emir Abdullah. In his assessment, Abdullah was prepared to accept a partition plan if it meant significant territorial gains favoring Transjordan.[40] During the deliberations, Rahman was less friendly toward the Zionists than Asaf Ali. While cross-examining the Jewish Agency testimonies before the committee as well as in his dissent note, Rahman exhibited a strong prejudice against Zionism and some of its principal figures.[41]

Was the stance taken by Abdur Rahman his own, or was he representing the views of the government of India?

Within hours of the formation of the UNSCOP, Asaf Ali reminded New Delhi of the prevailing consensus in New York that nominees to the committee should be "persons of high character and standing in public life [and] preferably with grasp of international affairs and *free from interference by nominating governments.*" He also reported that both the United States and Great Britain "are in favor of a declaration that members of the Special Committee will act on behalf of the United Nations as a whole and *will not (repeat not) be subject to direction by their government.*"[42] Iran took this sentiment seriously, and its representative, Nasrollah Entezam, told the session that the Iranian representative to the UNSCOP would be given complete freedom and would not receive any instructions from Tehran regarding his functions and recommendations. This, however, was not the case with India. Nehru actively intervened, diluted, modified, and even dictated the views of his nominee. The federal plan was Nehru's brainchild. Rahman merely acted as midwife.

When elected to the UNSCOP in May 1947, India was formalizing its independence, and Nehru was presiding over the interim government. Personally approving the nomination, on May 24, Nehru reminded Rahman of his role in the UNSCOP: "How to reconcile the two [Arab and Jewish] claims is the problem before us. I do not venture to express an opinion except vaguely to say that perhaps an autonomous Jewish area within an independent Palestine might lead to a solution. . . . The general attitude of India must necessarily be friendly to both parties but clearly indicating that an agreement must have Arab approval."[43] This largely reflected the prevailing thinking in the Congress Party over the future of Palestine. On the eve of World War II, it called for the establishment of a "free democratic state in Palestine with adequate protection of Jewish rights."[44] The need to seek an accommodation between Arab and Jewish rights dominated Rahman's functions in the UNSCOP.

Nehru did not forget the controversies surrounding Asaf Ali's role at the Special Session and was determined to avoid same mistakes. Therefore, he advised Rahman:

> We [India] should proceed, especially in this fact-finding committee, in a judicial manner as far as possible. It might be desirable not to say too much and to make any particular commitments at this stage. . . . *You will function as the representative of India on this committee and will naturally refer to us any particular matters that you think should be cleared up.* But you will also be a representative of the United Nations Organization, free to suggest what you consider fit and proper from the larger viewpoint of that Organization as well as of the Arabs and the Jews.[45]

The message was clear. As India's representative, Rahman should seek New Delhi's prior consent on any substantive matter and should refrain from adopting positions that might jeopardize India's interests. This was very different from the free hand that Iran gave to its UNSCOP representative.

Rahman's performance was also severely undermined and affected by events back home. The issue of India's partition figured prominently both in the testimonies and in his private conservations with other members of the committee. Reflecting on his Indian counterpart, the Guatemalan delegate Jorge Garcia-Granados remarked: "Throughout the following days, when we finally came to debate the merits of partitioning Palestine, Sir Abdur (as I was to learn later) labored under great strain, worrying as to the safety of his family in the post-partition riots in India."[46] The impending division of India also raised certain doubts in Rahman's mind concerning his legal status. He felt that he was an international personality and not India's representative. In his very first report on the activities of the committee, he informed Nehru that some of his colleagues had enquired "as to what the legal position of India would be after the division." He was confident that his position would not be compromised, because "I was nominated by the United Nations although on the recommendation of the Indian government, at a time when *India was a member of the United Nations.*"[47]

Nehru was in no mood for such far-fetched claims. He strongly refuted Rahman's assertions that the impending partition would affect the status of India in the United Nations and, therefore, Rahman's *locus standi* in the committee. On July 10, he informed Rahman that the partition of India

> does not affect the international status of India as a continuing entity, and all our old obligations continue. . . . Your position on the Palestine Special Committee is not affected in any way. I might point out that it is not quite correct to say that you were nominated by the United Nations. India was chosen as one of the countries to be represented on the Special Committee. The nomination of the representative from India was done by the Government of India and not by the United Nations.[48]

The matter, however, did not end with this categorical response from Nehru.

On August 10, less than a week before India's partition, Rahman observed that some committee members felt that following the division of the subcontinent and formation of two independent states India "would not continue to be a member of the United Nations, and I would consequently not be entitled to represent India on this Committee." Therefore, Rahman suggested that he would present his views "in a sealed cover with the Chairman of the Committee on the 14th August [the day of the formation of Pakistan], to ask him not to open it until the report of the Committee was ready."[49] His doubts over India's membership were misplaced. While Pakistan was admitted to the United Nations on September 30, 1947, India, being a founding member of the world body, emerged as the legal successor to British India. There was no legal impediment to either India's continued membership in the United Nations or the continuation of Rahman in the committee.

Within days, another problem arose. This time Rahman and New Delhi differed over the future of Palestine. He prepared two sets of reports. In his initial proposal, dated August 14, 1947, the very eve of India's independence, he made a strong case for a unitary Palestine. He felt that both the binational solution and the cantonal option were undemocratic and cumbersome. In his view, there were only two realistic solutions to Palestine: partition or a unitary state. He rejected the federal option as "unworkable as the desire to federate is lacking at present."[50] Outlining his proposal, Rahman cabled:

> Palestine should in accordance to promises given by British and French Governments be constituted into a democratic unitary Palestinian State and although Jewish ethnic, cultural, religious, educational and linguistic rights be reserved by constitution either unalterable or alternatively by a three-fourths majority. Yet there is no reason to deprive the majority of their legitimate right according to principle of self-determination to form a Government in which Jews should be allowed a share of one-third in all Government offices and posts proportionate to their present population.

On the question of *aliya*, the primary Zionist agenda, Rahman was prepared to accept immigration based on "religious and domestic but not political reasons."[51]

Rahman's August 14 unitary plan and his decision to place his recommendations in "sealed cover" rang alarms in New Delhi. On August 23, a week after India's partition, he was instructed to abandon his proposal and opt for a "middle course between what may be theoretically just and what is factually practicable." Disagreeing with Rahman's views, India expressed support for a federal Palestine, and Rahman was explicitly instructed not to pursue "a democratic unitary Palestinian State."[52]

Thus, in proposing a solution for Palestine, Rahman followed the broad parameters and guidelines set by the Indian government, especially Prime Minister Nehru. What, then, was the Indian plan?

Federal Palestine

As per the deadline set by the first Special Session, the UNSCOP submitted its report on September 1, 1947.[53] Most of its recommendations were unanimous or near unanimous. On issues such as the termination of the Mandate, the granting of independence to Palestine, transitional arrangements under the United Nations, the safeguarding of holy places, the plight of Jewish displaced persons in Europe, and the protection of minorities and economic unity, the committee members were unanimous. Guatemala and Uruguay refused to endorse the majority recommendation that declared that "any solution for Palestine cannot be considered as a solution for the Jewish problem in general."[54] On the core issue of the future political status of Palestine, the UNSCOP was divided. A seven-member majority consisting of Canada, Czechoslovakia, Guatemala, the Netherlands, Peru, Sweden, and Uruguay opted for a partition of Palestine, while India, Iran, and Yugoslavia put forward a federal plan. Australia refused to endorse either plan.

The majority plan recommended that Palestine be partitioned into independent Arab and Jewish states with an economic union between the two. The city of Jerusalem and its environs would be placed under an international *corpus separatum*. Justifying partition, the majority members argued: "The basic premise underlying the partition proposal is that the claim to Palestine of the Arabs and Jews, both possessing validity, are irreconcilable, and that among all of the solutions advanced, partition will provide the most realistic and practical settlement, and is the most likely to afford a workable basis for meeting in part of the claims and national aspirations of both parties."[55] Viewing the problem in Palestine as "a clash between two intense nationalisms," the plan rejected the maximalist demands of both the Arabs and the Jews. It recognized that any worthwhile, viable, and realistic solution would have to be one of compromise.[56] The partition plan has been too widely discussed, examined, and criticized to be repeated here. Instead, we will look at the federal plan, which was largely ignored by the international community.

As early as April 23, 1947, when the First Special Session of the UN General Assembly was in progress, New Delhi felt that any solution to the Palestine problem "must lie on the lines of the Arab state with the inclusion of an autonomous Jewish area."[57] This was in tune with the traditional Congress Party's position vis-à-vis Palestine, especially since 1939. The federal plan more or less reflected this stand. Even though Iran (an Islamic country) and Yugoslavia (which had a sizable Muslim population) endorsed it, the federal plan was primarily Indian in origin. Though hand delivered by Rahman, it was Nehruvian by design.

The principal Indian opposition to the majority plan revolved around the unworkable nature of partition. Its envoy argued that the plan aimed at "a union under artificial arrangements designed to achieve essential economic and social unity after first creating political and geographical disunity by partition, [hence the plan was] impractical, unworkable and could not possibly provide for two reasonably viable states."[58] In his dissent note, Rahman elaborated his reasons for rejecting the majority suggestions. His arguments can be broadly summarized as follows:

- Palestine was a predominantly Arab country, and any resolution of the conflict should not be to the disadvantage of the native Arabs;
- Palestine was not a solution for the Jewish problem;[59]
- it was not possible to create two viable states in Palestine;
- it was not possible to create a Jewish state without a very large Arab minority;[60]
- Palestine was too small to bear the burden of two governments;
- the Jewish state would be surrounded by hostile Arab states, which would only increase the possibility of war;
- the likelihood of Arab-Jewish cooperation would become remote;
- the division of Palestine would make the transportation of goods impossible, since commerce was already handicapped by Palestine's artificial borders with its Arab neighbors;
- the proposed distribution of land and resources between the two states under the partition plan were inequitable and strongly biased against the Arabs;[61]
- partition would create problems for Jews everywhere since they would be accused of practicing dual loyalties;[62]
- enforcement of the partition plan would require the use of force, since Arab-Jewish relations would deteriorate; and
- partition was against the principle of self-determination.

Critiques of partition were not new. The Woodhead Commission set up in 1938 to examine the division of Palestine was unsuccessful. Likewise commenting on partition, in 1946 the twelve-member Anglo-American Committee of Inquiry observed: "Partition has an appeal at first sight as giving a prospect of early independence and self-government to Jews and Arabs, but in our view no partition would have any chance unless it was basically acceptable to Jews and Arabs, and there is no sign of that today. We are accordingly unable to recommend partition as the solution."[63] Even within the U.S. State Department, there were differences over the feasibility of the majority plan of the UNSCOP.[64]

Abdur Rahman also used his dissenting note to challenge some of the positions held by the great powers vis-à-vis Palestine. He argued, *inter alia*, that the Balfour Declaration should not have been made;[65] that the mandate was incompatible and inconsistent with the Covenant of the

League of Nations;[66] that where the Mandate was found to be inconsistent with the Covenant, the latter would prevail; and that no nation had the right to create a Mandate over Palestine and impose its will without the consent of the inhabitants.

Rahman was challenging the basic premises of imperialism. At the time of the Balfour Declaration or when the Mandate and Covenant of the League were drafted, the "world" or "international community'" was either European or Eurocentric. Voices and rights of the "rest" did not matter to those who decided the destiny of humanity.

The partition plan received widespread attention both because it was endorsed by the majority members of the UNSCOP and because of its subsequent acceptance by a majority of the UN members. It was therefore closely examined, praised, or demonized. In contrast, the minority plan received no attention, and it has largely been left to the Indians to venerate its virtues. It is too tempting to believe that the federal plan was foolproof, flawless, and could have eliminated all the ills of erstwhile Palestine. The federal plan was not a remedy in 1947. It is not so six decades later. That it received meager attention should be seen as an indication of its relevance, or otherwise.

The main features of the federal plan were:

- Palestine would be a federal and independent state;
- while the Mandate would be terminated soon, there would be a transition administration whose tenure would not exceed three years;
- federal Palestine would consist of Arab and Jewish states;
- each state would enjoy internal autonomy excluding "national defense, foreign relations, immigration, currency, taxation for federal purposes, foreign and inter-state waterways, transport and communication, copyrights and patent";[67]
- the federal state would have a bicameral legislature; and
- the constitution would safeguard, among other things, the equality of all citizens with regard to political, civil, and religious rights of the individual and linguistic, religious, ethnic, and cultural rights of the people as a whole.

To ensure a smooth and functional transition, a three-year interim administration would be established toward preparing the necessary groundwork for federal Palestine.

Why Did the Indian Plan Fail?

The fundamental disadvantage of the federal plan was that it was rejected by both contending parties. This marked the only occasion when the Arabs and Jews were on the same side of the debate. A strong segment of the Zionist leadership was aspiring for the transformation of the whole of Palestine into a Jewish state. There were others who were prepared to settle for less. Even though the partition plan fell short of their expectations, mainstream Zionists recognized it as the best possible solution. Despite their disappointment over smaller territorial limits and the exclusion of Jerusalem, they saw the partition plan as the sign of international recognition of Jewish claims to Palestine. While the Arabs vehemently opposed it, the majority plan at least had the support of the Zionists.[68]

The Indian plan disappointed both parties. It offered only civic and religious rights to the Jews; they were aspiring for political rights and sovereignty. It placed *aliya* under joint federal control and thus restricted its scope. Irrespective of their ideological orientation, everyone in the *yishuv*, from the revisionists to the binationalists, was unanimous on unrestricted Jewish immigration. *Aliya* was the cardinal principle, indeed the *raison d'être* of Zionism. It was therefore unrealistic to expect the Zionists to subject this core issue to an Arab veto.

If the Jews opposed the Indian plan because it gave them too little, the Arabs rejected it because it gave too much to the Jews who emigrated to Palestine. Both inside and outside Palestine, the Arabs demanded immediate and complete independence, and they did not look kindly at Indian suggestions of autonomy for the Jews as the precondition. While they were demanding a unitary Arab state, the Indian plan called for greater and even unacceptable internal autonomy for the Jews. Both sides were quick to reject the Indian plan, and it was never discussed by the United Nations.

Second, the Indian plan was unrealistic. The UNSCOP unequivocally recognized that Arab-Jewish cooperation was impossible. The committee conceded that in Palestine "government service, the Potash Company and the Oil Refinery *are almost the only places where Arabs and Jews meet as co-workers in the same organizations*."[69] During much of the Mandate period, they largely operated independently of each another. Both communities maintained well-defined and clearly demarcated spheres of political, social, and economic activities. On July 15, a bewildered Rahman wrote to Nehru that "even the Communists in this country are divided into two parties, one Jewish and the other Arab."[70] While partition meant a severing of even the minimal contacts between the two communities, the federal plan rested on continued cooperation between two noninteracting communities. Given this state of affairs, the federal plan required a superhuman effort—if not divine intervention—to bring about mutual trust and cooperation between the two communities.

Third, the plan suffered from a number of operational difficulties. While proposing the constitution of a federal state, Rahman stipulated a number of conditions. They were aimed at safeguarding the rights and privileges of the Jewish minority in a predominantly Arab federation. These provisions encroached upon the proposed sovereignty of federal Palestine. Internal communal tensions between the two nations demanded active involvement of a third party (as with the Mandate) for its implementation. Otherwise, it would not be possible to protect the rights of the Jewish minority, and this in turn would have challenged the notion of independence.

Fourth, the success of the plan was predicated on tolerance and democracy. It is highly debatable whether in 1948 the Palestinian community could have maintained a democratic character within a federal arrangement. The members of the UNSCOP had serious reservations about the Palestinian leadership. They were skeptical about the structure and functioning of the Arab Higher Committee headed by the mufti, even though it represented a large section of the Arabs of Palestine. The UNSCOP did not hesitate to recognize the intimidation tactics used by the Arab Committee in preventing Arabs from testifying before the committee in Jerusalem.[71] This becomes far more complicated if one compares the mufti-dominated Arab community to the well-organized *yishuv*.[72] The federal state visualized by India would thus comprise a centralized and nondemocratic Arab unit and a decentralized, institutionalized, and functioning Jewish unit. One could not have found a worse systemic mismatch.

Fifth, the federal plan exposed India's own hypocrisy. The Indian representative signed the UNSCOP report on August 31, 1947, and by then the subcontinent was partitioned along communal lines. Nehru was advocating a solution for Palestine that he was not prepared to accept for India, where the conditions were far better. Hindu-Muslim relations in India were not as poisoned or insurmountable as Arab-Jewish relations were in Palestine. This was true even taking into account the communal bloodshed that followed partition. Even after the formation of the Islamic state of Pakistan, a substantial number of Muslims chose to remain in India. No such similarities existed in Palestine. Though a significant number of Palestinians remained in areas that became Israel, there was no Palestinian leadership, organized or unorganized, that was prepared to give partition a chance. The Indian government, through its UNSCOP representative, was aware of the intercommunity tension, animosity, and noncooperation in Palestine. Despite this, it chose to advocate a path that was rejected by Nehru and the Congress Party for the subcontinent.

Sixth, the federal plan highlighted contradictions between Rahman's public pronouncements and his private actions. Both in his minority report and in his dissenting note to the majority plan, he followed the traditional INC opposition to religion-based nationalism. He was highly critical of religion entering the political realm, especially in the nation-state discourse. In his report, he observed: "it is important to avoid an acceleration of the separatism which now characterizes the relations of Arabs and Jews in the Near East, and *to avoid laying the foundations of a dangerous irredentism there,* which would be the inevitable consequence of partition in whatever form."[73] He was more forceful in his dissenting note, stating that if the Jewish demand for statehood in Palestine was conceded, Jews elsewhere would be charged with "double loyalty." Upholding the principle of self-determination, he argued that it would be difficult to "refuse the majority, the right of forming the government."[74] On the religious side, he contended: "it is impossible to forget that the Jews as a whole, are not a nation but only a community which follows a particular religion. . . . Moreover the so-called nationalism is of too recent a growth to be any value . . . there is no reason why political considerations should be mixed up with religious considerations and why political rights in a state should be confused with religious rights."[75] His views reflected the prevailing INC position toward similar demands made by Islamic separatism in the subcontinent and spearheaded by Jinnah. In short, democracy was the rule of the majority, and church and state are distinct and separate spheres.

What Rahman did subsequently was rather ironic. Despite vehemently rejecting any links between religion and statecraft, shortly after the submission of the UNSCOP report, he emigrated to Pakistan, a state formed on the basis of the same arguments put forth by the Zionists.[76] He eventually retired as a judge of Pakistan's Federal Court.[77] Describing the prevailing mood among Muslims immediately after World War II toward communal divisions, one scholar aptly remarked: partition, "the only means of real freedom to the Indian Muslims, . . . was anathema to Muslims elsewhere."[78] In rejecting the majority proposal for Palestine but still emigrating to Pakistan himself, Rahman reflected the prevailing dilemma facing the Muslim League: partition was justifiable in India but was sacrilege in the Islamic land of Palestine!

These shortcomings aside, the Indian plan failed mainly on the political front. It failed to secure the support and endorsement of the international community, especially the two principal parties, the Arabs and Jews.

The Partition of Palestine

Following the submission of the UNSCOP report, the international focus shifted back to New York. For the next twelve weeks, the fate of Palestine was the main agenda of the annual session of the General Assembly. After a general debate, two subcommittees were established. The first subcommittee was asked to draft a viable partition plan.[79] The second subcommittee, composed largely of Islamic countries, was asked to produce a scheme for a unitary Palestine.[80] The federal plan so vociferously proposed by Nehru was not even considered by the United Nations and was quietly consigned to the archives.[81]

The Arab leaderships in Palestine and in the region were opposed to any dilution of their demand for a unitary Palestine. This contributed to the international indifference toward the Indian proposal. The entire drama also underscored the inability, unwillingness, or failure of Indian diplomacy in convincing the Arabs of the validity and advantages of the federal plan. A well-argued plan was rendered futile. On October 8, more than six weeks before the UN vote, Vijayalakshmi Pandit, the leader of the Indian delegation to the 1947 UN session, warned New Delhi: "The majority report satisfied [the] Jews. It is naturally opposed by [the] Arabs. The minority report, on the other hand, is acceptable neither to Jews nor Arabs. For us to advocate Minority report would please no one and lead us nowhere."[82] Even this last-minute advice went unheeded.

Things moved rather rapidly at the United Nations. The reports of the two subcommittees were submitted on November 19 and 11, respectively. After a lengthy debate, on November 24 the ad hoc committee rejected the unitary-state proposal.[83] The following day, the committee approved the majority partition plan by twenty-five votes to thirteen, with nineteen abstentions. It also altered the territorial limits in favor of the Jewish state. In a last-minute effort, the Arab states unsuccessfully sought to refer the entire question to the International Court of Justice. As the date for the final vote neared, it was unclear if the partition plan would secure the necessary two-thirds majority. This raised some hopes among the Indian delegation. Mrs. Pandit, who had been unenthusiastic about the federal plan in early October, revised her position and advised: "It is probable that the special committee will be re-convened immediately and set to work on the federal solution, which has increasing support. Canada, Netherlands and Belgium yesterday [November 26] expressed preference for such solution, though they would vote for partition, in the absence of another alternative."[84] Indian optimism was supported by Arab rethinking on the issue. For the first time, the Arab states were prepared to consider the Indian proposal for a federal Palestine.[85]

Commenting on the last-minute *volte face* of the Arab countries, Nehru lamented before the Constituent Assembly:

> [The Arab states were] so keen on the unitary state idea and were so sure of at any rate preventing partition or preventing two-third majority in favor of partition, that they did not accept our suggestion. When, during the last few days, partition somehow suddenly became inevitable and it was realized that the Indian solution was probably the best . . . a last-minute attempt was made in the last 48 hours to bring forward the Indian solution *not by us but by those who wanted a unitary state*. It was then too late.[86]

The rejection of the unitary plan and approval of the partition plan by the ad hoc committee had forced the Arabs to rethink. By then it was too late. On November 29, 1947, the UN General Assembly adopted Resolution 181, recommending the partition of Palestine. Both at the ad hoc committee and in the General Assembly, India was the most prominent non-Islamic country to vote against partition.

Even this UN endorsement did not diminish Indian zeal. The post-vote violence in Palestine offered another opportunity. Between November 1947 and May 1948, when the British were to complete their withdrawal from Mandate Palestine, New Delhi made another unsuccessful attempt to bridge the gap between the Arabs and the Zionists. This time, the task fell on the shoulders of Sir B. N. Rau, an adviser to India's

Constituent Assembly and a member of the Indian delegation to the United Nations. He drafted a proposal that Nehru described as "a half-way house between partition and some kind of federation."[87] Rau had outlined his plan just a few days before the UN endorsement of the partition plan and had "shown this note to Weizmann . . . who had been attracted to it."[88] As violence intensified in Palestine, Rau's ideas gathered momentum and eventually resulted in the convening of the Second Special Session of the UN General Assembly in April 1948. According to Rau, the violence following the partition vote meant "each side must yield a little ground [and] they may be in a mood to consider a *via media*."[89]

Afraid of its rejection, Rau was against giving a name to his proposal until all the details were finalized.[90] Moving away from the federal proposal, this plan called for separate cabinets for Arab and Jewish regions headed by a separate prime minister. For a specific number of years, Palestine as a whole would be governed by a single executive head appointed by the newly formed UN Trusteeship Council. Given the importance that Zionism attached to *aliya*, Rau suggested "regulated immigration without materially disturbing the existing proportions of the two communities."[91] It soon became clear that the Rau plan had no real chance of being considered by the United Nations. Not prepared to face yet another diplomatic embarrassment, New Delhi advised its UN delegation not to present the plan. Instead, it was advised to "persuade the Committee to adopt the cardinal principle of co-operation between Arabs and Jews."[92]

Meanwhile, the British decision to pull out by May 15, 1948, irrespective of the consequences, intensified the Arab-Jewish violence in Palestine. In a bid to restore peace and order, on April 16, 1948, the United Nations convened another Special Session of the General Assembly. In a sudden reversal of its earlier policy, the United States proposed a "suspension" of the partition resolution and placing Palestine under a temporary trusteeship. India saw this as an opportunity to bypass the partition resolution, found a common cause with the United States, and actively supported the suspension of Resolution 181.[93] It was included in a twelve-member subcommittee set up by the United Nations to formulate a provisional post-Mandate regime for Palestine.

As the second Special Session was bogged down in endless debates and procedural wrangling, on May 14, hours before the final British soldiers left Mandate Palestine, the *yishuv* leaders met in Tel Aviv and declared the formation of the State of Israel. Within minutes of this development, U.S. President Harry S. Truman accorded *de facto* recognition to the Jewish state. This was soon followed by others. As a result, the UN efforts to secure trusteeship became meaningless, and the Special Session abruptly ended on May 15.

Thus India's election to the UNSCOP provided the first opportunity for its leadership to articulate the position of the nationalists regarding the Palestine question in the international arena. The pro-Arab position adopted by the Congress Party during the freedom struggle gained substance at the United Nations. Even though its nominee initially favored the Arab demand for a unitary Palestine, Nehru advised him to modify this stand and recommended a "middle path." If the majority members of the UNSCOP viewed partition as a compromise between the extremist demands of Arabs and Jews, Nehru saw a federal Palestine as a compromise between partition and a unitary Palestine. While providing greater civic and social rights, it sought to preserve the Arab character of Palestine.

The contrast between the partition and federal plans is stark. The former sought political separation and economic cooperation between the Arab and Jewish communities; the Indian plan aspired to achieve cooperation and accommodation between the warring communities. While one granted political rights and sovereignty to both nations, the other bestowed religious and civil rights upon the minorities. The former was swayed by the historic suffering of the Jewish people; the latter was preoccupied with the historic rights of native inhabitants. Both the partition plan and the federal plan have their own shares of limitations and shortcomings. The partition plan succeeded mainly because it enjoyed the support and endorsement of at least one of the contending parties. India's federal plan failed because even the Arabs discarded it. Rejected by both parties, India's plan was never discussed at the United Nations and was quietly buried by the international community.

[Normalization] is a welcome decision, particularly because this issue had become an unnecessary irritant in our domestic discussion of foreign policy. Had India established full diplomatic relations with Israel in 1950, it would have been far better. In its absence, all kinds of speculations were made about the benefits that could have accrued to India had it established full diplomatic relations with Israel long ago.
—*M. S. Agwani*

6 Recognition Without Relations

The traditional pro-Arab position and opposition to the partition plan inhibited India from immediately recognizing the Jewish state. At the same time, Prime Minister Jawaharlal Nehru could not ignore Israel's existence and its recognition by the international community and United Nations. Even when India eventually recognized Israel in September 1950, it was not followed by the logical next step of normalization of relations. If recognition took more than two years to materialize, diplomatic relations had to wait for over four decades. The prolonged absence of formal ties resulted in speculations about the nature of Indian recognition. The Indian leadership, especially Nehru, wanted to establish normal ties with Israel. Had it happened in September 1950 or soon afterward, subsequent Indo-Israeli relations would not have been so controversial, partisan, and agonizing.

Before looking at the absence of ties, it is essential to answer the central question: why did India recognize Israel? We must also answer a set of related questions: How do we square India's pro-Arab stance with the recognition of Israel? Was it a fundamental shift that marked a reconciliation with the Jewish claims in Palestine, or was it merely an aberration in India's overall Middle East policy? Was Nehru keen on the normalization of relations? How does one explain the peculiar policy of recognition without relations?

While the issue of the recognition of Israel has been frequently commented upon, there is no unanimity among scholars.[1] Traditional understanding on this issue has been overtaken by later developments and fresh evidence. When was the request made? Within hours of its establishment on the Sabbath eve of May 14, 1948, Israel sought recognition from the international community. Prime Minister Nehru offered two different dates as to when Israel made a request to India. Speaking at the Constituent Assembly in August 1948, he declared: "A telegram was received *in the middle of June 1948* from Monsieur Moshe Shertok [later Sharett], Foreign Minister of the Provisional Government of the State of Israel, containing a request for recognition of the Jewish State."[2] Some still consider this to be accurate.[3] The mid-June date gives an impression that India was not high on Israel's list of priorities and that its delayed request was an expression of its displeasure over India's opposition to the partition plan.

The publication in 1985 of Nehru's *Letters to Chief Ministers* offered a new and earlier date. On May 20, 1948, in his fortnightly letter to the heads of Indian states, the Indian premier acknowledged that the government had received a formal request from Israel for recognition.[4] This is closer to the actual date. Israeli documents indicate that Shertok wrote to Nehru (who was also serving as India's minister of external affairs) for recognition. The cable was sent on Monday, May 17—the second workday after the declaration of Israeli independence.[5] It was received by the Indian foreign office on the following day.[6] Despite the Indian opposition to the partition plan, Israel was quick to seek formal recognition from New Delhi.

On May 19, Eliahu Epstein, the Washington representative of Israel's provisional government, met the Indian chargé d'affairs and handed over a letter notifying the proclamation of the state of Israel. He felt that because of "interruption of cable communication between Israel and other countries," an official communication might not have reached New Delhi.[7] On May 21, within a week of the establishment of Israel, the Indian Foreign Ministry prepared a note on recognition and highlighted the UN angle: "the admission of a State to membership in the United Nations will be effected by a decision of the General Assembly upon the recommendations of the Security Council. Israel's application will therefore be considered first by the Security Council. As we are not a member of the Security Council, it is not necessary at this stage to formulate our views on this question."[8] Without a request for recognition, there was no need to discuss Israel's possible membership in the United Nations.

In short, Sharett sends a cable on May 17, which reaches New Delhi on May 18. The following day, Israel's envoy in Washington communicates with the Indian embassy. On May 20, the prime minister refers to the Israeli request in his letter to the chief ministers, and on May 21, the Indian foreign office prepares a note regarding Israel's possible admission to the United Nations. Thus Nehru's statement to the Constituent Assembly of having received a request in June was a mix-up.

Awaiting the Indian move, Israeli missions in different parts of the world regularly sent official circulars and reports to their Indian counterparts. Because of the obvious diplomatic implications, the latter did not know how to respond. Thus in April 1949, the Indian embassy in Prague sought clarifications from New Delhi:

> This embassy has been receiving many such letters [from the Israeli Legation in Prague] from time to time. We shall be pleased to know what our attitude should be in such cases. So far, we have not acknowledged or replied to any communication from the Legation of Israel, nor has the Ambassador returned the cards of the Minister. The situation is not without its difficulties as almost every other foreign establishment here, apart from Egypt, is in official relations with the Legation, these countries having accorded recognition to . . . Israel. What we wish to know is whether our acknowledging such communications or accepting calls or invitations from the Mission will be tantamount to any recognition.[9]

The ministry responded by saying that under international law "recognition would be implied in acts like acknowledging communications, accepting calls or invitations etc., from a diplomatic representative of Israel." Because India had not granted recognition, it instructed the Prague mission that "all such communications should be quietly ignored."[10] Similar queries soon poured in from other Indian missions. On May 28, Foreign Secretary K. P. S. Menon issued a clarification to all Indian missions abroad. Declaring that India had "so far scrupulously avoided recognizing" Israel, he conceded that Israel's recent admission to the United Nations had "altered" the situation and that the question of recognition was being "reconsidered." In the meantime, Menon advised the missions to immediately inform the ministry of "any approaches" made by Israeli missions "without . . . any assurances being conveyed to them."[11]

India took as many as twenty-eight months to reciprocate the Israeli request for recognition. During this period between May 1948 and September 1950, there were a number of definite and incontrovertible signs indicating India's movement toward recognition.

Ginger Steps

Writing to state chief ministers in May 1948, within days after the establishment of the state of Israel, Nehru remarked: "We propose to take no action in this matter [that is, recognition] at present. India can play no effective part in this conflict at the present stage either diplomatically or otherwise. We can only watch events for the time being, hoping that an opportunity may come when we might use our influence in the interest of peace and mediation."[12]

While acknowledging the Israeli request, he opted to defer decision on the matter. A note prepared in October following the formation of the All-Palestine Government (APG) rationalized the official stand: "in May this year, when the State of Israel was proclaimed in Palestine, her Foreign Minister Mr. Shertok also sent a similar telegram. It was decided that time not to take any action on the telegram and the said telegram *was not even acknowledged* in the view of possible political complications."[13] Interestingly, its silence on the request for recognition from the APG was accompanied by its preparedness to communicate with Hajj Amin al-Husseini not as the head of the APG but as grand mufti of Jerusalem. In March 1949, India's chargé d'affairs in Cairo acknowledged the mufti's telegram, wherein he expressed his "gratitude and appreciation of the [Indian] Government's refusal to recognize Israel."[14]

Remaining cautious regarding the issue, in August 1948 Nehru informed the Constituent Assembly that "a new State [of Israel] was formed and we had to wait."[15] Expressing similar caution, in February 1949 he observed that the recognition of Israel would be "guided not only by idealistic considerations but also a realistic appraisal of the situation."[16] A month later, he reiterated that Israel "is undoubtedly a State which is functioning as such; and the honorable member's [H. V. Kamath] opinion about it having come to stay may be correct."[17] Meanwhile, on May 11,

1949, Israel's application for membership came before the UN General Assembly.[18] In tune with its earlier position, India voted against the motion, which was endorsed by the majority in the UN General Assembly.[19] New Delhi could not ignore Israel's eventual admission into the United Nations, and on June 3, 1949, Nehru conceded: "We shall have to consider our future policy in regard to it [Israel's UN membership]."[20] Through these public pronouncements and internal debates, Nehru conveyed a wait-and-see approach toward recognizing Israel.

This domestic caution was accompanied by a friendlier stance internationally. By September 1948, weeks after the second Arab-Israeli ceasefire came into force, Israeli diplomats felt that a favorable Indian decision was a foregone conclusion and only the timing remained uncertain. As Nehru was gathering domestic support for recognition, India exhibited a friendlier and sympathetic attitude toward Israel. On September 28, 1948, India's ambassador in Washington, B. N. Rau, met his Israeli counterpart and referred to normalization.[21] Interestingly, the envoy talked about "normalization" when India was still nearly two years away from recognition. The following May, Vijayalakshmi Pandit, who succeeded Rau in Washington, told her Israeli counterpart Elath that India would recognize the Jewish state at an appropriate time. She estimated that this "may happen soon after the settlement of the Kashmir dispute."[22] The next month, Rau, who had moved to the United Nations, dealt at length with the existing commonalities between India and Israel and noted that there was no conflict of interest between the two states.[23] In her meeting with Ambassador Elath in September, Mrs. Pandit observed that India was slowly moving toward recognizing Israel and that the decision could not be delayed further.[24]

In October 1949, Elath had a lengthy conversation with Nehru when the Indian prime minister visited the United States. Summing up this meeting, the Israeli ambassador cabled:

> Nehru listened attentively, obviously disturbed by mention [of] Turkey's recognition. In reply after announcing complete frankness he explained India's attitude [toward] Israel. People never anti-Semitic, Hitler made them friends of Jews. Many Indians admired in past Zionist and now most sympathetic [to] Israel. . . . He had to choose slow, long, way towards recognition [in] order [to] justify it objectively and minimize internal opposition. . . . He arrived [at the] conclusion recognition cannot be postponed much longer. . . . To my question

> whether he could mention possible date [of] recognition he replied [he] would deal matter immediately on return India early November and we could expect recognition before January [1950].[25]

Nehru was equally optimistic. Upon returning home, he declared that the recognition of Israel "cannot obviously be indefinitely deferred."[26] While recognition was not forthcoming immediately, India exhibited some diplomatic niceties. In January 1950, Rau invited Ambassador Aubrey S. Eban (later Abba Eban) to an official function in New York marking the ushering in of the Indian republic.[27]

Its waffling on recognition did not inhibit India from approaching Israel for technical assistance. On November 15, 1947, as the UN General Assembly was debating the partition plan, Chaim Weizmann (the future president of Israel) offered technical assistance to India, which Nehru accepted.[28] The Zionist leader was acting on the suggestions made by K. M. Panikkar and Shiva Rao, who were active in the Asian Relations Conference held earlier that year.[29] Following a series of discussions between the two sides,[30] in March 1949, India sought agricultural assistance from Israel. Since it had not recognized the Jewish state, the Ministry of Agriculture asked H. Z. Cynowitz, the representative of the Jewish Agency in India, to take up the request "*with your people in Palestine*."[31] Despite the curious wording, Israel viewed this request as a sign of Indian friendliness. The request "for a loan of agricultural experts showed that no real hostility existed."[32] In later years, reflecting similar sentiments, Nehru's biographer S. Gopal observed, "despite basic differences with Israel, Nehru sent some experts to that country to study the working of the cooperative movement."[33]

The most promising statement on recognition came in February 1950, when Prime Minister Nehru told the Provisional Parliament: "The fact that the State of Israel exists is of course recognized by the Government of India. But formal recognition involving an exchange of diplomatic mission has to be considered in connection with a number of factors."[34] These public statements, confidential remarks, and diplomatic gestures clearly indicate the thinking of the government and its willingness to recognize Israel. They also underscore the delicacy with which Nehru approached the issue.

The inordinate Indian delay, however, irritated Israeli officials. Walter Eytan, who aspired to be Israel's first ambassador to India,[35] summed up the general feeling that prevailed in the diplomatic community.

> Two years after the establishment of the State of Israel, India remains one of the few non-Arab, non-Muslim countries which have not recognized her. Israel had always attributed a special value to India's recognition, due to her prestigious status in Asia. During the past two years, considerable efforts have been invested in making contacts with high-ranking Indian personalities but despite many promises and demonstrations of friendship, India has not yet taken this step. Now that 60 countries have recognized Israel, recognition by an additional one is no longer a burning issue and Israel has ceased trying to persuade vacillating countries, including India. Moreover, belated recognition is of lesser political and moral weight than that accorded close to the state's establishment.[36]

This sour note was valid even four decades later, when India followed—not preceded—China in normalizing ties with Israel.[37]

Meanwhile, after months of waiting, by mid-September 1950 India began negotiating with Israel over the timing of recognition. Both sides agreed that a formal and simultaneous announcement would be made declaring that India's recognition would come into force on September 18, 1950. A communication to this effect was sent to the Israeli embassy in Washington.[38] On September 17, Nehru, in his capacity as foreign minister, sent a cable to Foreign Minister Moshe Sharett, which read: "In conveying to Your Excellency the decision of the Government of India to accord recognition to the Government of Israel as from September 18 of this year, I send the greetings of the Government and people of India to the Government and people of Israel."[39] A crisp official communiqué issued in New Delhi declared: "The Government of India have decided to accord recognition to the Government of Israel." Interestingly, the Indian "government" chose to recognize the Israeli "government."[40] By then, Israel had conducted its first Knesset election; India was still two years away from its first Lok Sabha elections. Given the circumstances surrounding Israel's formation, an explicit and unambiguous reference to the state of Israel would have been more appropriate. Exploiting this ambiguity, some Indian scholars suggested that India's recognition was temporary and could be withdrawn at any time.[41]

There was something amiss in the whole exercise. Neither the formal communiqué to Israel nor the official statement released in New Delhi referred to the establishment of diplomatic relations. Because of the delays and controversies surrounding recognition, the absence of any reference to diplomatic ties assumed greater significance. In hindsight, it is obvious that just as he was moving toward recognition, Nehru was also facing counterpressures from those opposed to such a move. Thus the absence of any direct reference to the establishment of relations was apparently a compromise. Because recognition was not followed by diplomatic ties, a number of controversies arose over the legal status of recognition. Was it de facto or de jure? According to K. P. Misra, India generally extends recognition without any reference to its de facto or de jure status.[42] In his February 1950 statement cited above, Nehru clearly stated that "formal recognition involving an exchange of diplomatic mission" would have to consider a number of factors. Not only was there no exchange of diplomatic missions, but India even refused to treat the Israeli Consulate in Bombay (Mumbai) as a diplomatic mission. Hence, some innovatively argued that "in the case India has accorded only de facto recognition . . . that has not been followed by full diplomatic intercourse or the conferment of diplomatic immunities upon their representatives."[43]

A careful analysis would dispel any doubts about Indian recognition and indicate that it was de facto as well as de jure in nature. Primarily, Nehru's February 1950 statement indicated that India had accepted Israel's de facto status even before its formal recognition. On a number of subsequent occasions, India maintained that its declaration was de jure. For example, in July 1971, the government informed the Lok Sabha: "India extended de jure recognition to Israel in September 1950."[44] An official report prepared by Israel's senior diplomat, Walter Eytan, offers interesting insights into the whole controversy. In early 1952, he visited India and met all the leading Indian figures, including Prime Minister Nehru. Upon his return to Israel, he submitted a long report called *New Delhi Diary*, where he observed:

> Miss [Leilamani] Naidu [who was dealing with Israel in the Ministry of External Affairs] also told me of the argument they had had in the Ministry at the time they recognized Israel—whether it should be *de jure* or *de facto*. The Secretary General [G. S. Bajpai], on being appraised of this problem, had consulted all their legal authorities and had come to the conclusion that he couldn't see what difference there was between *de facto* and *de jure* recognition; so they recognized us pure and simple.[45]

Thus, despite the perceived ambiguity, prolonged nonrelations could not be used to question the validity or the legal status of India's recognition.

If one looks beyond the legal tangle, why did India take more than two years to accord recognition?

Why Procrastination?

The most obvious explanation is the wait-and-watch attitude that countries normally adopt when deciding on recognition. Countries need to satisfy themselves that the newborn entity is stable, cohesive, and, above all, is prepared to assume and play its role in the community of nations. Like the rest of the world, India adopts a cautious approach regarding recognition and has normally followed rather than led the international community. Its stances on the recognition of Algeria, East Germany, or the PLO reflect this trend.[46] Indeed, delayed recognition of Israel was accompanied by its indifferent stance toward the APG proclaimed by the Palestinian leadership in September 1948.

With regard to Israel, however, there are a number of additional reasons. As discussed elsewhere, domestic public opinion, especially of the Muslims, played a considerable role. The second reason has to be found in the Arab factor. India was afraid that any hasty move would antagonize the Arabs and jeopardize its larger interests in the Middle East. The issue of recognizing Israel figured in India's deliberations with the Arab countries. Following his meeting with Prime Minister Nehru in Washington in October 1949, Elath cabled: "He [Nehru] recently discussed Israel with Arab and Muslim envoys [in] New Delhi, emphasizing necessity [of] reconciliation [with] realities and preparing them for our inevitable recognition by India."[47] According to another senior Israeli diplomat, the Iraqi delegation "brought strong pressure [on] the chief delegate [of] India to activate against Indian recognition [of] Israel."[48]

Nehru's biographer Gopal admits the Arab influence on India's approach toward Israel. According to him, "on the question of Israel's admission to the United Nations, his [Nehru's] first reaction was to abstain. *Later,* as part of the policy of co-operation with the Islamic States, he ordered the Indian delegation to vote against."[49] Less than two weeks after recognizing Israel, Nehru frankly admitted the Arab factor and informed the chief ministers, "We would have done this [recognition of Israel] long ago, because Israel is a fact. We refrained because of *our desire not to offend the sentiments of our friends in the Arab countries.*"[50] Similarly, its ambassador in Cairo also attributed the delay to Arab pressures. Speaking to the Egyptian media soon after recognition, he remarked:

> For some time now announcements were being made that India did intend to recognize Israel and that it was only a question of time. India's intentions were made known well in advance to the Arab diplomats in New Delhi and to the Governments in the Middle East through Cairo. Some of these Governments requested India to postpone her decision but India felt that any further postponement would not serve any useful purpose.[51]

Moreover, by the time India had recognized Israel, all the neighboring Arab states, including Egypt, had signed the armistice agreement with the Jewish state.[52] This move could be interpreted as the Arab acquiescence, if not tacit recognition, of Israel.

A note prepared by the Ministry of External Affairs in February 1950 even linked recognition to the question of *hajj* and added a host of preconditions such as the resolution of the refugee problems, boundaries, and the Jerusalem question.[53] Indian apprehension over Saudi displeasure and the possible repercussions upon *hajj* pilgrimages underscore the religious dimension. Fears over Pakistan and its moves among Arab and Islamic countries came to haunt India for the next four decades and contributed to the prolonged absence of formal ties with Israel.

If the above were the reasons for the delay, what influenced, if not compelled, the September 1950 decision?

Reasons for Recognition

From the available records, one can identify nine possible explanations for Indian recognition. Legally, India is committed to the Declaratory Theory of Recognition and, as one scholar concluded, in its position, "recognition registers but does not create a situation."[54] It scrupulously avoided creating a situation whereby its recognition alone would constitute a reality. Even in the case of Bangladesh, in whose formation it played the pivotal role, recognition did not come until December 1971.[55]

Second, it accords recognition to a newly formed state as soon the latter fulfills basic attributes of a state and expresses and exhibits its willingness to honor international commitments. Like many other states, India had misgivings over Israel's survival. However, Israel not only survived as a sovereign entity but showed its ability and willingness to shoulder responsibility as a member of the international community. India could not ignore this.[56]

Third, Israel had become a reality and was recognized by a large number of states. Long before the Indian move, two other states that had endorsed the federal plan, Iran and Yugoslavia, recognized the Jewish state. While Yugoslavia recognized Israel on May 19, 1948, within days of its establishment, Iranian recognition was obtained on March 15, 1950.[57] Moreover, during the crucial UN vote on partition, Yugoslavia abstained. Turkey, another major Islamic country, had recognized Israel well before India.[58] Even Indonesia was not indifferent, and its prime minister and foreign minister, Muhammad Hatta, sent a formal communication to Shertok acknowledging Israel's recognition of his country.[59] India could not have remained indifferent to the growing international accommodations toward Israel.

Fourth, in May 1949 Israel joined the United Nations. Explaining the link between recognition and UN membership, Nehru told the Indian parliament: "our policy [is] to recognize any country that was an independent functioning country represented in the United Nations."[60] Similarly, his close confidant V. K. Krishna Menon argued, "I have always taken the view that whatever country is recognized by the UN should be recognized by us."[61] Though Israel's admission was conditional,[62] it came against the background of similar membership requests being rejected by the UN Security Council. The cold-war rivalry blocked the memberships of countries such as Albania and Jordan, whereas Israel was recognized by the rival blocs. Even though he voted against Israel's entry into the United Nations, Nehru could not ignore the prevailing international view on Israel.

Fifth, Indian recognition was also influenced by its policy regarding the People's Republic of China. In its view, the political orientation of the regime in Beijing should not be an impediment to recognition.[63] As one of the first countries to recognize the new, communist China and ignore the breakaway Taiwanese republic, Nehru came under pressure, especially from lawmakers. Even though the Chinese and Israeli situations were different,[64] questions were asked about him adopting "various criteria" regarding recognition.[65] There were suggestions that a different stance regarding recognizing Israel "would have placed India in a paradoxical situation."[66] At least at the popular level, India would not be able to campaign for international recognition of communist China while denying the same privilege to the Jewish state.

Sixth, India appeared to be genuinely interested in playing a mediatory role in the Arab-Israeli conflict. Explaining the decision to recognize Israel, the official spokesperson for the Ministry of External Affairs observed: "continuing non-recognition is not only inconsistent with the overall relations but even limits the effectiveness of the Government of India's role as a possible intermediary between Israel and the Arab states."[67] Nehru felt the need to establish some balance in India's Middle East policy, especially vis-à-vis Israel.

Seventh, recognition enjoyed significant support inside the country and was often raised in the Constituent Assembly debates. The issue first came up in August 1948, when the socialist member of the Assembly H. V. Kamath questioned India's policy toward Israel.[68] Since then, it figured in every session of the Constituent Assembly and forced Nehru to articulate his stand.[69] Such debates provide an insight into the slow but gradual Indian advance toward recognition. Though relatively small in number, a few prominent Indians living abroad were also active in this direction.[70] Likewise, senior Indian diplomats such as K. M. Panikkar were favorably inclined toward recognition long before the official move.

Eighth, Israel carried out effective lobbying for recognition. Such efforts were made both directly by Israeli diplomats posted in Washington and New York and by U.S. officials sympathetic toward Israel. Israel established and maintained regular personal contacts with senior Indian diplomats in the United States and the United Nations; they included Asaf Ali, B. N. Rau, Shiv Rao, Vijayalakshmi Pandit, and Krishna Menon. The pro-India U.S. congressman Emanuel Celler played a role in this campaign and was present at the Nehru-Elath meeting in October 1949 in New York. According to Elath, Nehru "arrived [at the] conclusion [that] recognition cannot be postponed much longer. Here he turned [to] Celler saying it would be unwise to grant Israel recognition during his [Nehru's] stay [in the United States] because this [is] liable [to be] interpreted as American pressure."[71] Weizmann was in periodic correspondence with B. N. Rau, and following the establishment of Israel, he approached Rau for the same purpose.[72] Toward the same end, the Sanskrit scholar Immanuel Olsvanger, who had visited India in 1936, revived his old contacts in India.[73] Even before the formation of Israel, the renowned scientist Albert Einstein sought Nehru's support for the Jewish cause.[74] Given this worldwide, star-studded lobbying, India could only delay and not deny recognition.

Finally, the growing political contacts between Pakistan and leading Arab countries contributed to India recognizing Israel.[75] The erstwhile INC support for Arabs or Palestinians did not pay immediate political dividends. According to Gopal: "the vote cast by Farouk's Egypt against India on the Hyderabad issue in the United Nations disposed him [Nehru] towards accepting the fact of Israel and recognizing her."[76] Even while opposing Israel's admission to the United Nations, in May 1949, more than a year before recognition, Nehru remarked: "It is about time that we made some of these Arab countries feel that we are not going to follow them in everything in spite of what they do."[77] However, as we will see, even for Nehru this was easier said than done.

If India accorded a belated recognition to Israel, it was even more cautious toward the Gaza-based APG. On September 22, 1948, a few months after the formation of Israel, the Arab Higher Committee met in the Gaza and proclaimed an "All-Palestine Government" under the leadership of Ahmad Hilmi Pasha. On the same day, a twelve-member cabinet was formed with Pasha as prime minister and assumed control of "all Palestine, within the frontiers such as were established at the moment when the British Mandate ended."[78] At a Congress of Arabs held on October 1, Hajj Amin al-Husseini, the mufti of Jerusalem, was unanimously elected "President."[79] A day earlier, "Prime Minister" Ahmed Hilmi informed India of the formation of an "independent" Palestinian state and conveyed an "earnest desire of the All-Palestine Government to establish relations of cordiality and cooperation with your country."[80] New Delhi viewed both his request and his claims with skepticism and decided "not to take any action on the telegram, and the said telegram [was not to be] acknowledged in view of possible political implications."[81]

Because New Delhi did not recognize the Gaza entity, it is sufficient to look at some of the possible explanations. Even though it opposed the partition plan, India did not support the Arab proposal for a unitary Palestine. The APG in Gaza reiterated the unitary proposal and sought to annul the state of Israel. Thus the APG ran counter to the UN position vis-à-vis Palestine. Its recognition by India might have been construed as going against the prevailing international consensus. Other than a handful of Arab states, no major power inside or outside the Middle East had recognized the APG. Great Britain is an exception, and it tacitly recognized the Jordanian annexation of the West Bank.[82] Second, though backed by Egypt and other members of the Arab League, the APG did not exercise control over vast areas of Mandate Palestine. The Gaza Strip was under the military control of Egypt, and the APG had very little freedom of movement—let alone sovereignty—in that tiny piece of land. The much larger eastern Palestine (or later on, the West Bank) came under the control of King Abdullah of Transjordan (later Jordan), who had no intention of relinquishing control. Granting sovereignty to the mufti-led APG was out of question. Reflecting this reality, India felt that the claim of the APG "for recognition are no stronger than that of the Government of South Korea posing as the national government of all Korea. Realistic approach would suggest our ignoring this claim."[83]

Third, the APG soon became a major political embarrassment for the Arab League, as some of its members sought to expel Transjordan, one of the founding members, over its occupation of the West Bank. The Jericho Conference of December 1948 accentuated internal divisions among the Palestinians and the unpopularity of the mufti-led government. The APG did not survive, and before long key cabinet members left the mufti and joined hands with King Abdullah. Thus a hasty recognition of the APG would have placed New Delhi at loggerheads with Amman. And finally, there was a Pakistani dimension. Despite past Indian support, the Palestinian leadership, especially the mufti, drew closer to Pakistan and became its staunch supporter over the Kashmir dispute.[84] Ever since his February 1951 visit to Karachi to preside over the World Muslim Conference, the mufti had been frequenting Pakistan.[85] If one adds the traditional wait-and-see position adopted by India, nonrecognition of the APG was both logical and inevitable.

If India was so diligent and cautious toward recognizing Israel and not recognizing the APG, how does one explain its quick recognition of the state of Palestine, proclaimed on November 15, 1988? Indian recognition came despite the entity lacking the most fundamental characteristic of statehood: *control over territory*. This lack of sovereignty did not inhibit India or many other Third World countries from recognizing the Palestinian state and treating it as a sovereign entity. This was long before Yasser Arafat returned to the Gaza Strip in 1994 to establish the Palestinian National Authority (PNA). Given the extent of Israeli control, even the PNA could not be seen as a sovereign entity. But Indian recognition of the state of Palestine in 1988 was merely a political gesture that should be placed within the context of its pro-Palestinian policy.

Notwithstanding delays and ambiguities, its recognition of the Jewish state was a major development in India's Middle East policy. This came against the backdrop of traditional Indian sympathy for the Arabs, its unfriendliness toward the Jewish demand for a homeland in Palestine, its opposition to the partition plan, and its vote against Israel's admission to the United Nations. Its decision to recognize Israel, however, was complicated in the long run by the absence of formal ties between the two countries.

For more than four decades, the absence of normalization or recognition without relations remained the hallmark of India's Israel policy.

Nonrelations as a Policy

States rarely establish formal ties with all the countries of the world. The establishment of relations and the opening of residential missions are decided by political, economic, strategic, or cultural considerations vis-à-vis the recognized state. Conversely, the fewer shared interests, the greater the chances of nonrelations. If this was the rationale, the prolonged absence of formal ties with Israel would not be controversial. India's initial willingness to seek normal ties with Israel and its subsequent backtracking make the case rather unique. New Delhi's original intention to establish a residence mission in Israel did not receive adequate attention in the scholarly literature. And because of the absence of formal ties, recognition itself was often treated as a not-so-significant development.[86]

Nehru admitted that normalization was a logical step after recognition. Speaking in the context of relations with Spain in 1956 he told lawmakers, "a logical consequence of [recognition] was to exchange diplomatic mission, subject of course, to our having the personnel."[87] This appears to be the general Indian position on recognition and is true for Israel. A number of official statements support this understanding. An official note prepared on April 4, 1951, revealed a favorable disposition toward normalization: "In order to ensure that we obtain a clear picture of the Middle East, it is necessary for us to open a mission in Israel as soon as possible."[88] During his March 1952 visit to New Delhi, Eytan got a distinct impression that normalization was around the corner. According to him,

> Before Israel's representative [that is, Eytan] left New Delhi, he was informed that the Prime Minister [Nehru] had approved the proposal. . . . A draft budget for the Indian legation was being prepared, though

> the formal decision to establish diplomatic relations still remained to be confirmed by the Cabinet. This was to be done as soon as the new Government was set up following the elections [that is, to the first Lok Sabha] a few weeks later.[89]

Eytan further learned that the Indian government was working on the budget for its mission in Israel. The message was obvious: normalization was a foregone conclusion and Nehru just needed ratification from his cabinet. But it did not happen.

The view that India was committed to establishing a resident mission in Israel was shared by Nehru's biographer Gopal, who observed: "In March 1952 Nehru informed the Israeli government [through the visiting Foreign Ministry Director General Walter Eytan] that there was no major objection to the exchange of diplomatic representatives, but it might be better to wait for the formation of a new government after the elections [to the first Lok Sabha that were then underway]."[90] Similarly, in December 1952, India's ambassador in Moscow, K. P. S. Menon, informed Eytan: "I am very sorry that the exchange of Missions between India and Israel had not yet taken place. I hope and trust that it is now only a matter of few weeks. I shall do all I can from this end, as I am really keen that we should establish a Mission in Israel without further delay."[91] Angry over Nehru's broken promise, in 1959 Prime Minister David Ben-Gurion lamented: "I cannot understand how Mr. Nehru fits his behavior to Israel with [Mahatma] Gandhi's philosophy of universal friendship. Mr. Nehru gave definite promises to the Director-General of our Foreign Ministry eight years ago that he would soon establish normal diplomatic relations with Israel, but so far he has not kept his word."[92] Normalization would not materialize until January 1992.

Budgetary considerations seemed the primary reason for the initial absence of diplomatic exchanges. An official note prepared in December 1950 declared: "Owing to reasons of financial stringency, the case of Israel has presumably to wait for more propitious times."[93] This appeared logical. At that time, the absence of diplomatic relations was the rule and not the exception. As Krishna Menon told Michael Brecher, "We don't send Ambassadors to a lot of countries."[94] In 1947, for example, India's resident missions in the Middle East were confined to Cairo, Tehran, and Istanbul. Cairo had the only resident Indian mission in the entire Arab world![95]

The Indian Foreign Office needed to reduce its diplomatic budget through a number of administrative measures, including postponing new missions or concurrent accreditations. In early 1950, the ministry observed: "In view of the imperative need for all possible economies on expenditure, the proposal for establishing consular representation at Mehshed and Koramshahr [Iran], Basra [Iraq], Bahrain and Muscat [Oman] have been kept in abeyance."[96] Another report suggested that "as a measure of economy, the Heads of Mission in certain countries were concurrently accredited."[97] As a result, even in the mid-1950s, India's ambassador in Cairo was concurrently accredited to Jordan, Lebanon, and Syria.[98] Taking cognizance of this trend, at one time Israel even suggested the concurrent accreditation to Israel of India's ambassador to Turkey.[99]

Some of Nehru's statements vindicate the nonpolitical thinking taking place during this phase. A couple of months after recognition, he ruled out diplomatic exchanges with Israel due to "financial and other reasons" and added that his government was "anxious to avoid additional commitments abroad at present."[100] Two years later, India declared: "Owing *mainly* to the existing financial stringency it has not been found possible to establish missions in these countries [Israel, Saudi Arabia, and Yemen] *so far*."[101] While it opened embassies and consular offices in other parts of the Middle East, Israel remained an exception. As time went by, it became obvious that the budgetary issue was merely one of the reasons for the Indian hesitance and not the prime one. Over time, Nehru's reference to "other factors" in his December 1950 statement gained greater importance than before.

A formal and officially negative attitude concerning normalization was noticeable during the Suez Crisis of 1956. By then, three powerful forces came to influence India's policy toward Israel: (1) anticolonialist Afro-Asian solidarity, formally consecrated at Bandung in April 1955; (2) Israel's increasing identification with the imperial powers, as manifested by its coordinated aggression against Egypt during the Suez crisis; and (3) the growing personal friendship between Nehru and the Egyptian president, Gamal Abdel Nasser. Speaking in the Lok Sabha days after the Israeli invasion of Egypt, Nehru declared that "in view of the existing passion," diplomatic exchanges were not possible.[102] A couple of years later, at a press conference in New Delhi, Nehru maintained: "This attitude [toward Israel] was adopted after a careful consideration of the balance of factors. It is not a matter of high principles, but it is based on how we could best serve and be helpful in the area. . . . After careful thought, we felt that while recognizing Israel as an entity, we need not at this stage exchange diplomatic personnel."[103] Gradually, "the time is not ripe" became the standard Indian mantra on the normalization of relations with Israel.

Over the years, India began discovering new reasons to prolong the absence of formal ties. In December 1960, the prime minister informed the Rajya Sabha (the upper house of India's parliament) that India did not have a diplomatic mission in Israel because "the whole position is very much entangled in important and rather dangerous international issues."[104] In September 1963, India felt that "there is not enough consular work to justify a post."[105] On May 27, 1969, following the June war, Foreign Minister Dinesh Singh offered a new rationale. Speaking at a meeting of Indian envoys in the Middle East, he felt that India "had not established diplomatic relations with Israel because Israel had followed wrong policies against Arabs particularly the Palestinians. It was persisting with this policy and until there was a revision of this policy it would be difficult for India to revise her policy. One could also fully justify India's policy in this regard from the point of view of national interests."[106] Elaborating on this logic, some recalled differences with Israel over key issues. In their assessment, the official communiqué of September 17, 1950, underscored that recognition "did not mean that it had endorsed the Israeli position regarding its boundaries."[107]

At times, India sought to justify its nonrelations through a secular logic and its refusal to accept the notion that religion could become the basis for nationality.[108] This was aimed at countering Pakistan's efforts in the Middle East and at forging closer ties with secular Arab nationalism; while India is secular like most Arab states, Pakistan is closer to Israel in terms of its ideological and religious focus![109] In the light of later developments, India linked normalization to demands for Israeli withdrawal to the pre-June 1967 position, an endorsement of the right of self-determination of the Palestinians, and the support of a "just and honorable settlement" of the Palestinian problem.[110]

In hindsight, many Indian leaders, including Nehru, admitted that diplomatic exchanges should have occurred soon after recognition. Recalling his meeting with the Indian prime minister in 1961, the Israeli diplomat Gideon Rafael observed:

> After this minuet of preliminaries Nehru took over. India had recognized Israel in 1950 he said and indeed should have at that time established diplomatic relations. The sentiments in India towards Israel

> were good. Many people were keenly interested in its achievements. . . . The trouble was that there was a strong Arab reaction to the establishment of diplomatic relations between our two countries.[111]

This view was shared by others. Nehru's close confidant Krishna Menon told Michael Brecher that if India "had sent an ambassador at that time [that is, soon after recognition] there would have been no difficulties."[112] Morarji Desai, who was prime minister from 1977 to 1979, reflected similar sentiments.[113]

Bitter over India's posture, the veteran Israeli diplomat Ya'acov Shimoni observed that in the initial years, "our policy was to ask for an exchange of ambassadors on every possible occasion . . . but we have some pride left. . . . We were tired of being told, 'Please do not worry us' and being put off repeatedly."[114] Reflecting Israel's disappointments, Ben-Gurion remarked: "Nehru too claims allegiance to neutrality. . . . He is not even neutral in regard to Israel and the Arabs, for he has close ties and normal relations with the Arab countries—but he has stubbornly refused to establish diplomatic relations with Israel, and in his frequent visits to the Middle East he has on every occasion—and not by accident—overlooked Israel."[115]

Interestingly, in 1960 the Indian lawmaker and former minister Rajkumari Amrit Kaur visited Israel and met Prime Minister David Ben-Gurion. The latter explored the idea of inviting Nehru to Israel and extended a formal invitation on July 28, 1960.[116] Within a fortnight, Nehru expressed his inability, saying, "it is not easy for me to go abroad frequently," and chose to add the following: "it occurs to me that in the circumstances existing today, it will not be advisable for me to pay such a visit. Instead of improving international relations, it might have the opposite effect."[117] Such an attitude did not prevent Nehru from visiting the Gaza Strip during his visit to Egypt in May 1960.[118]

Consular Relations

While the establishment of diplomatic ties was bogged down in political controversies and supposed economic constraints, New Delhi was more flexible regarding the Israeli request for opening a representative office in India. The latter falls into two distinct categories, namely, an immigration office and a consular office. Even before the establishment of the Jewish state, India functioned as a major sanctuary for Jewish refugees. It offered refuge to the beleaguered Jews of Iraq, Afghanistan, and, to lesser extent, Europe. From India, these refugees eventually emigrated to Mandate Palestine and later Israel.[119] A large number of Jews from Europe took refuge in India during the late 1930s and 1940s, and Nehru actively sought their employment and absorption. Some of the Jewish refugees from Europe married prominent Indian figures, such as B. K. Nehru, Shiva Rao, and M. N. Roy.[120]

Facilitating the emigration of Jewish refugees, especially from Afghanistan and Iraq, became a priority for Israel, and at least since early 1949 the Jewish Agency kept a representative in Bombay.[121] A formal immigration office was established in the city shortly after India's recognition of Israel; Aryeh Gance was appointed as the representative.[122] This port city in western India is geographically closer to Israel than elsewhere in India and had a significant Jewish presence. A few months later, Gance was promoted to director of the Palestine Office of the Jewish Agency. As the urgency of refugee immigration gradually diminished, a separate consulate was established in Bombay, and immigration became part of the consular function. Separate representation by the Jewish Agency became redundant.

Israel's consular presence in India was much more complicated. Consular duties are normally confined to matters relating to trade, shipping, notary functions, issuance of passports and visas, and the registration of the births, marriages, and death of its nationals. In short, it has only commercial and functional duties, with no scope for diplomatic activities or responsibilities. However, even to secure this limited foothold in India, Israel had to invest considerable effort, time, persuasion, and diplomatic capital. The formal approach in this direction began as early as in May 1950, over five months before recognition. In a communication addressed to the Indian high commissioner in London,[123] it informed New Delhi of its decision to appoint F. W. Pollack as "Trade Commissioner of South East Asia."[124] It appears that there was some diplomatic misunderstanding between the two sides, and the matter did not proceed further. India's hesitation to recognize Israel largely contributed to its reluctance to acknowledge, let alone respond, to the Israeli move.

Israel revived the matter following the September 1950 recognition. Interpreting the earlier Indian silence, a senior Israeli official observed that if Israel did not "assume that the High Commissioner failed to inform his government, we would be compelled to presume that the Indian Government does not consider the term 'South East Asia' to include India in a way [that would] require the Indian Government to take cognizance."[125] Thus, in November 1950 Pollack's title was changed to "Trade Commissioner for Israel in South East Asia including India." As per the prevailing practice of coordinating through the Indian mission in London, Israel communicated Pollack's new designation through Krishna Menon.[126] This channel was not proving effective. Irritated over delays and difficulties in using London as the conduit, Israel "abandoned the procedure and started communicating directly with New Delhi."[127] India's recognition the previous September also emboldened this approach. Accordingly, on December 28, 1950, the Israeli Foreign Ministry sent a cable to its Indian counterpart informing the appointment of Pollack as "Trade Commissioner for India and South Asia."[128] After prolonged negotiations, correspondence, and clarifications, an official Indian notification to this effect was issued on March 1, 1951.[129]

Around this time, the economic division in the Israeli Foreign Office wanted to terminate Pollack's appointment as trade commissioner. Meager trade prospects made his continuation an unviable proposition. Ya'acov Shimoni, who was handling the Asia desk, was in favor of continuing the arrangement, because it had been secured after prolonged effort.[130] Israel settled for a compromise. To consolidate its foothold in India, especially as the latter was not moving on the issue of resident missions, Israel decided to concurrently appoint Pollack as its consular agent.

Because of the previous delays and inaction, a cable regarding Pollack's nomination was sent directly to Prime Minister Nehru, who was also India's foreign minister. This change of strategy had the desired effect, and on March 8, New Delhi responded favorably: "The President of India is pleased to recognize provisionally the appointment of Mr. F. W. Pollack as Consular Agent of Israel at Bombay." A formal gazette notification to this effect was issued on the same day.[131] Pollack, however, was unhappy with this new arrangement, and said that it was "not my intention to make official use the title Consular Agent which is much lower than that of Trade Commissioner for South East Asia."[132] Concurring with this assessment, Shimoni consoled him, saying that Israel viewed this "simply as a functional and technical arrangement, at least until we [that is, Israel] establish our legation in India."[133] While trying to persuade Pollack to formally submit the letter of his nomination, Shimoni cautioned that he was "accredited to the Government of India and not to the Government of Bombay [later on Maharashtra] and the sphere of your jurisdiction, I assume, in contrast to that of most of the foreign consuls at Bombay—[you are accredited to] the whole of India, and not Bombay only."[134] As subsequent events proved, Shimoni clearly misread the Indian situation. Pollack's successors were officially confined to the state of Maharashtra and could travel to other parts of India only as "private" foreign nationals.[135] Meanwhile, a formal notification regarding Pollack was issued on September 28, 1951. Issued in the name of President Rajendra Prasad, it bore the signature of Prime Minister Nehru.[136]

The whole arrangement took a different turn when the government of India enquired about the legal status of Pollack. Was he "an honorary or *decarriere* officer"?[137] Since Pollack was not a regular career diplomat, in January 1953 he was designated as the honorary consul of India. Simultaneously, effective January 1, 1953, the status of the Consular Agency of Israel was raised to the level of consulate, and Pollack was named honorary consul.[138] Within months, a regular arrangement was made, and on June 1, 1953, Gabriel Doron became Israel's first career diplomat to assume office in India. Between then and 1992, when full relations were established, sixteen Israeli officials headed the mission in Bombay.

This consular arrangement faced a number of problems. No evidence is currently available in the public domain in India regarding the territorial jurisdiction of the consulate. India often emphasized the Israeli presence in Bombay. But the Israelis contended that their emissary was accredited to the Government of India and hence its jurisdiction extended to the whole of the country. Israeli documents share this narrow interpretation. Following his interaction with the officials in New Delhi, in February 1960, Israeli Consul Michael Michael observed that Indian officials had advised him "to be satisfied with being on Indian soil, to keep a low profile and to refrain from attempting to win over public opinion. . . . [Mirza Rashid A.] Baig, Head of the Protocol in the Ministry of External Affairs, advised Michael to visit New Delhi *as seldom as possible*, and not to maintain contacts with heads of missions, apart from consulates."[139] In another report sent in October of that year, he maintained that due to Arab pressure, "the Indians interpret the 'status quo' in relations as limiting the Israeli consulate to activity in the narrow consular field. In contrast, Michael has asserted that the consulate is Israel's representative mission in the full meaning of the word, and its duty is to behave like any embassy in India."[140]

These internal tensions between the two sides exploded openly just before Nehru's death and firmly established some new ground rules. In April 1964, Consul Peretz Gordon decided to organize Independence

TABLE 6.1
Heads of the Israeli Consulate in Bombay (now Mumbai), 1950–1992

F. W. Pollack[a]	1951–1953
Gabriel Doron	1953–1956
Avshalom Caspi	1956–1959
Michael Michael	1959–1962
Arieh Ilan	1962–1963
Peretz Gordon	1964–1965
Reuven Dafni	1965–1969
Ya'acov Morris	1969–1971
Yair Aran	1971–1973
Yehoshua Trigor	1973–1976
Shlomo Armon	1976–1979
Yosef Hassin[b]	1979–1982
Immanuel Seri[c]	1982–1984
Oded Ben-Hur[d]	1985–1987
Amos Radian	1987–1989
Giora Becher	1989–1992

[a]Initially, he was appointed trade commissioner of Israel for Southeast Asia, and following Nehru's reservations over India not being part of Southeast Asia, on June 7, 1951, his designation was changed to consular agent for India. On October 20, 1952, he was made honorary consul and continued in this position until June 1, 1953, when a regular diplomat from the Foreign Ministry replaced him.

[b]Following a controversial media interview in June 1982, he was declared persona non grata.

[c]This position was downgraded to vice consul and continued until the mid-1980s.

[d]Ben-Hur and Radian were technical staff who were temporarily in charge of the mission because of the Indian refusal to authorize a regular staff.

Source: Avimor, ed., *Relations Between Israel and Asian and African States*, 6:382.

Day celebrations in New Delhi. Until then, such celebrations had been held in Bombay, where the Israeli Consulate was located. The Indian government was not prepared to accept this deviation and demanded the cancellation of the function, which was scheduled for April 15, 1964. When the consul did not respond to this request, the Indian government had the reservations at the state-run Ashok Hotel cancelled. The issue rocked the Indian parliament. Many friends of Israel were furious over the government's treatment and accused Nehru of being "discourteous."

Justifying the move, Foreign Minister Dinesh Singh told the parliament that such a function would not have been permitted anywhere in the capital.[141] During the debate, the lawmaker H. V. Kamath pointedly raised a vital legal question: Is it a fact that the Consul General of Israel is accredited to the entire territory of the Republic of India?"[142] This critical issue had never been clarified by the Indian government. As subsequent developments indicated, India behaved as if the consul was accredited not to the entire territory of India but only to the state of Maharashtra, whose provincial capital was Bombay. As mentioned above, while Israeli consuls were allowed to travel beyond Maharashtra, they could only do so as foreign nationals, not as consuls. According to various Israelis who had served in Bombay, until the early 1970s there were no visible restrictions on their movements, except to sensitive border areas. They had easy access to India's minister of external affairs and often met the Indian prime ministers.[143] Their official movements, however, were restricted to Maharashtra. In 1982, India even expelled the Israeli consul for a controversial media interview. It was only in 1989 that the consular jurisdiction was formally extended to the southern Indian state of Kerala, which has historic links to and a significant presence of Jewish people.

Diplomatic Contacts

Meanwhile, by late 1951 Israel was troubled by the absence of formal ties with India. Even a year after recognition, New Delhi was not taking any steps in that direction. Concerned by this, some within the Israeli foreign office proposed opening a legation in New Delhi without insisting on "reciprocity." Foreign Minister Moshe Sharett did not favor such an idea.[144] As it happened with China, he insisted on the propriety of mutuality. Though Israel was small and new, he was not prepared to forgo diplomatic protocols in favor of pragmatism. Gopal admitted that "the Israeli insistence on reciprocity created a deadlock."[145] Alternatively, it was felt that the Indian envoy in Turkey could be concurrently appointed as "Minister to Tel Aviv."[146] Either way, Israel was extremely keen to have some form of residential representation as soon as possible.

In the light of the similarities it found with India, formalization of relations was of paramount importance to Israel. Therefore, in an attempt to clarify the Indian stand and facilitate normalization, it sought to establish contacts at "the highest possible levels" and decided to depute the

Foreign Ministry's director general to India. There were some misgivings as to how Prime Minister Nehru would receive and respond to such a proposal. Israel broached the idea with the Indian ambassador in New York, B. N. Rau, who in turn conveyed it to New Delhi. Rau quickly secured the necessary clearance, with late February 1952 as the suitable meeting time.[147] Things began to move swiftly. Israel made a formal request for Walter Eytan's visit with Prime Minister Ben-Gurion, who was then the acting foreign minister, writing to his Indian counterpart. Nehru quickly extended an official invitation.[148] Eytan reached New Delhi on February 28 and spent a full week in India before leaving for home on March 7. For logistical reasons, he made a long stopover in Karachi both into and out of New Delhi. A closer look at his thirteen-page "New Delhi Diary" clearly indicates that the exchange of diplomatic missions was a foregone conclusion.[149]

During his stay, Eytan met a host of diplomats, public figures, and others, including President Rajendra Prasad, Nehru's daughter and future prime minister Indira Gandhi, Foreign Ministry Secretary-General G. S. Bajpai, Foreign Secretary K. P. S. Menon Sr., Commonwealth Secretary R. K. Nehru, Nehru's sister and India's ambassador in Washington Vijayalakshmi Pandit, Minister of Rehabilitation A. P. Jain, and the secretary of the Food and Agriculture Ministry and the secretary of the Indian Council of World Affairs, A. Appadorai. In short, the Israeli visitor met all those who mattered in the Indian capital. The culmination of his visit was a lunch with the prime minister on March 4, 1952, where Nehru explicitly referred to the domestic Muslim factor as a major concern but added that as soon as the newly elected government assumed office, the issue of normalization would be put before the cabinet and a positive decision would be available in about two months' time.

Walter Eytan was satisfied that the Indian bureaucracy was favorably disposed toward full diplomatic ties with Israel. R. K. Nehru, the Commonwealth secretary and a distant cousin of the prime minister, was the sole exception. During the visit, there were discussions about the level of diplomatic representation, and Prime Minister Nehru felt that the opening of legations should be reciprocal. Furthermore, an official in the ministry was asked to prepare the budget and other financial details for a resident Indian mission in Tel Aviv.[150] In March 1953, an Israeli diplomat updated Eytan on the normalization front: "(1) The decision to establish relations with Israel is still valid; (2) India's Muslim minority has nothing to do with the delay in the establishment of relations; (3) The main factor is rather the Kashmir dispute. India needs the support of Arab states at the UN and fears it will jeopardize its chances for such support by establishing a diplomatic representation in Israel."[151]

These developments clearly indicate that Nehru favored normalization and made a commitment as such to Eytan. Under his explicit instructions, the ministry worked out the budgetary provisions of an Indian mission in Israel. Dispelling early Israeli misgivings, Nehru insisted on reciprocity and dismissed suggestions of a nonresident Indian envoy to Israel. However, subsequent events belied not only Israeli expectations but also Nehru's firm commitments to Eytan.

Because of the absence of formal diplomatic ties with New Delhi, Israel began cultivating diplomatic contacts with India in a number of countries. Such contacts were usually maintained in Washington, New York, London, and in non-Western capitals such as Ankara and Rangoon. What were the motives? First and foremost, such contacts are part of normal diplomatic courtesies. Posted away from home, it was natural for Indian and Israeli diplomats to be friendly and cordial toward one another. In the earlier days, India was considerably admired by the Israeli elite and a number of Indian diplomats were favorably disposed toward Israel. Moreover, some of the Indians who were in close contact with the Zionists in the pre-1947 years had become ambassadors, and thus their contacts were strengthened. They included Panikkar, Rau, and Shiva Rao.[152] As the discussions between Rau and Eban in Washington and C. S. Jha and Eliahu Sasson in Ankara portrayed, both sides shared a genuine feeling of warmth. Indian missions abroad, at times, served as a conduit for Israel to convey various messages, proposals, and offers to the government of India.[153]

In some cases, diplomatic contacts with India in third countries proved helpful to Israel when the diplomat in question was posted back to New Delhi (as in the case of C. S. Jha)[154] or posted elsewhere (as with Panikkar). They were used for direct access to Indian leaders, including the prime minister. In a hitherto unknown meeting, an Israeli diplomat had a personal meeting with Nehru's senior cabinet colleague Maulana Abul Kalam Azad, when the latter was visiting Turkey. In June 1951, Indian Minister C. S. Jha took the initiative and organized a lengthy meeting between Azad and the Israeli diplomat Eliyahu Sasson. During this meeting, Azad did not object to the normalization of relations with Israel.[155] Likewise, personal contacts enabled Israel to explore and push for diplomatic ties. The observations of K. P. S. Menon, a secretary in the foreign ministry, a few months after Eytan's visit testifies to this. Lamenting on the situation, Menon informed Eytan that he was "very sorry that the exchange of Missions between India and Israel has not yet taken place. . . . I shall do all I can from this end, as I am really keen that we should establish a Mission in Israel without further delay."[156]

Indian diplomats proved to be a source of information for Israel regarding the Middle East. Such contacts filled Israel's information gaps regarding Arab countries and inter-Arab rivalry. One such lengthy rendezvous took place at the British countryside residence of the veteran historian Captain Basil Liddell Hart on September 6, 1953. He hosted Israel's ambassador in London, Elath, and India's ambassador in Cairo, Panikkar.[157] Similarly, Jha briefed his Israeli counterpart in Ankara about the activities and discussions surrounding the visit of Arab League Secretary General Azzam Pasha to Turkey in June 1951.[158] Such meetings also enhanced India's understanding of the Middle East and Israel's experiences with its Western allies. In the absence of official Indian documents, it is impossible to quantify and substantiate the benefits accrued to India through its diplomatic contacts with Israel in third countries.

Such extensive contacts, especially during the Nehru years, indicate the level of warmth between the two countries. These contacts were regular and periodic; they include interactions between Abba Eban and B. N. Rau in New York, Eliahu Elath and Vijayalakshmi Pandit in Washington and later in London, and Eliahu Sasson Sr. and C. S. Jha in Ankara. Moreover, personal contacts between Elath and Panikkar and Eytan and K. P. S. Menon Sr. continued even when they were no longer posted in the same capitals. Indian delegates to the United Nations such as Shiva Rao, Kitty Shiva Rao, Amiya Chakraborthy, and Sucheta Kripalani maintained contacts with Israeli personalities. There was also a surprisingly long meeting between Foreign Minister Dinesh Singh and his Israeli counterpart Abba Eban in October 1969. The meeting, which took place in New York, came shortly after the Rabat fiasco, when India unsuccessfully tried to attend the Islamic summit.[159]

Besides these connections, there were a number of bilateral visits even when both countries lacked formal ties. Most of these visits in the pre-1992 period are shrouded in secrecy, and a comprehensive list is impossible to compile. In March 1953, when Nehru was contemplating normalization, four senior state-government officials were sent "to study the Israeli cooperative system of agriculture and marketing."[160] In 1960, the Indian lawmaker and Nehru's former cabinet colleague Amrit Kaur visited Israel; as a sequel to this visit, Ben-Gurion extended a formal but rebuffed invitation to Nehru.[161] During this period, one of important visitors from India was Homi Bhabha, the chairman of the Atomic Energy Commission.[162] A few planned visits did not materialize: for example, upon his transfer from New Delhi to Moscow, Menon was unable to stop in Israel in 1954 to meet his old friend Eytan.[163]

Similarly, a number of Israeli leaders and officials visited India. Until the mid-1970s, when Indian visas became difficult for Israeli passport holders, a number of Israeli scientists came to India to participate in various international meetings. They were often used as a meeting point for scientists from both countries.[164] Israeli scientists came to India as part of various UN-sponsored programs. The Israeli labor federation Histadrut sponsored a number of visits to India, often at the invitation of the Indian National Trade Union Congress (INTUC), a trade union affiliated with the Congress Party.[165] In subsequent years, things deteriorated, and India refused to grant visas to Israeli nationals, including athletes, thereby preventing Israeli participation in a number of international meetings and events organized and hosted by India.

At the political level, a number of official and semiofficial visits took place during the nonrelations years. Among the notable visitors to India were Eytan (1952); Foreign Minister Moshe Sharett (1956); Labor Minister Yigal Alon (1964); Minister of Development Mordechai Bentov (1959); Ruth Dayan, the wife of Defense Minister Moshe Dayan (1968); and Foreign Minister Moshe Dayan (1977). The visit of Sharett took place in the midst of the Suez crisis, and despite his strong opposition to Ben-Gurion's adventure, the Israeli leader was forced to defend his government's actions when he met Prime Minister Nehru on October 30.[166] In late 1961, Foreign Ministry Director General Gideon Rafael, a successor of Eytan, met Nehru in New Delhi, during which the Indian prime minister reluctantly admitted that relations should have been established immediately after recognition.[167] Contacts also existed between India and international Jewry, notably the meeting between Nehru and Chairman of the World Zionist Organization Nahum Goldman in June 1957 in New Delhi. Coming shortly after the Suez crisis and severe Indian criticism of Israel, Goldman was trying to fathom, if not modify, India's position on normalization.[168]

In the end, such diverse contacts and diplomatic maneuvers were interesting but not fruitful. For over four decades, Israel was unable to make progress on the normalization front. At one time, Israel even contemplated shifting its consulate from Bombay to New Delhi. Such a move appeared logical in the wake of the Indian shift regarding diplomatic representation. In August 1953, it decided that effective September 15, "officers stationed elsewhere than at the headquarters of the Government of India will not be deemed to be members of the Diplomatic Mission, and will no longer be included in the Diplomatic List."[169] Transferring the consulate to New Delhi in accordance with the new regulations had drawbacks. In the early 1950s, Israel was still hoping for a reciprocal move from India on normalization. Speaking about diplomatic ties, Nehru highlighted the reciprocal nature of relations and clearly declared:

> Yes. If we send an Ambassador to Washington or Nanking, they may also send an Ambassador to New Delhi. The Australian Minister for Foreign Affairs has informally indicated to the Government of India that the Australian Government will be happy to raise the status of the Australian High Commissioner here to that of Minister. Naturally it means that our representative in Australia will also become a Minister.[170]

It was obvious that India favored reciprocal relations, and thus Israel would not be able to shift its consulate to New Delhi without the latter opening a resident mission in Israel, something Nehru had been resisting since the mid-1950s.

This dilemma perhaps explains why Israel explored the possibility of the Indian ambassador in Turkey being concurrently accredited to Israel. Such a move might have enabled Israel to have a consulate in New Delhi endowed with full diplomatic status. Others had a different view. They felt that a consulate in New Delhi, being of a lower representation, would attract undue attention, given that the Arab states had full-fledged embassies in the Indian capital.[171] However, by the time Israel was contemplating a consulate in New Delhi without any reciprocal arrangement, India's position on normalization had hardened, and any change in the status quo became remote.[172]

Following his visit to New Delhi to attend an annual conference of the World Health Organization in 1961, the Israeli diplomat Gideon Rafael remarked: "Besides regular meetings with leading representatives of India at the United Nations, sporadic friendly talks with Mrs. Pandit, Nehru's sister, and agitated and exasperating meetings with Krishna Menon, the Prime Minister's confidant, no official dialogue of consequence between the two countries had taken place in the intervening years [that is, since the early 1950s]."[173] This was true for most of the four decades since India's recognition of Israel.

If one looks at the Israeli experience, its diplomatic initiatives proved successful only in five major areas, and India does not figure in any of them. First, those countries with a sizeable Christian population and a better understanding of the Judeo-Christian heritage were quick to recognize Israel and normalize relations. Countries from Europe and Latin America fall into this category. Second, countries with a sizable Jewish population and thus Jewish influence recognized Israel rather early. The United States and the countries of Eastern Europe, including the Soviet Union, could be cited as examples. Third, countries with a hostile or unfriendly attitude toward the Arabs looked to Israel as a possible ally; non-Arab countries in the Middle East such as Iran and Turkey are the notable examples. Fourth, those seeking closer ties with the United States looked to Israel and its supporters in the United States as potential allies. The attitude of Turkey toward Israel amply exhibits this calculation.[174] And finally, Israel's technical-assistance program proved helpful for a number of newly independent countries in Africa who were either apprehensive of Western assistance or did not receive adequate attention in the West.

India came under a different category. Its politico-economic situation was relatively better than a number of newly independent countries of that time. Thus the need for Israeli assistance was limited. To complicate matters further, a sizeable domestic Muslim population brought India closer to the Arab perception of the Middle East and its problems. Thus, for a long time, nonrelations dominated India's Israel policy.

I am sorry, gentlemen, but I have to answer to hundreds of thousands who are anxious for the success of Zionism: I do not have hundreds of thousands of Arabs among my constituents. —*President Harry S. Truman*

7 Domestic Politics

Like the child in Hans Christian Anderson's fairy tale, one is tempted to shout, *But the Emperor has nothing on at all!* The domestic dimension is the most difficult aspect of India's Israel policy to research and analyze; it is hard to quantify and support with evidence. Political correctness, partisan politics, and a paucity of official papers compound the problem. The nonparochial and inclusive nationalist struggle undertaken by the Congress Party meant that its policies before and after independence have to be seen and presented within a secular paradigm. However, most scholars argue that India's Middle East policy is shaped by a host of factors, ideas, and currents, but not by domestic political calculations. The farthest that they will go is to discuss Pakistan's efforts toward creating an Islamic bloc to undermine and counter secular Arab nationalism. Any suggestion of other domestic factors influencing India's Middle East policy remains taboo. A. Appadorai, who was active at the Asian Relations Conference of 1947, remains the sole exception: he has discussed the Islamic aspects of the domestic roots of India's foreign policy.[1]

In the absence of documents, how does one establish that domestic political calculations substantially helped determine India's Israel policy?

Is it possible to establish the link between domestic and foreign policy with a reasonable degree of conviction? Do domestic calculations play a significant role? If so, should they be considered as appeasement or as a conspiracy to denigrate the secular ethos of the state? Has secularism been used to camouflage meaningful debate on the internal currents that shape foreign policy? Is there openness within the country over domestic dynamics? Can foreign policy remain immune and indifferent to various sectoral demands and aspirations?

As the following narrative highlights, domestic calculations played a significant role in shaping India's Israel policy. To argue otherwise is both untenable and questions India's credentials as a democracy. Instead of seeing the domestic factor as either appeasement or a right-wing conspiracy, it is essential to view it as part of the democratic discourse within the country. Put differently, if India is a democracy, can it remain indifferent to the views and aspirations of an important segment of its population, namely, the Indian Muslims?

The most serious challenge to a meaningful debate stems from the Indian obsession to secularize its foreign policy's logic and compulsions.

Political Correctness, "Secular" Paradigm

The most effective means by which Indian leaders and scholars sought to establish the secular credentials of its Middle East policy has been to highlight the Jewish character of Israel.[2] While Jewish nationalism was religious, the Arabs fought under the banner of secularism, they argued. As early as in 1933, Nehru categorically argued that the British "pit Jewish religious nationalism against Arab nationalism."[3] At times, Indian leaders used the "religious" character of Israel as a rationale for the absence of diplomatic ties. How can a secular country have normal relations with a country that was founded on a religious basis? Speaking in Cairo in 1966, within months of assuming office, Prime Minister Indira Gandhi declared that Indian support to Arab countries "is not only due to our traditional friendship towards the Arab people but to our belief in and commitment to socialism and to the principle that *states should not be carved out or created on the basis of religion.*"[4] In a similar vein, India explained its close ties with the Arab world in secular terms. An *Annual Report* of the Ministry of External Affairs declared that India "shares with the Arab world . . . common principles of . . . secularism."[5] In 1969, New Delhi used secularism to justify its nonrelations and argued that it could not accept the notion that religion could become the basis for nationality.[6]

Even before its formal recognition of the PLO, India described al-Fatah, the most prominent and powerful Palestinian group headed by Yasser Arafat, as a secular organization.[7] Najma Heptulla, the grand-niece of Maulana Azad, clearly articulates this argument when she observes that Azad, "one of the most prominent and vocal nationalist leaders in India, was vehemently opposed to the idea of creating a state of Israel in Palestine. It is important to note here that the Maulana's stand on Israel was in *no way influenced by the Muslim sentiments in India.* He was firm in his belief that one cannot divide the people on the basis of religion."[8] Likewise, others have argued that at least in the initial years of independence, "the Islamic factor did not figure prominently in India's dealing with Muslim countries."[9]

The notion that India's Middle East policy could be influenced by nonsecular considerations still remains anathema to many. Unfamiliarity with the Mahatma's endorsement of *Jazirat al-Arab* or his recognition of the prophet Mohammed's injunction over Islamic holy places serves them well. As one leading media commentator argues, "The *Collected Works of Mahatma Gandhi* as well as Jawaharlal Nehru's writings belie [the] claim that India traditionally supported the Palestinian cause on anything other than its merits."[10] Suggestions that domestic Islamic considerations ("vote-bank politics," in Indian parlance) were taken into account when Nehru was establishing the foundations of the country's Middle East policy is rejected as incorrect, misleading, and a political conspiracy. It is not uncommon to find arguments stating that "religious considerations have not played any role, either in the formulation of India's [Middle East] policy on the whole, or in prioritizing foreign policy goals vis-à-vis individual countries in the context of bilateral relations."[11] Though it is fashionable "to criticize Nehru and others of following a pro-Arab policy on account of 'vote-bank politics,' *religious considerations never played any role in the formulation of the* [Middle East] *policy.*"[12]

In their eagerness to dismiss Islamic influences, some are forced to give a clean bill of health to the Hindu nationalists. The Bharatiya Janata Party (BJP) is known for its traditional sympathies for Israel. Bilateral relations took an upward swing when it was in power during 1998 through 2004. The need to present Indian policy within a secular paradigm was so overwhelming that even the foreign policy of the BJP had to be explained within the secular construct. In the words of one scholar:

> [Atal Behari] Vajpayee as the Foreign Minister, under the Janata government [1977–1979] with its Jan Sanghi mix, could not alter the so-called "pro-Muslim" orientation of India's [Middle East] policy during the Cold War. Similarly, after the end of the Cold War, it was the Congress government, led by Narasimha Rao, which decided to establish full diplomatic relations with Israel. Furthermore, the NDA (National Democratic Alliance) coalition government, led by a rightist party [the BJP] has been intensifying its efforts to build bridges with many Islamic nations like Iran, Saudi Arabia and Turkey more than its predecessors led by the Congress and National Front.

He concludes that it is as "erroneous to accuse Nehru and others of being pro-Muslim as it is to apprehend that the BJP-led NDA would neglect Muslim countries" in the Middle East.[13] In other words, when it comes to the Middle East, even the BJP is secular!

If the BJP was able to pursue a secular policy toward the outside world, why did it fail to internalize this secular ethos? The party and its forerunner, the Jan Sangh, are known more for their anti-Muslim slant than for any of their other policy platforms. Although not every member of the BJP can be accused of being anti-Muslim, the party has been unable or unwilling to rid itself of its antiminority tag. The belated admission of Muslims within its rank and file has not transformed the party into a centrist force, and the Muslim leaders of the BJP are often decried as "poster boys" rather than party stalwarts. A more plausible explanation would be that when it comes to the Middle East, even a Hindu nationalist party like the BJP could not ignore the domestic dimension.

To claim that India's Israel policy is exclusively "secular" and that the domestic Muslim factor has no influence would be taking liberty with logic, common sense, and democratic values. Such an argument would be possible if India were to satisfy three basic conditions: (1) that it does not have a sizeable Muslim population; (2) that Muslims outside the region are not interested in Middle Eastern developments; and (3) that India is a nondemocratic state oblivious to views of different segments of its population. None of these conditions accurately describes India. The available data indicates that Islam has had a greater influence in India's Middle East policy than commonly recognized.

Muslims and the Middle East

Any discussion of the domestic factor has to recognize two objective realities: India's Muslim population and the general Muslim interest and involvement in Middle Eastern developments, especially regarding the Jewish-Arab and Israeli-Arab conflicts. Islam has been an important ingredient of India's sociocultural milieu. Arab invasion in the eighth century brought Islam to India, and it soon spread to different parts of the country. While the religion traces its origin to the Arabian deserts, most of its followers live in the Indian subcontinent. During British rule, India had the largest Muslim population in the world. This influenced not only British policy toward Palestine but also compelled both the *yishuv* and the emerging Palestinian leadership under the mufti of Jerusalem to look to India for political support.

The partition of the subcontinent in 1947 somewhat changed these demographics. While he succeeded in creating Pakistan, Mohammed Ali Jinnah could not solve the problem of the Muslims of the subcontinent. A large number of Muslims consciously chose to stay behind and become part of a multicultural, multireligious, and multiracial India, which emerged as the third largest Islamic center after Indonesia and undivided Pakistan. According to the 2001 census, India's Muslim population is estimated at 138 million, or 12.4 percent of its total population.[14] This makes the Indian Muslim population the third largest in the world, after Indonesia and Pakistan. To imagine that India could ignore or remain insensitive toward such a large segment of its population would be worse than irresponsible.

The second objective reality is the interests of Muslims in Middle Eastern developments. For a Muslim, the Middle East is not just another piece of land on Earth. As *Jazirat al-Arab,* it has religious importance and enjoys the sanctity of the prophet Mohammed. For Indian Muslims, the Islamic holy land also includes Jerusalem and historic Palestine. The religious and historic importance of the region evoke interest and passion among Muslims worldwide. Even an atheist would not dispute the Islamic significance of the region. From opposition to a Jewish national home in Palestine to recognizing Israel or accepting Jewish claims to Jerusalem, religion remains a dominant force in determining the position of Muslims the world over. Even when states adopt realistic or *Realpolitik* stances, the masses refuse to compromise. The normalization of Egyptian-Israeli relations, for example, has not made Egyptians friendlier toward Israel. The same holds true for Jordan. Though couched in liberal expressions such as justice, morality, and international law, the religious dimension is undeniable. As manifested by the Khilafat struggle, Indian Muslims passionately agitated over developments in the far-off Ottoman Empire. Seeds of their opposition to the British Empire were sown when their "temporal ruler" was threatened by imperial designs. Thus even those who venerate the secular nature of Nehru's policy had recognized the "overwhelming" support of the Indian Muslims to Palestinians.[15]

By "domestic," therefore, we refer to Muslims being a dominant factor in India's attitude toward Jews and Israel. The Islamic influence has to be located within India's sociopolitical context and its democratic polity. At one level, the involvement of domestic factors in the formulation of India's overall foreign policy since independence has been limited and marginal. If one excludes the New Delhi–based elite, vast majority of Indians have been indifferent toward developments in distant lands. Their daily struggle for survival, illiteracy, linguistic and religious barriers, and acute social problems involving caste have resulted in foreign policy becoming the hobby of a select and privileged segment. But over time, some changes have taken place. However, the liberalization and gradual globalization of Indian economy during the 1990s affected the lives of middle-class Indians. As a result, the debate on foreign policy has gradually expanded to the urban middle class and rural poor, whose lives are influenced by the kind of economic agreements and concessions that India makes to foreign countries and companies. Otherwise, the foreign-policy debate has little domestic impact or base of support.

There are two notable exceptions. India's policy toward its immediate neighbors has strong domestic inputs, especially from border provinces. Periodic tensions within Sri Lanka, for example, affect the southern state of Tamil Nadu, which has close ethnic links with the Tamils of that island republic. As exemplified by India's military intervention in the late 1980s, New Delhi's policies toward the ethnic conflict have largely been influenced, and at times dictated, by the popular sentiments and political compulsions in Tamil Nadu. This holds true for its policy on Pakistan and Bangladesh, where one notes strong domestic inputs from the states of Punjab and West Bengal, respectively. In times of crisis in Bangladesh, Pakistan, or Sri Lanka, the real and immediate impact are felt in the Indian provinces with a strong ethnonational linkage with those countries. In this way, India's policy toward its neighboring countries is shaped more by domestic political dynamics than by strict foreign-policy calculations.

The Middle East is the second example for this link between domestic dynamics and foreign policy. While a comprehensive treatment of the domestic inputs into India's Middle East policy has yet to be written, it is possible to sketch the larger contours. As the following narrative will indicate, India's interest and involvement in the Middle East, and more particularly Israel, since the early 1920s was influenced, and at times dominated, by the Islamic factor. Secularism thus does not mean the absence of Islamic inputs in India's Israel policy. With the notable exception of Mahatma Gandhi, Indian leaders and academics ignored or belittled the religious dimension and in the process settled for an unscientific and nondemocratic paradigm. Under such circumstances, how can we establish this link? Nehru's personal choices regarding the region offer some interesting insights.

Nehru's Choices

Unlike the Mahatma, it is not easy to establish that Islamic calculations influenced Nehru's views on Palestine. He was a socialist by conviction and had little interest in, knowledge of, or patience for religion. Much of his secularism was a sign of atheism rather than the traditional separation of church and the state. A scientific temperament, not religious sentiment, dominated his worldview. He understood the world through the emerging lenses of anticolonialism and anti-imperialism. At least in public, he did not view the problem in Palestine through a religious prism, as the Mahatma did.

Despite his secular bias, Nehru did not ignore the Islamic dimension of the problem. The "sentiments" of Indian Muslims figured prominently in his post-1947 policy toward the Middle East. In his conversations with Israeli diplomats, he sought their understanding of the trauma of partition and its effect upon the Muslims of India. He felt that the Muslims who had opted to stay in India after partition were already being pressured to prove their loyalty to India by distancing themselves from Pakistan, a state conceived as the homeland of the Muslims of the subcontinent. Spearheaded by the Jan Sangh, the Hindu right wing was accusing Indian Muslims of being a "fifth column" that was seeking to further fragment "Mother India." He confided to Israeli diplomats that Indian Muslims should not be burdened with further emotional strain over his Middle East policy.[16]

During the freedom struggle, Nehru's perceptions of the Jewish national home were couched in secular and ideological language. Anticolonialism dominated his views. But his understanding of the Middle East was largely influenced by two individuals, the historian Arnold Toynbee and the Indian Muslim leader Maulana Abul Kalam Azad. Both these individuals offered a partisan understanding of the Middle East, especially when it came to the Jews. As will be discussed, Azad was accused of sabotaging efforts to normalize relations with Israel. Much of Nehru's understanding of the Middle East stemmed from Toynbee's historic narrative. Known for his unsympathetic appreciation of Jewish history, Toynbee depicted Jewish and other minority groups that survived as "fossils."[17] When an official publication, *India and Palestine*, sought to dismiss Jewish claims to Palestine, it treated Toynbee's arguments as if they were the Ten Commandments.[18]

A more categorical appreciation of the Islamic factor could be located in Nehru's choice of candidates for critical assignments pertaining to Palestine. In 1947, he appointed his ambassador in Washington, Asaf Ali, as India's representative to the First Special Session of the UN General Assembly, which deliberated the Palestine question. This, perhaps, was a pure coincidence motivated by logistical considerations. But this selection angered Muslim League circles. Responding to some of his remarks at the Special Session, the Karachi-based *The Dawn* declared that Asaf Ali did not represent Muslims of India and was acting contrary to their views.[19]

When India was elected to the eleven-member UNSCOP, Nehru's choice fell on Abdur Rahman. A note prepared by the Foreign Ministry observed that India would have to find *"a suitable Indian Muslim with wide legal knowledge."*[20] India explicitly wanted a Muslim personality to be its representative at the UN committee. Indeed, even before the special session began, India was keen to be part of the forthcoming committee. Such a role, it felt, was essential, because the Palestine question would be a major issue on the international agenda. As discussed earlier, reflecting the prevailing INC thinking, the Indian representative vehemently opposed the idea of religion forming the basis of statehood. But shortly after the submission of the UNSCOP report, Rahman settled in Pakistan, a state created with religion as its basis.

In the post-1947 years, Azad functioned as Nehru's adviser on Arab affairs. As Michael Brecher argued, with Nehru's biographer S. Gopal concurring, it was Azad who sabotaged the normalization of relations in

1952. Nehru, who promised to secure formal cabinet approval shortly after the first Lok Sabha (the lower house of India's parliament) elections, could not do so largely because of Azad, who felt that normalization would harm India's position on Kashmir with the Arabs and would also antagonize domestic Muslim opinion.[21]

Nehru was quick to recognize the importance of the Palestine issue and felt that the future of Palestine was the most critical question that would affect the postwar Middle East. By articulating a strong stand on such an important development, he sought to establish India's imprint on the world stage. He hoped to achieve this by sending highly capable diplomats who could ably articulate the Indian position. At the same time, the choice of Asaf Ali, Abdur Rahman, and Maulana Azad for critical positions pertaining to the Middle East could not have been accidental. They were selected not just because they could articulate India's position. They were chosen primarily because, being Muslims, they could understand the problem better. As explicitly highlighted by the selection of Abdur Rahman, religious faith became the primary criteria for their selection. By giving responsible positions to Muslim personalities, Nehru was seeking to brandish the secular credentials of the Congress Party and repudiate the Muslim League's claims that only the latter could be considered the authentic spokesperson of the Muslims of British India.[22]

By choosing only Muslim personalities for matters relating to Israel, Nehru institutionalized the Islamic influence on his Middle East policy. This approach meant the nonavailability of alternative perceptions regarding Jewish history and their claims to Palestine. As a result, the divine rights of Jews to the land of their ancestors were questioned without any Indian ever challenging the *Jazirat al-Arab* being eternally under Islamic control and sovereignty. The nonappreciation of the Jewish claims to Palestine was partly facilitated and institutionalized by Nehru's reliance on Muslim personalities to express and explain India's stance regarding Palestine.

Far greater evidence is available on Azad's role.

The Azad Factor

Among individual statesmen, Maulana Abul Kalam Azad is the most important for a discussion on the absence of the normalization of ties with Israel. Azad had strong connections with the Arab world. He was born in Mecca; his mother was the niece of Sheikh Muhammed Zahir

Vatri of Saudi Arabia.[23] During the critical years between 1940 and 1946, he functioned as president of the Congress Party. Following India's independence, he became a key member of the Indian cabinet and, despite strong objections from the Mahatma, Prime Minister Nehru made Azad his education minister. While never formally in charge of foreign affairs,[24] he greatly influenced Nehru's policy toward the Middle East. Despite the obvious familial bias, Heptulla is accurate when she observed that in the formulation of India's Middle East policy, "Nehru was no doubt influenced by . . . Azad. Azad's contribution helped India to formulate a . . . policy which has withstood the test of time and besides standing firm behind the Palestinian cause helped develop friendly and cooperative relationship with the countries" of the region.[25] For example, in March 1948, when the question of opening an Indian legation in Saudi Arabia was being considered, Nehru advised the foreign office to consult Azad.[26] In fact, during Nehru's periodic foreign visits, "matters relating to External Affairs were referred to Maulana Azad."[27]

Many regard Azad as Nehru's adviser on Arab and Islamic affairs.[28] Although Azad's expertise and knowledge of the region is indisputable, describing him as Nehru's Arab adviser is problematic. The Arab factor was relevant for Israel but its overall impact upon India's foreign policy was rather marginal. When Azad passed away in 1958, there were only a handful of sovereign Arab states, and with the exception of post-1952 Egypt, most of them lacked any regional, let alone international, influence. Vast areas of the Arab world were still under direct or indirect control of the Western powers. The petroleum resources of the region were marginal and controlled, exploited, and exported by the Western "Seven Sisters." Thus calling Azad an adviser on a region of such marginal importance seems farfetched. It would be more appropriate to describe him as Nehru's adviser on Muslim rather than Arab affairs.[29] But recognizing him as an adviser on Muslim, rather than Arab, affairs would not be considered "secular," thus the title "Arab adviser."

There are two interesting interpretations of Azad's role regarding Israel. According to one Israeli document, he was not hostile toward the establishment of relations. Nehru's biographer Michael Brecher, on the other hand, holds Azad singularly responsible for the absence of diplomatic relations.

Eliahu Sasson, the Israeli emissary in Ankara, had a lengthy meeting with Azad when the Indian leader visited Turkey in 1951. Sasson observed in his report:

> Speaking of the Orient, Abu-al Kalam Azad told me that it is his wish to see the settlement of Israel's conflict with her neighbors and the establishment of a continuous and whole hearted cooperation between all the countries of the Orient. When I remarked that this is also Israel's desire and that we [are] perpetually making efforts to this end, [Abul] Kalam Azad informed me that during the conversations he has had, in the course of the last three years, with the Arab leaders he has never ceased to explain to them that Israel is a factual reality which has to be recognized. [He] met the Arab Chiefs in India, Egypt and other parts of the world and describing his attitude towards the Israeli question, he pointed out to them that, as a Muslim, he would have preferred that Palestine be remaining in the hands of the Arabs and that there should not be a state of Israel. But as an Oriental statesman he cannot help realizing that the interests of his country and of the whole East compel him to be realistic and to see facts as they are. It is in this spirit that he talked to the Arab leaders and that he supported Nehru's suggestion to the Indian government for the recognition of Israel. [He] mentioned that his understanding attitude in this connection enabled Nehru to enforce the Government's decision in a country like India where there are 40 million Muslims, without giving rise to hostile reactions. Abu-El Kalam Azad added that he very much regrets that his friends and co-religionists, the Pakistanis, do not follow India's example and that they still cling to religious fanaticism and support the Arab's intransigence. . . . Before taking leave, I told the Minister of Education that I hope there will soon be an exchange of diplomatic representatives between Israel and India. Abu-El Kalam Azad replied that, to the best of his knowledge, the Indian government has no objections against [*sic*].[30]

In short, while he was not happy with the establishment of Israel, Azad was realistic enough to accept its existence and supported India normalizing relations with the Jewish state.

However, Brecher's personal interviews with various Indian personalities led him to a different conclusion. He wrote in 1959: "India's staunch support for the Arab states in their conflict with Israel and its refusal to establish normal diplomatic relations with the Jewish state . . . were largely due to Azad's advice."[31] Subsequently, he elaborated this point in *The New States of Asia*. The visit of Walter Eytan to New Delhi in early 1952 did not result in normalization, as promised by Nehru. Commenting on this, Brecher remarked:

> The "sudden change of mind" in the spring of 1952 was due to the forceful intervention of Maulana Azad, intimate friend of Nehru. . . . Until his death in 1958, the Maulana exerted great influence on India's Middle East policy. . . . *As a Muslim, Azad was naturally pro-Arab.* He was also fearful of the consequences of diplomatic relations with Israel on India's position in the Arab world. An unstated but bitter rivalry with Pakistan for Arab support on the Kashmir dispute was then at its height. . . . Azad [and Nehru] was also concerned about the possible impact of a welcoming gesture to Israel on India's large and insecure Muslim minority. Pakistan would probably have fanned the flames of communal hatred in India by reference to Israel. This might have affected the loyalty of India's Muslims and would, in any event, have been a shock to their already bewildered state of mind following the Partition riots and mass migration, with the aftermath of distrust among Hindus. Was an exchange of diplomatic missions with Israel worth all these risks? Azad firmly argued against the proposal. Nehru may have been convinced—for the case was strong in terms of India's "national interests." At any rate, he yielded to Azad's advice.[32]

Moreover, according to Eytan, Nehru had suggested that the question of normalization would be referred to the cabinet. Commenting on Nehru's role in foreign affairs, Brecher concluded:

> In no other state does one man dominate foreign policy as does Nehru in India. Indeed, so overwhelming is his influence that India's policy has come to mean in the minds of people everywhere the personal policy of Pandit Nehru . . . he has impressed his personality and his views with such overpowering effect that foreign policy may properly be termed a private monopoly. . . . No one in the Congress or the government, not even Sardar Patel, ever challenged his control in this sphere.[33]

Azad therefore becomes the only minister who could have questioned Nehru's proposal for normalization. Since cabinet decisions in India must be unanimous, it is likely that the issue was not put to vote. Thus, more than any other single individual, it was Azad who compelled Nehru to abandon his promises to Israel on normalization.

Under normal circumstances, Brecher's assessment could be treated as his personal views and could even be dismissed as being personally or politically motivated. His biography of Nehru, which contained a brief reference to Azad's role, was published in 1959. This was shortly after Azad's death in 1958, but Nehru was still in office. Hence it is difficult to imagine that the Indian prime minister was not aware of Brecher blaming Azad for nonrelations. *The New States of Asia*, which contained a much detailed assessment of the issue, was first published in 1964, shortly after Nehru's death in May of that year. More than a decade later, Nehru's other biographer, S. Gopal, gave credence to Brecher's assessment. Gopal admitted that Nehru had informed Israel that there were no major objections to normalization and that Israel would have to wait for the formation of a new Indian government after the elections. But then Gopal adds: "Even then nothing was done. This inaction has been attributed to the influence of Azad."[34] The source was not any cabinet or other official papers which were available to him; Gopal consulted *The New States of Asia*.

Not surprisingly, others have not commented upon Azad's role in delaying the normalization of diplomatic relations. At one level, it was difficult to challenge Brecher's assessment, especially after Gopal endorsed his claims. On the other hand, to concur with the assessment that Azad sabotaged normalization would undermine the "secular" arguments explaining India's Israel policy. The objections supposed to have been raised by Azad were not new and were valid when the Indian prime minister promised normalization to Eytan. They were probably given additional importance by Azad, which led to the deferment. Given the results, even those who argue about Azad's role and influence upon Nehru's Middle East policy carefully avoid discussing Brecher's assessment. This deafening silence ironically becomes the loudest confirmation available in India regarding Azad's role. There are also other indications.

Grudging Admissions

In July 1948, within weeks of the formation of Israel, an Indian intelligence report noted that some influential Muslim leaders in the state of Bihar had launched a campaign to collect money and volunteers for the aid of Arabs in Palestine. These "volunteers and the collected money are to be dispatched to Jeddah, a centre of war activities of Arabs, by the end of this month."[35] Around the same time, the nizam of the princely state of Hyderabad in southern India "has been collecting subscription for lending 14,000,000 [pounds] sterling to Arabs to buy arms to help them in attaining their objectives in Palestine."[36]

The following month, speaking in the Constituent Assembly, Banarsi Prasad Jhunjhunwala referred to a cable that was sent by the *Jama'at-ul-ulemai-Hind* to U.S. President Truman and Vice Chairman of the Soviet Council of Ministers Vyacheslav Mikhailovich Molotov. In this cable, the *Jama'at* conveyed the resentment of Indian Muslims toward their recognition of the Jewish state.[37] A fortnight later, Begum Aizaz Rasul, the only female Muslim member of the Constituent Assembly of India, raised the following question: "Will the Hon'ble Prime Minister keep in mind the fact that there are a large number of people living in the Indian Dominion whose wishes and sentiments in this regard should be kept in view regarding the recognition of the State of Israel and they are definitely opposed to it?"[38] While Nehru did not directly answer this query, the message was loud and clear. A "large number of people," namely, the Muslim population, was not in favor of India's recognition of Israel. S. Gopal highlights the domestic factor when he observes that the "weight carried by Muslim opinion in India," *inter alia*, "strengthened [Nehru's] inclination to support the Arabs."[39] Elsewhere he maintains that Nehru "did not immediately follow [recognition] with the establishment of a legation in Tel Aviv, *perhaps* mainly because of Muslim sentiment within India."[40]

However, many Indian leaders, including Nehru, were forthcoming in their interaction with Israeli officials. Analysis of Israeli documents show that on numerous occasions they referred to the feelings of India's Muslims toward Israel and had candidly linked this to delays in recognition and normalization. While visiting the United States in November 1949, Nehru met Israel's ambassador in Washington, Eliahu Elath. At this meeting, also attended by U.S. Congressman Celler, the prime minister was candid and forthright. According to the summary of the meeting prepared by Elath, Nehru referred to the impact of the "painful" partition upon Indian Muslims. For Nehru, Pakistan turning "theocratic" had seriously hampered the "assimilation" of Indian Muslims. Given the trauma of partition, his government would have to tread with caution on the issue of the recognition of Israel. He reminded the Israeli diplomat that over the years the question of Palestine had a deep impact upon the Indian Muslims and had been "a constant source of agitation." Therefore, Nehru cautioned his interlocutor that India "must treat the thirty million Muslims most carefully."[41] One normally does not find such frankness in domestic Indian discussions on Israel.

A similar account is presented by Eytan following his meeting with Nehru on March 4, 1952. According to the Israeli diplomat, Nehru frankly admitted that difficulties pertaining to personnel and financial constraints or problems of Arab reaction were irrelevant. What then was the problem for normalization? According to Eytan,

> [Jawaharlal Nehru] said . . . that what had held the thing up in the past was his consideration for India's Muslims. We [that is, Israel] must realize he said, that the Indian Muslims had suffered a great shock by partition; they were now a minority whose leaders had all abandoned them for big jobs in Pakistan; and though individual Muslims occupied leading positions in India, the Moslem community as a whole was depressed and fearful of the future—though less so now than two or three years ago. The Indian government had always shown understanding for their delicate position and had not wanted to heap shock on to shock if it were not absolutely necessary. This was what had delayed diplomatic relations with Israel in the past, but it was clear that the positions would now have to be reconsidered.[42]

Financial considerations and the absence of personnel, according to Nehru, were secondary to his concern and sensitivities toward India's Muslim population and their possible response to normalization.

As the issue of Indian recognition was being raised regularly in the Constituent Assembly, in February 1950, the Ministry of External Affairs prepared a long note explaining the reasons for the delay regarding recognition. Given the near blackout imposed by the National Archives of India, this note speaks volumes:

> The consensus of opinion expressed by our Missions in Arab countries, as a result of their conversations with knowledgeable persons in these countries and as a result of their own study of the question, is that the recognition of Israel by India would displease the Arabs and be treated as an unfriendly act and would certainly aggravate our relations with Pakistan. It has been brought to our notice that Saudi Arabia would be particularly concerned at our recognition of Israel. Our missions have, therefore, emphatically advised us against our

> recognition of Israel till the outstanding question of (i) settlement of Arab refugees; (ii) boundary between Israel and the Arab world; and (iii) Holy places of Jerusalem are satisfactorily settled. The view has also been expressed that any premature recognition of Israel might affect the position of Indians in Bahrain, Kuwait and other places in the Persian Gulf and the Middle East. The displeasure of Saudi Arabia may also have serious repercussions on *Hajj* pilgrimage by Indian Muslims and thus give rise to domestic difficulties.[43]

A "hasty" move toward recognition could upset Saudi Arabia, which might retaliate by creating hurdles for the annual pilgrimage. This in turn would generate a serious domestic crisis. It is highly debatable whether India, with its large Muslim population, could have been the target of such a reprisal, although it is true that Saudi Arabia has not been averse to using its unique religious status to further its political agenda. Until the late 1970s, for example, Riyadh refused to recognize Israeli travel documents. This in turn prevented Israeli Muslims from performing the *hajj,* one of the five pillars of Islam.[44] If and when the official Indian documents are available, one might find similar candidness and open admission. Meanwhile, we have other circumstantial evidence.

India's gatecrashing at the Rabat Islamic conference in September 1969 exposed the secular façade behind its Middle East policy. Reflecting on the fiasco, M. S. Agwani lamented that Nehru's

> directive of 1955 outlined New Delhi's approach to various Muslim conferences of pan-Islamic character. . . . Nehru stressed that need to oppose any Islamic grouping, but added that non-official delegations might participate in Islamic conferences. Dilution of the latter part of the directive in the post-Nehru era resulted in official delegations being sponsored for the various Islamic conferences. That this was both unnecessary and unwise was subsequently revealed by the distasteful Rabat episode.[45]

With the sole exception of apologists within the country, no one ever described the Rabat conference's agenda or composition as secular. The monarchs of Saudi Arabia and Morocco, the principal protagonists, had no such pretensions.

In his memoirs published in 1974, Morarji Desai (who became prime minister in 1977) recollected an incident that occurred in 1967 when he was the deputy prime minister under Indira Gandhi. Drawing a parallel between the Jews in the United States and Indian Muslims, Desai told his American interlocutor: "There must not be more than five million Jews in the USA. If this is considered a very large population and you have to be influenced by this, there are fifty-five million Muslims in India. Would that not be considered as a very strong argument for India?"[46] As prime minister, Desai hosted the incognito visit of Moshe Dayan, the Israeli foreign minister, in 1977. His decision to keep the visit under wraps was interpreted by the Israeli leader as an attempt to prevent any negative reactions from the domestic Muslim population: "If the news of my visit to him [Desai] now were to be published, he said, he [Desai] would be out of office."[47]

The desire of Prime Minister Indira Gandhi to disclose Dayan's secret visit during the state assembly elections in 1980 was primarily motivated by electoral considerations. Foreign policy had rarely been an election issue in India, but raising this during elections to the state assemblies was a move driven by political calculations. By highlighting the Janata leaders' playing host to the Israeli foreign minister, she accused the opposition of abandoning the traditional Indian position and moving closer to Israel. This implied that Muslims should not place their faith in parties that were warming to Israel. The pressure was so intense that the leader of the Janata Party, Jagjivan Ram, had to meet Arab ambassadors in New Delhi and reiterate his party's commitments to Arabs and Palestinians.[48] Some senior functionaries even sought to distance the party from Dayan's visit.[49]

Commenting on the Indian position during the Kuwait crisis, one academic observed:

> What is especially unfortunate is that Indian freedom of action has been curtailed by tailoring Indian goals in the region of west Asia to what are believed to be predominant views of Indian Muslims. . . . Instead of developing internal consensus through open debate, India's West Asia policy has become a phenomenon of domestic appeasement of Indian Muslims, without understanding the prudent and legitimate interests of all Indians, including Indian Muslims.[50]

Not only the government but even the INC, which was then the main opposition party, led by Rajiv Gandhi, "took a pro-Iraq stand in order to win the Muslims' vote."[51]

Domestic calculations again came to the fore when Prime Minister Rao sought to change India's four-decade-long nonrelations with Israel. In a candid but unprecedented move, Foreign Secretary J. N. Dixit, who had announced normalization to the media, subsequently disclosed:

> The Prime Minister discussed this crucial issue with senior cabinet colleagues [on or around January 23, 1992]. The only person who maintained a sulking silence after murmuring some initial doubts was [Human Resources Minister and Deputy Prime Minister] Arjun Singh. Arjun Singh felt that this decision might affect Muslim support for the Congress and went on to imply that establishing relations with Israel would be a departure from the Nehruvian framework of our foreign policy.[52]

As a result, when Singh became the most senior cabinet minister to visit Israel in 1994, a section of Indian academia mildly disapproved. Singh's "secular credentials" became suspicious. How could a person who had adopted a strong position against the demolition of the mosque at Ayodhya visit Israel?[53]

A relatively candid official admission had to wait until the summer of 2000, when Foreign Minister Jaswant Singh visited Israel. During a talk organized by the Israel Council on Foreign Relations on July 2, he admitted: "India's Israel policy became a captive to domestic policy that came to be unwittingly an unstated veto to [*sic*] India's larger West Asian policy."[54] This remark was quickly picked up by the Indian media, and Singh was castigated for not only discussing domestic issues on foreign soil but also for casting aspersions on India's "principled" policy toward the Palestinians set out by Mahatma Gandhi and Nehru.[55] In the words of one leading commentator, Jaswant Singh's assertion "was as demeaning as it was factually untrue. He owed no apology or explanation to Israel for a policy pursued by predecessors, Jawaharlal Nehru included, a policy which incidentally earned rich dividends at the United Nations—to Pakistan's chagrin—and was indeed rooted in Gandhi's and Nehru's perceptions on the merits of the Palestine question."[56]

Any lingering doubts that scholars might have had over the importance of domestic compulsions were settled during the run up to the controversy surrounding Iran's nuclear program, when the International Atomic Energy Agency (IAEA) was preoccupied with the matter. There were doubts in Washington regarding the Indian position. Would its energy ties compel New Delhi to side with Iran, or would its newly found friendship with the United States tilt the balance in that direction? Added to these doubts was a new factor: the Shia population. Addressing a press conference in New York on September 16, 2005, Prime Minister Manmohan Singh observed: "We have world's second largest Shia population in our country. So we have to weigh all these factors."[57] While in the past, Indian leaders were reluctant to admit the Muslim factor, the controversy surrounding Iranian nuclear ambitions compelled even the INC leaders to admit the Shia factor. Not to be left behind, even the opposition harped on this. Protesting the government's decision to side with the United States over Iran, the opposition held a massive public rally in November 2005 in Lucknow, a major Shia center in India.

At times, to appreciate the domestic dimension, one has to demystify academic vagueness. Examining Nehru's policy, Heptulla claims that initially he wanted to adopt a "neutral" stance on the Arab-Israeli conflict. He preferred a position that was favorable to Arabs but not hostile to Jews, because "Nehru did not want the issue to affect the Muslim populace of India [and] that the *separatist elements* in India be given a boost by this rise of pan-Islamism."[58] In plain English, this meant that Nehru feared losing out the minorities if he adopted a pro-Israel stand.

Even after the normalization of relations, India was reluctant to forge closer ties with Israel. In early 1993, the media partly attributed the refusal to sign a civil-aviation agreement to Civil Aviation Minister Ghulam Nabi Azad's "fear of alienating a large section of the Muslims in the country."[59] Remarks by Defense Minister Sharad Pawar about cooperating with Israel on counterterrorism evoked criticism from some Muslim lawmakers.[60] Frequent official denials of any military cooperation with Israel was due to domestic pressure. Despite the secular-left fig leaf, many of the protests in New Delhi and other parts of India against the September 2003 visit of Prime Minister Ariel Sharon were organized by various Muslim organizations.[61] Even those who had been reconciled to normalization often take exception to military cooperation with Israel. Reflecting this argument, one scholar observed that "India is capable of tackling the Pakistani threat by itself and on the basis of its own capability and experience. But to give the impression that India will tackle this threat with [Israeli] expertise or experience, sends the wrong signal to many people both at home and abroad."[62] People "at home" is a euphemism for Indian Muslims; "abroad" refers to Arab and Islamic countries.

During the cold war, Pakistan and its diplomatic activities offered Indian leaders and academics a useful foreign-policy logic to camouflage the domestic angle. Though extremely important, it enabled them to avoid highlighting the internal dimension. The absence of relations and increasing unfriendliness toward Israel was squarely blamed on Pakistan and its "mischief" in the Arab and Islamic world. One can even call Pakistan India's whipping boy on Israel. The Israeli consul, Yosef Hassin, was not wrong when he accused India of competing with Pakistan for favors from Arab countries.[63] But such an excessive preoccupation enabled India's leaders and scholars alike to ignore the more pressing domestic dimension of nonrelations. Hence, when he met the senior Israeli diplomat Gideon Rafael in late 1961, Prime Minister Nehru could blame Pakistan and the Arabs for nonrelations without having to address the domestic angle.[64]

Even those who harped on the domestic dimensions of U.S. policy on Israel conveniently sidestepped the similar dilemma faced by India. "Vote-bank politics" are relevant *only* in the understanding of U.S. Middle East policy but cannot be used in the Indian context. The grim picture painted by John Mearsheimer and Stephan Walt about the power of the "Israel Lobby" has often resonated in India and is widely commented upon. In the words of one columnist: "In the Islamic world there was little doubt that the rich and politically powerful Jewish lobby in the US was, to a great extent, dictating the superpower's agenda when it came to resolving the Israeli-Palestinian conflict."[65] During the 2000 U.S. presidential elections, it was observed that Vice President Al Gore "and his wife need the support of the American Jewish lobby and Mr. Clinton is giving signs that he will soon have to bend to the imperatives of domestic politics."[66] Such arguments are never internalized and used to examine India's Middle East policy.

Indian Muslims do not have an organization similar to the America Israel Public Action Committee (AIPAC). Nor is lobbying a legal and organized endeavor in India, as it is on Capitol Hill. This does not diminish the effectiveness of Muslims as a pressure group, especially regarding Middle Eastern matters. Commenting on the role played by Jews in shaping U.S. policies, one U.S. congressman observed: "Israel succeeds in the Congress for the simple reason. Two or three percent of the voters care intensely about it and the rest are uninformed and don't care."[67] This is equally true for the Muslims of India, but it is not politically correct to draw a favorable parallel between the Jews of America and the Muslims of India.

However, a discussion of the domestic angle is incomplete without mention of the pro-Israeli sentiments that are prevalent in India.

Pro-Israeli Sentiments

During the prolonged absence of relations, the Indian parliament functioned as the principal forum for articulating nongovernmental viewpoints. The Constituent Assembly, for example, discussed the Jewish state in December 1947, more than five months *before* the formation of the state of Israel.[68] Since then Israel figured prominently in the Constituent Assembly Debates and subsequently in both houses of India's parliament.[69] In the wake of Nehru's decision to recognize Israel, attention shifted to normalization, and the opposition regularly raised objections over India's Israel policy.[70] The socialist parties, especially the Praja Socialist Party (PSP) and Samyukta Socialist Party (SSP) had fraternal ties with the Israeli labor movement and looked "upon the Jewish state as a beacon of democratic socialism" in the Middle East.[71] *Mapai*/Labor rule in Israel until 1977 favored the pro-Israeli orientation of Indian socialists. Their participation in various international gatherings such as Socialist International and the Asian Socialist conferences proved useful for forging bilateral ties.[72] The socialists had long campaigned to reverse the official policy toward Israel. The socialist weekly *Janata* discussed Middle Eastern developments and gave the widest possible coverage to pro-Israeli views in the country.[73] Support for Israel also came from the Swatantra Party, known for its pro-Western orientation and opposition to the Soviet controlled-economy model and antidemocratic social order.

However, the most prominent and vocal support came from groups that viewed Israel through the Islamic prism. Taking a more lenient view of the situation, Heptulla attributed right-wing support to Israel to the trauma of partition for Hindu refugees from Pakistan.[74] Partition along religious lines had an adverse impact upon the scores of Hindus and Sikhs who were uprooted from the land that became Pakistan. Their immediate grievance against Muslims, whom they held responsible for partition, was transformed into a fondness for "enemies" of Muslims. Their unfriendliness and suspicions toward the Muslim population within India was externalized. They viewed Israel primarily as a state opposed to Islam and Muslims, and were thus favorably disposed toward it. Their criticism of the domestic policy of the Congress Party as an appeasement toward Muslims was extended to the foreign-policy realm. For pro-Hindu and pro-Sikh parties like the Jan Sangh and Akali Dal, the Congress Party's Israel policy was a hallmark of its Muslim appeasement.

Two examples will illustrate the pro-Hindu mindset of the Jan Sangh. The manifesto of the party for the first Lok Sabha elections in 1952 declared that secularism "as currently interpreted in this country, however, is only a euphemism for the policy of Muslim appeasement. The so-called secular composite nationalism is neither nationalism nor secularism but only a compromise with communalism of those who demand a price even for their lip-service loyalty to this country."[75] Reflecting similar sentiments, on December 23, 1953, a Bharatiya Jan Sangh member of Lok Sabha demanded that Muslims should not be "allowed in the army, navy, air force and police and they should not be allowed to occupy any key posts including the officers of Ministers [and] one hundred miles on the borders of Pakistan should be cleared of people who are likely to have leanings towards Pakistan."[76] In other words, Jan Sangh perceived both the domestic and foreign policy of the Congress Party as one of appeasing the Muslim minority; in its assessment, the INC was pro-Muslim domestically and pro-Arab externally.

The Jan Sangh was a prominent critic of India's Israel policy from the outset. While it was critical of the "artificial division" of Germany, India, Korea, and Vietnam, it was favorably disposed toward the partition of Palestine.[77] It demanded immediate Indian recognition and normalization of relations with Israel.[78] As early as 1949, the right-wing Hindu Mahasabha deplored "the discriminatory policy of the Nehru government in refusing recognition" to Israel.[79] The partition of Punjab witnessed the emergence of large scale anti-Muslim sentiments among the Sikhs; the Akali Dal leader Master Tara Singh even offered to fight for Israel. Though their overall influence on Indian foreign policy has been marginal, one cannot ignore the anti-Muslim roots of their pro-Israeli sentiments. Even K. M. Panikkar viewed possible Indo-Israeli rapprochement through a postpartition Hindu paradigm. Writing on the eve of independence, he hoped that "Hindu India" would be more favorable toward the Zionists after partition.

While the influence of the Muslim population upon Middle East policy did not receive adequate treatment, the anti-Muslim sentiments of the Hindu right figure prominently in mainstream Indian discourses.[80]

There is a general agreement that the right-wing parties, especially the Jan Sangh and its successor, the BJP, have been pro-Israeli because they are anti-Muslim. In the words of one scholar, "The Jan Sangh, ever suspicious of the Muslim Arab states, saw in the latter's adversary, Israel, a potential ally of India."[81] This anti-Muslim and pro-Israeli convergence was tested in 1998 when the BJP-led National Democratic Alliance (NDA) came to power. Bilateral relations with Israel flourished significantly from 1998 to 2004, when Atal Behari Vajpayee served as prime minister. For the critics, especially from the left, closer ties with Israel were merely an extension of the anti-Muslim policies of the BJP. They argued that the BJP and Israel shared a common hatred for Muslims. In the words of Communist Party of India-Marxist (CPI-M) General Secretary Prakash Karat:

> The chauvinist positions and military attacks by Sharon and his rightwing government find a positive response amongst the BJP and its RSS mentors in India. The war against the Palestinians is seen through the prism of the *Hindutva* war against Muslim minorities in India. Some of the barbarism which is taking place in Gujarat finds a parallel in the Israeli atrocities in the West Bank. That is why the Vajpayee government has remained silent throughout except for a muted expression of concern for Yasser Arafat during the siege. There is no indignation or revulsion at the savagery of the Israeli onslaught. The nexus with the Israeli regime established by the BJP rulers needs to be exposed and thwarted.[82]

The communist parties could not discover any other logic for Indo-Israel ties, even though normalization was achieved by an INC government and despite the fact that even the communist-ruled state of West Bengal was engaged in building strong economic ties with Israel.

Presenting Indo-Israeli ties though an anti-Muslim prism, however, was not confined to the communist parties. Writing on the controversial demolition of the Babri Masjid by Hindu militants in December 1992, one academic observed, "in some circles, there is a growing suspicion of a nexus developing between Israel, BJP and its allies ranged against Muslims of India with the U.S. appearing as an innocent spectator, which could have implications for the unity and integrity of India."[83] Making a similar argument, the French Indologist Christophe Jaffrelot argued that the emerging "alliance" between India and the United States is "based on the fact that Islam is the common enemy now. It has reassured them in their own orientation and it gave them more means from abroad certainly."[84] There are those who felt that, with the sole exception of the left, the "bulk of the Indian elite today is utterly unconcerned about the fate of the Palestinians; it may well be only a matter of time before the Indian government's position on the Palestine issue becomes effectively indistinguishable from the general Israel- and U.S.-leaning postures of most Western European governments."[85] In short, they felt that the anti-Muslim sentiments of the BJP were manifest in both its domestic agenda and its foreign policy, resulting in its closer ties with Israel!

This anti-Muslim rationale for Indo-Israeli relations eventually boomeranged when the INC-led UPA government, which came to power in May 2004, refused to alter the existing close ties with Israel. Having presented Indo-Israeli ties as an outcome of the anti-Muslim conspiracy of the BJP, the communists have become a prisoner of their own paradigm. The CPI-M leader Sitaram Yechury reflected this dilemma when he lamented that while he could "understand" the previous government seeking closer ties with Israel because the BJP shares "the common hatred for Muslims and the Arab world . . . it is a great pity that the Congress and the UPA government are not conscious of the need to differentiate from this pro-Israeli stance."[86]

When it comes to the domestic factor, two possible conclusions can be drawn. The Muslim factor played a role in Nehru's hesitation in recognizing Israel and the subsequent absence of relations. To a large extent, this was a continuation of the pro-Arab and pro-Palestinian stand adopted by the Congress Party since the early 1920s. Similarly, anti-Muslim sentiments of the Hindu right, especially the Jan Sangh and the BJP, contributed to their pro-Israeli posture. They were not only critical of the prolonged absence of relations but warmly welcomed Narasimha Rao's decision in 1992 to normalize ties.

The differences between these two conclusions, however, are also interesting. Much of the history of Indo-Israeli ties is a study of nonrelations, and these nonrelations were maintained while the Congress Party was in power. Hence, the Muslim factor played a role in the formulation of that policy. Despite its pro-Israeli sentiment, the Hindu right was mainly in opposition and could not be held responsible for either the prolonged absence of relations or the normalization in 1992. By the time the BJP came to power in 1998, bilateral ties were firmly in place, with growing political, economic, and military relations between the two countries.

During its six years in power, the NDA government promoted greater cooperation with Israel without ignoring India's economic and political ties with principal Islamic countries such as Iran and Saudi Arabia. Its perceived anti-Muslim sentiments did not spill over into foreign policy. While the pro-Muslim sentiments of the Congress Party inhibited India from normalizing ties with Israel, the anti-Muslim sentiments of the Hindu right were unable to reverse that policy. If one looks at the post-1992 picture, the anti-Muslim sentiments of the BJP or its supporters alone are not responsible for the growing political, economic, and military ties between the two countries.

Rather than presenting the BJP's foreign policy as secular, as some tend to do, one should look at its rapprochement with Islamic countries such as Iran and Saudi Arabia as a vindication of the pro-Muslim and pro-Arab undercurrents of India's foreign policy. As discussed earlier, even when it opposed the policy pursued by Indira Gandhi, the Jan Sangh was also critical of Israel's actions during the June 1967 war. When it was part of the Janata government in the late 1970s, it was unable to modify India's Israel policy. In short, even a Hindu nationalist party such as the BJP had to recognize and accommodate the domestic factor when pursuing its Middle East policy.

Thus, having opted for democracy, India could not ignore the demands and aspirations of different segments of its population. Muslims are no exception, and the Middle East is not unique. However, rather than discussing it as part of the democratic discourse, aided by official secrecy, many took refuge under the "secular" umbrella, missing the colorful rainbow.

8 International Factors

Belated recognition and Jawaharlal Nehru's commitment to the normalization of relations between India and Israel were important milestones in India's Middle East policy. They were significant departures from the past and signaled a new approach. Eventual progress, however, was minimal, and the absence of relations remained the hallmark of its foreign policy for over four decades. If domestic concerns over Muslim populations played a crucial role, was the international climate more favorable? If the Congress Party could not find a common cause with the *yishuv*, did independent India look for political common ground with Israel? Was there at some point a fundamental transformation in India's view of the Jewish state? Did the formation of Pakistan alleviate pressures for supporting the Palestinians, or did it accentuate the Arab factor? If nonrelation was its policy, how did India deal with the growing international support for the Palestinian issue? Did Israel's endorsement by the rival blocs of the cold war indicate a more favorable climate for the Jewish state?

The basic climate within which the Indian nationalists viewed the Jewish nationalist aspirations remained after 1947 but took a different outward form. Political convergence and a commonality of interests were overlooked in favor of ideological differences. The Congress Party–Muslim League rivalry transformed into an intense competition between India and Pakistan, which was substantially played out in the Middle East arena. In the process, Indian commitments to the Palestinians acquired greater prominence.

The Cold War

While the Eurocentric cold war was not instrumental in India's Israel policy, it provided, especially in the later years, a strong ideological basis for opposition to Israel. The emergence of anticolonial and anti-imperialist sentiments in various parts of the decolonized world eventually turned into a generalized hostility to the West. A number of Western countries, such as Britain, France, and Italy, were also former colonial powers; this made the task of defining the "other" easier. As discussed, its identification with the European powers during the Suez crisis made it easier for Nehru and his allies to lump Israel with imperialism. Their reluctance to recognize Zionism as a national-liberation movement was vindicated when David Ben-Gurion joined with imperial powers against a fellow member of the Afro-Asian world. For many, Israel's exclusion at the Bandung Conference a few months earlier was justified. But was there really nothing in common between the decolonialized, newly independent countries and Israel?

The Indian equation of Israel with the colonial, Western powers prevailed even as Israeli leaders and diplomats stressed the identical policies that India and Israel were pursuing. Two Israeli documents illustrate this point. In June 1949, nearly fifteen months before India's recognition of Israel, Abba Eban, the Israeli ambassador to the United Nations, met his Indian counterpart, Sir B. N. Rau, in New York City. Following the meeting, the Israeli diplomat prepared an aide-mémoire:

> It is suggested that the Government of India might be willing to reconsider its attitude to Israel in the light of the following considerations:
> 1. There is no conflict of interest between the two countries . . .
> 2. Israel, like India, seeks a conciliatory and unprejudiced position in the conflict between East and West . . .
> 3. India and Israel, almost alone amongst the new liberated States of Asia, lay emphasis on the economic and social factor in national liberation . . .

4. Both India and Israel are faced with difficult problems arising from exclusive and expansionist movements in the Moslem world . . .
5. If normal political relations can be envisaged, there are good prospects for free and fruitful inter-change in the scientific and cultural fields.
6. [On questions such as] Italian colonies, the Franco regime in Spain, the treatment of Indians in South Africa, enquiry into the positions of aborigines in Latin America, the Israeli attitude coincided precisely with that of the Indian delegation.
7. Israel has always attempted to understand the special interests and problems which have made it difficult for India to take an objective and detached view in the dispute between Israel and the Arab states.[1]

By listing the commonalities between the two, Israel was suggesting that these provided sound reasons for India to expedite recognition and normalization of relations.

Lack of progress on normalization resulted in Israel sending its director general of the Ministry of Foreign Affairs to India. In February and March 1952, Walter Eytan came to India and met a number of Indian leaders and diplomats, including Prime Minister Nehru, who hosted him over lunch. Eytan handed over an official memorandum to his Indian counterpart, G. S. Baipai. In this communication Israel declared:

1. Israel desires to establish full diplomatic relations with India.
2. Israel is a parliamentary democracy—probably the only true democracy in the Middle East . . .
3. Israel's foreign policy is one of strict independence, identifying itself with that of no other country or *bloc* of countries . . .
4. In pursuit of this independence in foreign affairs, and because she has always felt to be an integral part of Asia, Israel was among the first countries to recognize the People's Republic of China [in January 1950]. She had maintained friendly relations with that republic ever since. No other country in the Middle East has recognized the People Republic of China.
5. Israel is a vital, vigorous, hardworking, progressive society. She has carried out large-scale projects of social and economic reform . . .
6. It is one of Israel's primary aims to raise the productivity of her soil. . . . Israel has no unemployment thanks in part to Government's program of public works . . .

7. During the first half of 1949, Israel was able to conclude armistice agreements with her four immediate neighbors—Egypt, Lebanon, Jordan, and Syria. These agreements are still in force.
8. Israel has made strenuous efforts to bring about a settlement of outstanding issues between the Arab states and herself, but so far without success . . .
9. Twenty-four countries are diplomatically represented in Israel today [March 1952]. These include USA, USSR, Great Britain, almost all the countries of Europe [East and West] Turkey, leading Latin American states and others.[2]

Israel was arguing that both countries had adopted similar stances toward a number of international developments, and its positions on issues such as nonalignment ("nonidentification," in Israeli parlance), Asian solidarity, recognition of communist China, socialism, peaceful co-existence, and democratic rule were close to Nehru's. By mentioning Turkey establishing diplomatic ties, Israel was hinting at its acceptance by a prominent Islamic country and was attempting to allay India's apprehensions over possible, perceived, or potential Islamic opposition to normalization. Above all, as discussed in the introduction to this book, Israel was using the foreign-policy statement that Nehru had made in the Lok Sabha to explain and communicate its own understanding of the world situation and its approach to emerging global problems.[3]

Yet the conventional wisdom has been that the Israeli leadership was no different from the *yishuv* and had nothing in common with India, whereas the Arab countries were favorably disposed toward India. In the words of G. H. Jansen, the Zionists "were only interested in having the support of [Mahatma] Gandhi, with his worldwide reputation; they made no attempt to contact the Indian National Congress, a fact which underlines their basic lack of concern with Asian nationalism as such. The Congress *consequently* identified itself fully with the Arab nationalist movements in West Asia."[4] Contacts between the Arab nationalists and their Indian counterparts figure prominently in Indian discourses on the Middle East.[5] This trend does not obtain in discussions on Zionist-Indian contacts. As discussed earlier, Zionist-Indian contacts were rich, diverse, and at times colorful. Shared values with the Arabs such as anti-imperialism, decolonization, and Afro-Asian solidarity are widely recognized, while Israel's pro-Western policies and linkages to imperial powers (especially during the 1956 crisis) were used to justify Indian indifference and alienation. The areas where the two countries' interests converged were conveniently forgotten.[6]

Nehru endorsed Israel's omission at Bandung and thereby institutionalized its exclusion from the emerging bloc of Afro-Asian countries. When Yugoslavia hosted the first summit of the Non-Aligned Movement (NAM) in September 1961, Israel's absence was considered normal. The Belgrade Summit extended its support "for the full restoration of all rights of the Arab people of Palestine in conformity with the Charter and resolution of the United Nations."[7] Because the NAM operates by consensus, had Israel been present, it would also have urged the Arabs' acceptance of the UN partition resolution.[8] Israel's absence meant there was no need for balance, and before long NAM pronouncements on Israel became stronger and virulent. By the 1970s, anti-Israeli rhetoric became an integral part of NAM meetings and other Third World gatherings. Earlier, the Indian nationalists had not viewed Zionism as a genuine national-liberation movement. Following independence, they did not consider Israel to be part of the emerging Afro-Asian bloc. Willing or otherwise, Nehru was a handmaid in the whole process.

If this was not enough, the Congress Party–Muslim League rivalry took a turn for the worst.

The Pakistan Factor

There is a parallel between the Congress Party–Muslim League rivalry of the preindependence years and the post-1947 Indo-Pakistan rivalry. During the freedom struggle, especially since the mid-1920s, the Congress Party was entangled in an intense rivalry with the Muslim League to secure the support of Indian Muslims. The INC embrace of the Khilafat struggle and the prominence given to the Palestine issue were partly motivated by its desire to enlist the support of the Muslims, who were very concerned over these developments. After independence, Pakistan occupied a central position in India's foreign policy. Its overall policy, especially on issues such as nonalignment, anticolonialism, and anti-imperialism has been relatively independent from the Pakistan factor. But its Middle East policy, particularly on Israel, has been heavily colored and dominated by New Delhi's preoccupation with Islamabad.

Both India and Pakistan pursued their interests in the Middle East by highlighting their consistent support for the Palestinians. While Pakistan used Islam as a means of asserting its pro-Arab credentials, India used secular logic to explain its support.[9] Israel became a hostage to this Indo-Pakistani rivalry. K. M. Panikkar's prediction of free India taking a more sympathetic view of Jewish political aspirations never materialized. On the contrary, driven by need to counter, minimize, and circumvent Pakistan's initiatives, India became more unfriendly toward Israel. Two closely linked issues, namely the Kashmir dispute and concerns over an Islamic bloc, shaped India's preoccupation with Pakistan.

The Kashmir problem became international when Nehru chose to refer the dispute to the United Nations on January 1, 1948. Since then, Kashmir has dominated its foreign-policy calculations. New Delhi feared that the United Nations would impose either an unacceptable settlement or one that would undermine India's vital national interests. Hence, Kashmir figured in Indian discussions with Israel. Indian leaders felt that a settlement to the Kashmir problem would enable India to move closer to Israel. In May 1949, for example, Vijayalakshmi Pandit, Nehru's sister and the leader of India's UN delegation, suggested that recognition of Israel "may happen soon after the settlement of the Kashmir dispute."[10] This was supposed to be one of the reasons suggested by Maulana Azad for his opposition to normalization of relations in 1952.[11] India's accommodation of the Arab veto over Israel at Bandung could be linked to the Kashmir issue. In 1961, when Prime Minister Nehru blamed the Arab factor for the absence of relations, he was merely highlighting India's vulnerability over Kashmir.[12] A number of observers have noted Pakistan's role in influencing India's Middle East policy.[13] When the Kashmir issue first came up for discussion in the United Nations, there were six Arab states.[14] As this number grew over the years, India became apprehensive of losing Arab support to Pakistan. It soon became a simple function of the math: one Israel versus many Arab states.

Kashmir was not the only problem. Recognizing India as a secular and cosmopolitan state undermines the raison d'être for Pakistan being a Muslim homeland in South Asia.[15] Thus India's secular credentials had to be discredited. Pakistan often expressed concerns over the welfare of Indian Muslims and charged that they were being persecuted by the Congress Party. It is not uncommon for many Pakistanis to see a conspiracy between the "Hindu India" and "Jewish Israel" not only against Pakistan but also against the wider Islamic world. They periodically highlighted Gandhi's "Zionist friends," and some went to the extent of describing the Mahatma, some of whose writings caused much pain and anguish in the *yishuv*, as "a stooge in [Jewish] hands."[16] India's recognition of Israel and the presence of an Israeli consulate in Bombay figured prominently in Pakistani discourses. They were presented as evidence for India's "duplicity" vis-à-vis the Arabs. While professing friendship with the Arabs, Pakistani scholars argued that India was pursuing a sinister course inimical to the *ummah*.

The second Indian concern revolved around Pakistan's efforts to forge an Islamic bloc. During the pre-1947 years, the Muslim League was primarily interested in Islamic issues. Since the abolition of the caliphate in 1924, pan-Islamic movements made numerous efforts toward reinstating a caliph or forming a political forum for the *ummah*.[17] The Indian Muslim community played a significant role in some of these efforts.[18] External contacts of the Muslim League during this period were restricted to the Middle East, and they were useful when Pakistan's foreign policy was centered on the region. Liaquat Ali Khan, Pakistan's first prime minister, "and Chaudhury Khaliquzzaman, a prominent Muslim League leader, were in the forefront of initiating and sponsoring numerous Islamic conferences. Several international Islamic organizations had been established with headquarters in Karachi."[19] Beginning with the World Muslim Congress in 1948, Pakistan hosted and organized a number of official and semiofficial Islamic meetings and conferences.[20] The mufti of Jerusalem was a frequent visitor to Pakistan. The ideological opposition of Pakistan to secular Arab nationalism led by Nasser was accompanied by its desire to forge close ties with conservative regimes in the Middle East, such as Saudi Arabia and Iran under the shah. Its support for the pro-Western Hashemite Kingdom resulted in strong military cooperation with Amman.[21] Its relations with Turkey, another pro-Western country, manifested through their joint membership in the U.S.-sponsored blocs such as the Baghdad Pact (later renamed the Central Treaty Organization, CENTO) and Regional Cooperation and Development (RCD). While formation of the Organization of the Islamic Conference had to wait until 1969, Pakistan's efforts resulted in a number of Islamic gatherings adopting positions that were unfriendly toward India.

As a result, India's diplomatic activities in the Middle East were overwhelmingly obsessed with Pakistan. The assessment of Eliyahu Elath, Israel's ambassador in London, aptly summed the prevailing situation. After a gap of few years, on September 6, 1953, Elath met his old friend and now India's ambassador in Cairo, Panikkar. Reporting on this daylong rendezvous in the English countryside, Elath remarked that when

Panikkar "was appointed to Cairo, Nehru told him to do his utmost to prevent the Arab countries from identifying themselves with Pakistan."[22] Similarly, another Israeli diplomat, Eliahu Sasson, observed: "Talking about politics in general, the Indian Minister [in Ankara, C. S. Jha] brought the topic of what seems to be the *center of gravity of his interest,* namely: Pakistan."[23] Indian preoccupation with Pakistan becomes apparent in the manner in which it handled some of the major developments in the Middle East. It was largely due to this that India was prepared to endorse Israel's exclusion from the Bandung Conference. As Krishna Menon admitted subsequently, "Indonesia might have been persuaded at that time, but Pakistan made use of our attitude to Israel's presence at Bandung in propaganda with the Arabs."[24] A far more direct involvement of the Pakistani factor became apparent when India gatecrashed the first Islamic summit in Rabat in September 1969.

Arab-Islamic Influence

Even without Pakistan, Islam plays a significant role in India's calculations. As one scholar has reminded us, with a few notable exceptions, India is surrounded by countries with large Muslim populations.[25] Its vital trade routes to Europe and Pacific pass through Islamic countries whose importance ironically increased following the Arab defeat in the June war and the subsequent marginalization of secular Arab nationalism. The formation of the OIC and the growing influence of conservative ideas in the Middle East and elsewhere have influenced India's Israel policy. As highlighted by the Rabat fiasco, commitments to secularism did not inhibit India from wanting to partake in an explicitly religious political gathering.

At least during the initial years of independence, "the Islamic factor did not figure prominently in India's dealing with Muslim countries."[26] There are those who presented the emergence of a North-South dialogue among developing countries through an Islamic prism. In the words of G. H. Jansen, "without Islam the Afro-Asian movement would probably have aborted. And without the Afro-Asian movement there would have been no 'non-aligned' group of nations, and without that group there would not have been the economic Group of Seventy-Seven, the underdeveloped South in the current North-South dialogue."[27] Even though Islamic considerations were not the foundation of the Third World, the

Islamic countries have played a very significant role in the development and consolidation of solidarity among its member states.

Besides anti-imperialism, India's policy toward Israel was also shaped by the growing politico-strategic importance of the Arab world. The Arab factor is one of the very few determinants whose influence can be felt throughout the years. Since the days of the Khilafat struggle and until after the normalization of relations in 1992, the Arab factor permeated Indian thinking and calculations vis-à-vis Israel. Egypt had long dominated Indian thinking. As early as 1949, New Delhi declared that "the pre-eminent position of Egypt in the Arab world makes our relations with that country of particular importance."[28] Commenting on Cairo's importance, Onkar Marwah observes that due to "its status in the Arab world—and also for its geostrategic location—Egypt was an obvious choice for Indian attention, especially at a time when several Arab countries were being persuaded to enter into military alliance by the West. Israel could not be expected to play a role as significant as Egypt's in this sequence of international politics."[29]

Egypt's importance was more acutely felt during Nasser's time. Beginning with their first meeting in Cairo in 1953, the Nehru-Nasser friendship blossomed into a unique relationship, and each had a great influence upon the other.[30] According to Mohamed Hassanein Heikal, between February 1953 and July 1955 alone they met as many as eight times.[31] If Cairo provided "a convenient refueling stop" during Nehru's voyages to Europe, Nasser offered political support to Nehru.[32] Their convergence, first witnessed at the Bandung Conference, soon transformed into closer relations between the two countries, which were largely sustained until Nasser's death in 1970. India's unwavering support for Egypt during the Suez crisis and the June war was part of this trend. While the former was never challenged, unqualified support for Egypt during the June 1967 war drew bitter domestic criticism. The opposition castigated the INC-led government for its imbalance but could not bring about any changes in the pro-Egyptian policy.

Moreover, the strategic importance of the Suez Canal also compelled India to support Egypt. Justifying Egyptian nationalization of the canal, Menon remarked:

> I knew well that in no circumstances could any Arab could do other than [what] Nasser was doing . . . neither he nor anyone else could get the population to agree to the idea of ships going through the Suez

> Canal with an Israeli flag flying. It may not be rational; it may not be politically sensible . . . we got Nasser to agree at first that Israeli goods could go in other ships. . . . [Nasser] said "we are at war with Israel and we are not going to allow enemy to go through." He was right. . . . I think the UN convention [that is, the UN Security Council resolution of September 1951 demanding freedom of navigation for Israel through the Suez Canal] *was wrong*. In any case, said Nasser, we cannot have Israeli ships going through [Suez]. . . . Which Arab government could permit the Israeli flag in their home waters, even in the name of freedom of navigation? The Arabs would not agree to this; a red rag to a bull is the Israeli flag. It may be the fault of the Arabs—but no Arab government, no Egyptian government could agree to Israeli ships going through the Canal. The Arabs claim that they are at war with Israel. We tried some way to help solve the Israeli problem—conditions were more suitable for them before the Suez invasion.[33]

These were Menon's views when Michael Brecher interviewed him in 1964 and 1965. By then, he had resigned from the government following the 1962 Sino-Indian War and was slowly fading away. However, his remarks assume importance because of his close association with Nehru and his involvement in formulating policy during the Suez crisis. From his observations, it is obvious that India wholeheartedly endorsed and embraced the Arab viewpoint. It accepted the Arab contention that they were at war with Israel and thus would not abide by international obligations or the demands of the UN Security Council. In short, India would not endorse Israel's right of passage through the Suez Canal. This partisan approach toward the Middle East, especially during the June 1967 war, caused acrimonious debate and criticism in the Indian parliament and the media.

The importance of the Arab countries is further enhanced by India's strong economic ties, which date back to the pre-Christian era. The arrival of Arabs and later European powers on Indian shores and the hinterland were primarily driven by economic incentives and opportunities. During the colonial period, much of India's export of raw materials to and import of finished produce from Britain passed through the Middle East.[34] It was this geostrategic and geoeconomic importance that partially led to the British endorsement of the Balfour Declaration. Palestine was seen as a major staging area for British interests in India. The importance of the region only increased after India's independence, as it offered a host of trade, commerce, and investment opportunities. The Arab countries also provided important trade and aviation links to Europe. Before the advent of long-haul aircraft, Cairo and Beirut were "important halting stations for India's West-bound air services."[35]

Since the oil boom of the 1970s, three additional items were added to India's list of interests in the Middle East: trade opportunities, energy security, and the presence of a large skilled, semiskilled, and unskilled Indian workforce in the Persian Gulf. All three worked against Israel. Indo-Arab trade was growing, but India's bilateral trade with Israel was meager and negligible. In 1960, the government informed the Lok Sabha that the size of the Israeli market was small and thus offered little incentive for Indian exports.[36] A few years later, another highlighted that bilateral trade was noncomplementary and competitive.[37] The Indo-Arab trade, on the contrary, has been complementary. The oil boom and resultant increase of cash flows into the Arab states rapidly expanded India's export potential to this region. A significant growth in India's trade with the littoral states of the Persian Gulf can be directly traced to the post-1973 boom. By the end of the twentieth century, the Gulf region emerged as India's fifth-largest trading partner.

Second, the oil crisis contributed to a massive construction boom in the Persian Gulf, and a large number of Indians found gainful employment there. These expatriates also contribute valuable foreign-exchange remittances to India. For example, in 2006 expatriate remittances to India stood at over US$20 billion, constituting about 3 percent of the GDP. The bulk of the Indian workforce can be found in the oil-rich Arab countries of the Persian Gulf, especially Saudi Arabia, the United Arab Emirates, and Kuwait. Estimates of their presence range from three to four million. This process not only provides direct employment to a large workforce but also indirectly sustains much larger dependent populations back home. As highlighted during the 1991 Kuwait crisis, the expatriate population and their welfare became an important input into India's Middle East policy.[38]

Third, the oil-rich Arab countries are pivotal for India's search for energy security. Economic liberalization has increased its demand for hydrocarbon resources. Since the early 1990s, more than two-thirds of its oil needs are met by imports, and according to the Paris-based International Energy Agency, by 2030 as much as 87 percent of India's oil needs will have to be met by imports.[39] Arab countries such as Saudi Arabia, Qatar, the United Arab Emirates, and Sudan currently supply the bulk of India's oil needs.[40]

It is, however, essential to recognize that issues such as trade opportunities, energy security, and expatriate laborers became prominent only in the wake of the oil crisis. They significantly contributed to the consolidation of India's pro-Arab policy but were not its foundations. The hardening of India's policy in the 1970s was linked to the economic dimensions of Indo-Arab relations. But their actual role in the formulation of India's policy, especially when Nehru deferred the normalization decision in early 1952, was minimal. Although economic arguments strengthened the status quo, they were not the root cause.

But this assessment is not true for the Arab threat of political and economic boycott, which adversely affected Israel's political fortunes, sustained its prolonged international isolation, and undermined economic progress.[41] These boycotts influenced Israel's bilateral relations with a number of countries and regional forums. Through the effective use of boycotts, Arab countries influenced and at times radically altered the policies of a number of countries. Even the United Nations was not free from such pressure tactics. The Arab demand, for instance, compelled Israel to seek membership in other regional groupings even though it resides in the Asian or East Mediterranean zone. This was more acute during the cold war. Since the regional headquarters of various UN bodies and agencies such as the Food and Agriculture Organization (FAO); International Civil Aviation Organization (ICAO); United Nations Educational, Scientific, and Cultural Organization (UNESCO); and World Health Organization (WHO) were situated in Cairo, their services were long denied to Israel.[42] Enlarging the scope of its political boycott, on May 19, 1951, the Arab League declared that its members "would not boycott international conferences of which Israel was a member but would not participate in or would seek to have Israel excluded from regional conferences called by one country and would not give Israeli delegations visas to participate at such conferences in any Arab country."[43] This proved fatal when Indonesia hosted the Afro-Asian conference in Bandung, in 1955. For the same reason, for decades, Israel was not attached to any regional groupings in the United Nations and thus was ineligible for election to the Security Council.[44]

The economic dimension of the Arab boycott predates not only the formation of the state of Israel but also the establishment of the British Mandate over Palestine.[45] The earliest Arab boycott can be traced to 1908, when the Arab newspaper *al-Asmai* called for the boycott of Jewish goods.[46] The formation of Israel radically altered the nature and scope of the Arab boycott. All commercial and financial transactions between Arab states and Israel were banned; postal, radio, and telegraphic communications were cut off; and a land, sea, and air embargo was enforced. These measures included a host of secondary and tertiary boycotts.

Some suggest that India appeared as a late entrant on the Arab blacklist.[47] But as early as November 1947, Indian cargo passing through the Suez Canal came under the provisions of the Arab boycott and was confiscated by Egyptian authorities.[48] In line with its overall policy of not antagonizing the Arabs, India often took pains to declare that there was no need for Indian cargo vessels to pass through Israeli ports.[49] By 1976, at least 128 Indian firms and organizations were on the Arab blacklist.[50] They included some of the leading names in the country, such as Birla, Colgate Palmolive, Gestetner, Mahindra & Mahindra, Kirloskar, Praga Tools (an undertaking of the Indian government), Velco, Vikram Enterprises, and Voltas. Their inclusion did not imply that these firms had any direct trade or commercial links with Israel. A 1975 report prepared by the Federation of Indian Chambers of Commerce and Industry (FICCI), the most important body of Indian industry, highlighted this problem. Following a visit to the Middle East, a FICCI delegation concluded:

> The delegation would like to draw attention to the manner in which the Arab boycott of Israel is operating, as it affects our trading opportunities. A number of Indian firms continue to be blacklisted and borne in the register maintained at the headquarters of the Arab Boycott of Israel office in Damascus. *In quite a number of cases* the Indian companies figure in the register because they have collaboration arrangements with some foreign companies, say Great Britain, Germany and the United States in which, there may be an Israeli on the Board of Directors. In many such actions where requisite actions have been taken by Indian companies, delays have occurred in getting the names removed from the boycott list.[51]

To remedy the situation, the January 1975 report suggested that in view of the "friendly relations between India and the Arab world, diplomatic efforts at the appropriate level should be made to ensure that no Indian company remains on the list unless there are overriding reasons for doing so."[52]

The power of the economic boycott reached its apogee when the Arab states managed to convince the NAM to endorse their economic boycott.

Not satisfied with Israel's political exclusion, the fourth NAM summit in Algeria in 1973 called on the international community, "particularly the United States of America, to refrain from supplying Israel with weapons, and from any political, economic or financial support, which would enable it to continue its aggressive and expansionist policy."[53] It welcomed the decision of some African countries to break off diplomatic ties with Israel. Demanding similar moves from others, it called on the member countries "to work for a boycott of Israel in the diplomatic, economic, military and cultural fields and in the sphere of maritime and air traffic in accordance with the provisions of Chapter VII of the United Nations Charter."[54] In short, the NAM unreservedly endorsed the Arab boycott of Israel. Given the post-1973 economic leverage of the Arabs and political clout of the Arab League, India had little choice regarding the boycott, even if it wished otherwise.

The other Arab input into India's foreign policy is the Palestinian factor.

The Palestinian Factor

The long absence of ties with Israel might give an impression that India had a Palestinian, not Israeli, policy. The Indo-Arab contacts and pronouncements dating back to the Mandate years add to such claims. During the freedom struggle, Indian nationalists had contacts with Arab leaders of Mandate Palestine, including the mufti of Jerusalem. Since independence, the Palestinian factor figured prominently in India's bilateral relations with countries of the Middle East and in multilateral forums such as the NAM. Above all, India's only official publication on the Arab-Israeli conflict was curiously titled *India and Palestine: The Evolution of a Policy*. Published following the widespread uproar in the country over the June 1967 war, it traces and justifies Indian policy toward Israel through a Palestinian prism. In their enthusiasm to exhibit their pro-Palestinian credentials, both the government and independent scholars often claim that India "was the first non-Arab state to recognize the PLO as the sole and legitimate representative of Palestinian people."[55] This honor, however, actually goes to China, which recognized the PLO as far back as 1965.

In any case, the history of India's eventual recognition of the PLO indicates a different trajectory. Formal and official contacts between India and the Palestinian leadership occurred only after President Nasser established the PLO as an outlet for Palestinian nationalist aspirations. Between 1947 and 1964, India's support for the Palestinians was expressed through its overall pro-Arab policy and its closer ties with countries such as Egypt. For nearly a decade after the formation for the PLO, contacts were few and progress slower. Following his visit to Cairo for the second NAM summit, Lal Bahadur Shastri, India's prime minister, hosted a PLO delegation in November 1964.[56] In September 1969, al-Fatah, which had since joined the PLO, sent a three-member delegation at the invitation of the left-leaning Indian Association for Asian Solidarity. During this visit, described as "private," the Palestinians tried to establish official contacts with the Indian government and were eager to open a representative office in New Delhi, but the latter was cautious and unenthusiastic.[57] The visit was a partial success, as the delegation managed to enlist the support of Indian communists.

The communist parties played the same role for the Palestinians that the socialists played for Israel—political lobbying. In August 1970, Bhupesh Gupta of the Communist Party of India added two amendments to the official motion in the Rajya Sabha on international relations. One called on the government "to extend its support to the struggle of the Palestinian Arabs to return to their homeland and in particular, to the al-Fatah which is leading this struggle." His other demand was that al-Fatah should "be allowed to open an information office in New Delhi."[58] Taking cognizance of such sentiments, a few months earlier, the Indian government declared that the PLO, "of which al-Fatah is the most widely known constituent, is assuming growing importance as a political force. The organization has become more viable and effective due mainly to its success in the unification of their different groups."[59] In March 1970, the Indian government depicted al-Fatah as "a secular organization fighting for the liberation of Palestine."[60]

Around this time, the PLO was gaining international acceptance and recognition. It was admitted to the NAM consultative meeting held in Belgrade in July 1969. Its status was somewhat confusing, as it attended the meeting as a "participating country."[61] In subsequent years, the PLO was designated as an "observer." At the Lima ministerial meeting in August 1975, the PLO once again became a "participant."[62] It formally entered the NAM as a full member at the Colombo summit in August 1976.[63] These changes were reflected in India's postures. Referring to the participation of the PLO in the Darussalam meeting in April 1970, Foreign Minister

Dinesh Singh declared that "as far as PLO is concerned there was no question of the recognition; it was allowed to make a statement along with other liberation movements from colonial territories."[64] India was reacting cautiously to PLO's entry into the NAM.

The sixth Arab summit in November 1973 at Algiers was a milestone in the history of the PLO. Coming within weeks after the Arab "victory" in the October war, the summit formally declared the PLO to be "the sole representative of the Palestinian people."[65] This enhanced the status of the PLO, which was under a cloud following a spate of hijackings in the early 1970s. This eventually compelled even King Hussein of Jordan to accept the reality on the ground. The Arab consensus vis-à-vis the Palestinian leadership enabled the United Nations to recognize the PLO and grant it an "observer" status in the General Assembly. On November 13, 1974, PLO Chairman Yasser Arafat made his famous "gun and the olive branch" speech.

Around the same time, India formally acknowledged that it was maintaining contacts with the PLO through various diplomatic channels.[66] In December 1974, roughly thirty parliamentarians demanded that India grant diplomatic status to the PLO, to coincide with the tenth anniversary of the "Palestine Revolution."[67] These efforts culminated on January 10, 1975, when India's ambassador in Beirut, S. K. Singh, signed the necessary official documents with Arafat. Through this agreement, India recognized the PLO and permitted an independent office in New Delhi.[68] According to Arafat, the Indian decision should have come earlier. Speaking to the state-run All-India Radio soon after recognition, he disclosed that "at the last interview between me and her Excellency Gandhi, in Algiers, during the nonaligned countries conference, I remember what she had promised me, and now we can say that what she promised me, has been fulfilled."[69] If he is correct, India was contemplating recognition even before a similar move by the Arab League.

Since its recognition, India has been consistently championing the participation of the PLO in the Middle East peace process as an equal partner.[70] In March 1980, India granted full diplomatic recognition to the PLO by upgrading its office to that of an embassy endowed with all diplomatic immunities and privileges.[71] This was one of the first foreign-policy initiatives undertaken by Indira Gandhi upon returning to power in January. Gradually, the India-PLO ties were strengthened through increased contacts, meetings, and exchanges. In April 1981, an Indian delegation headed by Lok Sabha Speaker Balram Jakhar attended the fifteenth session of the Palestine National Council (the Palestinian parliament-in-exile) in Damascus. This was the first time that an Indian delegation was present at a PNC meeting.[72] In November 1988, India became one of the first countries to recognize the state of Palestine proclaimed at the Algiers meeting of the PNC.

Considering these developments, Indo-Palestinian relations can be divided into three broad phases: the prepartition years, the period between the partition of Palestine and the emergence of the PLO in 1964, and the post-1964 phase. India's position on partition of Palestine was one of vehement opposition to territorial division along religious lines, and it explained its support for the Arabs in terms of self-determination and secularism. The establishment of Israel fundamentally challenged and slowly changed this worldview. The Arab-Israeli war of 1948 and subsequent developments revealed the absence of any viable Arab leadership and the onset of inter-Palestinian and inter-Arab rivalries and schisms. Hence in the second phase, India's policy was one of ambiguity. While generally supporting the Arabs, it left the details undefined, except for the right of refugees to return enshrined in UN General Assembly resolution 194. This trend was largely a reflection of the prevailing Arab thinking on the whole issue and continued even after the formation of the PLO. It was only after the October 1973 war and the Arab summit in Algiers that the empowerment of the PLO truly began. India then established formal ties with the PLO and made it an important plank of its Middle East policy.

It broadly supported the Palestinian position on a host of issues, including self-determination, political rights, and statehood. On the sensitive issue of refugee rights, India sided with the Palestinians.[73] It differed with the Israeli position that the Arab states and people could not escape from their responsibility for the creation of the refugee problem.[74] As the official statement issued at the time of its recognition of Israel declared, both sides differed in their "attitudes" toward various issues including Jerusalem, borders, and refugees.[75] Its recognition of Israel "does not mean that there is no difference between India's attitude and that of Israel over questions like the status of Jerusalem and Israel's frontiers. These questions would be judged by India on merits and due regard would be given to Arab claims."[76]

Regarding the territorial limits of Israel, in 1967 India felt it necessary to highlight the importance of partition resolution 181 and insisted that under the UN partition plan, "the Jewish State was to get approximately

5,500 square miles of the territory of the Palestine, which as a whole was 10,423 square miles. The present [that is, the pre-1967] area of Israel, according to the latest figures available, is said to be 7,993 square miles, that is to say 45 percent in excess of that authorized by the UN Resolution."[77] Interestingly, India was not vocal in expressing its opposition to the Jordanian annexation of the West Bank and east Jerusalem following the 1948 Arab-Israeli war. Likewise, it is difficult to accept that New Delhi was unfamiliar with the PLO covenant, which explicitly called for the destruction of Israel, until its annulment following the Oslo Accords.[78] The Jordanian action and PLO charter clearly ran counter to India's recognition of Israel. A more likely explanation could be that it had reservations but was reluctant to spell them out due to political compulsions.

On the sensitive issue of terrorism, India has adopted a mixed approach. In an official statement about the Munich massacre, issued on September 6, 1972, India declared that the tragedy "shocked us. Sports and terrorism go ill together. We thought it a good augury that Arabs and Israeli sportsmen were participating in the Olympics in the traditional spirit of sportsmanship."[79] This was one of the strongest Indian statements on terrorism.[80] However, when questioned about the political status of al-Fatah, in 1970 Foreign Minister Dinesh Singh declared that "there is no question of al-Fatah being a terrorist organization. It is a revolutionary organization in West Asia of considerable importance."[81]

At the international level, India's general attitude was one of sympathy and understanding toward the Palestinians. While the NAM maintained a complete silence on the Munich massacre, it condemned Israel for its rescue operation in Entebbe. The political declaration of the 1976 summit in Colombo categorically stated:

> The conference noted with serious disappointment the failure of the United Nations Security Council to condemn the Israeli military aggression against Uganda on 4 July 1976. The Conference expressed grave concern at the tragic loss of human life, damage and destruction of Ugandan property caused by the Israeli aggression.
>
> The Conference strongly condemned Israel's flagrant violation of the Republic of Uganda's sovereignty and territorial integrity and the deliberate and wanton destruction of life and property at Entebbe Airport and further condemned Israel for thwarting the *hu-*

> *manitarian efforts by the President of Uganda* to have all the hostages released.[82]

In short, according to India, which endorsed this stance, Israel was the aggressor at Uganda. It had nothing to say about the Palestinian guerrillas who hijacked the Air France plane and separated Jewish and non-Jewish passengers with the intention of executing them. India was willing a partner in this partisan revisionism.

On the whole, however, India has followed the general consensus in the Middle East regarding the Palestinians. The only notable exception was its refusal to recognize the All-Palestine Government of September 1948, which was recognized by some Arab states. Otherwise, it has followed the general Arab sentiments of recognizing the political rights of the Palestinians and the PLO. Its reservations regarding the PLO covenant that called for the destruction of Israel, a state recognized by India, were never explicitly stated. The same was true for the Jordanian annexation of the West Bank, and before 1967 India never invoked the "inadmissibility" of the acquisition of territory through war. This became a constant Indian theme vis-à-vis Israel following the June 1967 war. On the issue of terrorism, it sided with Palestinians even though the wanton killing of innocent civilians went against the Gandhian concept of *ahimsa* or nonviolence.

Thus, the Pakistan factor and the growing importance of Arab and Islamic countries resulted in India recognizing the political usefulness of a pro-Arab and pro-Palestinian position. With the Soviet Union providing an ideological ambiance for such a policy, during the cold-war years, India's policy on Israel ranged from unfriendliness to outright hostility. As Israel's circle of friends began diminishing following the Arab oil embargo, India became increasingly hostile toward Israel. Only a major international upheaval would be able to jolt India out of its position.

Once the present Muslim policy of a separate Islamic state in India (popularly known as Pakistan) is realized, which it will be in the course of the next two years, Hindu opinion on the question of Palestine will find its natural and untrammeled expression. —*Historian and diplomat K. M. Panikkar*

9 Nehru and the Era of Deterioration, 1947–1964

Panikkar's prognosis, which he made in April 1947, was quickly proved wrong, either because of misreading or wishful thinking. Within months of his observation, India not only opposed a Jewish homeland in Palestine but also had voted against the UN partition plan. Jawaharlal Nehru did not radically alter India's policy toward the Middle East. If he was the chief foreign-policy spokesperson for the Congress Party during the nationalist phase, he laid the foundation of free India's policy. Earlier, Nehru had to compete with Mahatma Gandhi's towering personality; now he emerged as the uncrowned monarch on foreign-policy issues. As such, much of India's foreign policy was designed and institutionalized by him. No account of India's external policy or relations would be complete without understanding and recognizing the Nehruvian model. As Michael Edwards observes: "No other democratic Prime Minister has ever had such a free hand in the formulation and execution of his country's foreign policy."[1] For his entire seventeen-year tenure as prime minister, he was also India's foreign minister and personally nurtured the ministry.[2] His influence was so overwhelming that even the non-INC governments that came to power long after his death could only change the style and not the substance of India's foreign policy. "Continuity and change," the perennial Indian mantra, is primarily a reaffirmation of Nehru's vital contributions.

India's policy toward Israel is primarily a study of nonrelations or the absence of normalization. For over four decades, the changing international political situations, the Eurocentric cold war, compulsions of interests, and domestic electoral calculations meant that the absence of normalization was prominent in India's Israel policy. Nonrelations did not mean that the two countries were not interacting with each other. At least in the early years, both countries were cooperating internationally. Slowly, they drifted apart, and India soon emerged as the principal non-Arab and non-Islamic country to castigate Israel for its policies and practices.

Between the formation of Israel in 1948 and the normalization of relations in January 1992, India had seven prime ministers.[3] With the exception of the Janata government (1977–1979) and two coalition governments from 1989 to 1991, the Congress Party ruled India for much of this period. Of these, the longest, the Nehru era (1947–1964), was the defining period for Indo-Israeli relations. Most critical decisions regarding Israel were taken during Nehru's reign. It was under his leadership that India advocated the federal plan, voted against the partition plan, and grudgingly recognized the Jewish state. Nehru played a crucial role in the organization of the Afro-Asian movement that eventually culminated in the formation of the Non-Aligned Movement. As will be discussed, Nehru backed Israel's exclusion from this bloc of newly independent countries, which in turn signaled and consolidated Israel's isolation from the Third World. The Nehru years witnessed two major conflicts, namely the Suez crisis of 1956 and the Sino-Indian war of 1962. These crises both highlighted India's policy toward Israel and underscored some of its weaknesses. We begin with Nehru's decision to invite the *yishuv* to the first Asian conference, which offered a brief window of opportunity.

Asian Relations Conference, 1947

Convened on the eve of India's independence, the Asian Relations Conference provided the first opportunity for leaders of the newly independent and near-independent countries of the continent to meet and understand one another. Nonofficial in character, the Congress Party organized the conference in New Delhi. Nehru, heading the interim government since September 1946, was its moving spirit. The preparatory work began in April 1946. Formally inaugurated on March 23, 1947, the conference ended on April 2 with a valedictory address given by Nehru. The primary purpose of the conference was to promote greater understanding of Asia (Egypt was the only non-Asian invitee). As a result, "not only controversial issues involving these countries, but even matters like defense and security which concerned powers outside Asia were excluded from the agenda, which listed only such innocuous subjects as national freedom movements, migration and racial problems, economic development and the status of women."[4]

The conference offered an opportunity for the *yishuv* to interact with India's nationalist leadership as well as those from other Asian countries. Hugo Bergmann, a professor of philosophy at the Hebrew University of Jerusalem, headed a ten-member "Jewish Delegation from Palestine."[5] The delegation felt that they represented only the Jewish community in Palestine and not the whole of Palestine. In spite of "our constant efforts to call ourselves, 'Jewish Palestine Delegation,' and to maintain that we represent only the Jewish part of Palestine, we were considered, sometimes consciously and sometimes implicitly, as a delegation of Palestine as a whole"[6] or as a "Hebrew University Delegation."[7] Some members of the delegation felt it was an "endeavor not to mention and not to refer to *Jewish* Palestine."[8]

There was a near total absence of Arabs at the conference. Out of the thirty-two countries that were invited, twenty-eight countries and a few observers attended the New Delhi meeting. While the Arab League was represented by an observer, six Arab countries (Iraq, Lebanon, Saudi Arabia, Syria, Transjordan, and Yemen) "did not accept individual invitations."[9] The Jewish delegation felt that this was due to the "request and pressure" from the Indian Muslim League, which boycotted the conference.[10] The Egyptian delegation linked Arab nonattendance to the participation of the Jewish delegation.[11] One observer could not hold back his sarcasm and remarked that the conference had "delegates from seven Arab countries numbered six in all—five from Egypt and one observer from the Arab League representing the other six countries."[12]

The *yishuv* saw the invitation and participation as a official recognition of the Jewish nation as a legitimate member of the Asian family of nations.[13] Reflecting this optimism, the Jewish delegation felt that "the most important and positive aspect of our participation is . . . the mere fact that we have taken part. This participation in itself has established

Jewish Palestine as part of the Asian continent and as a member of the family of nations of Asia."[14] The conference provided an opportunity for the *yishuv* to establish formal and, at times, first contacts with various Asian persons who were to become the future leaders of their respective countries. While personal contacts were important and useful, there were doubts if sympathetic statements could be converted into political support for Zionism. In these interactions

> we met outspoken sympathy for our case. . . . It need not be pointed out . . . that this sympathy may be considered, in most cases, a matter of politeness and conversational manners and that even in cases where it has been sincere and real, it need not commit not only the Government of the countries concerned, but even the personalities themselves who expressed it, in a political sense.[15]

Bergmann reminded the conference that Jews were an

> old Asian people . . . settling down in our old-new homeland. . . . This lesson Europe was unable to teach us. We do not want to be ungrateful to Europe. We have learned many important lessons there. We learned to appreciate logical reasoning and methodical thinking. . . . But one thing we could not learn in Europe: the mutual cooperation of groups of men belonging to different races and creeds.

He hoped that Palestine, "notwithstanding present difficulties, will not go the European way of 'solving,' so to speak, problems by dispossessing population."[16] In a radio broadcast, Ya'acov Shimoni referred to the "hopes of an ancient people driven from his native Asiatic country 1,800 years ago."[17]

Bergmann's speech at the conference, however, was challenged by the Arabs. While the observer from Arab League spoke of the Jewish community in Palestine taking advantage of the "British bayonets," an Egyptian delegate rejected the idea that "British rule [was] to be replaced by that of European Zionists." A drama quickly unfolded. According to the report prepared by the Jewish delegation, "Dr. Bergmann, quite reasonably, asked for the floor to exercise his right of rebuttal, but Nehru, who was presiding, refused his request and after a brief, angry exchange with [Nehru],[18] Dr. Bergmann and his delegation walked out. Some of the Indian delegates hurried after them and persuaded them to return."[19]

Eventually, Bergmann "ascended the dais amid a storm of applause and under a second storm of applause approached the Observer of the Arab League and shook hands with him."[20] In his closing speech, "Pandit Nehru expressed regret that Professor Bergmann should have been hurt by him, and apologized."[21]

However, Nehru did not miss the opportunity to reiterate the position of the Congress Party. Expressing sympathy for the prolonged suffering of the Jewish people, he stated: "the people of India, necessarily for various reasons into which I shall not go, have always said that Palestine is essentially an Arab country and no decision can be made without the consent of the Arabs."[22] He still hoped that following the withdrawal of the "the third party," the issue would "be settled in cooperation between them and not by any appeal to or reliance upon any outsiders."[23] Bergmann and his delegation were not happy with Nehru's overall attitude during the conference. In the words of one, "most [of] us had the feeling that during the whole Conference that Pandit Nehru was not very keen to greet us or meet us in the Hall or Lounge, the Dining Room or wherever he happened to meet us in public."[24]

At the same time, according to Shimoni, who drafted the main report, there were some "positive" outcomes.[25] The Bergmann incident "aroused a special interest in our affairs, bringing them into the limelight and giving them a publicity they might never have attained otherwise." Partly to assuage their feelings, all delegates "endeavored to be even more polite and sympathetic, at least formally." The controversy also "brought us into contact with more people," and this resulted in David Hacohen[26] being "elected Chairman for two days of the Economic Round Table Group." Above all, Shimoni was certain that the dinner invitation with Nehru "was an outcome of this incident."[27] During this meeting, Nehru agreed to extend the stay of the Afghan Jewish refugees in India for six more months.[28] The conference enabled the delegation to meet a number of officials, nonofficial leaders, business figures, and members of the Jewish community in India. Their meeting with Mahatma Gandhi "lasted only ten minutes."[29] The anger and disappointment of the Zionists over his 1938 statement explains its brevity.

Once the conference ended, the delegation traveled to different parts of India and met a number of persons. The most important meeting took place in the princely state of Bikaner. Its prime minister, Sardar K. M. Panikkar, put forth some interesting ideas. He strongly felt that following the partition of the subcontinent, public opinion in India, especially among the Hindu population, would change in favor of the Zionists. He therefore urged the Zionist leadership to make up for their prolonged neglect of India.[30] In the wake of its interactions with various Indian leaders during and after the conference, the Jewish delegation offered a number of suggestions to the Jewish Agency for Palestine:[31] to establish a Jewish Palestine unit of the Asian Relations Organization, to send a permanent political representative of the Jewish Agency to India, to create a desk for India and Asia at the Political Department of the Jewish Agency, to induce the Palestinian press to act as stringers for the Indian press, to explore the possibility of establishing an economic-liaison office in Bombay, to consider establishing a chair for Judaism at the University of Banaras (that is, Banaras Hindu University), and to use pro-Indian U.S. politicians "who are at the same time pro-Zionists . . . for our cause." As one delegate lamented, India "is a great chance that has been neglected far too long."

Some of these suggestions eventually materialized, and an *aliya* office was opened in Bombay shortly after India's recognition. The Israeli unit of the Asian Relations Organization functioned until June 1955, when the Bandung Conference formally ended the parent organization.[32] While some in the *yishuv* were happy over their participation, others were concerned over Nehru's remarks about the Arab character of Palestine and felt the need to do more "to bring home to Asiatic people the realities of Palestine—that the Holy Land is inseparable from the people of Israel."[33]

The overall effects of the Asian Relations Conference, however, were negative. The New Delhi meeting was the first and last occasion when a delegation from the *yishuv*/Israel was invited to such a political gathering. Despite its stated objective of seeking interstate cooperation by avoiding controversial issues, the conference could not avoid heated arguments over the Palestine question. Even the nearly total absence of Arab countries did not prevent Jewish-Arab discord from coming into the open. Tension between the two sides set the stage for future acts. Bergmann's declaration against "dispossessing population" was not vindicated by subsequent events surrounding the Arab-Israeli war of 1948. Jewish-Israeli exclusivism in Palestine ran counter to Nehru's vision of a partitioned but genuinely multiracial, multireligious, and multicultural India. Summing up the outcome, one Indian academic observed: "even as the Jewish spokesman made the solemn declaration before the Conference, the Zionist movement irrevocably committed itself to an exclusive Jewish State, snuffing out all hopes of genuine multi-racial, multi-religious and multi-cultural co-existence and cooperation in Palestine. The Zionists [therefore] were excluded from all subsequent Asian conferences."[34] Thus the Asian Relations Conference, though important, did not result in mutual appreciation of each others' concerns and anxieties. India failed to appreciate the underlying causes for the particularistic Jewish nationalism. For its part, the *yishuv*/Israeli leadership failed to alleviate New Delhi's concerns over imperialism. These differences influenced India's subsequent stand at the United Nations, especially over Israel's membership.

UN Membership

From the beginning Israel was keen to join the United Nations, especially as its creation was recommended by that world body. In March 1949, the rival cold-war blocs both endorsed its request for membership. The Soviet Union, which opposed Jordan's membership, was favorably inclined toward the Israeli request. At the same time, the world body expressed concerns over Israel's policies toward sensitive issues such as Jerusalem, Palestinian refugees, the assassination of UN mediator Count Bernadotte, and Israel's ability and willingness to shoulder and live up to its international commitments. For Israel, membership thus was of critical importance. Major powers including the United States and the Soviet Union had already granted recognition. UN admission, it hoped, would signal international disapproval of the Arab refusal to come to terms with its existence and a rejection of their efforts to isolate and strangle the newly formed state.

What was India's response? Keeping with its "consistent" attitude on the entire question, New Delhi voted against the Israeli request. On May 11, 1949, with a margin of thirty-seven votes to twelve, with nine abstentions, the United Nations admitted Israel as a member. According to Nehru's biographer S. Gopal, India was originally planning to abstain but then reversed its position and voted against Israeli admission.[35] Speaking on the occasion, India's ambassador in New York, M. C. Setalvad, argued that his country "could not recognize a state which had been achieved through the use of force and not through negotiations."[36]

Not everyone was happy with Nehru's decision, and there were voices of dissent within the Indian establishment. Shiva Rao, who was active during the Asian Relations Conference of 1947, was one. In 1949, he was part of the Indian delegation to the General Assembly session and, even before the final vote, he registered his disagreement. In a note dated April 30, he declared:

> As I have told the PM, I think we are making a great mistake in continuing our opposition to Israel's coming into the UN. On general principles we are not maintaining such an attitude toward any other state. We believe in every state coming into the UN. Also it does not seem to me right that we should seek Israel's help in matters of primary value and significance to us and yet maintain this hostile attitude.[37]

Rao was referring to Nehru seeking technical agricultural assistance from Israel.[38]

The legal and political implications of the Indian position require some explanation. During this period, the major powers had vetoed the UN membership of states that were seen to be closer to the rival bloc. For example, the Soviet Union vetoed the applications of Ireland, Portugal, and Jordan; the United States and United Kingdom opposed the membership of Albania. In a verdict delivered in May 1948, International Court of Justice in the Hague ruled that a member state voting on the application of a state for admission to the United Nations "is not juridically entitled to make its consent to the admission dependent on conditions not expressly provided by Paragraph 1 (of the Article 4 of the UN Charter).[39] Similarly, a legal memorandum prepared by the UN Secretariat concluded that "a member could properly vote to accept a representative of a government which it did not recognize or with which it had no diplomatic relations and that such a vote did not imply recognition or a readiness to assume diplomatic relations."[40] The converse was also true: "there is no suggestion that recognition binds the recognizing state to vote for the admission of the candidates."[41] Therefore, its nonrecognition of the Jewish state could not legally bind India to oppose Israel's membership application.

On the political front, India had always emphasized the universal character of the United Nations. During the San Francisco Conference in 1945, some countries sought to restrict the membership of the new body by adding certain preconditions and requirements. India, still a British dominion, forcefully argued in favor of universal UN membership.[42] Elaborating on this aspect in 1949, one senior Indian diplomat felt that "refusing admission to peace-loving and sovereign states on grounds which had nothing to do with the merits of their application would be disastrous both for the organization's prestige and authority."[43] Despite these earlier positions and declarations, India chose to vote against Israel's admission to the United Nations. Principles were given up in favor of pragmatism and political calculations. This approach became more pronounced during the Bandung conference.

The Bandung Boycott, 1955

The first Afro-Asian conference in Bandung in April 1955 was a major milestone for Israel, albeit for all the wrong reasons. This meeting legitimized its political exclusion from the emerging bloc of Third World countries. The conference recognized Arab veto power over Israel's participation in various regional organizations. From then on, organizers of such gatherings were forced to choose between one Israel and many Arab countries. At the bilateral level, Israel "lost" China to the Arab countries and had to wait for over three decades to establish ties with Beijing.[44] On the Indian front, Nehru was coming under the influence of Gamal Abdel Nasser, the Egyptian president. As Israel gradually came to realize, Bandung marked the beginning of its isolation from Asia, compelling it to consolidate the Eurocentric outlook of the *yishuv* period.

The immediate background for Bandung can be traced to the Colombo Conference held in April 1954. Hosted by Prime Minister Sir John Kotelawala of Ceylon (now Sri Lanka), the conference was attended by the prime ministers of Burma (now Myanmar), India, Indonesia, and Pakistan. The leaders discussed the prevailing regional and international situation and the need for greater cooperation among the newly independent countries of Asia and Africa. As they deliberated their future course of action, Prime Minister Mohammed Ali of Pakistan introduced a resolution on Palestine that declared the establishment of the state of Israel as a violation of international law. It condemned Israel's "aggressive policies" toward its neighbors and expressed grave concern over the plight of Palestinian refugees.[45]

By that time, India had already recognized Israel and was in principle committed to establishing diplomatic ties. Thus Nehru was unable to endorse Pakistan's position that the creation of Israel was a violation of international law.[46] Burma and its leader U Nu had good relations with Israel. Sri Lanka had recognized the Jewish state and Indonesian leaders had acknowledged Israel's recognition of their country's independence from the Dutch. Pakistan, which had sided with the Arabs during the partition vote in 1947, was vociferous in its opposition.[47] Eventually, all five leaders agreed to include the following passage in their joint communiqué issued on May 2, 1954:

> In considering the situation in the Middle East the Prime Ministers indicated grave concern over the sufferings of Arab refugees in Palestine. They urged the United Nations to bring about and expedite the rehabilitation of these refugees in their original homes. The Prime Ministers expressed deep sympathy with the Arabs of Palestine in their sufferings and affirmed their desire to see a just and early settlement of the Palestine problem.[48]

The absence of any reference to Israel and the unconditional demand for the return of the Arab refugees was a harbinger of bad news for Israel.[49] Even though the final wording fell far short of its expectations, Nehru's opposition provided an opportunity for Pakistan to present itself as a vigorous champion of the Arabs and set the tone for future Indo-Pakistani confrontations over Israel.[50]

That opportunity came a few months later, when Indonesia floated the idea of holding an Afro-Asian conference.[51] In December 1954, the same five prime ministers met at Bogor, Indonesia, to work on the agenda for the Bandung Conference. The conference aimed "to promote goodwill and cooperation" among Afro-Asian nations.[52] They felt that the newly independent countries of Asia and Africa "should become better acquainted with one another's point of view" and agreed to invite "all countries in Asia and Africa, which have independent governments." However, the issue of inviting the People's Republic of China caused some anxious moments. India was adamant that any Afro-Asian meeting would be incomplete without China, whereas a number of countries were not friendly toward communist China. Out of the twenty-six countries that eventually attended the Bandung Conference, as many as eighteen had not recognized the communist takeover in Beijing.[53] Therefore, to allay their concerns, the Bogor communiqué contained a rider:

> The Prime Ministers wished to point out that acceptance of the invitation by any one country would in no way involve or even imply any change in its view of the status of any other country. It implied only

> that the country invited was in general agreement with the purposes of the Conference. They had also bear in mind the principle that the form of government and the way of life of any one country should in no way be subject to interference by any other. Any view expressed at the [forthcoming Bandung] Conference by one or more participating country would not be binding on or be regarded as accepted by any other, unless the latter so desired.

In short, recognition or nonrecognition of one country by the other was irrelevant. The primary purpose was to promote a meaningful dialogue among member states of Asia and Africa.

Despite such an accommodative position regarding the participants, the Bogor meeting decided to exclude Israel from the Bandung Conference. As the operative part stated "*with minor variations and modification of this basic principle*," it decided to invite twenty-four independent states of Asia and Africa. As many as eight Arab countries were invited, and the communiqué extended its support for the people of Tunisia and Morocco in their struggle for "national independence and their legitimate right to self-determination."[54] But Israel was excluded from Bandung,[55] and out of the twenty-nine participants, as many as twelve were Muslim-majority states.[56]

During the Bogor deliberations, Nehru concurred with his Burmese counterpart that "Israel ought to be invited, but pointed out that if she were present the Arab states would stay away, which would mean that almost the whole of West Asia would be absent. The conference would therefore be so unbalanced that India would have to reconsider whether her own attendance would be worth while."[57] According to G. H. Jansen, while Ceylon wanted to take up the issue with Arab states, "Indonesia said this was pointless since their view was known and the Arab League had recently issued a warning on this very point." In the end, Burma, which at one time had threatened to boycott the conference over Israel's exclusion, fell into line with the emerging consensus.[58] The first Afro-Asian meeting aimed at promoting dialogue among the newly independent states would begin without Israel.

There were two primary reasons for Israel's exclusion: the Arab determination to block Israel and Pakistan's attempt to outmaneuver India. New Delhi yielded to both pressures. By early 1950, the Arab League resolved that the Arab states would refrain from hosting any international conference in which Israel could participate.[59] In May 1951, it went a step further and decided that "participation in regional conferences organized on the initiative of one country or by an international organization could not be attended if Israel were also invited."[60] In a bid to reiterate its determination, in December 1954, only a few days before the Bogor meeting, the Arab League declared that the Arab states would not "participate in any regional conference where Israel is represented. The Arab states do not have any doubt that Israel will not be invited to this conference [Bandung] and will not participate therein."[61] This Arab ultimatum worked. This hamstrung India, which was uncomfortable about Israel's exclusion. In the words of S. Gopal, Nehru's close confidant V. K. Krishna Menon "was for an invitation to Israel with an explanation to the Arab states that the presence of Israel committed them to nothing; Nehru, wishing to avoid dissension even on the question of the composition of the conference, agreed with reluctance that an invitation to Israel should be extended only if the Arab countries agreed to it."[62] Nehru was even prepared to antagonize Sir Anthony Eden over China, but he meekly accepted Arab dictates over Israel.[63]

Speaking to Michael Brecher a year after the Bandung Conference, Nehru admitted:

> Conditions were and still are that the Arab nations and Israel don't sit together. They do sit at the United Nations, but apart from that, they just don't sit. And one is offered this choice of having one or the other. It is not logical, my answer, but there it is. When the proposal was made for Israel to be invited . . . it transpired that if that were done the Arab countries would not attend. . . . Our outlook on this matter was based on some logical approach. Our sympathies are with the Arab nations in regard to this problem. We felt that logically Israel should be invited but when we saw that the consequences of that invitation would be that many others would not be able to come, then we agreed. Our approach, obviously, if I may add, is that it is good for people who are opponents to meet.[64]

Devoid of diplomatic niceties, the choice was between one Israel and many Arab states, and Nehru opted for the latter.

Krishna Menon went a step further and attributed Nehru's buckling under Arab pressure to Pakistan. In his long interview to Brecher shortly after Nehru's death, Menon disclosed that the leaders of Burma

> said, "we won't come without Israel." We said our position is the same but we have got to carry the Arabs with us. We will do whatever the Congress agrees but we will vote for an invitation to Israel. And we were three to two, Ceylon, Burma and India for, and Pakistan and Indonesia against; but Pakistan was the leader. They made propaganda against us . . . and issued leaflets terming us a pro-Jewish country.[65]

In his opinion, even "Indonesia might have been persuaded at that time, but Pakistan made use of our attitude to Israel's presence at Bandung in propaganda with the Arabs."[66] Had he maintained normal relations with Israel as had U Nu, perhaps Nehru would have been more determined and forceful. Israel's exclusion turned Bandung into an anti-Israeli forum. By refusing to negotiate with Israel, the Arab states, led by non-Arab Pakistan, challenged the core of the partition resolution of the United Nations and merely settled for demanding the right of the refugees to return to their homes.

For many, however, Bandung presented "a front of Asian unity." Menon reflected the general Indian euphoria when he remarked:

> Bandung was like Geneva and Locarno [1925]. These are old expressions now; people don't even know where Locarno is, whether it is in Italy or in Switzerland, but still Locarno is a spirit. . . . Bandung had become a world-known name. If you ask a lot of Canadians where is Bandung they wouldn't know, but probably they would know it is in Asia, or even in Indonesia. At any rate there is a Bandung spirit.[67]

In other words, its importance "was in what it began rather than what it did."[68] And Israel was not a part of it. Seeds were sown for its exclusion from the emerging Afro-Asian bloc, the forerunner of the Non-Aligned Movement. Bandung institutionalized the process of the exclusion of Israel, not only from regional political gatherings but also nonpolitical forums devoted to sports, scientific cooperation, and so on.

Israel was aware of the fallout. Following the Bogor decision, it approached a number of countries to reverse the move. Prime Minister and Foreign Minister Moshe Sharett wrote to his Indonesian counterpart expressing his "astonishment and regret."[69] According to Krishna Menon, an Israeli ambassador met Prime Minister Nehru at Bandung "coming through Burma."[70] The Israeli media perceived the whole episode as an indication of their country's political isolation.[71] The episode was partly due to the absence of relations between Israel and countries in Asia. By 1955, only seven Asian countries had recognized Israel, and out of these, five had Israeli legations, and the first Israeli embassy in Asia was established in Rangoon in 1957, *after* Bandung.[72] In April 1955, none of the Asian countries had a resident mission in Israel.

For India, the whole episode underscored Pakistan's role in shaping its Israel policy. At Bandung, it formally acknowledged and bowed to Pakistani dictates. It was the Pakistani factor that precluded Nehru from normalizing ties with Israel. Despite all his commitments to dialogue, independence, and the moral high ground, when it came to the Arab-Israeli conflict, Nehru often fought with Pakistan and succumbed to its political pressures. Menon was rather candid and conceded to Brecher that the Arabs "wouldn't come to dinner" with the Israelis and would not sit with Israel anywhere except in the United Nations.[73] For him, Pakistan only "makes anti-Israeli speeches." This made things difficult for Nehru. India could not be indifferent to Pakistan as other states could, because the Russians "can afford to have somebody in Israel because they are a big power. We have got Pakistan on our borders, and the West supports Pakistan, and we cannot go and create more enemies than we have at the present moment."[74] As the years went by, Pakistan began to occupy a prime place in India's Israel policy. Its defiance of the West over issues such as the recognition of communist China, the Suez crisis, Hungary, Czechoslovakia, and Afghanistan could not be imitated vis-à-vis Pakistan over Israel.

Bandung symbolized both Israel's exclusion from the emerging group of newly independent states and underscored its isolation from Asia. Major countries such as India and China started moving away from Israel, and the smaller ones, such as Burma, were unable to withstand the pressures exerted upon them. For both India and China, the Arab world offered better political opportunities, especially over the issues that were critical for them at the United Nations, namely the Kashmir dispute for India and UN membership for China.

It is difficult to say whether this bitter experience pushed Israel closer to Europe, but post-Bandung, Israel turned its back on Asia. In the wake of the Sinai war and adverse Asian reactions, Prime Minister David Ben-Gurion was unapologetic about his priorities. In terms of Israel's interest, "the friendship of one European nation [namely, France] which we have secured from July [1956] until the present [January 1957] is worth more than the opinions prevailing at this time among the Asiatic people."[75] Its isolation in the Middle East did not allow Israel to be indifferent toward the Asian countries, but in the post-Bandung years, its interest in the continent decreased considerably. Any lingering doubts about India's Israel policy were settled during the Suez crisis, which broke out a few months later.

The Suez Crisis, 1956

The crisis following the nationalization of the Suez Canal in mid-1956 provides a number of insights into India's Israel policy. It highlighted the depth of India's closeness to Egypt. Simultaneously, it underscored Nehru's disengagement from his earlier commitment to normalize relations with Israel. The causes and consequences of the war are too widely known to need fresh elaboration.[76] The general Indian position regarding the crisis leading up to the war can be summarized as follows:

1. India did not question Egypt's right to nationalize the Suez Canal, even though it had reservations over how President Nasser handled the situation. Speaking at the London Conference on September 20, 1956, Krishna Menon, India's defense minister, felt that nationalization "was an act which was within the competence of the Egyptian government. . . . We would like to have seen that nationalization carried out in the normal way of international expropriation, where there is adequate notice, and the way of taking over is less dramatic and does not lead to these consequences."[77]

2. India believed that a failure to find a peaceful solution to the crisis could lead to a military confrontation. On August 8, Prime Minister Nehru told the Lok Sabha that he would be failing in his duty "if I do not say that threats to settle this dispute or to enforce their [that is, British and French] views in this matter by display or use of force, is the wrong way."[78]

3. India had serious economic and strategic interests in the canal and was concerned over its unhindered operation.

4. India declared that it would "decline participation in any arrangements for war preparations or sanctions or any steps which challenge the sovereign rights of Egypt."[79]

5. During the London Conference, Krishna Menon spelled out a six-point formula as the basis for a settlement.[80] Even after the failure of two

rounds of the London Conference, New Delhi played a significant role in the adoption of Resolution 118 by the UN Security Council, which demanded "free and open transit through the Canal without discrimination, overt or covert, both political and technical aspects."[81]

However, once the conflict began on October 29, 1956, with the Israeli offensive, India was swift and unequivocal in declaring its indignation over the "flagrant violation of the United Nations Charter and . . . all the principles laid down by the Bandung Conference."[82] Having endorsed Israel's exclusion from that Afro-Asian meeting, Nehru now demanded Israel's adherence to the spirit of Bandung!

Nehru's position hardened further following the entry of Britain and France in the war, and he sent a blunt message to Prime Minister Anthony Eden of Britain. Depicting it as "a clear aggression and a violation of the United Nations Charter," he argued that for many countries of Asia and beyond, "this is a reversion to a previous and unfortunate period of history when decisions were imposed by force of arms by Western Powers on Asian countries. We had thought that these methods were out-of-date and would not possibly be used in the modern age."[83] In a similar tone, he told his citizens that, though they were well into the twentieth century, "we are going back to the predatory methods of the eighteenth and nineteenth centuries. But there is a difference now. There are self-respecting, independent nations in Asia and Africa which are not going to tolerate this kind of incursion by colonial Powers."[84] In short, Nehru was categorical in his condemnation of the aggression against Egypt, a fellow member of the Afro-Asian bloc.

This unequivocal stand over the Suez crisis unfortunately boomeranged on Nehru when he abandoned his opposition to external aggression against Hungary.[85] Far from condemning the Soviet invasion, he seemed to justify the developments in eastern Europe. Accused of adopting double standards, he was strongly criticized both within and outside his country.[86] After a long deliberation on November 5, 1956, Nehru expressed his public sympathy for the people of Hungary. By then, Menon had depicted the developments in Hungary as the "domestic affairs" of a sovereign country.[87] Not prepared to abandon his partisanship, on November 20, Nehru told the Lok Sabha that many countries felt "relief that it happened in Hungary so that attention might be diverted from Egypt to Hungary."[88] As Escott Reid, the Canadian high commissioner in India during this turbulent period reminds us, the converse was also equally true.[89]

The Suez crisis assumed strategic importance for Israel, because of India's stance regarding the freedom of navigation. Even while endorsing the principle of nondiscriminatory treatment, India's position crucially differed from that of Israel. In the United Nations, New Delhi declared that a legal controversy existed over the right of passage through the Gulf of Aqaba, pronounced the entire gulf an "inland sea," and claimed its waters were Egyptian "territorial waters." Krishna Menon argued that "various states have held that the gulfs and bays indenting their territories with mouths wider than that of the Gulf of Aqaba as territorial."[90] This position regarding the Gulf of Aqaba became relevant in 1967, when India endorsed the Egyptian closure of the gulf to Israeli shipping, a move that precipitated the June war.

India's stance on the Gulf of Aqaba was political and disregarded reality. In its eagerness to support Egypt, it overlooked a number of crucial but uncomfortable geographical facts: (1) The Gulf of Aqaba has a multilateral shore, and even if Israel were to be excluded, the gulf has three other independent littoral states;[91] (2) the examples cited by Menon to justify the Gulf of Aqaba as territorial waters were fundamentally different, because the other examples wash the shores of only one sovereign state;[92] (3) the Gulf of Aqaba is the only sea outlet for Jordan, and thus declaring it as Egyptian territorial waters was harmful to the Hashemite Kingdom; and (4) the area claimed as territorial zones by the four littoral states far exceeded the total breadth of the gulf.[93] Taking these facts into consideration, India's future arguments during the 1967 crisis become weaker.

At another level, the Suez crisis marked a clear deterioration of Indo-Israeli relations. Soon after the tripartite aggression, Nehru formally ruled out the normalization of relations.[94] His strong support for Nasser brought some benefits, and the Egyptian leader overwhelmingly supported India's inclusion in the newly formed United Nations Emergency Force (UNEF), which was deployed along the Egyptian-Israeli border. This was in sharp contrast to Nasser's refusal to allow Pakistani participation in the UNEF. The only consolation for Israel was Nehru's unsuccessful attempts to stop Nasser from deporting Jewish persons from Egypt.[95]

This overt unfriendliness toward Israel, however, did not prevent Nehru from seeking its help in times of crisis.

The Sino-Indian War, 1962

The complexities of India's Israel policy came to forefront during the Sino-Indian war of 1962. The conflict along the Himalayas clearly exposed India's military weaknesses and the political naiveté of Nehru's China policy, and, above all, it shook his faith in nonalignment. The war came just a year after the Belgrade Conference, which heralded the NAM. While India had unequivocally joined the chorus against Israel during the Suez crisis, Egypt stayed neutral during the Sino-Indian war. President Nasser chose not to condemn China, although Nehru had hoped he would. Nasser felt a neutral stance was essential if Egypt planned "to mediate" between India and China.[96]

Military defeat, political isolation, and the abandonment of a friend resulted in Nehru seeking military help from Israel. Following the outbreak of the border war, he made a universal appeal for assistance and personally wrote to various international leaders, including Prime Minister David Ben-Gurion.[97] His negative attitude toward normalization and his high-profile criticism of Israeli aggression against Egypt in 1956 were temporarily forgotten, and he explicitly sought military aid from Israel. Sharing India's concerns, the Israeli premier extended political support and supplied certain quantities of small arms.[98] According to the veteran Arab journalist and Nasser's confidant Mohamed Hassanein Heikal, Nehru stopped his "dealings" with Israel as soon as the Egyptian leader raised objections.[99]

India was rather coy in acknowledging Israeli assistance; however, it was more than willing to remember and recognize the "understanding attitude" of the Arab states.[100] Such a duality is true also of the Indian intelligentsia, who justified and rationalized Nasser's neutrality but ignored Nehru seeking military help from Israel in times of crisis.[101] This Indian duality is neither new nor an aberration. In the late 1940s, India sought agricultural assistance from Israel even while opposing Israel's membership in the United Nations. In later years, it obtained help from Israel during military conflicts with Pakistan in 1965 and 1971 but was not prepared to admit them publicly.

Thus India was not averse to approaching Israel for security assistance, and Nehru himself established this precedent. At the same time, driven by other interests in the Middle East, it was unwilling to recognize such help in public. It was only after normalization that India gradually began admitting military-security help from Israel, and even this was slow and reluctant. But the absence of formal relations and lack of progress in that direction overshadowed the occasional bonhomie between the two states. So when Nehru passed away on May 27, 1964, normalization became an even more remote possibility, and India's unfriendliness gradually turned into hostility. Normalization became possible only when powerful and far-reaching international changes occurred. Those, however, were not immediately forthcoming.

In retrospect, it was perhaps a big blunder on India's part not to have established full diplomatic relations with Israel soon after it recognized the Zionist state in 1950. That would have at least spared some, on both sides, the grandiose speculations about the benefits that might have accrued to India had it exchanged diplomatic missions with Israel an early date. —*M. S. Agwani*

10 The Years of Hardened Hostility, 1964–1984

By the early 1960s, the absence of relations with Israel was well established, and India began to use this to further its interests in the Middle East. Following the death of Jawaharlal Nehru in May 1964, Lal Bahadur Shastri became India's prime minister. As far as foreign policy was concerned, his tenure, which lasted less than two years, was a transitory one. Shastri had the disadvantage of being overshadowed by Nehru's personality and legacy. Following Nehru's footsteps, especially on foreign policy, was the only option available to him. His maiden foreign visit as prime minister was to Cairo to attend the second summit of the Non-Aligned Movement. Unlike the Belgrade Summit of 1961, this meeting was more vocal on Israel. Hosted by President Gamal Abdel Nasser, it unequivocally condemned the "imperialistic policy pursued in the Middle East" and endorsed "the full restoration of all the rights of the Arab people of Palestine to their homeland, and their inalienable rights to self-determination." It also expressed its support for "the Arab people of Palestine in their struggle for liberation from colonialism and racism."[1] More than a decade before the notorious 1975 UN resolution on Zionism, the NAM perceived and presented the Palestinian problem as a struggle against racism. The willingness of the NAM to embrace a narrow Arab agenda was partly due to the absence of leaders such as Nehru and U Nu, who had exerted a moderating influence. As the host, Nasser had greater influence and leverage in formulating a hardline position.

As a sequel to the summit, in November that year, New Delhi hosted a delegation from the Nasser-sponsored and newly formed Palestine Liberation Organization. In a similar move, it became friendlier toward the Arab League. The Arab Information Office, which had been functioning in New Delhi since 1959, was granted diplomatic status in July 1965.[2] If one compares this upgrading to the April 1964 controversy over Israeli Independence Day, the contrast is obvious. The differential treatment reaffirmed India's predisposition in the Middle East. While the Israeli mission was a consulate in far-off Bombay, often seen as India's "diplomatic Siberia," the Arab League was represented by an embassy in the national capital and enjoyed immunities similar to those conferred upon the UN mission in India.[3]

The Indo-Pakistani war, which broke out in September 1965, tested the seriousness of Shastri's Israel policy. The general attitude of the Arab states ranged from noncommitment to overt sympathy for Pakistan. Most had not been prepared to support India in its war with atheist, communist China a few years back, and to expect them to be more supportive in 1965 was unrealistic. Backing India now would have to mean opposing the Islamic state of Pakistan, something the Arabs could not contemplate. New Delhi appreciated this Arab dilemma and played down the region's attitude to the war. While expressing its disappointment at individual Arab countries, such as Jordan and Saudi Arabia, it consoled itself in that "by and large" the Arab countries had shown an understanding of its position. India did not even complain about Iranian assistance to Pakistan during the war, feeling that such help had to be viewed within the context of the Central Treaty Organization (CENTO), of which both countries were members.[4] The role played by President Nasser, especially at the Casablanca Arab Summit in September 1965 in adopting a "balanced" position, received Indian appreciation.[5] At the same time, as in the past, during the conflict India approached Israel for limited military assistance, which it was given.[6] While following the policy of his predecessor, Shastri gave an institutional framework to India's pro-Arab policy, as exhibited through developments surrounding the NAM, Arab League, and PLO. However, a real deterioration in relations with Israel began when Indira Gandhi, Nehru's daughter, took over the reins of power. Both domestic and regional compulsions led to a downward spiral.

The Indira Gandhi Years (1966–1977)

In terms of its longevity and eventfulness, the initial stages of Indira Gandhi's administration were critical in hardening India's policy toward Israel. When she assumed office in January 1966, following the sudden death of Prime Minister Shastri in Tashkent, retaining the status quo was the best one could have hoped for. Instead, the world witnessed a gradual deterioration in bilateral interaction, with India becoming publicly hostile toward the Jewish state. This uninterrupted downward slide was due to the changing political scenario both within and outside the country. Soon after she came to power, the opposition made significant political gains in the 1967 Lok Sabha elections and eroded the strength of the Congress Party in the parliament and various state legislatures. The fluctuating popularity of the Congress Party resulted in Mrs. Gandhi being dependent upon small parties, especially the communist parties, which were critical of Israel, for her political survival.

These changes had a clear impact on domestic and foreign policy. In Nehru's time, parliamentary debates on foreign policy were initiated by the government. The official motion on the "international situation" was an annual fixture, and Nehru enjoyed responding to the opposition's queries and criticisms. This changed dramatically under Indira Gandhi. Despite the presence of a full-fledged foreign minister, it was the opposition that launched major debates on foreign policy over issues such as the June war, the Czechoslovakian crisis, the Rabat fiasco, or the recognition of East Germany. One could even suggest that under Mrs. Gandhi the government lost the initiative to a more articulate and well-prepared opposition. Official policy on Israel came under greater scrutiny and criticism. It was only after her party swept the 1971 Lok Sabha elections that the government became more confident on foreign policy.

If Nehru's tenure ended with a diplomatic row over Israel, Mrs. Gandhi's tenure began with one.

Diplomatic Discourtesy, 1966

In March 1966, less than two months after Indira Gandhi became prime minister, President Zalman Shazar of Israel made a seven-day state visit to Nepal, a country with whom Israel had good relations since the early 1950s.[7] Because of flight schedules, he made a brief stopover in New Delhi and stayed overnight in the eastern city of Calcutta. While no Indian official received him in the capital, the Israeli leader was greeted by a small demonstration in Calcutta.[8] When the opposition criticized the government for its "discourtesy," Foreign Minister Dinesh Singh admitted that no one "from the Ministry of External affairs received him. . . . But the arrangements were known to him."[9] The issue did not die down, and a few weeks later he informed the *Rajya Sabha*: "It is not that we extended our hospitality. We only extended our courtesies."[10]

The handling of another visit in the same month underscores the Indian attitude. Deputy Prime Minister Margarete Wittkowski of East Germany visited New Delhi before India had formally recognized East Berlin. She was received by none other than Foreign Minister Dinesh Singh. Though India had recognized Israel as early as September 1950, it chose not to extend any courtesy to President Shazar. India's assertion that Shazar was on a "private visit" through India was technically correct. But he was on a state visit to the neighboring country of Nepal and was compelled to stop in India for technical reasons.[11] The whole episode highlighted that India was not prepared to extend normal cordialities toward Israel. Before long, this attitude manifested more clearly.

The June War, 1967

The Arab-Israeli war of 1967 was a hotly contested foreign-policy issue in independent India's history. Neither the aggressive opposition nor the watchful media were prepared to accept the arguments and rationale put out by the government or the Congress Party. While they were unable to bring about any change, the government was certainly put on the defensive. Tension in the Middle East was mounting following President Nasser's decision on May 16 to demand the withdrawal of the United Nations Emergency Force (UNEF) from the Sinai Peninsula. This eventually culminated in a complete pullout of the UN peacekeeping force. A few days later, on May 25, India announced its position on the unfolding drama. This was only days away from Israel's first decisive move toward confrontation, namely, the appointment of Moshe Dayan as defense minister. More than ten days before the commencement of actual hostilities, in identical statements before both houses of parliament, External Affairs

Minister M. C. Chagla outlined the Indian position,[12] which had five important aspects. Each requires a close look.

1. *The creation of Israel had given rise to tension between Israel and the Arab countries.* In a somewhat similar fashion in 1958, Prime Minister Nehru told the Lok Sabha: "Ever since Israel came into existence, it has been a source of constant irritation to the Arab countries."[13] While Nehru's observation went unnoticed, Chagla's pronouncement sparked an acrimonious debate in parliament.

2. *The sovereign right of Egypt to demand the withdrawal of the UNEF could not be questioned.* This was in accordance with the Indian position since the formation of the UN peacekeeping force in November 1956.[14] In hindsight, it is clear that this move precipitated a full-fledged war.

3. *India appreciated the reasons that compelled President Nasser to demand the withdrawal of the UNEF from Egyptian soil.* This was in agreement with its general policy of supporting the Arab countries, especially in their conflict with Israel.

4. *The Gulf of Aqaba was part of the territorial waters of Egypt, and India appreciated their closure to Israeli shipping.* As discussed earlier, geographical fact does not support the Indian position. Hence, Nasser's action of closing the Gulf of Tiran in the Red Sea to Israeli shipping could only be interpreted as an act of belligerency.

5. *India foresaw a threat of aggression from Israel.* New Delhi anticipated Israeli aggression more than ten days before the commencement of the actual hostilities. Strangely, the government came to this assessment without a resident mission or even an Indian journalist being present in Israel. In the absence of first-hand information, let alone assessment, the government would have relied on reports filed by its missions in the Arab countries. In short, India was in no position to make an independent assessment of the unfolding drama in the Middle East.

According to Chagla, this controversial statement "was drafted by my Ministry [of External Affairs and] was finalized and approved by the Political Affairs Committee of the Cabinet."[15] Despite repeated pleas from the opposition, the government refused to modify its May 25 position.[16] Thus India approached the June war with this set of preconceived ideas and subsequently hardened its position as events unfolded.

Its stance on the Israeli offensive was unequivocal. Rejecting the opposition's suggestion for caution, Prime Minister Indira Gandhi declared:

"We have not made our mark in the world by being cautious. We have made our mark in the world by taking a firm stand where justice was concerned."[17] Following the war, the official position toward the war was summarized by Chagla, in a statement to the parliament on July 18: (1) it was not open to a country to start a war merely because it feels that a threat to its security exists, (2) no aggressor should be permitted to retain the fruits of its aggression, (3) it was not permissible for a country to acquire the territory of another state in order to be able to bargain from a position of strength, and (4) rights could not be established and territorial disputes cannot be settled through armed conflict.[18] These positions became pertinent when the UN Security Council (with India as a member) was deliberating the text of UN Resolution 242, adopted on November 22.[19]

Despite claims to the contrary, India's official policy did not enjoy the unanimous support of the Congress Party, parliament, the press, or the wider public.[20] The resolution adopted by the All-India Congress Committee on June 23 revealed internal divisions within the governing party. While expressing its concern and anxiety over the "recent developments which escalated into a war," it did not condemn Israel. This was in contrast to the official position, which had condemned Israel even before the first shots were fired.[21] Likewise, the statements of the government did not refer to "recent developments"—something the opposition wanted the government to take note of before condemning Israel. Furthermore, the AICC resolution did not refer to the killing of Indian soldiers, which Prime Minister Gandhi repeatedly highlighted to shore up support for the government in parliament.[22] Underscoring the internal divisions within the party, Chagla conceded: "I found that not only the opposition but even a section of our own party was opposed to our policy."[23] A public-opinion survey conducted in July 1967 revealed large-scale disapproval of the government's policy toward the June war.[24]

Sections of the Indian foreign office had serious reservations over the pro-Arab policy of the government. C. S. Jha, India's foreign secretary (permanent undersecretary in the ministry), was unusually candid in his memoirs, which were published more than a decade after the June war, when views sympathetic toward Israel were politically controversial. But Jha admitted:

> I felt that as a sincere friend of Egypt we should advise Nasser to rest on the withdrawal of the United Nations forces from Sinai and to go slow over the closing of the Straits of Tiran so as to avoid a disastrous

> war which would ill-serve the Arab countries. . . . I drafted a message from the Prime Minister to President Nasser pointing out the gravity of the situation and urging that Israel should not be given a pretext for going to war. . . . In the light of subsequent developments I have often regretted that we did not send that message and I have blamed myself for not pursuing further the proposal with [Foreign Minister] Chagla and with the Prime Minister.[25]

When and as official papers become public, one will find more evidence of internal disagreements. Undeniably, there was substantial opposition to the official policy.

The widespread disapproval of official policy, however, should not be considered support for the Israeli occupation of the West Bank, Gaza Strip, and Sinai Peninsula. Criticisms of the official policy were accompanied by a strong disapproval of Israeli actions. Even right-wing parties such as the Jan Sangh were not silent. As Craig Baxter observes, when it comes to the Middle East,

> the Jana Sangh opposed the openly pro-Arab position of the Government of India. It called on the Arabs to recognize and negotiate with Israel but said that *Israel should recognize its place in Afro-Asia, work with the Afro-Asians in scientific and technological cooperation, and not be "an instrument to western diplomacy."* Israel should withdraw its forces from occupied Arab territories and should work to resettle the refugees.[26]

Their primary complaint was the absence of "balance" in the official policy. As highlighted by the watered-down INC resolution and Chagla's remarks, this was true even for a section of the Congress Party and the foreign office.

The anti-Israeli stance adopted by the Indian government on the eve of the June war took a turn for the worse when Indian units of the UNEF faced the initial Israeli onslaught. The contingent had come to maintain peace between Egypt and Israel, got caught in the crossfire, and started taking casualties. By the time Israel completed its capture of the Gaza Strip, five Indian soldiers were killed and scores injured. India not only had a large presence in the UNEF[27] but also contributed "a Chief of Staff from April 1958 to February 1960 and two commanders Lt. Gen. Prem Singh Gyani from February 1960 to 1964 and [Maj. Gen. Inder Jit Rikhye] from February 1966 till the Force was withdrawn."[28] The killing of Indian peacekeepers created a major uproar in parliament. Passions ran high. In a hard-hitting statement, Prime Minister Indira Gandhi squarely blamed Israel for the death of the Indian peacekeepers. Expressing "grief and indignation" over the incident, she attributed the death to a "wanton Israeli artillery attack and subsequent strafing by Israeli aircraft." She described the attack as "deliberate and without provocation in spite of clear and unmistakable UN markings and identification of our contingent." Calling on the United Nations to ensure "their safety and early evacuation from the area of conflict," she declared: "There can be no justification for Israeli armed forces to have attacked our forces, whose whereabouts, identification markings and intention to withdraw were clearly known to the Israeli authorities."[29]

Foreign Minister Chagla told lawmakers that the government had registered a formal complaint with the Israeli government over the attack on the UNEF. A protest note was given to the Israeli ambassador in Moscow by his Indian counterpart; a copy was handed over to the Israeli consul in Bombay.[30] Subsequently, India rejected Israel's offer to pay compensation to the victims because "Israel refused to accept responsibility for the attack." Partly concurring with Indian anger, Maj. Gen. Inder Jit Rikhye, the commander of the UNEF in Gaza, observed that Indian troops

> were equally incensed by the allegations made by the Israelis and taken up by the Jews and pro-Jewish elements in other parts of the world, notably in the United States, that the Indian contingent had sided with the Arab forces in Gaza. The allegations were made without any foundation, and had apparently been triggered by incorrect reports filed by foreign press sources in Cairo to the effect that India and Yugoslavia had ordered unilateral withdrawal of their forces on 16th May when General [Mahmoud] Fawzy's letter was delivered to me. There were also reports, equally inaccurate, that India at the United Nations had urged the immediate withdrawal of UNEF, once Egypt had requested it. In fact, India's permanent representative [in New York], Ambassador G. Parthasarathy, in advising the Secretary-General had agreed with his Yugoslav colleague that Egypt had the right to withdraw its consent for the continued presence of UNEF on its soil, *yet had expressed caution on the question of the actual withdrawal of the Force.*[31]

Because it had initiated hostilities, Israel could not escape from criticism over the death of the peacekeepers.

At the same time, it is essential to recall that when India reacted to the killing, it was reacting on the basis of unconfirmed media reports. A detailed firsthand account of the hostilities and casualties was available only after June 26, when Rikhye reached New York and was contacted by the military adviser of India's UN mission.[32] This was nearly three weeks after the commencement of hostilities. Based on Rikhye's published account, a more complicated picture surrounding the Indian casualties emerges: (1) "It was the Arab mines placed on the railroad crossing south of Gaza that killed Captain Vijay Sachar and his fellow passengers in the car."[33] (2) Both Israeli shells and Arab mortar bombs killed and wounded soldiers at Camp Delhi near the Dier al-Balah railway station. (3) The Indian supply convoy returning from Rafah was caught in the advancing Israeli armor near Khan Yunis. (4) Consequent to the initial attacks, Indian soldiers took shelter in Egyptian trenches, and when the trenches were overrun by Israelis, they were taken prisoner. "The Israelis found the Indians carrying their personal weapons and assumed that they had been fighting along with the Egyptians."[34] (5) The Indian camp in Dier el Balah and the Palestinian defenses were in close proximity.[35] (6) The early withdrawal of the Canadian contingent seriously affected air transport and quick evacuation of the UNEF contingent in Gaza. (7) India, which was the first country to accept Nasser's demand for the withdrawal of the UNEF, "never earmarked any military air transport to support its contingent in Gaza."[36] (8) The baggage of the Indian contingent that reached Gaza via a chartered ship was an additional impediment to airlifting the troops, because "converting a shipload to an aircraft seemed an insuperable difficulty."[37] In other words, the unfortunate death of members of the Indian contingent was not as premeditated and cold blooded as New Delhi portrayed.

One could view the entire controversy differently. By focusing on the death of the Indian soldiers, it became relatively easier for New Delhi to enlist popular support for its policy toward the war. With mounting criticism from the opposition during the run up to the war, the UNEF episode enabled the government and the Congress Party to partly offset domestic resistance. The absence of relations with Israel and political compulsions to support Nasser further aggravated the tension over the casualties. Scores of Indian soldiers were killed in various peacekeeping operations both before and after the June war, but the UNEF episode remained a poignant moment for India and set the tone for the next crisis with Israel.

Rabat Conference, 1969

On August 21, 1969, a fire broke out in the al-Aqsa mosque in the old city of Jerusalem, again refocusing India's Middle East policy. The arson attack was carried out by a deranged Australian Christian tourist, and it enraged Muslims all over the world.[38] While physical damage to the mosque, the third-holiest shrine in Islam, was limited and subsequently repaired, it called into question the safety and well being of holy sites in the Israel-occupied old city of Jerusalem. Various countries witnessed large protests and demonstrations against the "burning" of the al-Aqsa mosque. With its large Muslim population, India was no exception. The government headed by Indira Gandhi refused to recognize the incident as an Islamic issue.[39] In its view, the episode raised questions about the rights of the Palestinians and the preservation of holy and sacred places. It joined other states in demanding the immediate implementation of the UN Security Council resolutions on Jerusalem.[40]

Expressing the "shock and pain" over the action, on August 26, Foreign Minister Dinesh Singh told the Lok Sabha: "I am sure the House will join me in expressing our strong condemnation of this act of desecration." He attributed this to the "continued occupation of Jerusalem by Israel in defiance of the resolutions of the United Nations."[41] A couple of days later, he depicted it as a "barbaric act." In his assessment, this was not a "Muslim question" but "the question of the right of conscience of humanity." He was joined by other parliamentarians who urged the government to seek UN sanctions against Israel. Some left-wing members blamed the United States as the real culprit and accused it of "encouraging" Israel to perpetrate such actions.[42] Speaking at a public rally in New Delhi on September 9, Prime Minister Indira Gandhi described it as an "unholy" and "deplorable" action.[43] The Muslim community was outraged; widespread protest rallies were held in different parts of the country. On August 29, an estimated ten million Muslims abstained from work in the eastern city of Calcutta. The rally warned Israel and its supporters that Muslims "all over the world will shed the last drop of their blood to restore sanctity to their holy places."[44] Similar rallies were held in Bombay, Hyderabad, Lucknow, and Kanpur.[45]

Apart from domestic considerations, India was worried over the rapidly changing political landscape of the Middle East. The defeat of Nasser in the June war robbed India of the ideological basis for its Middle East policy. Marginalization of the icon of Arab nationalism forced it to look for alternative powers with whom it could forge closer ties and redefine its policy. These considerations led Indian leaders to conveniently sidestep their commitments to secularism and jump on the conservative bandwagon. The al-Aqsa issue soon went to the UN Security Council. At that time, India was not a member of the council, but Pakistan was. This led to India seeking and securing an invitation to participate in the council deliberations. Its delegate argued:

> With its firm belief in secularism, [India] had felt especially grieved at the desecration of a place of worship, and numerous and religious leaders of many faiths had expressed their profound shock. Nevertheless, it must not be believed that the question before the Council was a *religious issue*. Any attempt to create such a division would do incalculable harm and present fresh difficulties in solving the West Asian problem. India considered that the incident was a direct consequence of the illegal occupation by Israel of Jerusalem and other Arab areas. Israel thus could not be absolved of its responsibility for the incident of 21 August 1969.[46]

As with many other incidents involving the Arab-Israeli conflict, the Indian leadership, especially the Congress Party, sought to give a secular spin to the al-Aqsa incident.

The countries of the Middle East, for whom the matter was serious, saw it through a simpler religious lens. An initial Egyptian suggestion for an Arab summit to discuss the issue was overruled in favor of a larger Islamic gathering. For the conservative monarchs of the region, the al-Aqsa incident presented a unique opportunity to formally marginalize Nasser and his secular brand of Arab nationalism. If his humiliating defeat in 1967 was a setback to his firebrand radical socialism, the al-Aqsa incident provided an opportunity to formalize the demise of Nasserism. Capitalizing on popular anger over the incident, King Faisal of Saudi Arabia joined hands with King Hassan of Morocco to call for an Islamic conference to discuss the al-Aqsa fire. This eventually led to the formation of the Organization of the Islamic Conference (OIC).[47]A two-day preparatory meeting comprising representatives from the Arab world

(Morocco and Saudi Arabia), Asia (Iran and Malaysia), and Africa (Niger and Somalia) was held in early September. It decided to convene a summit conference at Rabat, from September 22 to 24, 1969. It set two basic criteria for the invitees: countries with a Muslim-majority population or with a Muslim head of state.[48]

Even if one takes a politically correct interpretation of secularism, India did not meet the necessary conditions for attending the Rabat conference. Though it had one of the largest Muslim populations in the world, Muslims made up only about one-sixth of India's population. India had neither a Muslim majority nor was its head of state a Muslim, but it was keen to go to Rabat, pleading "that since it contains the third largest community of Muslims in the world, it should not be excluded from the Summit."[49] It feared that its absence would result in Pakistan dominating the deliberations, perhaps even forcing the participants to adopt an anti-India posture. As the region was so much outraged and unified over the incident, New Delhi wanted to express its sympathy and solidarity with the Arab and Islamic countries.

Apparently, there were no written invitations. As A. G. Noorani eloquently put it: "The preparatory conference of the Rabat conference did not invite India. How then did we come to be invited by the conference itself? Because we pressed for an invitation."[50] A more plausible explanation for the Indian interests came from the parliamentarian Saifuddin Soz, who observed:

> The question is whether India should have tried for an invitation or not? I feel strongly in favor of India's insistence for an invitation although the effort for participation was not vigorous enough to put India's case in proper shape. Egypt and Malaysia had supported India's claim to be invited to the Conference against Pakistan's tooth and nail opposition. [The Saudi monarch] King Faisal's compromise suggestion to allow an Indian delegation to represent Indian Muslims was finally approved. But, then a procedural mistake was committed which gave psychological advantage to President Yahya Khan of Pakistan. The moment it was announced that India's Industrial Development Minister Fakhruddin Ali Ahmed would lead India's delegation the next day and till then Ambassador Gurbachan Singh would represent India, Yahya Khan created a virtual hell for the conference questioning the credentials of Gurbachan Singh who was a non-Muslim.[51]

In the words of Surjit Mansingh: "The first Islamic Summit Conference opened with a hall filled with internationally known Muslim leaders, plus a fully bearded and turbaned Sikh representing India."[52] Echoing similar sentiments, J. N. Dixit, the former foreign secretary, remarked that while India was invited, "we botched up the opportunity by indulging in an impractical exercise in assertive secularism by deciding to depute our Sikh Ambassador in Morocco to represent India at this meeting. Pakistan took full advantage of this ineptitude of ours and ensured our exclusion from the OIC, despite our having the second largest Muslim population in the world."[53] No one could have scripted a greater irony: a turbaned Sikh diplomat at an Islamic gathering!

Pakistan capitalized on this ironic situation, and anti-Muslim riots in some parts of India provided additional ammunition. President Yahya Khan was joined by countries such as Iran, Jordan, and Turkey in eventually forcing India to "withdraw" from the Rabat conference. While India responded by recalling its ambassadors from Morocco and Jordan, the Rabat fiasco soon snowballed into a major domestic crisis and provided an opportunity for the opposition to challenge Mrs. Gandhi, who had just split the Congress Party and marginalized the powerful Syndicate faction within the party. The opposition moved a censure motion over Rabat, but the government managed to defeat it convincingly, by 306 to 140 votes.[54] The government relied on its secular spin and sought to convince parliament and the nation that "in spite of its name, [the Rabat conference] was a political conference and it was in India's interest to be represented in it."[55] Writing to a member of parliament, the prime minister observed that although it "formally styled itself as Islamic, its contents were intensely political."[56] However, when the watchful opposition demanded the government to table the "invitation," Prime Minister Indira Gandhi was unable to produce it.[57]

Certain broader issues emerge from the examination of the protracted and often acrimonious debates in both houses of parliament.

1. Despite India's peculiar interpretation, Rabat was an Islamic gathering in name, content, composition, and future course of action. If the conference was not religious but political, as claimed by India's government, Noorani's pointed challenge during the controversy becomes relevant: "why were such powerful supporters of the Arab cause as Russia and China not invited to the First Islamic Summit Conference?"[58]

2. Since the mid-1930s, Indian leaders had explained and justified their support for the Arabs in secular terms (as opposed to the religious logic of the Muslim League and, later on, Pakistan). Thus the Rabat fiasco was a setback to that logic.

3. The primary motive of the two sponsors, Saudi Arabia and Morocco, was to consolidate the defeat of Nasser and his brand of secular Arab nationalism, a principal plank of India's Middle East policy since the mid-1950s.

4. The Rabat conference underscored the emergence of Islamocentric politics (as opposed to Nasser's brand of secular Arab socialism) in the Middle East, and India was responding to these winds of change. Unfortunately, it could not be as vociferous as Pakistan. Thus its attempts in that direction proved counterproductive.

5. The Rabat episode was not unique. India had faced a similar humiliation at the World Muslim Conference in Somalia in December 1964.[59]

6. It was ironic that while India was keen to participate, two secular regimes in the region, Ba'athist Iraq and Syria, chose to stay away.

One thing was certain. India wanted to be at Rabat to counter Pakistan and present itself as a steadfast champion of the Palestinians. With the rapid raise of religious conservatism in the Middle East, it would have been prudent to abandon its secular framework in favor of the Islamic paradigm. India sought instead to gain some support in the Islamic world by presenting the al-Aqsa incident through a secular framework. This strategy misfired.

For much of the time, the Rabat conference was bogged down in resolving Indo-Pakistan tensions over Muslim representation. Reflecting on this irony, *The Washington Post* remarked that the Indo-Pakistani "conflict plunged the Islamic Summit Conference into disarray and set back Arab hopes of rallying the world's 500 million Muslims to support the Arab cause against Israel."[60] The conference almost collapsed over Indian participation, and India's secular credentials were dented irreparably. There are still voices within India that advocate institutional linkages with and even membership in the OIC.[61]

The Bangladesh War, 1971 and After

The Indo-Pakistan war of 1971 provided an opportunity for the government to test Arab goodwill. The civil-war situation that persisted in what was then East Pakistan since March of that year culminated in the secession and formation of Bangladesh in December 1971. Since India was largely instrumental in the whole process, how much support and understanding did it receive from the Middle East? Three distinct trends are noticeable.

First, the war once again highlighted the Arab and Middle Eastern commitment to Pakistan. For them, the situation in 1971 was more acute than during the Indo-Pakistan war of 1965. This time, India was instrumental in "cutting Pakistan to size." For the Arab states and Iran, this was blatant intervention in the "domestic" affairs of an Islamic state. Their support for Pakistan's territorial integrity far overwhelmed their sympathy for the victims of the brutality unleashed by the Pakistani military junta starting on March 25. Over two million civilians were killed or maimed, and thousands of women were raped by the army. Yet the Arab and Islamic countries were not prepared to support India. Countries such as Iran even provided limited military assistance to Pakistan. Even after the war, the Islamic world remained cautious in accepting the independence of Bangladesh. Reconciliation between the Islamic world and Bangladesh began only at the second OIC summit, hosted by Pakistan in Lahore in February 1974.

Second, the Indian interpretation of the Arab position is rather interesting. At one level, it was disappointed at the Arab attitude and their inadequate understanding of the crisis over Bangladesh.[62] Medical supplies and other assistance provided by the Arab countries figured prominently.[63] As in the past, India downplayed its disappointment with the political stance taken by the Arab countries.

Third, India had carefully avoided mentioning the aid provided by Israel during the crisis. It was not politically correct to admit receiving help from Israel when it was "dividing" an Islamic state. An open admission would have sent a wrong message to Islamic countries sympathetic to Pakistan. It was only after repeated questioning that the government acknowledged that on June 23 the Israeli Knesset had adopted a sympathetic resolution and that Israel offered to provide medical personnel to treat the millions of refugees who had fled to India.[64]

The unfriendly Arab attitude during the crisis rekindled fresh demands for a reassessment of India's policy toward the Arab states and Israel. The government was clear about its priorities, and Foreign Minister Swaran Singh told the parliament: "No passing of disappointment should mar these close relations [that is, between Arabs and India] which are in our mutual interests."[65] To put it mildly, India was more understanding of Arab support for Pakistan than the Arab countries were of the Indian position on Bangladesh.

The post-Bangladesh period witnessed a further deterioration in India's attitude toward Israel. A host of domestic and external factors contributed to this trend. The massive mandate secured by Indira Gandhi in the 1971 Lok Sabha elections and the military success over Bangladesh in December strengthened and consolidated her position and power. Coming out of the shadow of being Nehru's daughter, Indira Gandhi emerged as India's undisputed leader. The opposition, which had been needling the government over its Middle East policy, was decisively defeated. Parties sympathetic toward Israel, such as Swatantra and Jan Sangh, faced serious electoral reverses. These developments virtually eliminated the type of real opposition that was witnessed during the June war and the Rabat fiasco. Around the same time, Israel was facing increasing international isolation and condemnation over its policy regarding the territories it had occupied during the June war.

As a result, India's support for the Arabs during the October war of 1973 was a foregone conclusion. Even without the Arab threat of an oil embargo, it was overwhelmingly supportive of the Egypt-initiated war. It squarely blamed Israel for its refusal to vacate the occupied territories. "Intransigence" on the part of Israel, it argued, was the basic reason for the hostilities.[66] In December 1973, Foreign Minister Swaran Singh maintained that the "arrogance" of Israel and the active support it received from its "mighty friends" (an obvious reference to the United States) "had driven the Palestinians to measures of desperation."[67] Unlike the past, the official position was not seriously challenged either in the parliament or by the press. The post-1973 years witnessed the growing influence of the PLO. In October 1974, the Rabat summit of the Arab League recognized the PLO as the "sole and legitimate" representative of the Palestinians. This was followed by the decision of the United Nations to bestow "observer" status upon the PLO; the Palestinian leader Yasser Arafat addressed the world body on November 13, 1974. These events resulted in India recognizing the PLO and permitting an independent office in New Delhi.

India's Israel policy reached its nadir on November 10, 1975, when it joined with the Arab and Islamic states and voted for the notorious UN General Assembly Resolution 3379, which described Zionism as a form of racism and racial discrimination.[68] Justifying its stance, India argued, "in its impact on the people in the Middle East suffering from the consequences of Zionist occupation and operation, Zionism was clearly a form of racial discrimination."[69] Surprisingly, India's neighbors Bhutan and Nepal abstained during the controversial vote. Appreciation of Indira Gandhi's domestic situation partially explains India adopting such an extreme position. Having been disqualified for her electoral malpractices, she was fighting for political survival. Midnight, June 26, 1975, she imposed a state of internal emergency, arrested thousands of opposition leaders and activists, muzzled political dissent, and censored the media. Until the emergency was lifted, following Indira Gandhi's defeat in the Lok Sabha elections in March 1977, there was very little parliamentary discussion and none whatsoever on foreign affairs. Since freedom of expression was severely curtailed, it was unlikely that anyone would have offered any alternative views, let alone critical comments, on Israel.

These events highlight the pronounced pro-Arab thrust under Indira Gandhi. Even while being reluctant to normalize relations, Nehru had avoided making harsh public remarks against Israel. The converse was true for his daughter. Adopting an openly belligerent position was perceived to be in India's interest. There were not many known political or nonpolitical contacts with Israel during her tenure. It was during this period, especially after the October war, that India added a new hurdle, refusing visas to Israeli passport holders. A significant number of Israeli scientists, professional athletes, and other leading figures were denied permission to attend international gatherings hosted and organized by India.[70] This policy was briefly relaxed during the tenure of the Janata government, but it was revived with vigor after Indira Gandhi returned to power in 1980. Thus, when Indira Gandhi lost the elections in March 1977, Indo-Israeli relations were at their worst.

Janata and After (1977–1980)

In early 1977, the Janata Party, an amalgamation of various opposition parties that contested the election on an anti-INC platform, won an unexpected victory in the Lok Sabha elections. They formed the first non-INC government in New Delhi, under the leadership of Morarji Desai.[71] Despite its brief tenure, which was riddled with infighting and lacked focus, the Janata government ushered in some noticeable changes regarding Israel. Its coalition consisted of erstwhile noncommunist opposition parties such as Jan Sangh and the Praja Socialist Party, who were supportive of Israel and were critical of the policies of the INC governments. Atal Behari Vajpayee, a Jan Sangh leader and vocal supporter of Israel, became foreign minister. Naturally, there were hopes that India would reverse the past INC policy on Israel. However, political parties and individuals tend to behave differently once they assume positions of responsibility, and the Janata Party was no exception. Vajpayee was quick to allay fears over impending normalization of relations with Israel. In his first public statement, he declared that while recognizing Israel's right to exist, India could not support the forcible occupation of the Arab lands. The formation of a separate Palestinian state, he felt, was an essential precondition for peace in the Middle East.[72] At the same time, a couple of developments during Desai's tenure revealed that the new government was not averse to pursuing a different course on Israel. One was the Camp David accords signed between Israel and Egypt in September 1978; the other was the incognito visit of Moshe Dayan, Israel's foreign minister, to India.

Broadly speaking, the government of Morarji Desai was favorably disposed toward the first peace agreement between Israel and an Arab country. Welcoming direct talks between the warring nations, India hoped that a peaceful resolution would result in the Israeli withdrawal from the occupied territories. Adopting a more liberal interpretation of UN Security Council Resolution 242, it hoped that "boundaries between states should be settled through negotiations and not by force and all states in the region, including Israel, should have the right to exist in peace within secure boundaries."[73] This formulation reflected the true spirit and substance of the UN resolution, namely, "within secured and recognized boundaries." In the past, India had harped on the Israeli occupation and demanded unconditional withdrawal as a precondition for peace. Furthermore, at that time Israeli peace proposals included phrases such as "negotiated settlement" and "secured borders." That New Delhi was now using similar terminology underscored a significant concession to Israel.

The Camp David accords were not popular in the Middle East. A number of players, including Iraq, Syria, and the Palestinians were vehemently opposed to President Anwar Sadat abandoning Arab rejectionism enshrined in the Khartoum Declaration of September 1967.[74] For them, Sadat, who advocated a negotiated political settlement with the Jewish state, was abandoning larger Arab interests in favor of narrow Egyptian national interests. For making peace with Israel, Egypt paid a political price: it was excluded, isolated, and eventually expelled from the Arab League. This regional unpopularity naturally influenced the Indian stance, and it began underlining the deficiencies in the Egyptian-Israeli peace accord.[75] It felt that the question of Palestinians and their inalienable rights were ignored and that the Camp David agreement was silent on the status of Jerusalem.[76] Not to antagonize the Arab countries, at the Havana NAM summit in September 1979, it joined with other nations and condemned the Camp David accords. Egypt, however, had one consolation. Despite strong pressure from some Arab members, India refused to endorse their demand to expel Egypt from the NAM.[77] The NAM was one of the very few multilateral forums that retained Egypt as its member while it was expelled from the Arab League and OIC. Those were the punishments for making peace with Israel.[78]

A more sympathetic view of the Desai government emerged after the secret visit of the former Israeli general Moshe Dayan. There are different accounts about the timing of the incognito visit of the Israeli foreign minister. In his memoirs, Dayan placed it in August 1977, or within weeks after the Janata government came to power.[79] According to Desai, however, the visit took place in early 1978.[80] During an election rally in May 1980, Prime Minister Indira Gandhi claimed that Dayan had come to India more than once.[81] External Affairs Minister P. V. Narasimha Rao went a step further and, intervening in a debate in the Lok Sabha in June 1980, he declared: "While we have complete information about Moshe Dayan's visit to Delhi in August 1977, the statements of the leaders of the Janata and the BJP point to the possibility of more visits than one, namely, one in 1977, another in 1978, and perhaps a third in 1979."[82] Evidently, the issue gave some political mileage to the Congress Party to belittle and discredit the already trounced Janata Party.

Discussions, both inside and outside the parliament, indicate the following broad points:

- Despite the controversy surrounding the exact timing and frequency, there was no doubt that Foreign Minister Moshe Dayan came to India when Desai was prime minister. According to Foreign Minister Rao, the visit took place on August 15, 1977, the day India was celebrating its thirty-first independence day; Dayan left for Bombay the following day.[83]

- Since the visit of Israeli Minister Yigal Allon to attend an international conference in 1965, this was perhaps the first visit to India by an important Israeli functionary.
- The visit was due to the Israeli desire to explore the possibilities of a improvement in relations in the wake of political changes in both countries.[84]
- Conceding that India should have established full relations soon after its recognition in September 1950, Desai expressed his inability to modify the situation unless Israel withdrew from the occupied territories.[85]
- The visit was not made public because of its explosive nature, and in the words of Dayan, "If the news of my visit to him [Desai] now were to be published, he said, he [Desai] would be out of office."[86]
- The INC government, which came to power in January 1980, claimed there were no official records on the substance of the meeting.[87]
- Dayan was unable to achieve his basic objective, namely, an improvement in Indo-Israeli relations. Some suggested that Dayan's primary goal was "to upgrade the Israeli Consulate in Bombay to a Consulate-General and further to shift it to Delhi."[88] Even this did not happen.
- A sensitive foreign-policy matter became a domestic political battle when Prime Minister Indira Gandhi disclosed Dayan's visit during an election rally on May 10, 1980. There followed a heated debate both inside and outside the parliament.[89] Foreign Minister Rao, however, maintained that the visit was first disclosed by a New York newspaper, *News and Cine India*, on April 26, 1979, and was picked up and repeated by various other media outlets, including Israel Radio.[90]
- The government of Indira Gandhi maintained that Dayan's visit had "damaged India's image" and "lowered India's prestige" in the Arab world.[91]
- The visit was apparently organized by the Israeli businessman Shoul Isenberg.[92] Around the same time, he initiated military ties between Israel and China, long before normalization of relations between the two countries.[93]

The incognito visit was not entirely futile, as there were some noticeable changes in India's overall policy. Without disclosing Dayan's visit,

Desai apparently suggested ways of settling the Arab-Israeli problem and "shared his ideas and the Israeli reaction with Egyptian Vice President [Hosni] Mubarak and the Syrian President [Hafiz al] Assad, when they visited Delhi."[94] There were other high-level contacts between the two countries during the Janata period, including a reported meeting between Desai and Defense Minister Ezer Weizman.[95] New Delhi also relaxed passport regulations, and Israel was dropped from the list of countries where Indian passports were declared "not valid."[96]

The Desai government's favorable disposition toward Israel, especially over the Camp David accords, did not go down well with a large segment of the political circles. During the campaign for the Lok Sabha elections, Jagjivan Ram, a senior cabinet colleague of Desai and now the leader of the Janata Party in parliament, met Arab ambassadors in New Delhi and assured them of the continued support of the party.[97] During the election campaign, various parties vied with one another to express and exhibit their pro-Palestinian credentials.[98] For its part, the Congress Party and its leadership used Dayan's visit to depict the Janata Party as an anti-Muslim force during the state elections in the early 1980s. There were disagreements even within the Janata ranks. Secretary General of the Party Madhu Limaye publicly declared that India "has no reason to extend a welcome to the Camp David accord."[99] Another senior leader, Jagjivan Ram, a former defense minister, took exception and claimed that the cabinet "generally was not informed about the visit."[100]

The policy of the Janata government toward Israel was one of "continuity and change": *continuity* in the sense that it was unable to normalize relations and *change* because it was prepared to explore new avenues. Even while adhering to India's support for the Palestinians, it was not averse to establishing formal and informal contacts with Israel. Considering the internal differences within the ruling coalition and its short tenure, it is futile to speculate how India's policy toward Israel would have evolved had Desai's government continued in power for a full five-year term.

Indira Gandhi, 1980–1984

Internal squabbles and disagreements among the coalition partners led to the premature demise of the Janata experiment. Capitalizing on the lack of governance, Indira Gandhi won the January 1980 Lok

Sabha elections and returned to power. Dayan's secret visit became a political football when assembly elections were held that summer. She sought to discredit the opposition by presenting them as being unsympathetic toward the Palestinians and of trying to bring India closer to Israel. At the bilateral level, Indira Gandhi strengthened the pro-Arab policy. In one of her first major foreign-policy moves, in March 1980 she granted full diplomatic recognition to the Palestine Liberation Organization. The Palestinian mission in New Delhi was upgraded to an embassy and endowed with full diplomatic immunities and privileges. The Israeli consular mission was still languishing in Bombay. Though staffed by career diplomats, New Delhi continued to treat the Israeli mission merely as a consular office and rejected periodic requests to raise its status to that of a consul general or to extend its jurisdiction beyond the state of Maharashtra.

Even this limited Israeli presence was curtailed following a controversial interview by Israeli Consul Yossef Hassin. Speaking to the Bombay-based weekly *Sunday Observer* near the end of his tenure, he charged that Indian politicians "are afraid of the Arabs, they are afraid that Iraq will cancel their contracts, Saudi Arabia will stop accepting laborers. . . . India is always asking for floor at the UN and other international forums to denounce Israel and prove to the Arabs that you are doing more than Pakistan. That way you think you will impress the Arabs."[101] He was not saying anything new. Opposition figures had long accused the INC government of reducing India to the "fourteenth Arab state" or *chaprasi* (a peon or messenger, depending on the context) of the Arabs. This time, the criticism came from a foreign consul, and the government was not prepared to accept such an undiplomatic and intemperate outburst—especially given that bilateral relations were anything but cordial. To make matters worse, the interview appeared on June 27, 1982, less than three weeks after the Israeli invasion of Lebanon and mounting international criticism. The Israeli consul was declared *persona non grata* and was asked to leave the country within forty-eight hours. This was the first time in the history of India that a foreign official was forced to leave the country for making hostile remarks.[102] There were speculations that it was only under intense American pressure that New Delhi resisted the temptation to close the Israeli mission.[103] While Hassin was promoted within the foreign ministry, Israel had to wait for more than six years to nominate his successor. In the interim, the consulate in Bombay was manned by technical personnel.[104]

India hosted the ninth Asian Games in 1982. This event once again highlighted Israel's misfortunes. Ever since India had hosted the first games in 1951, Israeli participation had been erratic. While Iran was prepared to invite Israel, with whom the shah had good relations, countries such as Indonesia were not prepared to accept Israeli athletes. To overcome this problem, during the 1982 New Delhi Games, a new Olympic Council of Asia was formed without Israel; this institutionalized Israel's exclusion from the Asian Games.[105] Moreover, under Indira Gandhi, India was highly restrictive in granting visas to Israeli passport holders, and Israeli citizens and athletes could not attend various conferences and competitions hosted by India. Even Israeli citizens of Indian origin faced difficulties in obtaining visas to visit their families in India.

If all this was not enough, since the mid-1970s, international attitudes turned hostile toward Israel. Due to the dynamics of the cold war and oil crisis, many Third World countries felt it prudent to join with the Arab countries and began curtailing their political and economic contacts with Israel. Even African countries, which benefited from Israel, turned their back on the country following the oil crisis. Anti-Israeli rhetoric became the theme song of NAM summits, and Israel's political interaction was increasingly confined to the West. When Prime Minister Indira Gandhi was assassinated in October 1984, Indo-Israeli relations were at rock bottom. They could only improve. And they did improve, eventually.

The international situation has no doubt changed considerably but my gut feeling is that even if Indira Gandhi or Rajiv Gandhi were in office today, they would still be wearing blinkered glasses. In contrast [Prime Minister P. V. Narasimha] Rao, though an elder statesman, comes out as a refreshingly pragmatic and unorthodox politician. —*Joseph Leibler, co-chairman, World Jewish Congress*

11 Prelude to Normalization

On January 29, 1992, India became the last major non-Arab and non-Islamic state to establish full diplomatic relations with Israel. While the final credit went to Prime Minister P. V. Narasimha Rao, much of the ground work was done by Rajiv Gandhi. During his tenure as prime minister between 1984 and 1989, Gandhi made a number of small but significant moves toward Israel, repaired some of the damages of the past, and started a process that eventually bore fruit a few years later. He approached the Middle East with an open mind and had a genuine desire to explore new avenues. His failure to take the process to its logical conclusion underscored not only the limitations of India's Israel policy but also Gandhi's own personality.

The 1980s saw Rajiv Gandhi's political baptism, ascent to the highest elected office in the country, electoral debacle, and brutal assassination. On October 30, 1984, literally hours after security guards assassinated his mother, Indira Gandhi, Rajiv was sworn in as India's youngest prime minister. Until that moment, he had never held any official position.[1] He showed himself to be a different kind of politician. His absence of ideological orientation and refusal to see things within a narrow historical context were his greatest assets as well as his impediments. Notwithstanding limited political experience and acumen, he led the Congress

Party to a spectacular victory in the December 1984 Lok Sabha elections. He secured an unprecedented four-fifths majority in parliament, a feat that eluded even his grandfather, Jawaharlal Nehru. Despite his limited exposure to international diplomacy—or because of it[2]—he had a keen interest in foreign policy and traveled widely, met every major political leader in the world, took part in numerous conferences, and addressed a wide range of international gatherings.[3]

Though he promised to tread a traditional path, the ideological rhetoric of the past had no attraction for the young leader. From the very beginning, Rajiv opted for modernization and carrying the country forward into the twenty-first century. Moving away from the socialist tradition of the Congress Party, he looked to liberalization as a key instrument in India's economic progress and prosperity. His commitment to technology and modernization endeared him to the West. His penchant for summits, accords, agreements, and other political adventures should be seen in this context. Indeed, his interest in foreign affairs continued even after he lost the election in 1989. During the Kuwait crisis he sought, for the first time in Indian history, to conduct a parallel foreign policy from the opposition ranks. Though the eventual results of his efforts were mixed and remain questionable at times, these initiatives highlighted his openness towards foreign policy. This fresh approach was also visible in his Israel policy. The younger Gandhi had the opportunity, desire, and, above all, a massive parliamentary mandate to approach the Middle East differently. And he did.

The prevailing international climate of the 1980s was favorable toward his style of governing. There was a substantial reduction in international tension, despite the Soviet occupation of Afghanistan and prolonged Iran-Iraq war. Even these two problems were showing signs of stalemate. Until the outbreak of the Palestinian intifada in December 1987, the overall climate in the Middle East was relatively favorable and less hostile toward Israel. For the first time in many years, the Jewish state was not seen as the root cause of regional instability. Around the same time, Mikhail Gorbachev arrived on the international scene and slowly heralded the end of the cold war, a move that immensely benefited Israel. The later half of the 1980s saw a renewal of low-level contacts between Israel and the countries of eastern Europe. The international media was rife with reports of Sino-Israeli military relations even while Beijing continued its public rhetoric against the Jewish state.[4] The communist bloc that provided the ideological basis for Third World hostility gradually sought rapprochement with Israel. Notwithstanding the Camp David accords, Egypt was being admitted into the Arab League and the Organization of Islamic Conference (OIC). This signaled an Arab and Islamic inclination toward a possible reconciliation with Israel. Within India's neighborhood, Sri Lanka showed that it was possible to cooperate with Israel even in the field of intelligence without inviting Arab retribution. These developments clearly underlined that if handled properly, ties with Israel would not evoke hostile reactions from the Middle East.

How did Rajiv Gandhi capitalize on these favorable circumstances? How much did he differ from his predecessors in dealing with Israel? What were the changes he introduced regarding Israel? How were they received both within and outside the country? Despite his intentions, why did he fail to carry the process forward and normalize relations with the Jewish state?

Improving Signs

Unlike his predecessors, Rajiv Gandhi openly met Israeli officials and U.S. groups promoting Israel's foreign-policy interests. While he avoided making any categorical statement in favor of normalization, his actions revealed a shift in Indian perceptions. The issue of normalization figured prominently in his discussions with leading American officials and was widely reported in the Indian media. There appears to be a link between these meetings and the gradual relaxation of India's position on Israel. Through these less visible gestures, Gandhi sent positive signals toward Israel.

Like many of his predecessors, Rajiv Gandhi was under considerable pressure from Jewish and pro-Israeli organizations in the United States over normalization. Since the late 1940s, Israel figured prominently in the Indo-U.S. dialogue, and during his tenure these pressures became more frequent and reasonably successful. While seeking to promote Israel's interests, its supporters in the United States did not hesitate to occasionally use pressure tactics against India. For example, partly to influence New Delhi's decision regarding the Davis Cup tennis tie with Israel, in May 1987 the influential Anti-Defamation League of B'nai Brith (ADL) brought out an indictment against India.[5] Recalling a series of past incidents when India refused to grant visas to Israeli nationals and highlighting its "anti-Israel" statements and actions, the report warned that the international community should "let India know that unless it ceases to inject its anti-Israeli politics into events aimed at furthering the spirit of international cooperation, it will be forced to forfeit its frequent role as host nation." It also condemned India for its "frequent disregard for minimum standards of civility and law required among nations." This harsh report was followed by a move by the U.S. Congress to reduce aid to New Delhi from US$60 million to US$35 million.[6]

On April 18, 1985, a few months after Rajiv Gandhi's electoral victory, the Israeli radio reported that the National Unity Government headed by Shimon Peres had asked a British Jewish businessman to explore the mood in New Delhi. A few months later, during the fortieth UN General Assembly session, Prime Minister Gandhi met Peres. This was probably the first meeting between the prime ministers of the two countries since 1948. Unlike similar high-profile encounters at the United Nations between Israeli and Chinese leaders, the Rajiv-Peres meeting did not lead to any dramatic changes. It was important simply because of the absence of such high-level contacts in the past. One small result of this meeting was that a few months later, Israel was able to post a regular vice-consul at Bombay. Ever since Yosef Hassin was declared *persona non grata* in 1982, India had refused Israeli requests to send a successor. According to one leading Indian commentator, this should have happened earlier but was delayed due "to obstruction by South Block [where the Indian Foreign Ministry is located] officials."[7] Like the US State Department, the Indian foreign-policy establishment had its share of Arabists who were comfortable with the status quo.

A couple of years later, Rajiv Gandhi met a group of pro-Israeli leaders in New York.[8] Before reaching American shores, Gandhi undertook a high-profile state visit to Syria, where he reiterated New Delhi's traditional commitment to the Arab position. Besides a long working meeting with President Hafez al-Assad of Syria, the Indian leader visited the ruins of Kuneitra, destroyed by Israel during the June war. Gandhi had a different agenda in New York. This "casual encounter," as it was depicted in the Indian media, was arranged by Congressman Stephen Solarz, a Democrat from New York City, the chairman of the House subcommittee on Asian and Pacific Affairs, and a champion of Indian issues in the U.S. Congress. Prominent among Gandhi's interlocutors during the June 8, 1988, meeting were Morris Abrams, the head of the Conference of Presidents of Major Jewish Organizations, a powerful umbrella body of thirty-eight Jewish associations, and his deputy Malcolm Hoenlin.

The question of diplomatic relations and the difficulties facing Israelis in securing Indian visas figured in the hour-long discussion.[9]

The mood in Israel was upbeat, and a possible diplomatic breakthrough with India became a political battle between Prime Minister Yitzhak Shamir and Foreign Minister Peres, the rival leaders of the National Unity Government. Hours after Gandhi met Solarz and his friends, the Israeli media quoted Peres as saying that the upgrading "was supposed to happen a week ago or something like that. Take another two weeks. History can wait for another two weeks." At the same time he cautioned by saying that "it will be a limited rise. By the way, we are not talking about a substantial rise." Interestingly, when this news was leaked, Gandhi was still in the United States, and the Indian foreign office did not know much about the meeting and its contents. There were no dramatic announcements, as some had wished. But before long, Amos Radian, the Israeli vice-consul in Bombay, was elevated to the pre-1982 position of consul. In early 1989, he was succeeded by Giora Becher, who became the first Israeli to be sent to Bombay as consul since 1982. Indian officials maintained that Gandhi's New York encounter and this elevation were "a pure coincidence." In the words of one official: "The decision was taken much earlier. The meeting with Jewish leaders in New York was a *fait accompli* and we could hardly say no."[10]

In January 1989, India hosted two American groups that were working toward ending Israel's diplomatic isolation. A three-member ADL delegation and Congressman Solarz, who visited New Delhi, had a common agenda: normalization. While the ADL mission did not meet Prime Minister Gandhi, it met Foreign Minister Narasimha Rao and the ministry's joint secretary, P. K. Singh.[11] Two members of the ADL delegation, Burton S. Levins and Abraham Foxman, were signatories to the 1987 ADL report that was highly critical of India's visa policy. Upon returning to the United States, the third member, Jesse N. Hordes, concluded that the "basic decision to change direction had already been made." At the same time he warned: "anything short of full diplomatic relations within a reasonably limited timeframe will constitute a great disappointment for Israel's friends."[12] Shortly after the visit, the government of India instructed the state-government authorities in Maharashtra to invite the Israeli consul to all official functions. In the past, he was pointedly excluded from such occasions, which was a major embarrassment for Israel. The question of normalization figured prominently in the talks between Indian leaders and Solarz. Foreign Minister Narasimha Rao took the unprecedented step of briefing the U.S. visitors about the steps that India had taken in that direction, such as upgrading the consular mission in Bombay. Shortly before the visit, consular jurisdiction was extended to the southern Indian state of Kerala, which has a significant Jewish population.[13]

Rajiv Gandhi's approach toward Israel was also influenced by shared security concerns over Pakistan, which was India's major preoccupation, especially during his tenure.

Since the early 1980s, security debates inside India were dominated by Pakistan's strategic ambitions and its clandestine nuclear-weapons program. Such concerns led to growing speculations of India following Israel's example and conducting an Osiraq-type preemptive strike against Pakistan's nuclear facility at Kahuta.[14] Its leaders had dismissed such reports publicly as farfetched speculations. In an interview to *Le Monde* in June 1988, Rajiv was emphatic: "We try not to conduct ourselves as certain other countries do." When the same interviewer asked about normalization of diplomatic relations, he observed: "If Israel changes its attitude on a number of subjects, yes. But for the moment, we consider Israel to be very bellicose and oblivious to the problems it has created."[15] Media speculation, however, did not die down. In July of that year, with the help of satellite photos supplied by the convicted U.S. spy Jonathan Jay Pollard, senior Israeli diplomats reportedly met Rajiv Gandhi's emissary in Paris. Both sides discussed the common threat posed by Pakistan's nuclear program.[16] For operational and political considerations, Israel apparently sought India's active participation and cooperation. The air base in Jamnagar, near the Indo-Pakistani border, was mentioned as a possible refueling site. Quoting the former Israeli military intelligence chief Aharon Yariv, the Indian journalist Bharat Karnad disclosed that "several approaches [were made] over the years . . . to New Delhi, *some predating the 1981 Israeli bombing of the Iraqi reactor near Baghdad*, for assistance in hitting Pakistani nuclear installations."[17]

Rajiv Gandhi's frequent references to Pakistan's nuclear program and some of his controversial statements added fuel to the preemptive-strike theory. For instance, addressing the officers of the National Defence College in October 1985, he warned: "We know and are fairly sure that the program has been financed not solely by Pakistan but also by other countries. Will this mean that the weapon will be available to these countries? How will these countries use the weapons?"[18] A couple of years later, he again referred to external financial assistance for Pakistan's nuclear program. In early 1987, the *Washington Times* quoted him as saying that an Arab-funded Pakistani bomb would be Islamic and could be made available to Arab countries. Such accusations were not new. Since the late 1970s, various Indian and Western studies focused on the Islamic aspect of Pakistan's nuclear program.[19] Fears were expressed over the possibility of Islamabad reciprocating Arab financial support by sharing its nuclear technology with the donors. Gandhi became the first and so far the only Indian leader to express such an apprehension in public. His concerns vis-à-vis Pakistan coincided with the commonly held view over the nonconventional ambitions of "irresponsible states," but his public remarks displeased the Arabs.

The much-hyped Osiraq-type attack against Pakistan never materialized. The Indian reluctance to join with Israel and pursue a military option against the Pakistani nuclear program was logical and inevitable. While it would gain certain tactical benefits, a preemptive strike against Islamabad's premier nuclear facility would have gone against India's larger interests. With vital national installations such as oil refineries, nuclear facilities, and other economic targets lying within the striking range of retaliatory air strikes by Pakistan, the long-term strategic benefits of an Osiraq-type operation were limited and indeed remain counterproductive. Any open collaboration with Israel on an aggressive defense policy was politically costly for India, especially when it lacked the type of superpower guarantees that Israel managed to secure following the Osiraq bombing. Interestingly, much of the speculation occurred against the backdrop of the December 1985 understanding between Rajiv Gandhi and President Zia ul-Haq of Pakistan, whereby both countries agreed not to target each other's nuclear installations. Delays in implementing this oral understanding partly contributed to the continued speculation.[20]

However, the most visible manifestation of a shift in India's Israel policy manifested in the nonpolitical arena, especially sports. Rajiv Gandhi's decision to host the Davis Cup quarter-finals tennis match in July 1987 was the most crucial development that indicated a reappraisal of India's Israel policy.[21] It was also the most controversial Indian decision since the incognito visit of Moshe Dayan in 1977, when the Janata government was in power.[22] Lobbying in favor of the match, the Indian tennis star Vijay Amritraj vehemently argued that the tie against Israel "might be our last big chance to go some distance in Davis Cup."[23] The likely punitive sanction from the International Tennis Federation was a major consideration.[24]

Unlike the "ping-pong" diplomacy between China and the United States,[25] the Davis Cup tennis tie did not mark any dramatic change in India's policy. It, however, generated a lively debate over the prolonged absence of diplomatic relations with Israel. Saner voices were heard not only over the depoliticization of sports but on the need to reevaluate India's policy. Until then, the negative publicity over the Israeli invasion of Lebanon and the Sabra-Shatila massacres prevented any meaningful debate over normalization. The Davis Cup atmosphere changed that. Senior figures such as C. Subramaniam, the former cabinet minister under Indira Gandhi, joined Israel's traditional supporters. He sought to break the popular tendency of linking Israel with apartheid South Africa and publicly asked: "[Do] we need to be more Arab than Egypt?"[26] The issue dominated the front pages of Indian newspapers for well over four months. Rajiv Gandhi eventually gave the games the green light.[27]

There were also noticeable changes in India's attitude regarding the granting of visas to Israeli passport holders. Thanks to dual passports, preventing Israelis from entering became a futile exercise.[28] Even when tighter visa restrictions were in force, some Israeli diplomats managed to visit and tour India using their second passports.[29] When the ADL highlighted some prominent cases where visas were denied, Rajiv Gandhi relaxed the procedures. The restrictions imposed upon Israelis of Indian origin were lifted, and the Israeli consulate in Bombay was authorized to coordinate the processing of their visa applications with the government of Maharashtra.[30] During his tenure, individual and group tourists from Israel were given Indian visas. In the absence of representation in Israel, the task was given to Indian missions in New York and London, which processed the visa applications. Israeli participation in international conferences in India was allowed under certain conditions: the participation had to be in their individual capacity and not as the official representatives of Israel. Local organizers were encouraged to avoid publicity about Israeli participation.[31] In practice, there was no uniformity. In October 1988, an Israeli was elected president of the International Hotel Association during its conference in New Delhi. Ironically, the conference was inaugurated by Rajiv Gandhi.[32]

Bilateral trade also showed some improvement. Existing trade was dominated by a group of Indian diamond merchants based in the Tel Aviv suburb of Ramat Gan. They began operating in the late 1970s and emerged as the prime force behind trade in precious stones. This relatively unpublicized activity came into the open in 1986, when the Damascus-based

Arab Boycott Office blacklisted twenty-nine Indian diamond firms for trading with Israel. Following Rajiv Gandhi's assassination in May 1991, the Indian diamond community in Israel issued a public advertisement in the *Jerusalem Post* mourning the tragic loss.[33] It is also worth noting that in November 1988 the Manufactures Association of Israel and the All-India Association of Industries signed a cooperative agreement in Bombay.

Rajiv Gandhi's openness toward Israel was manifested in India's reaction to some of problems facing the Middle East.

At one level, the Indian leader was not eager to play any mediatory role in the Arab-Israeli conflict. On more than one occasion he expressed reluctance to get entangled in the Middle East cobweb. Dismissing any role in the peace process, in 1986 he candidly admitted: "There are already so many parties involved, we would not like to add one more hand in the complicated situation. We prefer to watch for a while and see how things turn out before actively trying to take an interest in it."[34] At the same time, he was tacitly signaling the need for the Arabs to seek a negotiated settlement with Israel. In June 1985, few months after assuming office, Gandhi paid a state visit to Egypt and reaffirmed India's longstanding support for Arabs and the Palestinians. Since the early 1950s, Egypt had dominated India's Middle East policy and, during Nehru's times, even dictated India's agenda toward Israel. This bonhomie began to wane in the wake of the Arab debacle in the June 1967 war and the resurgence of conservative forces in the Middle East. Thus the timing of Rajiv Gandhi's visit to Cairo is interesting. Egypt had yet to recover from regional opposition to its peace with Israel. While it managed to stay within the NAM, thanks partly due to India, it still remained suspended from the Arab League and the OIC. Gandhi's visit to Egypt was a welcome relief to the beleaguered Egyptian leader, Hosni Mubarak, and an affirmative move in favor of the Camp David accords and peace with Israel. Signs of Indian moderation were visible toward the Palestinians as well. At one level, it strongly condemned Israeli air raids against the PLO headquarters in Tunis in 1985 as "aggressive and expansionist" and portrayed them as a "threat to peace and security."[35] Simultaneously, it was not prepared to go along with the Arab states in expelling Israel from the United Nations. Likewise, even in the wake of the intifada and its decision to recognize the state of Palestine, India reiterated its commitment to Israel's right to exist in peace.

Despite these favorable signs and tentative steps, the overall transformation of the policy toward Israel eluded the Indian leader. While his moves eventually worked in favor of normalization, Rajiv Gandhi was unable to carry the course to its logical conclusion. There were factors that facilitated some tangible moves toward Israel. But there were also forces that worked in the opposite direction. These in turn prevented him from proceeding toward Israel. One can identify four closely linked impediments to normalizing relations with Israel.

Impediments to Normalization

The outbreak of the Palestinian intifada in December 1987 was a major deterrent against any Indian rapprochement toward Israel. The uprising eroded traditional support for the Jewish state even among liberal elements the world over and evoked universal condemnation. Benevolent or humane occupation ceased to be acceptable to the vast majority of international community, and the intifada reiterated the centrality of the Palestinian problem in Middle East politics. Given its historical disposition, India's sympathy and support for the Palestinians was inevitable. Another outcome of the intifada was the Algiers Declaration of November 15, 1988, in which the PLO declared its belated acceptance of the 1947 partition plan and proclaimed the "state of Palestine." India became one of the first countries to recognize the move and received PLO Chairman Yasser Arafat as a head of state. The intifada also influenced India's refusal to play the Davis Cup relegation playoff tennis match in Israel in April 1988.[36]

In addition, a pro-Israeli policy remains unlikely to win elections in India.[37] For economic, political, ideological, and religious reasons, a pro-Palestinian stance has a strong base of support. While communal calculations play a very important role, a pro-Palestinian policy enjoys widespread support in India. The same does not hold for a pro-Israeli policy. Support for closer ties with Israel comes from a variety of interest groups, such as pro-Western, anticommunist, Hindu and Sikh fundamentalists, anti-Muslim elements, socialists, idealists, or realists. Individually or collectively, none of these groups ever had sufficient influence to alter the policy. Domestic political dividends for normalization has always been marginal and unattractive. On the contrary, unless handled judiciously, the potential political fallout would be enormous for any political party or government. For the opposition groups, normalization was largely a political tool against the Congress Party. Since the days of the partition, the socialists, for example, periodically harped on the need for close ties with

Israel, yet when they were in power from 1977 to 1979, they were unable to transform their demands into concrete policy.

Moreover, under Rajiv there was no parliamentary opposition. In the 1984 Lok Sabha elections, the pro-Israeli Bharatiya Janata Party (BJP) won just two seats in the 542-member parliament.[38] The dogmatic Communists, who had won more seats, were never strong allies of Israel. The emerging third force, namely the Janata Dal under V. P. Singh (who subsequently became prime minister in 1989), was too eager to cultivate Muslim groups to adopt an overtly pro-Israeli stand.[39] If Rajiv Gandhi was not prepared to take that step, there also was no opposition to force it.

Third, since the middle of 1987 Rajiv Gandhi had been embroiled in a multimillion dollar bribery scandal involving the Bofors Company, of Sweden. Much official attention and effort were diverted to countering charges that the prime minister and his close friends were involved. The allegation snowballed into a major controversy and resulted in a rapid erosion of Gandhi's popularity. Before long, the Congress Party started losing various crucial elections. With the next parliamentary elections around the corner, normalization with Israel would have definitely complicated the Congress Party's support base among Muslim voters. Partly with an eye on the election, in November 1989 India presented the Jawaharlal Nehru Award for International Understanding to Arafat.[40]

Finally, Israeli involvement in Sri Lanka and its military-intelligence help to Colombo caused consternation and anxiety in New Delhi.[41] Israel's involvement in the ethnic conflict was viewed negatively in India.[42] The Sri Lankan civil war has serious ethnic and political ramifications in India, especially in the southern state of Tamil Nadu. India feared that Israeli involvement would only strengthen Colombo's drive for a military solution. As a result, under the July 1987 Indo–Sri Lankan accord, Gandhi and President J. R. Jayewardene of Sri Lanka agreed that both "will reach an early understanding about the relevance and employment of foreign military and intelligence personnel with a view to ensuring that such presence will not prejudice Indo–Sri Lankan relations."[43] Israeli involvement in this ethnic crisis partially dampened Gandhi's desire to pursue closer ties with Israel.

New Delhi was also worried over Israel's interests in Fiji, especially in the wake of the 1987 military coup led by Col. Sitiveni Rabuka. Establishment of diplomatic relations with Israel was the first major decision taken by the coup leaders.[44] Fiji provided an opening for Israel in the Pacific region, and Foreign Ministry Director General Avraham Tamir visited the island just before the coup. Rabuka not only overthrew a democratically elected government but also adopted an overtly racist stance regarding the ethnic Indian population of the island. When New Delhi was campaigning for international pressure for the restoration of democracy in Fiji, Israel was the first country to send an ambassador to the new regime. Under these circumstances, Israeli overtures in Fiji were seen as unpleasant developments.[45] During this period, some leading media commentators also expressed concerns over possible cooperation between Israel and Pakistan.[46] These developments considerably reduced the space for diplomatic maneuvers.

The Twilight Moments

Rajiv Gandhi attempted to take a new look at India's Israel policy and even took small steps in that direction. Though he had four different foreign ministers, he himself conducted the foreign policy. Unlike others, his government was more inclined to meet those who actively campaigned on behalf of Israel, and some of these contacts took place in India. He sought a *modus vivendi* with Israel and its supporters in the United States on issues such as Pakistani weapons proliferation. Even in 1989, a few months before the Lok Sabha elections, he allowed the Israeli consul to operate beyond Maharashtra. Israel was probably one of the few issues where progress was consistently made during Gandhi's tenure. But he could not take that giant leap to normalization.

Dogged by corruption charges, administrative inefficiency, and internal dissent, the November 1989 Lok Sabha elections witnessed an anti-INC wave, and Gandhi was voted out of office. The two minority governments that succeeded him headed by V. P. Singh and Chandra Shekhar were too preoccupied with their own political survival to make any far-reaching foreign-policy decisions, particularly on Israel. Moreover, Singh's electoral strategy was based on forging common cause with self-appointed Muslim leaders such the Shahi Imam of New Delhi's Jama Masjid. This strategy eliminated any hopes of normalization of relations with Israel. Confronted with growing instability, in the summer of 1991, President R. Venkataraman called for midterm Lok Sabha elections. While addressing an election meeting near the southern Indian city of Madras (now Chennai), Rajiv Gandhi was assassinated by a female suicide bomber belonging to the Liberation Tigers of Tamil Eelam (LTTE).[47]

As a result, Narasimha Rao, who did not even contest the parliamentary elections, emerged as the consensus candidate of the Congress Party and on June 21 was sworn in as India's prime minister. His tenure began on an ominous note. On June 27, less than week after he assumed office, Kashmiri militants killed an Israeli tourist and kidnapped another. This tested the official policy toward Israel, especially as Israelis became the victims of the ongoing militancy in Kashmir. Rao waived normal restrictions imposed upon the Bombay-based Israeli consul and offered full cooperation in resolving the unfolding situation. In an unprecedented gesture, he approved the visit of the senior Israeli diplomat Moshe Yegar to coordinate diplomatic efforts with Consul Giora Becher. During his brief visit, the director of the Asia Desk at the Israeli Foreign Ministry held talks with Junior Foreign Minister Eduardo Falerio and senior officials in New Delhi. He also spoke at the Institute for Defense Studies and Analyses (IDSA), the government-funded think tank. After days of hectic behind-the-scenes negotiations, the issue was amicably resolved with the release of the kidnapped Israeli tourist.

Soon after the Kashmir episode, the Indian media started what could be termed as a concerted campaign for normalization. Erstwhile critics of Israel began reexamining their earlier position. Spearheaded by the well-known strategic analyst–turned-academic C. Raja Mohan, the realists saw normalization within the context of the emerging post–cold war global order. There emerged a growing willingness to revisit some of the earlier justifications for the anti-Israeli policy. While pro-Palestinian elements continued to insist on taking the moral high ground and cited Mahatma Gandhi as justification, other critics of the status quo urged India to recognize and capitalize on the new Middle Eastern reality opened up by the Kuwait war and Madrid Peace Conference.

This time around, the Indian government was not far behind public opinion. If Yegar's July visit was presented as a "humanitarian gesture," India signaled a new policy shortly after the Madrid Conference. On December 16, 1991, it joined the majority in the United Nations and voted to repeal the notorious 1975 resolution that equated Zionism with racism. As India had been one of the original supporters of the resolution, this was a significant move.[48] By taking this step, Rao exhibited India's determination to move away from the past. Engagement, not isolation, and constructive dialogue, not condemnation, became the new mantra. Even while professing to follow the policies of his predecessors, Rao signaled a new approach toward Israel. The UN vote was followed by a meeting between Indian and Israeli diplomats in Washington. In the second week of January 1992, the senior Israeli diplomat Yoseph Hadass met India's Deputy Chief of Mission Lalit Mansingh.[49] This meeting in the Indian embassy was a precursor to normalization. The final confirmation came when Rao hosted Yasser Arafat in the third week of that month. Arafat's public statement that India could pursue a policy that served its national interests was interpreted as a sign that the Palestinians were coming to terms with the inevitable. But the traditionalists felt that India was snubbing the Palestinian leader. In their assessment, on December 18, a few days after the UN vote, the Palestinian leader had sought an audience with the Indian prime minister to register his "protest" over the Zionism vote.

> The President of the State of Palestine, who, in earlier times, visited this country more frequently than any other world leader, was in for a surprise this time. His visit kept getting postponed on flimsy pretexts—that the Prime Minister was preoccupied with two foreign dignitaries and with the preparations for the Republic Day [which falls on January 26]. . . . What was more ironical probably was that while Arafat was having a difficult time in meeting the Indian Prime Minister, hectic efforts were on to facilitate the meeting of Indian and Israeli diplomats in the US. . . .
>
> Finally, New Delhi took the initiative and gave a date which was not so suitable for the PLO leader as he was tied down by the outgoing [*sic*] West Asia peace negotiations. But still he had to make it in view of the far-reaching developments. The reception accorded to the visiting Palestinian dignitary was lackluster at the worst and make belief [*sic*] warm at best.[50]

In short, it was easier for them to admit and recognize Arafat's "busy schedule," but the same reason by the Indian prime minister was dismissed as an "excuse." However, in his elliptical way, Narasimha Rao set the stage for a radical departure from the past. Professing to continue on the path set by Mahatma Gandhi, Jawaharlal Nehru, and others, in January 1992 he irreversibly altered India's Israel policy.

It has taken thirty-three years and a bang on the head to get my values right.
—Sterling Moss

12 Normalization and After

On January 29, 1992, hours before Prime Minister Narasimha Rao left for New York for the summit meeting of the UN Security Council, India announced its decision to establish full diplomatic relations with Israel. The significance of the decision was so palpable that the foreign secretary chose to make this announcement to the media.[1] More than four decades after its recognition, India finally decided to take the next logical step: normalization. This was the most visible foreign-policy shift India had made since the end of the cold war. What was promised by Jawaharlal Nehru in 1952 eventually happened under another INC leader. Given that more popular and charismatic leaders had shied away from normalization, how had the colorless and unassuming Rao managed to take that leap? Was he helped by domestic or international shifts? Was he not concerned about the Muslim factor? How did the decision play out in the region? How did Rao square the circle? His determination to change the direction of India's policy was facilitated by a host of international as well as domestic developments.

Rationale

First and foremost, the end of the cold war and collapse of the Soviet Union significantly enhanced Rao's endeavor. While Eurocentric politics was not directly responsible for nonrelations, the cold war did provide a strong ideological rationale and support for India's unfriendliness toward Israel. The post-1967 Soviet hostility toward Israel partly contributed to its isolation in the Third World. As the "natural ally" of the nonaligned world, Moscow's pro-Arab and anti-Israeli policies had resonance in different parts of the world. Support for the Palestinians became a sign of progressive orientation against imperialism. Thus the disintegration and disappearance of the Soviet Union significantly diluted the ideological component of the foreign policies of many states. In practical terms, this meant the weakening of the Non-Aligned Movement and a reduction of the anti-Israeli climate. The sudden disappearance of the Soviet Union meant that the new world order would be dominated by the sole surviving superpower, the United States. Like many other countries, India would have to learn to live with this new reality. Having thrived on a diet of anti-Americanism, especially during the 1970s and early 1980s, this was a tall order for India.

India needed U.S. backing for another reason. Prime Minister Rao inherited a serious economic crisis that forced him to mortgage the national gold reserves in London to pay for desperately needed imports.[2] Any economic recovery was conditional upon massive aid from multilateral institutions such as the International Monetary Fund (IMF) and the World Bank. In practical terms, this meant unqualified American support. It was obvious to Rao that the absence of relations with Israel was an impediment to a better connection to industrialized countries, especially the United States.[3] It was therefore not accidental that the decision to establish relations with Israel was announced on the eve of Rao's visit to New York, where he would be meeting with President George H. W. Bush. Though important, one should not overemphasize the U.S. factor.[4] If the United States was so important, how did India manage to ward off such pressure since the late 1940s? As the post–cold war trajectory indicates, improvement in Indo-U.S. relations has been possible because both countries are prepared to abandon their past misgivings and seek closer ties. In short, Indo-U.S. bonhomie enhances Indo-Israeli relations and not the other way around.

Second, the end of bloc politics and the Kuwait war of 1991 improved Israel's diplomatic fortunes. The weakening of the Soviet Union meant that the Arab states lost their patron and their counterweight to American support for Israel. The military option became less viable for countries such as Syria. Political negotiations, not military confrontation, with Israel became the new slogan. The Middle East Peace Conference, which began in Madrid on October 30, 1991, signaled an Arab willingness to seek a negotiated settlement with Israel. Even the Palestinian leadership was not averse to a compromise solution. This relaxed atmosphere vis-à-vis Israel was reflected in the desire of major powers such as the Soviet Union and China to reassess their hostilities and normalize ties with Israel. While Moscow renewed its relations in October 1991, China recognized the Jewish state in January 1992.[5] India could not remain indifferent to this newly found international rapprochement with Israel.

Third, the Palestinian factor, a key element in India's Middle East policy for over sixty years, was considerably weakened. The Palestinian support for President Saddam Hussein of Iraq during his invasion, occupation, and annexation of Kuwait proved costly. Key Arab states such as Kuwait and Saudi Arabia perceived this as a sign of betrayal and ingratitude.[6] The regional importance of the PLO waned considerably, and while Arab states were still supportive of the Palestinian cause, they were less willing to endorse its leadership, especially Yasser Arafat.[7] It was no longer possible for India to further its interests in the Middle East by playing up its "consistent" support to Arafat. Fourth, the unfolding Middle East peace process was a major post–cold war development. The willingness of the Arabs and Israel to seek a political settlement through direct negotiations was groundbreaking, and many countries were eager to play a part. India was no exception. But its ability to play any role in the Middle East peace process depended upon its willingness to establish normal relations with all the parties to the Arab-Israeli conflict, including Israel.[8] To avoid being left out of the process, New Delhi announced its decision within days of the Chinese move.[9]

Fifth, the domestic situation within India was favorable to Israel. Domestic political calculations had long influenced India's Israel policy. The principal opposition party, the Bharatiya Janata Party (BJP), had been a staunch supporter of the normalization, and this in turn ensured greater political support for Rao. In the words of Efraim Inbar, the ascendance of the BJP "removed some hesitations about Israel."[10] Moreover, during the

1991 Lok Sabha election, prominent Muslim leaders of north India abandoned the Congress Party and endorsed the Janata Dal led by V. P. Singh. As a result, the INC was less worried about Muslim leaders than they had been. Opposition to normalization was confined to the communist parties and marginalized groups such as the Janata Dal. Domestic opposition was also partly mitigated by changes in the Arab attitude toward Israel. The Madrid conference was possible because prominent Islamic countries such as Saudi Arabia lent their full backing. The willingness of Arafat to support the process significantly weakened Islamic opposition to dealing with Israel.

Sixth, it is difficult to ignore the security element in Rao's decision. The absence of diplomatic relations did not inhibit India from seeking Israeli assistance in the past. During national crises such as the conflict with China in 1962 and war with Pakistan in 1965, India sought and obtained a limited quantity of small arms and ammunition from Israel.[11] Due to political compulsions, it had rarely acknowledged the help provided by Israel. At the same, these incidents reveal that despite hostile public postures, many Indian leaders, including Nehru, considered Israel in friendlier terms and during critical times sought understanding, if not friendship, with it. In recent years, many have admitted the existence of prolonged intelligence cooperation with Israel. Such cooperation existed even during the premiership of Indira Gandhi (1966–1977; 1980–1984), periods generally considered unfriendly toward Israel. According to one published account, the Research and Analysis Wing (R&AW, the external-intelligence arm of India's intelligence services)

> has always had links with the Israelis and the US. In the late 1970s, it engineered the visit of Moshe Dayan to India; it also played an important role in trying to get the Israeli defense industry a foothold in India. RAW sent its personnel to Israel for specialized training and in late 1984, in the wake of Indira Gandhi's assassination, it also [sought the advice of] . . . a senior Israeli security specialist on the Prime Minister's security systems.[12]

Furthermore, a former intelligence official disclosed that soon after the formation of R&AW in September 1968, its chief, Rameshwar Nath Kao, "with the approval of Indira Gandhi, had set up a secret liaison relationship with Mossad."[13] Following normalization, security issues have become a major agenda item in Indo-Israeli cooperation. Thus it would be safe to conclude that security was one of the factors that influenced Rao to normalize ties with Israel.

Finally, Rao's decision appears to be a well-conceived plan aimed at seeking balance and pragmatism in Indian foreign policy. By becoming a prisoner of its rhetoric, it had divorced itself from political reality. "Consistency" was its guiding principle regarding the turbulent Middle East. It extended political support for the Arab and Islamic countries of the region without demanding or ensuring reciprocity. Even the political and military support some of these countries gave to Pakistan during the 1965 and 1971 wars did not result in any modification. Normalization was partly aimed at remedying this anomalous situation. Shortly after the establishment of relations, India's foreign secretary,[14] J. N. Dixit, publicly retorted: "What have the Arabs given us, if I may ask? Did they vote for us in the Kashmir issue? Were they supportive of us when we had the East Pakistan crisis [in 1971]?"[15] In the past, such harsh words came only from opposition-party leaders who were highly critical of the official policy on Israel.[16] Some Arab countries were not happy with the Indian move, but normalization did not evoke any adverse response from the region. Contrary to past fears and apprehensions, newly established relations with Israel enabled India to pursue productive ties with a number of countries in the region. Growing bilateral relations with countries such as Iran and Saudi Arabia indicate that Indo-Israeli normalization did not inhibit Middle Eastern countries from seeking and improving their relations with India. On the contrary, Indo-Israeli relations forced key states of the Middle East to take India seriously. Not everyone, however, was happy with Rao's decision.

Internal Criticisms Continue

Support for normalization was overwhelming but not unanimous. A vast majority took a sober view of the prevailing world order, but there were voices of dissent that longed for the past. Having grown up with a heavy and often unverified historical legacy, they were not prepared to accept normalization easily. What were their principal criticisms?

It was hasty. Significant segments of the Indian intelligentsia were unable and unwilling to recognize and appreciate the need for close political relations with Israel. They viewed normalization as an aberration and betrayal of the traditional commitment to the Palestinian cause. According to this view, nothing substantial had changed to warrant an abandonment of a policy that had survived for over four decades. Mahatma Gandhi's arguments were resurrected to question the need to abandon the past. For them, India should not have supported the 1991 UN decision on Zionism. When Israel "was founded and continues to exist on the basis of a racist ideology, that is, Zionism," what was the need for India to change its stance?[17] The establishment of relations was seen as a hasty, untimely, and even unnecessary move. Such sentiments were expressed by the leaders of the communist and Janata Dal parties. Some even blamed Dixit "for the unseemly haste with which he has tried to improve relations with Israel."[18] According to these critics, India should have "waited" until the resolution of the Palestinian problem and the creation of an independent Palestinian state. In the words of one critic, Prime Minister Rao "should have waited till the ground realities in the West Asian theatre changed substantially so as to remove the very basis of our decades-old anti-Israeli policy."[19] While the Palestinians and Arab states were ready to negotiate with Israel, critics wanted India to continue with its policy of nonrelations. This more-Catholic-than-the-Pope attitude can only be characterized as an ideological hangover.

Ideological hangover. Criticism of normalization came largely from those who were shocked at the demise of the Soviet Union and the end of the cold war. Having lived on a diet of anti-imperialism for decades, they were unable to adjust to the new reality. The disappearance of communism in the Soviet Union and rapid changes in eastern Europe orphaned them ideologically. For this segment of population, opposing Israel and its policies was a sign of a "progressive" worldview. The Soviet Union's demise not only ended the ideological debate but also forced them to see Israel as a normal state, if not as a friend. Some found this ideological transformation too sudden and harsh to digest. The attitude of Mani Shankar Aiyar, a former career diplomat and a close aide of Rajiv Gandhi, highlights this point. In May 1993, Foreign Minister Shimon Peres became the first official visitor from Israel. Describing the Israeli leader as "a known terrorist with forty-five years of national and international experience of terrorism," Aiyar lamented: "Judas betrayed Jesus for thirty pieces of silver. Foreign secretary J. N. Dixit has been rushed to Tunis to explain to the Palestinians that we are not about to betray Tirupati for thirty sprinkler-irrigation sets from Israel. I am glad that I left the foreign service before it came to this."[20] His membership in the ruling Congress Party did not prevent Aiyar from being a prominent critic of the

Oslo accords.[21] Such a negative attitude regarding normalization was shared by opposition figures closely identified with the left. Some attributed normalization to Rao's willingness to comply with American dictates in order to secure financial assistance from the World Bank. The establishment of "full diplomatic relations with Israel was a correct decision . . . but to do so under American pressure was unwise."[22]

It was anti-Muslim. Senior Cabinet Minister Arjun Singh warned Rao of the consequences of normalization, especially regarding Muslim support for the party. In the words of one senior Indian diplomat who attended the crucial cabinet meeting, "Arjun Singh felt that this decision might affect Muslim support for the Congress and went on to imply that establishing relations with Israel would be a departure from the Nehruvian framework of our foreign policy."[23] Arjun Singh, still hoping to become prime minister, was trying to position himself as a savior of minority interests. What could be more attractive than opposing normalization with Israel! At the same time, he was not ready to ignore the overwhelming support for normalization, and thus, though expressing his reservations inside the cabinet, he went along with the majority view. This two-faced approach earned the education minister some negative publicity. Singh came under criticism from some Muslim circles when he made an official visit to Israel in June 1994.[24] Partly due to the domestic political calculations, the former prime minister and then leading opposition figure V. P. Singh registered his opposition to normalization. Reflecting this trend, one scholar even viewed Rao's decision as an "anti-Muslim alliance," if not a conspiracy. Rationalizing the move, he argued that the government and its supporters sought to counter the Pakistani factor "by forging an anti-Islamic alliance along with [*sic*] Israel."[25] A few prominent Muslim leaders were also critical of the decision, calling it "ill timed and hasty."[26]

Wearing blinkers. The critics of Narasimha Rao were reluctant to recognize, let alone adjust, to the new international reality. Both the global order and Middle Eastern realities had changed radically. They were not ready to admit the weakened position of the PLO. Having taking a pro-Saddam position during the Kuwait crisis, many Indian intellectuals could not fault Arafat for doing the same. Their quick endorsement of the Iraqi decision to obliterate the existence of Kuwait meant that their sympathies were with the Palestinians, who viewed Saddam as their savior.[27] This in turn prevented them from recognizing the weakened status of the PLO after Operation Desert Storm. In a number of Persian Gulf countries,

Arafat became a liability in promoting India's interest. But Rao's critics were not ready to admit the new realities and hoped that New Delhi could still promote its interests by playing the PLO card. Blinded by ideological rhetoric, they were unable to see the new challenges and opportunities facing Rao.

Israel has nothing to offer. Some were critical over the kind of relations that India might develop with Israel following normalization. Even before 1992, counterterrorism was frequently mentioned as a possible area of cooperation. This evoked strong criticism. Because of its own "failures" to curb terrorism, they argued, Israel's assistance would not be helpful. Even those who were otherwise reconciled to normalization reacted strongly over security cooperation with Israel. In their view, India had both the capacity and experience to overcome any threats from Pakistan without outside help. "To give an impression that India will tackle this threat with [Israel's] expertise or experience . . . sends the *wrong signal to many people both at home and abroad.*"[28] While bilateral relations could facilitate a "mutually beneficial relationship in the field of science and technology," another warned that "India must exercise utmost caution in considering interactions with Israel in regard to security and international terrorism. Any such move could create avoidable complications in our dealings with other states in the region and might eventually prove counterproductive."[29]

Despite these criticisms, the overwhelming view toward normalization was favorable. Things moved swiftly and both countries tried to make up for lost time. Israel temporarily shifted its consular official to New Delhi and opened its embassy in February; the Indian embassy was opened in Tel Aviv on May 15, 1992. Israel soon became a favorite destination of Indian leaders, officials, and businesspeople. The progress made since 1992 indicates that both countries are determined to reverse the past by identifying and pursuing new areas of cooperation. Neither has allowed external factors and extraneous considerations to unduly affect the bilateral relationship. Narasimha Rao thus elevated India's Israel policy to the next stage.

Stage 2: Parallel Ties

Normalization marked the second stage of Indo-Israeli relations. During the cold war, New Delhi treated the Arab-Israeli conflict as a zero-sum game. Support for the Palestinians, it felt, demanded not only unfriendliness toward Israel but also opposition to normal diplomatic interaction. By denying formal relations with Israel, it sought to project its pro-Arab credentials. Its preoccupation with Pakistan's diplomatic moves in the Middle East and domestic concerns over Muslim sentiments prevented its leaders from differentiating between bilateral issues and multilateral concerns. Just as Pakistan clouded India's overall foreign-policy formulations during the cold war, it also forced India to see relations with Israel within an "either/or" paradigm.

Normalization was a paradigm shift. India recognized and admitted that it was possible to establish normal relations with Israel without abandoning its support for the Palestinians. This approach toward the Arab-Israeli conflict was a new experience for India. Major powers have recognized the need to maintain normal ties with all parties involved in the conflict, and even if they are not prepared to mediate, relations with Israel have become a precondition for international credibility.[30] Continuing past hostility and absence of formal ties with Israel only meant marginalization in the Middle East. Even before the fall of the Berlin Wall, eastern European countries and China initiated low-level contacts with Israel and were giving sufficient indications of normalization. While the cold war was not responsible for the Arab-Israeli conflict, it definitely intensified the problem and contributed to Israel's political isolation.

Contrary to some critics, normalization did not mean that India had abandoned or betrayed the Palestinians. Nor was it a surrender to imperialism.[31] Prime Minister Narasimha Rao's decision did not dilute India's position on the right of self-determination of the Palestinians or the support for Palestinian statehood. Nor was normalization an endorsement of Israeli claims vis-à-vis Palestinian political rights. Rao was merely stating that support for Palestinians did not mean isolating Israel. Some of India's earlier actions (for example, the Zionism resolution of 1975) and studied silence over extremist Arab rhetoric might incorrectly suggest that New Delhi shared the Arab desire for the destruction of Israel. Though this was never touted, India always opposed the extremist demands among the Arabs and Palestinians regarding Israel. This was part of Nehru's legacy. In 1947, he opposed the unitary plan proposed by the Arabs and suggested a federal alternative. When this idea did not get any attention at the United Nations, he did not support the unitary solution. Likewise, the reluctance to establish diplomatic relations with Israel did not mean that India endorsed Arab calls for the destruction of the Jewish state. Its refusals to normalize were often accompanied by its willingness to accept Israel's existence.

During the cold war, a negotiated settlement was remote, partly because of the infamous "Three Nos" of the September 1967 Arab summit in Khartoum.[32] India felt that given the prevailing international climate, its pro-Arab policy demanded absence of formal ties with the Jewish state. In the post–cold war and post-Madrid era, isolating Israel became unwise and counterproductive. When the Arab states were eager to negotiate with Israel, even a pro-Palestinian policy would require India to support the Madrid process. The most tangible means of doing this was to have relations with all parties to the conflict, including Israel.

This interpretation of the normalization of ties is supported by events since 1992. First and foremost, India presented relations with Israel as a contributing factor to the peace process. Active engagement with other nations bestowed greater self-confidence to Israel and increased its trust. Both were essential if Israel was to overcome its inherent security concerns vis-à-vis a Palestinian state. Even if India's actual contribution to the peace process was limited, Rao was prepared to be a part of the international endeavor aimed at minimizing Israel's mistrust of the outside world.[33]

Normalization was not accompanied by any radical departure from past positions vis-à-vis the Palestinian question. India is still committed to the establishment of a Palestinian state and views the fulfillment of the Palestinian political aspirations as a precondition for lasting peace in the Middle East. It continues to recognize the PLO as the sole and legitimate representative of the Palestinians and recognizes the legality and powers of the Palestine National Authority. It has treated the Palestinian mission in New Delhi as a full-fledged embassy since March 1980. Following its recognition of the state of Palestine in November 1988, New Delhi received Yasser Arafat and later Mahmoud Abbas as heads of state. In the initial years, it had coordinated critical diplomatic moves on Israel with Chairman Arafat. While the nuances have undergone changes, India's basic postures on some of the key issues have not been diluted. While it has abandoned its tendency to sermonize and employ anti-Israeli rhetoric, it has not switched sides. Much to Israel's annoyance and displeasure, it continues to support the Arab stance regarding the Palestine question in various forums, such as the United Nations and the NAM. On issues such as Jewish settlements, borders, status of Jerusalem, and refugees, there is no major difference between India's pre-1992 and post-normalization positions.

There is, however, one significant departure from the past. India has become more sensitive to Israel's security concerns. Unlike the past, it counsels caution and restraint on "both" sides. For example, in the initial days of the second Lebanese war (2006), it was critical of Hezbollah's abduction of Israeli soldiers, which precipitated the crisis.[34] Its stance on the controversial security fence highlights this shift. In November 2005, it told the United Nations that "no one could have objections to the construction of the wall in areas coinciding with the green line. However, its encroachment on Palestinian land and interests creates great hardship for the people affected by its construction and exacerbates the situation."[35] Its primary concerns were not the security fence per se but its actual location in an area whose claims still remain disputed and unresolved. Prior to normalization, India would have been less restrained and probably would have employed fiery rhetoric.

Of late, however, Indo-Israeli relations have entered a third and more complex phase.

The Complex Stage 3

While the seeds for elevation of bilateral relations were sowed when the non-INC National Democratic Alliance (NDA, 1998–2004) government was in power, it was the Congress Party that cemented the third phase of Indo-Israeli relations. India has begun differentiating bilateral interests from its differences over the peace process. This has been the policy of the West. Countries such as Britain, France, and Germany do not allow their strong disagreements over the peace process to impede bilateral ties and interaction. Stronger criticisms of Israel are often accompanied by robust bilateral linkages and interactions. To paraphrase the *yishuv*'s position on World War II, India *promotes bilateral ties as if there were no peace process and disagrees over the peace process as if there were no bilateral relations.*[36]

In the absence of official documents, it is difficult to pinpoint the exact timeframe, but a decade after normalization, Indo-Israeli relations have clearly entered a third and interesting phase. If the 1990s marked India's desire to differentiate normalization and the support for the Palestinians, the early part of the twenty-first century presented a new shift. Without articulating it formally, India has made a distinction between its differences with Israel over the peace process and the need to strengthen bilateral ties. The willingness of the UPA government to promote joint missile research (July 2007) signals that disagreement over the Palestinian issue does not impede both countries from pursuing converging interests.[37] This decision came against the background of prolonged demands of the Indian left to suspend or freeze military cooperation with Israel.[38]

Operationally, this approach creates extra diplomatic space for India. To garner domestic support for closer economic and military ties with Israel, New Delhi has to highlight and even overemphasize its differences over the peace process. That way it not only reiterates support for the Palestinians but also justifies its security dealings with Israel. In the past, strong disagreements over the peace process prevented India from talking to Israel politically. In this third phase, Indo-Israeli relations play out along two parallel tracks: convergence over bilateral ties and strong differences over the peace process. Such a complex approach is inevitable for the furtherance of Indo-Israeli relations. By adopting a dual posture toward Israel, various political parties could rally around the bilateral relations. It is in this context that one should view the willingness of the UPA government (2004–) to enhance its economic and political relations with Israel. A complex and nuanced approach toward Israel is essential to enhance and expand the support base for bilateral ties. In other words, disagreement over the peace process is a political price that Israel will have to pay if bilateral ties are to flourish.

Such disagreements are not painful for Israel. Historically, except in matters closer to its immediate neighborhood, India has not been proactive. Nehru led the struggle against colonialism because it was a political movement that did not demand any major sacrifice on India's part. Its active involvement in resolving various international conflicts and tensions virtually came to an end following the 1962 Sino-Indian conflict. Its endorsement of various national-liberation movements were expressed through political support, not military aid. This differed from the Chinese practice of providing ideological and material support to various radical movements, including the Palestinian Fedayeens. Even at the height of its pro-Arab policy, India had not armed Israel's adversaries, something that China and Russia mastered during the cold war. Thus India's disagreements with Israel over the peace process are primarily political and do not pose any strategic challenges to Israel.

Within this broad contour, how have the bilateral relations progressed since 1992?

Political Contacts

There are growing political interactions between the two countries, and hosts of official, semiofficial, and unofficial visits have taken place since 1992. There exists a genuine domestic consensus regarding Israel, especially regarding normalization. Political opposition to some of Israel's policies vis-à-vis the Palestinians did not impede Indian leaders from recognizing the benefits of normalization. Issues like agricultural cooperation, technology transfer, foreign investments, tourism, and military-strategic cooperation generated positive sentiments about Israel. Those who entertained reservations over Rao's decision gradually muted their opposition and came to terms with the need to benefit from Israel rather than continuing with past anti-Israeli rhetoric.

India avoided a high-profile approach toward Israel and thus its political dealings with Israel have been somewhat asymmetrical. While Israeli leaders were eager to visit New Delhi, the latter adopted a cautious and at times even cool approach toward such requests. There were signs that Prime Minister Yitzhak Rabin wanted to visit India as part of his Far East trip in late 1993. Prime Minister Rao was reluctant even when the Israeli leader was hosted by Islamic countries like Indonesia.[39] Likewise, during the visit of President Ezer Weizmann in late 1996, it was agreed that his Indian counterpart would make a reciprocal visit to Israel. A decade later, this has not materialized.[40] Likewise, prolonged persuasion from the Indian military establishment preceded the political leadership agreeing to post a defense attaché in Israel.[41]

For a while, India sought to "balance" its contacts with Israel by making similar gestures toward the Arabs. Days before announcing the normalization of relations with Israel, for example, Prime Minister Rao hosted Arafat and appeared anxious to secure his approval before moving closer to Israel. During Rao's tenure, India's high-profile contacts with Israel were either preceded or followed by similar contacts with the Palestinian leadership. As long as Arafat was alive, even the BJP followed this trend, albeit with less frequency.[42] The opening of the Maulana Abul Kalam Center in Cairo in 1992 and the awarding of the Jawaharlal Nehru Prize for International Understanding to President Hosni Mubarak in 1997 were aimed at mitigating some of Egyptian concerns over normalization. The general reluctance of Indian ministers to visit Israel has to be seen within the context of "Arab sensitivities." For the same reason, Indian leaders have long denied any defense procurements from Israel.

At least until the late 1990s, India appeared to be bending over backward in preventing its new relations with Israel from affecting its ties with Arab countries.

A noticeable shift was visible toward the end of the 1990s, especially following the formation of the BJP-led NDA government under Atal Behari Vajpayee. Either out of growing Indian confidence or due to the historic pro-Israeli baggage of the BJP, the Indian leaders were more willing to publicize the friendship with Israel. This was also the time when India adopted a softer line toward various developments concerning the peace process. The onset of the al-Aqsa intifada and the subsequent intensification of international criticism over Israel's policy toward the Palestinians did not hamper India from seeking closer ties with Jewish state.

Bilateral relations immensely benefited from the Indian provincial governments. Even in the early 1990s, the state governments were free from the political compulsions that inhibited the central government from pursuing active relations with Israel. Enjoying the new openness and opportunities offered by economic liberalization, various state governments directly dealt with foreign countries to promote their economic agendas. From the very beginning, INC-ruled states such as Haryana, Gujarat, Madhya Pradesh, Maharashtra, Orissa, and Punjab were in the forefront of forging strong ties with Israel. Without attracting undue publicity, their chief ministers visited the Jewish state and sought cooperation in agriculture, water management, and foreign investment.[43] Even if the actual progress was moderate, state governments entered into numerous agreements and understandings with various Israeli companies and organizations. Indeed, the participation of state governments in promoting Indo-Israeli relations has rarely been appreciated. For their part, Israeli leaders and businesspersons found it easier to deal with the state governments, whose primary agenda was economic, especially when the central leadership was preoccupied with political correctness.

Some of the non-INC opposition parties were helpful in Rao's overtures to Israel. As they had been since the days of the Constituent Assembly, the socialists were in the forefront of seeking closer ties with Israel. When the Congress Party remained aloof and was busy with anti-Israeli rhetoric, it was the opposition parties, especially the Jan Sangh, the Praja Socialist Party, and the Swatantra Party that campaigned for moderation and modification. Following normalization, these groups and leaders were quick to embrace the opening provided by Rao. These developments led to the emergence of a national consensus and, until the outbreak of the al-Aqsa intifada in September 2000, even those who had some reservations in the past came around to strengthening and benefiting from bilateral relations.

A real shift in Indo-Israeli relations coincided with the formation of the BJP-led NDA government in 1998. It is tempting to attribute this trend to the shared right-wing ideologies of the BJP and the Likud, which emerged as the dominant force in Israel since 1977. Writing on the controversies surrounding the demolition of the Babri Masjid in Ayodhya, one academic felt that "in some circles, there is a growing suspicion of a nexus developing between Israel, BJP, and its allies ranged against Muslims of India with the US appearing as an innocent spectator, which could have implications for the unity and integrity of India."[44] Although this ideological affinity cannot be discounted, there were other forces that also enabled India to pursue a more open approach to Israel.

Among the political parties, the Congress Party has remained extremely cautious in its approach to Israel. Normalization was presented within the traditional Indian slogan of "continuity and change."[45] Rao was not prepared to project normalization as a radical departure from the past or that he was reversing a policy set by Nehru. Rao's successors were also equally careful in floating closer ties with Israel. Both under Rao and later Manmohan Singh, bilateral relations flourished but without any hype or undue media attention. There was some opposition within the Congress Party and, as discussed earlier, leaders such as Arjun Singh and Mani Shankar Aiyar were critical of Rao's decision.[46] As a result, during Rao's tenure (1991–1996) only two cabinet ministers visited Israel, and during the first four years of Singh's tenure (2004–2008), no cabinet minister went to Israel. The only visit of a foreign minister took place when the NDA was in power (1998–2004). When Prime Minister Sharon visited India in September 2003, it was uncertain if the opposition leader and Congress President Sonia Gandhi would meet the Israeli leader. Though the meeting eventually took place toward the end of Sharon's state visit, no pictures of their meeting ever appeared in the mainstream Indian media.

On the contrary, the Hindu-nationalist BJP was far more forthcoming. Whether in or out of power, it had no qualms about exhibiting its friendliness toward Israel. As opposition leader, L. K. Advani visited that country in July 1995 and was received by its senior leaders. He again went to Israel in June 2000, this time as home minister, and admitted that India shares "with Israel a common perception of terrorism as a menace, even more so when coupled with religious fundamentalism. Our mutual determination to combat terrorism is the basis for discussions with Israel, whose reputation in dealing with such problems is quite successful."[47] Not only did he choose Israel as the destination for his maiden foreign trip as home minister, but he was accompanied by senior officials responsible for internal security.[48] Back in the opposition, in February 2007 Advani hosted an interreligious dialogue attended by Hindu, Jewish, and Islamic scholars. Moreover, since the visit of Rajasthan's chief minster (later India's vice president) Bhairon Singh Shekhawat in June 1994, various state leaders of the party have traveled to Israel. It was during the reign of the BJP that India gave a red-carpet welcome to Prime Minister Sharon.

The attitude of the leftist parties was complex and at times contradictory. They were not enthusiastic about Rao normalizing relations with Israel, but, overwhelmed by the tragedy of the disintegration of the Soviet Union, the communists were fighting for self-preservation. With both of the largest parties, the Congress Party and the BJP, supporting normalization, there was very little they could do. Reflecting the prevailing national consensus, the left eventually came around to the idea that forging closer ties with Israel was in India's interest. In the summer of 2000, the chief minister of West Bengal and veteran communist leader Jyoti Basu visited Israel. Around the same time, Somnath Chatterjee, another communist personality and, later, speaker of the Lok Sabha, led a business delegation to Israel to promote investment opportunities in his home state of West Bengal. These two visits marked a diplomatic coup for Israel and signaled the larger Indian consensus on normalization.

The spoiler came in the form of the al-Aqsa intifada, which began in September 2000 and prompted the Indian left to revert to its cold-war ideological rhetoric. Disapproving of Israel's handling of the Palestinian uprising, it demanded that the Indian government recall its ambassador. The BJP being in power during this period added a domestic twist to the communist logic, which perceived the Indo-Israeli ties as part of the anti-Muslim agenda of the BJP. Senior leaders of the CPI(M) argued that by seeking "special ties" with Israel, the BJP had abandoned the Palestinians and brought shame to the country. In the words of CPI(M) General Secretary Prakash Karat:

> The chauvinist positions and military attacks by Sharon and his right-wing government find a positive response amongst the BJP and its RSS mentors in India. The war against the Palestinians is seen

> through the prism of the *Hindutva* war against Muslim minorities in India. Some of the barbarism which is taking place in Gujarat finds a parallel in the Israeli atrocities in the West Bank. That is why the Vajpayee government has remained silent throughout except for a muted expression of concern for Yasser Arafat during the siege. There is no indignation or revulsion at the savagery of the Israeli onslaught. The nexus with the Israeli regime established by the BJP rulers needs to be exposed and thwarted.[49]

When the Congress Party returned to power in 2004, the leftist parties hoped that the UPA coalition government, which depended upon their support, would bring about a "course correction" and freeze military imports from Israel.[50] The refusal of the Congress Party to abandon its course challenged the anti-Muslim paradigm presented by the left.

The attitude of other parties, such as the Janata Dal and Samajwadi Party (SP), were rather mixed. At one level, they opposed normalization, viewing Rao's decision as an anti-Palestinian move and criticizing him for reversing Nehru's policy. At another level, they were active in promoting bilateral relations. The actions of H. D. Deve Gowda, the Janata Dal leader who was prime minister from June 1996 to April 1997, depict this contradiction. In February 1995, Israel was the first foreign country he visited as the chief minister of Karnataka. As prime minister, he hosted President Weizmann in December 1996, and the following February he met Benjamin Netanyahu during the Davos economic summit. Despite these, Gowda was in the forefront of opposition when Sharon visited India in 2003. The same applies to the SP leader, Mulayam Singh Yadav. His self-portrayal as the champion of Muslims meant a criticism of and distancing from Israel. However, the first known visit to Israel of Scientific Advisor A. P. J. Abdul Kalam (later India's president), in June 1996, took place when Yadav was India's defense minister. A more robust picture can be found in the growing economic ties between the two.

Bilateral Trade

The pace of bilateral trade gives credence that both countries are determined to make up for the lost decades. Bilateral trade stood at just $200 million in 1992 but passed the billion mark before the end of that decade and is now close to four billion. This massive increase in just over a decade is phenomenal and unprecedented. By the end of the 1990s, Israel emerged as India's fourth-largest trading partner in the wider Middle East. It trades more with Israel than with Egypt, with whom it has had close political ties since early 1950. In some years, the volume of trade with Israel has been larger than its trade with Iran. Such rapid growth makes Israel one of India's top twenty trading partners in the world and among the top five in the Middle East.

Economic relations should not be measured merely by trade. Both countries are engaged in a host of joint ventures in agriculture, water management, and horticulture whose true value and importance cannot be quantified in dollars. Despite economic liberalization and globalization, the Indian economy continues to be heavily dependent upon agriculture. Thus Israeli expertise in the production of high-yield crops and irrigation systems has been sought by various state governments, who face the perennial problem of drought and water shortages. Expertise on arid-land management is another area that is attractive for states such as Rajasthan.

A third area of economic cooperation is investment. A number of Indian and Israeli companies have invested in one another. Since 1992, Israel has emerged as one of the largest players in India's foreign direct investments sector. Israeli companies are actively investing in areas such as irrigation equipment, medicine, and textiles, and lately have entered into the booming construction industry. Various business forums such as the Confederation of Indian Industries (CII) and the Federation of Indian Chambers of Commerce and Industry (FICCI) have ongoing arrangements with their Israeli counterparts and organize regular trade visits by leading businesspeople. According to one estimate, as many as 150 bilateral agreements were signed during the first fifteen years of normalization.[51]

Economic relations, unfortunately, have a flip side, and the rosy trade picture hides certain uncomfortable facts. Indo-Israeli trade is largely a single-commodity trade, namely diamonds. India imports uncut diamonds and precious and semiprecious stones and re-exports them to Israel as a finished product. This segment constitutes about two-thirds of the total bilateral trade. As table 12.1 indicates, during 1996 to 2006, the diamond trade accounted for between 52 and 71 percent of the total trade. It is true that India's trade with other Middle Eastern countries is also a single-commodity trade, namely, energy. However, there is one notable

TABLE 12.1
India's trade with Israel and the share of diamond trade (in million US$)

Year	Total imports	Diamond imports	Total exports	Diamond exports	Total trade	Share of diamond trade (%)
1996–1997	260.69	175.55	211.41	123.39	472.10	63.32
1997–1998	335.63	196.37	353.24	197.36	751.24	52.41
1998–1999	350.27	217.22	355.21	216.70	705.48	61.51
1999–2000	581.94	424.38	499.70	344.13	1081.64	71.05
2000–2001	432.48	299.51	472.29	273.75	904.77	63.36
2001–2002	427.75	246.69	428.02	257.77	855.77	58.95
2002–2003	602.68	329.01	634.54	412.80	1237.22	59.96
2003–2004	669.76	399.16	723.98	477.03	1393.74	62.87
2004–2005	988.11	547.09	1005.76	698.00	1993.87	62.45
2005–2006	1031.19	576.30	1201.50	814.21	2232.69	62.28
2006–2007	1088.57	497.83	1320.39	875.33	2399.24	57.23

Source: Adapted from Export-Import Data Bank, Director General of Foreign Trade, New Delhi, http://dgft.delhi.nic.in.

difference: energy-related trade benefits both India and the supplier countries. The principal beneficiaries of the diamond trade are a group of Indian business families who are settled in Israel and operate from the Diamond Exchange in Ramat Gan. They "export" uncut diamonds and stones to their family companies in India and, upon polishing and value addition, these goods, often supplied through credit arrangements, are "imported" into Israel. Their true value addition is thus marginal.

Real progress in bilateral relations, however, is happening in an arena that neither side is willing to discuss: defense cooperation.

Defense Ties

In just over a decade, Israel has emerged as a major player in India's defense and security calculations.[52] It has become the second-largest defense supplier to India after Russia,[53] and India has emerged as the largest export destination for Israeli arms. Though primarily revolving around the air force, the bilateral-defense ties include other areas, such as upgrades, small arms, border management, intelligence cooperation, naval patrol, and counterterrorism. India's search for technological modernization and Israel's needs for economizing defense research are complementary and should lay the foundation for sustained long-term partnership. Both countries share certain common objectives in pursuing their strategic policies and seek technological independence and qualitative superiority over their adversaries. The numerous strategic programs currently pursued by both countries are complementary. These include *Lavi* (India's Light Combat Aircraft), *Merkava* (Arjun tank), Jericho-I missile (*Prithvi*), and Jericho-II missile (*Agni*). The same can be said about a number of other Indian programs, including remotely piloted vehicles (RPVs) and an airborne early-warning system. Although Israel has an edge in several of these arenas, India has acquired considerable experience and expertise in space and satellite programs.

Because of increasing acts of terrorism and cross-border infiltration, Israeli expertise in intelligence gathering, innovative and proactive counterterrorism policies, and electronic surveillance along international borders have become key areas of cooperation.[54] India has adapted some of the Israeli techniques and methods in combating threats emanating from across the international border and line of control with Pakistan. Israel is one of the few countries with whom India has carried out regular discussions on counterterrorism within the framework of Joint Working Group. On the very day that terrorists struck the World Trade Center and the Pentagon in September 2001, Israeli National Security Adviser Major General Uzi Dayan was holding high-level discussions with Indian officials in New Delhi on terrorism.

Some of the major defense deals involving both the countries since 1992 include the procurement of the Barak anti-missile system; import of Heron UAVs and searcher drones; the upgrading of aging MiG fighter planes; import of two Super Dvora Mk II fast attack craft (FACs) and licensed production of four more at Goa Shipyard; purchase of three Phalcon advance airborne early-warning systems at an estimated cost of US$1.1 billion; a series of defense contracts estimated at $2 billion for the supply of long-range surveillance equipment, night-vision hardware, and ammunition, signed in August 2001;[55] a US$2.5 billion program to jointly develop missile defenses, agreed to in July 2007;[56] and the January 2008 Indian launch of an Israeli spy satellite into orbit.

In May 2007, in an unprecedented move, Defense Minister A. K. Antony informed the parliament that defense purchases from Israel during

2002 through 2007 totaled "over US$5 billion."[57] Besides these purchases, the military and intelligence chiefs of both countries visit one another periodically, and there is a regular and ongoing consultation between their national-security establishments. There is also an institutional consultation mechanism between the two foreign ministries. Indian naval vessels make periodic port calls to Israel. As part of the exercise, India joined the UN peacekeeping operations in the Middle East and began contributing troops to the UN Interim Force in Lebanon (UNIFIL) in November 1998 and joined the UN Disengagement Observer Force (UNDOF) along the Israel-Syria border in March 2006.

How do these diverse political, economic, and military relations between India and Israel play out internationally?

External Reaction

The improvement in Indo-Israeli relations questions some of the conventional wisdom regarding Israel and its usefulness in "opening many doors in Washington." Many Israelis and others have argued that countries seeking closer ties with the United States often make overtures toward Israel or issue pro-Israeli statements.[58] Ever since he came to power in 1981, for example, President Mubarak's visits to the United States have been preceded by some high-level political contacts with Israel. Like some of his predecessors, President Pervez Musharraf habitually made pro-Israeli statements before his trips to the United States. Similar tactics have been used by Turkey to circumvent the Greek and Armenian lobbies in the United States. The American dimension naturally became prominent as Indo-Israeli bilateral relations began to flourish. Desire for U.S. political support, technological assistance, and economic investment influenced Rao's decision to move away from India's traditional hostility toward Israel. The timing of the announcement, which came literally hours before Rao's visit to New York, did not go unnoticed. It was widely believed that normalization would spur the friends of Israel in the United States, especially on Capitol Hill, to work toward improving Indo-U.S. relations—and it did.

But the big picture is more complicated. It is beyond doubt that since the end of the cold war Indo-U.S. relations have improved considerably.[59] Washington hosted three Indian prime ministers; New Delhi witnessed two presidential visits. Even the tensions over the 1998 nuclear tests did not last long, with both nations settling for reconciliation, accommodation, and a commitment to forge closer ties.[60] Just as the United States has learned to abandon its prolonged nonproliferation policy toward India, the latter has learned to abandon its erstwhile anti-American rhetoric, which peaked during the early 1980s. The July 2005 nuclear agreement not only signaled a new phase of Indo-U.S. relations but also compelled other countries of the world to look to India as a potential partner. In short, improvement in its relations with the United States has opened many doors to India.

It is essential to recognize that the qualitative improvements in Indo-U.S. relations especially since 1998 did not come because of the normalization of relations with Israel. This happened primarily because of India's economic growth and its willingness to adopt a market-friendly economic liberalization program. Had it remained a Soviet-modeled closed economy with limited economic opportunities, greater state intervention, and an anti-American ideology, friends of Israel would not have brought about any Indo-U.S. rapprochement. It was the fundamental transformation in India's worldview and its growing economic clout, not normalization, that led to the warming of relations with the United States. While one does not rule out the positive role played by the American friends of Israel, the core reason for improvement in Indo-U.S. relations has to be found in changes that occurred inside India since 1991 and its post–cold war worldview.

For its part, India has been extremely wary of the U.S. role in disturbing closer ties with Israel, especially in the military-security arena. In the past, U.S. displeasure and disapproval resulted in Israel abandoning or scaling down its military exports to countries with which the United States had problems. The shift in U.S. policy, for example, compelled Israel to abandon the lucrative South African market during the dying stages of apartheid. This interventionist policy forced Israel to abandon military exports to China, including the Phalcon early warning system.[61] India sought to avoid the same trap.[62] It did not wish to find itself in the situation China found itself in, where military ties with Israel would be subjected to American whims. New Delhi decided to synchronize its Israel policy with Washington. By keeping the United States on board and in the picture, it hopes to minimize U.S. intervention. It is in this context that one has to examine some of the statements made by Indian leaders, especially when the NDA was in power. For example, addressing a dinner hosted by the American Jewish Committee in May 2003, Brajesh Mishra,

India's national-security adviser, observed that these three countries "have some fundamental similarities. We are all democracies, sharing a common vision of pluralism, tolerance, and equal opportunity. Stronger India-U.S. relations and India-Israel relations have a natural logic."[63] By bringing the United States into its bilateral relations with Israel, New Delhi sought to quarantine a potential American veto.

The reaction of the Middle Eastern countries is interesting. Compared to domestic criticisms, their reactions to normalization were muted almost to the point of indifference. Major powers who had a stake in the Madrid peace process were favorably disposed toward normalization. By accepting Israel and ending its diplomatic isolation, they hoped to contribute to peace in the Middle East. A more confident Israel, they felt, would be more willing to make political concessions that were essential for the success of the peace negotiations. For their part, the Arab countries were equally reconciled to the prospect of other countries modifying their policy toward the Jewish state. Having abandoned the "three Nos" of Khartoum, they could not counsel other states against talking to Israel, especially when these countries lack any bilateral disputes with Israel. The willingness of hardliner states such as Syria to go to Madrid meant that constructive engagement and not political isolation was the order the day.

There were some exceptions. Still reeling under the influence of the Ayatollah Khomeini, Iran was not ready to embrace the idea of Indo-Israeli normalization. Since its early days, hostility toward the Jewish state has been a cornerstone of the Islamic revolution. At the same time, post-Khomeini Iran was gradually seeking to end its political isolation both within and outside the Middle East. Hence, beyond minor criticism in the initial stages, Iran did not allow Indo-Israeli relations to impede its desire to seek closer ties with New Delhi. One could go to the extent of suggesting that while Israel was preoccupied with Indo-Iranian relations, Tehran was almost indifferent toward Indo-Israeli ties, including the growing military relationship.[64]

This is not true for Egypt. New Delhi initially feared that its new overtures toward Israel might generate negative vibes in the region, especially from Egypt. The same month it declared normalization, India announced the establishment of a cultural center in Cairo named after Maulana Abul Kalam Azad. This, India hoped, would assuage Egyptian sensitivities and thereby convey a strong message to the larger Arab world that its decision to establish relations with Israel was not anti-Arab. A few years later, India went to extent of conferring the Jawaharlal Nehru Award for International Peace upon President Hosni Mubarak. These efforts were not fruitful and did not remove the Egyptian displeasure with India.[65]

Other states were more accommodating. Despite some initial reservations, the principal Middle Eastern states have not allowed Indo-Israeli relations to affect their bilateral ties with India. Contrary to popular perception, while in power even the BJP was more sensitive to strengthening India's ties with the Islamic world.[66] Countries such as Iran and Saudi Arabia have been more than willing to promote closer economic and energy ties with India and are less worried about India's Israel policy. Far-reaching improvements in India's relations with Iran happened after and not before Indo-Israeli normalization. Likewise, significant improvements in its political and economic ties with Saudi Arabia happened after 1992. For its part, India was determined to decouple Pakistan from its Middle East policy. This approach paid dividends. In January 2003, it hosted President Mohammed Khatami as the chief guest of the Republic Day celebrations; King Abdullah of Saudi Arabia enjoyed that privilege three years later.

This growing confidence in dealing with Israel was exhibited when India decided to give a red-carpet welcome to Prime Minister Ariel Sharon in September 2003. Since the early days of the state, controversies dogged Sharon. For the critics of Israel, Sharon personified all that was wrong with Israel and Zionism. Even those who were sympathetic toward Israel were extremely wary of meeting the maverick Israeli leader in public. Not many Western countries were ready to host the Israeli leader following his February 2001 election as prime minister. Belgium even sought to initiate a war-crimes trial against Sharon over the Sabra and Shatila massacre of 1982. Thus to host Sharon under such circumstances was no ordinary feat for any country, let alone for India, which had a huge amount of historic baggage. One might even describe it as a political gamble.

Naturally, Sharon's visit generated widespread protests. Led by the communist parties, protest rallies were joined by various Islamic organizations and groups that were critical of Israel's heavy-handed policy toward the al-Aqsa intifada. No foreign visit had previously generated so much attention, controversy, and protest in India.[67] Sharon's visit also highlighted the other aspect of the bilateral relations: Arab and Islamic indifference. Even countries such as Iran, which has serious problems with the Jewish state, were not prepared to hold their relations with New Delhi hostage to Indo-Israeli ties. This enabled both countries to pursue serious discussions, dialogues, and dealings even in the military/security arena. Prolonged neglect and indifference did not inhibit India and Israel from pursuing military transactions and cooperation, and the tacit regional acceptance if not endorsement made things a lot easier.

This regional acceptance and emerging national consensus enabled India to pursue a relatively confident policy toward Israel unconcerned about the erstwhile drive for "balance." Even though Indian leaders were still meeting Palestinian leaders including Arafat, they were not inhibited from pursuing closer ties with Israel or in publicizing their preference for Israel in fighting terrorism. Neither the deportation of suspected Hamas militants in December 1992 nor the Hebron massacre of February 1994, in which scores of Muslim worshippers were killed, evoked adverse reactions from the INC government in India. This subtle pro-Israeli position was more clearly manifested when the BJP was in power during 1998 and 2004. While Indian officials continued to meet the Palestinian leader when they visited Israel, the shift was discernable. The World Conference Against Racism held in Durban in August 2001 was an important moment in Indo-Israeli relations. Under Arab pressure, the conference agenda included a strong condemnation of Israel and depicted Zionism as a form of racism and racial discrimination. Capitalizing on the international condemnation over the al-Aqsa intifada, Arab and Islamic countries sought to resurrect the 1975 UN resolution that had been annulled in December 1991. Despite pressure from some Islamic countries, India, which had supported both the original resolution describing Zionism as a form of racism and its subsequent revocation in 1991, was not prepared to go back to the past.

The response of the Indian government to the outbreak of the intifada and prolonged violence was also muted. Unlike the past, it limited its reactions to counseling restraint on both sides. The Israeli policy of assassinating key Palestinian political and military leaders evoked only a mild rebuke. It was not prepared to condemn Israel and its leaders for their repeated personal threats against Yasser Arafat. Such an attitude was strongly criticized by the leftist parties. In the words of CPI(M) General Secretary Harkishan Singh Surjeet, "Even the U.S. state department felt compelled to urge Israel to keep its promise of not harming Arafat. But the Vajpayee government is not prepared to issue even such an appeal."[68] This shift was more blatant when in January 2003 the Indian government took exception to the presence of the Palestinian ambassador Khalid al-Shaikh at an opposition meeting critical of anti-Muslim riots in Gujarat. Not prepared to tolerate his "interference" in Indian domestic affairs, it requested that Arafat recall his emissary in India; the Palestinian leader was quick to comply.[69] If further proof were needed, the visit of Prime Minister Sharon took place while the Palestinian leader was confined to his Ramallah headquarters.

Thus, having remained aloof for much of the twentieth century, both India and Israel have shown a serious desire and commitment to pursue a mutually productive relationship. Even fifteen years after normalization, Israel still attracts widespread interest, attention, and publicity in India. Unlike other larger countries and bigger economies, it still dominates the front pages of the English and vernacular media. The fascination is not confined to those who view relations with Israel in a positive light. The obsession with Israel is equally dominant among the critics of India's Middle East policy.

Even the defeat of the BJP and the formation of the INC-led UPA government in May 2004 did not radically alter India's policy. The government of Manmohan Singh was quick to dispel any misgivings. In his address to the parliament, President Abdul Kalam outlined the policy of the new government and declared that relations with Israel, "which have developed on the basis of mutually beneficial cooperation, are important, but this in no way dilutes our principled support for the legitimate aspirations of the Palestinian people."[70] After some initial hesitation, it reiterated its commitment to maintaining and improving ties with Israel. As one commentator bitterly observed, even as Arafat was struggling for his life in the Percy military hospital in Paris, "the Indian government was busy preparing for the high-level political consultations with Israel."[71] Far from "correcting" the course chalked out by the BJP, the UPA government was prepared to pursue long-term strategic ties with Israel in the form of joint missile development. What, then, is the big picture?

13 Conclusion

"Jerusalem has been a holy city for Christians, Muslims, and Jews. Lately, it has also become a holy city for the Indian armed forces."[1] Though odd—and some might say controversial—this formulation aptly reflects the newly found Indian fondness for Israel. Since the establishment of relations in January 1992, India has come a long way. Within a short span of time, bilateral relations have flourished considerably, often frustrating countries whose historic ties with India could not match the profile that Israel has acquired within a decade of normalization. The transformation has been astronomical.

In 1947, represented by the Congress Party, the Indian nationalists opposed the partition of both India and Palestine. They were not prepared to accept the notion that religion could be a defining identity for nationalism. Recognizing the Muslims as a separate "nation" that entails a separate state would have opened a Pandora's box. The presence of over five hundred princely states at the time of the British withdrawal frightened them. Endorsing a religiously based self-determination was seen as detrimental and disastrous for India, a country of diverse ethnic, religious, linguistic, and caste-based divisions and cleavages. The Indian leaders were equally realistic. Despite their deeply seated reservations and disapproval, they were prepared to accept the partition of the subcontinent along communal lines. A large portion of the Muslim community rejected Pakistan and stayed behind in a predominantly Hindu but secular India. This not only vindicated the ideological stand of the Congress Party but also provided an opportunity for free India to establish its secular credentials.

India exhibited the same political realism vis-à-vis Israel. Its advocacy for a federal solution and opposition to the partition plan in the UN Special Committee were part of its larger position regarding religious nationalism. During its freedom struggle, India saw Zionism as the external version of the Muslim League and subsequently Israel as another Pakistan. As with the partition of the subcontinent, New Delhi was prepared to accept the political situation of the Middle East. Israel had become a reality and was recognized by a host of countries, including the rival bloc of the cold war. The hopes for a Palestinian state never materialized because of inter-Arab squabbles and aggrandizement. India thus had to approach Israel realistically. If it could accept a "religious partition" in its neighborhood, how could it adopt a different position with respect to the Middle East?

There was a fundamental problem, however. While the Indian readiness to accept Pakistan was quick, formal, and complete, Israel was less fortunate. Indian recognition took more than twenty-eight months to materialize, and it was not followed by normal relations. In the initial years, it was eager to establish full relations with Israel, and Prime Minister Jawaharlal Nehru made a formal commitment when the senior Israeli diplomat Walter Eytan met him in New Delhi on March 4, 1952. Nehru even asked the foreign ministry to prepare a budget for a resident Indian mission in Tel Aviv. This never materialized, and normalization became entangled in Indian domestic politics.

Nehru's cabinet colleague and close confidant Maulana Azad was often blamed for the situation. But the problem was much larger. Since the early 1920s, the Indian nationalists perceived the Middle East, especially Jewish political aspirations in Palestine, through an Islamic prism. Mahatma Gandhi was more honest and candid than most of his contemporaries and successors. He was prepared to see the Arab opposition to Jewish aspirations in Palestine as an Islamic and not a nationalist issue. He openly endorsed the concept of *Jazirat al-Arab* and argued that the Islamic lands of Palestine must not be handed over to non-Muslim rule. He accepted the divine injunctions of Prophet Mohammed over Islamic places and explicitly ruled out non-Muslim sovereignty.

As a country with the largest Muslim population in the world, British India could not ignore the Islamic dimension of the problem. The Congress Party sought to expand its support among Muslims and counter the efforts of the Muslim League by adopting pro-Muslim and pro-Arab positions on the Middle East. The Congress Party, however, projected this pro-Arab policy through secular rationales. Anticolonialism, anti-imperialism, and opposition to religion-based nationalism became its main arguments regarding the *yishuv*.

This Congress Party–Muslim League rivalry took a different turn after 1947. Contrary to the expectations of the historian and future diplomat K. M. Panikkar, free India did not adopt a "Hindu" view toward Zionism, if this had ever been feasible. It still had a large Muslim population, and Israel became a Middle Eastern pawn in the Indo-Pakistan rivalry. If the Congress Party was competing with the Muslim League in the past, now the competition operated at two levels. Domestically, the support of the Muslim population was essential not only for the electoral success of the Congress Party but also to maintain its secular credentials vis-à-vis the Hindu nationalist parties on the right. Externally, India was competing with Pakistan for political favors from the Islamic countries, especially over the Kashmir dispute. To complicate matters, Nehru had to deal with Israel's regional isolation, India's strong political and economic ties with the Arab world, and his own evolving friendship with the Egyptian leader Gamal Abdul Nasser.

The domestic dimension has perhaps been the most important factor in shaping India's understanding of the Jewish history and political struggle. While the Pakistan factor has received considerable attention internally, the domestic dimension still remains taboo. There are honorable exceptions, such as Appadorai, but for the most part mainstream scholars carefully avoided and still avoid discussing the influence of the domestic Muslim population upon India's Israel policy. Such an inquiry was dismissed as communalization, partisanship, or as being part of a right-wing agenda. It never occurred to them that the foreign policy of a democracy is a function of its domestic politics and that Indian Muslims have strong historic, cultural, and religious links with the Middle East. The absence of dispassionate debate regarding the domestic inputs into India's Middle East policy remains a major challenge. This is further compounded by India's policy of not releasing official papers pertaining to even Nehru's tenure as prime minister (1947–1964).

The absence of relations and avoidance of serious debate over the domestic dimension have made Israel the most controversial aspect of India's foreign policy. Ever since the issue was first raised in the Constituent Assembly in December 1947, more than five months before its establishment, Israel remained a hotly contested and passionately debated foreign-policy issue in India. For the non-INC opposition parties, Israel became an important political instrument to criticize the government. During upheavals like the June war, the Indian parliament witnessed heated, uproarious, and acrimonious debates. At times, the Indian government found itself on a shaky wicket, for example during the row over the September 1969 Rabat fiasco.

India's Israel policy is not exclusively domestic. Such an understanding would be wrong, misleading, and incomplete. While domestic concerns regarding the Muslim population resulted in India viewing the Jewish-Israeli problem through an Islamic prism, there are also other secular and nonreligious considerations. Its concerns vis-à-vis Pakistan in the Middle East are driven by calculations of national interest. The numerical strength of the Arab and Islamic countries and Pakistan's efforts to forge an Islamic front dominated its thinking. This competition at times resulted in India making controversial choices, like its futile attempts at attending the Rabat conference.

Indeed, for decades Pakistan functioned as India's litmus test for its relations with the outside world. This, however, could not be implemented in the Middle East. Its pro-Palestinian stance did not yield political dividends in the Middle East, and on numerous occasions it was disappointed over Arab support for Pakistan.. The lack of Arab reciprocity during conflicts with Pakistan did not result in any dramatic Indian moves. India could neither demand reciprocity nor retaliate for the Arabs' pro-Pakistan position. In fact, India could not even publicly criticize the Arabs for letting their old friend down during crucial moments. If its political leverage, especially after 1962, was limited, its economic leverage was nonexistent. It was vulnerable to Arab economic and energy pressures. India settled for the least resistance: suffering in silence. By not openly discussing the Arab reaction and by praising their "understanding," it sought to minimize any negative fallout. By not responding forcibly, it hoped to convince the Arabs to reexamine their pro-Pakistan position. Thus India never took the Arabs to task for their prolonged pro-Pakistan stance and their refusal to accommodate India despite the latter acceding to their demands on Israel. Thus India kept Israel at a distance to placate the Arabs, but the latter had no qualms about cozying up to Pakistan during its conflicts with India. This Indian path led to a peculiar development when it acknowledged Arab "help" during its conflicts even while it was receiving unacknowledged military assistance from Israel.

When Prime Minister Narasimha Rao decided to establish full diplomatic relations with Israel in January 1992, he completed a process that began over four decades earlier. India became the last major non-Islamic country to establish full relations with the Jewish state. Through normalization, Rao put an end to India's treating its relations with Israel as a zero-sum game. No longer would India assume that support for the Arabs and Palestinians had to be accompanied by a total absence of formal ties with Israel and that even a modicum of relations would be a betrayal of the Palestinians.

This shift was possible both because of the end of the ideological divide in international relations and due to specific circumstances that enabled India to revisit and reorient its Israel policy. The international community, especially in the Middle East, has been less hostile to Israel since the end of the cold war. For the vast majority of Arab and Islamic countries, there is no military solution to the Arab-Israeli conflict. In practical terms it is no longer an "either/or" question. Unlike the past, India can maintain cordial ties with Israel and with the Palestinians. Its new desire for great-power status and its growing economic strength have resulted in India gradually diluting the Pakistani factor from the Middle East. The region has ceased to be a battleground for Indo-Pakistan diplomatic rivalries.

The domestic Muslim opinion has shown signs of accommodation on Israel. Improvement in Israel's diplomatic status in the Islamic world resonates among Indian Muslims. Although their pro-Arab sentiments are visible and palpable when the peace process turns violent, they are not blind to the growing political recognition of Israel by countries such as Saudi Arabia. Rabid opposition to Israel's right to exist is largely confined to marginal radical elements. The mainstream Islamic world has serious differences with Israel's policies but less with its existence.

During the cold war, the Indian approach to the Middle East had the peculiar feature of being a zero-sum game. It was unable to decouple its bilateral relations with Israel from the wider problems in the Middle East. In its assessment, the furtherance of its interests in the Arab world demanded not only remaining distant from Israel but even treating it as an outcast. By not establishing formal ties with the Jewish state, it sought to promote its interests in the Middle East. It was unable to make a distinction between bilateral ties and multilateral problems. It had yet to learn the art of conveying its disagreements with the policies of Israel while maintaining formal ties. It is often forgotten that even those parties that clamored for the normalization of relations were equally critical of Israel's occupation of the Arab lands following the June war. Normalization did not have to be an endorsement of Israel's policies. But India was not pursuing a nuanced approach.

Thus the establishment of full diplomatic relations with Israel in January 1992 has to be seen within the wider context of the far-reaching domestic changes that were happening within India. Despite the obvious shortcomings both within and outside the country, there are today suggestions of a "rising" India and unmistakable signs of great-power aspirations. The tone for this grand self-imagery, both problematic and exaggerated, was set by some of the critical decisions taken by the Rao government, which signaled the arrival of a new India. While pretending to adhere to the "continuity" of Nehru's sociopolitical model, the Congress Party made nuanced changes. Its leadership signaled a reorientation of foreign policy and in the process redefined India's role on the world stage. Abandoning the Soviet model, the Indian leadership also opted for economic reforms that fundamentally changed its domestic and foreign-policy priorities. The transformation was slow but decisive, and it resulted from a set of complex social, political, and economic factors and compulsions that affected every aspect of the Indian polity.

The period between the late 1980s and the early 1990s was one of immense political instability, social turmoil, and economic crisis. Political violence and separatist militants in Punjab, Kashmir, and the northeast undermined internal security. These challenges were complicated by political ineptness, raising doubts about national unity and cohesion. Within a span of six years, both Prime Minister Indira Gandhi and her son Rajiv fell to terrorists. Perpetual discord over caste and communalism threatened social cohesion. The decision to empower members of lower castes through increased affirmative action resulted in a backlash from those wedded to meritocracy. Around the same time, Hindu-Muslim community harmony reached its nadir. Decimated in the earlier elections, the Hindu right sought better political fortunes by raising the question of the Babri Mosque in Ayodhya. There were widespread tensions and communal passions in different parts of the country, which, coupled with the shortsightedness of political leaders, considerably weakened many institutions of the state and undermined the principle of secularism enshrined in the Indian constitution.

These in turn adversely affected the Indian economy. The Soviet Union, its principal supporter during the cold war, was preoccupied with its own survival and was not in a position to come to India's rescue. Mikhail Gorbachev was increasingly sucked into the political and economic mess of the Stalinist model of state capitalism. In 1991, India had the dubious distinction of having to fly out and mortgage two hundred tons of its gold reserves just to pay for a two-week import of essential commodities. The defeat of the Congress Party in the 1989 Lok Sabha elections unleashed the phenomenon of coalition politics and weak and unstable governments at the center. The Congress Party lost its hegemony in Indian politics and was forced to share power with various regional parties, factions, and leaders. Their unfamiliarity with foreign policy proved costly when India endorsed the Iraqi annexation of Kuwait by closing its embassy in Kuwait City in early August 1990. The international climate was equally challenging. The cold war was moving to a close, and the Soviet Union was crumbling along with the Iron Curtain. The Iraqi action against Kuwait shifted global attention from the Israeli-Palestinian conflict to the Persian Gulf.

In short, this period witnessed India undergoing an organic crisis. The convergence of domestic turmoil and major shifts in international politics remain the key to understanding the trajectory of the post–cold war foreign policy of India.

Democracies either find a way to confront grave threats or they cease to exist. To survive, the Indian political elites adapted themselves to the new situation and readjusted India's overall economic and foreign-policy orientation. Both great-power aspirations and coalition compulsions prevented them from completely abandoning the past or capitulation. Under the leadership of Rao, they initiated a cautious path toward integration with the global market and reached out to the Western world, especially the United States. Driven by economic reforms, India consciously engaged Washington, and, discarding the ideological blinders of the cold war, the Indian establishment began to see the United States in friendlier terms. Those who for decades had harped on the entry of *USS Enterprise* into the Bay of Bengal during the Indo-Pakistan war of 1971 began recognizing the usefulness of Washington in furthering India's great-power aspirations. Democracy and shared political values with the United States gained prominence.

To mend relations with Washington, India needed to convince the world that it was prepared to make a clean break from the past. If its cold-war worldview was truly obsolete, it had to make a visible foreign-policy gesture. This came in the form of normalizing full diplomatic relations with Israel. Besides political and geostrategic calculations, one cannot ignore the symbolic nature of the decision. Normalization of relations was announced literally hours before Prime Minister Rao left for New York to attend the summit meeting of the UN Security Council.

In making a break from the past, India did not take a U-turn. Such a move would have been detrimental to its aspirations of influence in the wider world. While normalization marked a new beginning, a zigzag policy would have been disastrous. Nor did the domestic and coalition situation enable the Congress Party to abandon its past policy regarding Palestine. This is marked by continued Indian support for the political rights of the Palestinians and their rights for statehood.

Normalization of relations with Israel marked a definite break from the past. Rao's new approach to Israel was followed by mainstream political forces within the country. Despite occasional pressures from some Muslim and communist groups, India resolved not to revert back to the old ways of treating Israel as an outcast.

Interestingly, normalization also undermined some of the conventional wisdom regarding Indian foreign policy. Normalization did not happen when India was witnessing political stability, economic growth, or Hindu-Muslim communal harmony. On the contrary, it happened when all of them were absent or most unfavorable. Indeed, within months after the establishment of relations with Israel, religious tensions reached its height when the controversial Babri Mosque in the sleepy north Indian town of Ayodhya was destroyed by right-wing Hindu activists, burying secularism in its rubble.

Likewise, the conventional wisdom argues that in parliamentary democracies weak governments cannot undertake strong, assertive, and far-reaching foreign-policy decisions. Political stability and single-party domination are often seen essential for a break with the past. The Indian example, however, exhibited the opposite. Rao indeed did not have a simple majority when he reversed the four-decade-old policy initiated by Nehru. Not only Israel but even a larger rapprochement with the West since the early 1990s was brought about by centrist coalition governments. There has been remarkable continuity in India's foreign policy since the end of the cold war. Regardless of the hue of the coalition that forms the government in New Delhi, India's foreign policy has been more realistic. Despite their differences when in opposition, both mainstream parties, namely the Congress Party and the BJP, have pursued a markedly pro-U.S. policy when in power.

Finally, India's new foreign policy has abandoned its erstwhile binary shibboleths. Normalization and its new friendship with Israel has not meant the abandonment of the Palestinians. This approach has not been confined to the Middle East: there are other examples. Since the early 1990s, India has strengthened its relations with the United States without weakening its ties with the Russian Federation. Likewise, India seeks closer ties with both Tehran and Washington.

Normalization marked the second phase of India's relationship with Israel, in which India recognized that it was possible and necessary to maintain closer ties with Israel and the Arabs. In this pragmatic worldview, India's new relationship with Israel was not an abandonment, let alone betrayal, of the Palestinians. Given that the Palestinians and other Arab neighbors were seeking a negotiated political settlement with the Jewish state, there was no compelling reason for India to treat Israel as an outcast. Once the Madrid Middle East peace process began in October 1991, where was the need to be more Palestinian than Arafat?

Even nearly two decades after normalization, Israel continues to draw considerable attention within India. While progress has been slower than many have hoped, relations have blossomed. Even the al-Aqsa intifada could not bring about a "course correction," as many on the left demanded. Domestic pressures do result in India not favoring any high-profile contacts with Israel, the visit of Prime Minister Ariel Sharon in September 2003 being an exception. With the sole exception of Egypt, most of the Arab and Islamic countries have come to terms with Indo-Israeli bilateral ties. Significant improvements in its relations with principal Islamic countries such as Iran and Saudi Arabia happened after and not before Indo-Israeli normalization. Even Pakistan, which in the past was paranoid about an Indo-Israeli "conspiracy against the Islamic world," is not averse to moving closer to Israel.

India's relationship with Israel has slowly moved into a third and more complex phase: namely, the delinking of bilateral relations from the vagaries of the Middle Eastern peace process. It has strong reservations over the direction and substance of the peace process and differs with Israel over key issues such as Jewish settlements in the occupied territories, national boundaries, the question of Jerusalem, and combating Palestinian violence. Even the Hindu-nationalist government was not prepared to endorse Israel's assassination of Palestinian leaders. During the second Lebanon war, even traditional supporters criticized Israel's attacks against the civilian population. These disagreements have not prevented India from forging closer economic and military ties with Israel. By expressing its reservations over the peace process, India is contributing to the consolidation of domestic support for bilateral relations.

Vocally distancing itself from Israel's controversial peace policies is essential if India is to consolidate bilateral ties. This is rather un-American: a robust bilateral relation with Israel accompanied by strong criticism over the peace process. Therein lies the long-term stability of Indo-Israeli relations.

Notes

1. Introduction

1. *Harijan* (November 26, 1938), in Gandhi, *The Collected Works of Gandhi*, 68:137.
2. The Khilafat movement refers to the agitation by the Indian Muslims for the protection and preservation of the Ottoman Empire, whose sultan also held the office of caliph.
3. *Debates CA*, first session, party II (December 4, 1947): 1258.
4. Rafael, *Destination Peace*, 89.
5. Brecher, *India and World Politics*, 79.
6. Personal interview with Morarji Desai on October 22, 1987, in Mumbai. When he was prime minister, Moshe Dayan, Israel's foreign minister, paid an incognito visit to India.
7. Agwani, *Contemporary West Asia*, 253.
8. L. Panjabi to H. Z. Cynowitz (March 26, 1949), ISA, 2555/5.
9. Raman, *The Kaoboys of R&AW*, 127.
10. Panikkar, *In Two Chinas*, 12.
11. Olsvanger to Tagore (October 7, 1936), and A. K. Chanda, secretary to Tagore to Olsvanger (October 23, 1936), CZA S25/3583.
12. The *Times* (London) (November 13, 1959), quoted in Mudiam, *India and the Middle East*, 160.
13. Eliahu Sasson to S. Divon (December 28, 1950), ISA, 53/6b. Emphasis added.

14. Accepting the UN resolution continues to remain the main bone of contention between the mainstream Fatah and the militant Islamic group Hamas.
15. Eytan to Shiloah (August 11, 1949), ISA, 2441/2.
16. Abba Eban to B. N. Rau (December 8, 1950), ISA, 71/14b.
17. As *ahl al-kitab* ("Possessors of the Scripture" or "People of the Book"), Islam guarantees certain protections to followers of Judaism, Christianity, and, in the Iranian context, Zoroastrianism. Bernard Lewis offers a sympathetic portrayal in his *The Jews of Islam*. For a more critical depiction of *Dhimmi* life, see Ye'or, *The Dhimmi* and *Islam and Dhimmitude*.
18. According to the historian Mushirul Hasan, *Jazirat-al-Arab* included "Constantinople, Jerusalem, Medina and above all Mecca, with its Baitullah, the focal point of daily prayers and the annual Haj." *Nationalism and Communal Politics in India, 1885–1930*, 112–113.
19. *Young India* (April 6, 1921), in Gandhi, *The Collected Works of Gandhi*, 19:530.
20. For the text of the resolution adopted at the Gaya Congress of 1922, see Zaidi and Zaidi, eds., *Encyclopedia INC*, 8:542. In subsequent years, the Islamic rationale never figured formally in the pronouncement of Indian nationalists. Even these earlier pronouncements were explained within the context of the need to support the Muslims of India. Thus, in the mid-1920s, support for the Arabs of Palestine was depicted as part of the larger anticolonial and anti-imperial struggle and support for national liberation.
21. *UNSCOP Report*, 2:42, 2:45.
22. Thus, for some the disintegration of Pakistan and the formation of Bangladesh in 1971 vindicated India's stand against the rationale of Pakistani nationalism and partition along communal lines.
23. "Memorandum on India Before the United Nations, 1950" (September 16, 1950), ISA, 2413/28.
24. Statement of M. R. Masani, *Hindustan Times* (June 5, 1967). Meaning "messenger," the expression has the derogatory connotation of being unimportant.
25. The Jan Sangh lawmaker M. L. Sondhi in parliament, *Debates LS*, series 4, vol. 4 (June 8, 1967), 3937.
26. *Iftar* is the evening meal for breaking the daily fast during the holy month Ramadan and is normally organized as a community event. In India, various non-Muslim political leaders host *Iftar* parties for both Muslim and non-Muslim invitees.

2. Mahatma Gandhi and the Jewish National Home

The epigraph to this chapter is taken from a statement given by Mahatma Gandhi to Kallenbach on Zionism in July 1937, CZA, S25/3587. Emphasis added.

1. *Harijan* (November 26, 1938), in Gandhi, *The Collected Works of Gandhi*, 68:137.

2. Among others, see India, Ministry of External Affairs, *India and Palestine*, 11; Agwani, *Contemporary West Asia*, 152, 220; Heptulla, *Indo-West Asian Relations*, 153.
3. *Congress Marches Ahead, January 1996–December 1997*, 199–200. This formulation is inaccurate. Gandhi talked of Arabs and not Palestinians. Also see Foreign Minister Natwar Singh's speech at Jamia Milia Islamia on October 6, 2004, available online at http://meaindia.nic.in/speech/2004/10/06ss02.htm.
4. Shourie, *The Only Fatherland*.
5. In its obituary for the Palestinian leader Yasser Arafat, *People's Democracy*, the official organ of the Communist Party of India (Marxist) declared, "in 1938 . . . Mahatma Gandhi denounced the illegal occupation of Arab land. Since then India had always stood behind the Palestinians who were fighting for their freedom." "Left Salutes Comrade Arafat," *People's Democracy* (November 28, 2004), available online at http://pd.cpim.org/2004/1128/11282004_arafat%20condolence.htm.
6. Jafferlot, *The Hindu Nationalist Movement in India*, 87.
7. *Harijan* (November 26, 1938), in Gandhi, *The Collected Works of Gandhi*.
8. Shimoni, *Gandhi, Satyagraha, and the Jews*, 12.
9. Ibid., 11.
10. Among others, see Shimoni, *Gandhi, Satyagraha, and the Jews*; Chatterjee, *Gandhi and His Jewish Friends*; and Gordon, "Indian Nationalist Ideas About Palestine and Israel," 221–222.
11. *Harijan* (November 26, 1938), in Gandhi, *The Collected Works of Gandhi*.
12. Ibid.
13. Shimoni, *Gandhi, Satyagraha, and the Jews*, 12.
14. *Harijan* (May 27, 1939).
15. For detailed discussions on the Khilafat struggle, see Neimeijer, *The Khilafat Movement in India, 1919–1924*; and Minault, *The Khilafat Movement*.
16. *Young India* (March 23, 1921), in Gandhi, *The Collected Works of Gandhi*, 19:472.
17. *Young India* (April 6, 1921) , in Gandhi, *The Collected Works of Gandhi*, 19:530.
18. Ibid. Emphasis added.
19. Shimoni, *Gandhi, Satyagraha, and the Jews*, 24.
20. Chatterjee, *Gandhi and His Jewish Friends*, 164.
21. *Harijan* (November 26, 1938), in Gandhi, *The Collected Works of Gandhi*, 68:137.
22. *Harijan* (May 27, 1939), in Gandhi, *The Collected Works of Gandhi*, 69:289. Emphasis added.
23. They include "Gandhi and the Jews," *The Jewish Advocate* (Bombay) (December 2, 1938); "Jewish Satyagraha," *The Jewish Advocate*; "Mr. Gandhi on the Jewish Problem," *The Jewish Tribune* (Bombay) (December 1938); "Open Letter to Mahatma Gandhi," *The Jewish Advocate* (December 30, 1938); "Mr. Gandhi and the Jews," *The Jewish Tribune* (June 1939); and "We Are Treated

as Sub-Human, We Are Asked to Be Super-Human," *Jewish Frontier* (New York) (March 1939).

24. At that time, Magnes was the president of the Hebrew University of Jerusalem.
25. Buber and Magnes, *Two Letters to Gandhi.*
26. Ramana Murti, "Buber's Dialogue and Gandhi's Satyagraha," 605. Emphasis added.
27. Shimoni, *Gandhi, Satyagraha, and the Jews,* 47.
28. *The Jewish Advocate* (December 2, 1938): 2.
29. Shimoni, *Gandhi, Satyagraha, and the Jews,* 3.
30. Moshe Shertok to Herman Kallenbach (July 15, 1936), CZA, S25/3239.
31. Jansen, *Zionism, Israel, and Asian Nationalism,* 169.
32. The meeting took place on January 14, 1931, on the eve of Shaukat Ali accompanying the body of his brother Mohammed Ali to Jerusalem for burial. Chaim Weizmann to Lord Passfield (January 14, 1931), CZA, S25/3048.
33. Kupferschmidt, "The General Muslim Congress of 1931 in Jerusalem."
34. Note of the interview by Selig Brodetsky (October 15, 1931), CZA, S25/3535.
35. Shertok to Kallenbach (July 15, 1936), CZA, S25/3239.
36. Shimoni, *Gandhi, Satyagraha, and the Jews,* 36.
37. Before he could undertake this trip, Andrews died in 1940.
38. Likewise, Brodetsky met Polak before he and Sokolov met Gandhi in London in October 1931.
39. Shimoni, *Gandhi, Satyagraha, and the Jews,* 37–55; Jansen, *Zionism, Israel, and Asian Nationalism,* 177–179; Buber and Magnes, *Two Letters to Gandhi; The Jewish Advocate* (Bombay); Fischer, *Gandhi and Stalin,* 42.
40. Weizmann to Kallenbach (July 22, 1937), in Weizman, *The Letters and Papers of Chaim Weizmann,* series A, 18:182.
41. Shimoni, *Gandhi, Satyagraha, and the Jews,* 31. A more detailed and annotated account of Olsvanger's visit and the English translation of his dairy can be found in Ben-David, *Indo-Judaic Studies,* 14–44.
42. Shertok to Arthur Lourie (September 28, 1936), CZA, S25/3239.
43. *Report on the Inter-Asian Conference* (April 6, 1947, and April 17, 1947), CZA, S25/7485.
44. Statement given by Mahatma Gandhi to Kallenbach on Zionism in July 1937. Since Kallenbach referred to this statement in his letter to Weizmann (July 2, 1937), it should have come on or before July 2, 1937. For a typed copy of this statement, see CZA, S25/3587.
45. The journal described itself as "the official organ of Bombay Zionist Association and Keren Hayesod (Palestine Foundation Fund) and Keren Kayemeth (Jewish National Fund)."
46. Eliahu Epstein to Arthur Lourie (December 21, 1938), CZA, S25/3587. See also Epstein to Shohet (December 21, 1938), CZA, S25/3587.
47. Eliahu Epstein to Arthur Lourie (December 21, 1938), CZA, S25/3587.
48. Shohet to Epstein (March 24, 1939), CZA, S25/6315.
49. Ibid.

50. Shimoni, *Gandhi, Satyagraha, and the Jews*, 40.
51. Zangwill, "The Return to Palestine," 627.
52. Kallenbach to Weizmann (July 4, 1937), CZA, S25/3587.
53. Statement given by Mahatma Gandhi to Kallenbach on Zionism in July 1937. Emphasis added.
54. *Harijan* (November 26, 1938), in Gandhi, *The Collected Works of Gandhi*, 68:140.
55. This contrasted with the position of the Zionists toward the war. They were caught between the need to fight Nazism in Europe while opposing the White Paper of 1939, which repudiated British commitments to the Balfour Declaration. Hence they adopted a unique posture "to fight the War as if there is no White Paper and to fight the White Paper as if there is no war."
56. *Harijan* (June 21, 1942), in Gandhi, *The Collected Works of Gandhi*, 76:216.
57. Resolution adopted at the Haripura annual session of the Congress in February 1938. Zaidi and Zaidi, eds., *Encyclopedia INC*, 11:427.
58. Jawaharlal Nehru to Olsvanger (September 25, 1936), CZA, S25/3583.
59. *Young India* (April 6, 1921), in Gandhi, *The Collected Works of Gandhi*, 19:530.
60. *Young India* (May 25, 1921), in Gandhi, *The Collected Works of Gandhi*, 20:129. Emphasis added.
61. For the text of the resolution adopted at the Gaya Congress of 1922, see Zaidi and Zaidi, eds., *Encyclopedia INC*, 8:542.
62. Fischer, *Gandhi and Stalin*, 42. Emphasis added. However, for a different version of what Gandhi told Silverman, see Jansen, *Zionism, Israel, and Asian Nationalism*, 177–179. It should be remembered, however, that Fischer's work was published while Mahatma was still alive, whereas Jansen's version came out in 1971, more than two decades after the Mahatma's death.
63. Gandhi, *The Collected Works of Gandhi*, 87:262.
64. Ibid., 87:417. Emphasis added.
65. Ibid., 88:48.
66. *Harijan* (November 26, 1938), in Gandhi, *The Collected Works of Gandhi*, 68:138–139.
67. *Harijan*, (December 17, 1938), in Gandhi, *The Collected Works of Gandhi*, 68:191–192.
68. *Harijan* (November 26, 1938), in Gandhi, *The Collected Works of Gandhi*, 68:140.
69. In 1939, communicating with a Muslim friend, he remarked: "My mind goes back to the days of Khilafat agitation . . . when at a meeting of the Muslim League before 1920 I asked for supreme sacrifice, two or three names were given . . . but I believed that many would come forward at the right time. And they did. But looking back upon those days I see that I compromised nonviolence. I was satisfied with mere abstention from physical violence." *Harijan* (June 17, 1939), in Gandhi, *The Collected Works of Gandhi*, 69:314.
70. One could draw a parallel between the Arab opposition to Jewish immigration to Palestine and the current Israeli opposition to the unrestricted Palestinian right of return to their homes.

71. "An Open Letter to Mahatma Gandhi," *The Jewish Advocate* (December 30, 1939): 3–4.
72. Shimoni, *Gandhi, Satyagraha, and the Jews,* 18–19.
73. Theologically, Judaism has more in common with Islam than Christianity. Indeed, both the Judeo-Christian heritage and Judeo-Islamic animosity are of recent origin.
74. Michael Brecher, "Israel and China: A Historic 'Missed Opportunity,'" 221.

3. The Congress Party and the *Yishuv*

The epigraph to this chapter is taken from a letter from Immanuel Olsvanger to Selig Brodetsky (December 2, 1937), CZA, S25/3588.

1. For the text of the resolution adopted at the Gaya Congress of 1922, see Zaidi and Zaidi, eds., *Encyclopedia INC,* 8:542. According to the historian Mushirul Hasan, *Jazirat al-Arab* included "Constantinople, Jerusalem, Medina and, above all Mecca with its Baitullah, the focal point of daily prayers and the annual Haj." Hasan, *Nationalism and Communal Politics in India,* 112–113.
2. Quoted in Hasan, *Nationalism and Communal Politics in India,* 113.
3. In December 1924, the All-India Congress Committee (AICC) adopted a resolution on the "Egyptian crisis." This was the first non-Khilafat Congress Party statement on the Middle East. For the text of the resolution adopted at the Belgaum session, see Zaidi and Zaidi, eds., *Encyclopedia INC,* 8:681.
4. Quoted in Dastur, "India and the West Asian Crisis," 27.
5. Zaidi and Zaidi, eds., *Encyclopedia INC,* 9:538.
6. Ibid., 11:153.
7. Ibid., 11:260.
8. Ibid, 11:400.
9. Ram Manohar Lohia to Immanuel Olsvanger (October 13, 1936), CZA, S25/3583.
10. Zaidi and Zaidi, eds., *Encyclopedia INC,* 11:427. It should be noted that while the *modus operandi* of the Jews was questioned, the INC did not pronounce its position on the central issue of the Jewish national home. A similar resolution was adopted by the AICC during its Delhi meeting in September 1938. Ibid., 11:445–446.
11. CWC resolution adopted in Wardha in December 1938. Ibid., 11:497. It is interesting to note that the proposition "in" was used instead of "of."
12. Ibid., 12:159–160.
13. The Congress motion moved by T. S. Avinashilingam Chettier was adopted by fifty-seven votes in favor and forty-three against. For the complete debate, see India, *Legislative Assembly Debates, Official Report, Fifth Legislative Assembly* (February 3, 1939), 1:170–200.
14. There was some ambiguity in the adoption of the resolution. The amendment was not put to a vote separately. Even though it also demanded India's

withdrawal from the League of Nations, its rationale was different. Only Qaiyum, a sponsor, referred to the British role in Palestine. Referring to the ambiguous situation, Sir Abdur Rahim, the president of the Assembly, remarked: "The question has arisen whether the Chair can put the amendment to vote. There is no precedent that the Chair can find and the Chair does not know whether any question like this has arisen before." Ibid., 200.

15. Similarly, there was no direct reference to the Mandate being granted to the British.
16. Ram Manohar Lohia, in his capacity as the secretary of the Foreign Department, wrote in October 1936: "The battles of the persecuted Jews have to be fought out in the different countries where such persecution is practiced in common with other freedom loving colonial and progress forces." Lohia to Olsvanger (October 13, 1936), CZA, S25/3583. While it took a keen interest in the welfare of the Arabs, the INC was silent on the Jewish problem.
17. Bandyopadhyaya, *The Making of India's Foreign Policy*, 286.
18. Nehru, *Glimpses of World History*, 762–763.
19. Ibid., 764.
20. There is no evidence to suggest that Arabs sought Zionist cooperation in their fight against the British in Palestine. On the contrary, until the Arab revolt of 1936, the Arab leadership, especially the mufti of Jerusalem, was also cooperating and benefiting from the British.
21. Nehru, *Glimpses of World History*, 764–765.
22. Nehru, *Eighteen Months in India, 1936–1937*, 129.
23. Ibid., 130.
24. Ibid., 136–137.
25. Nehru to A. E. Shohet (August 26, 1937), in Nehru, *Selected Works of Jawaharlal Nehru, Series I*, 8:714.
26. Nehru to Husseini (September 4, 1937), in Nehru, *Selected Works of Jawaharlal Nehru, Series I*, 8:723.
27. Nehru, *Glimpses of World History*, 767.
28. Nehru, *Selected Works of Jawaharlal Nehru, Series II*, 2:511.
29. Nehru, *Eighteen Months in India, 1936–1937*, 136–137.
30. Jawaharlal Nehru to Immanuel Olsvanger (September 25, 1936), CZA, S25/3583.
31. Zaidi and Zaidi, eds., *Encyclopedia INC*, 11:497.
32. Ibid., 12:160.
33. Quoted in Sareen, "Indian Responses to the Holocaust," 56.
34. Ibid.
35. Ibid., 57.
36. Ibid., 58.
37. Nehru, *Selected Works of Jawaharlal Nehru, Series I*, 9:224ff.
38. Sareen, "Indian Responses to the Holocaust," 59.
39. Bergmann and Shimoni, "Report on the Inter-Asian Conference" (April 17, 1947). After the war, India served as a transit point for a number of Iraqi and Afghan Jews prior to their emigration to newly formed state of Israel.

As prime minister, Nehru was more than accommodative and repeatedly extended their stay in India. It was in this context that Nehru permitted the opening of a Jewish Agency immigration office in Bombay shortly after India recognized Israel in September 1950.

40. Quoted in Jawaharlal Nehru's letter to Subhas Chandra Bose (April 3, 1939), in Nehru, *Selected Works of Jawaharlal Nehru, Series I*, 9:537.
41. Nehru, *Discovery of India*, 422. However, one cannot underestimate or ignore the political rivalry between the two and the challenge that Bose posed to Nehru's political future. Quoting German sources, one Jewish periodical claimed that Bose had argued that "anti-Semitism must become a part of the Indian freedom movement since the Jews—he alleged—had helped the British to exploit and suppress the Indians." Report in the *Jewish Chronicle* (London) reproduced in *The Jewish Advocate* (Bombay) 12, no. 3 (November 1942): 22.
42. Quoted in Jawaharlal Nehru's letter to Subhas Chandra Bose (April 3, 1939), in Nehru, *Selected Works of Jawaharlal Nehru, Series I*, 9:537. Emphasis added.
43. Indeed, during the war the United States closed its borders to Jewish refugees who were fleeing Europe and on occasions contributed to their eventual execution by Nazi Germany. For an opposing argument, however, see Desch, "The Myth of Abandonment: The Use and Abuse of the Holocaust Analogy."
44. *United Nations Special Committee on Palestine, Report to the General Assembly*, 1:46. Only Guatemala and Uruguay refused to endorse this recommendation.
45. Agwani, "The Palestine Conflict in Asian Perspective," 456. "Sympathy for the Jewish victims of Nazism was not lacking among the Asian nations. But the idea of visiting the sins of Nazi Germany upon the Palestinians did not appeal to them." Ibid., 461. For similar arguments, see Hasan, "To Arafat, in Anguish."
46. Brecher, *The New State of Asia*, 126.
47. Agwani, "The Palestine Conflict in Asian Perspective," 443.
48. For an interesting study on this issue, see Rose, *The Gentile Zionists*.
49. Lewis, *The Jews of Islam*, 4.
50. India, Ministry of External Affairs, *India and Palestine*, 6.
51. Glucklich, "Brahmins and Pharisees," 14.
52. Quoted in Teslik, *Congress, the Executive Branch, and the Special Interests*, 36.
53. Pirzada, ed., *Foundations of Pakistan*; Zaidi, *Evolution of Muslim Political Thought in India*, vol. 2: *Sectarian Nationalism and Khilafat*.
54. A formal resolution to this effect was adopted at the twenty-third session of the Muslim League, held in Delhi in November 1933. For the text see Pirzada, ed., *Foundations of Pakistan*, 2:225–226.
55. A well-known poet during the nationalist struggle, Tagore was awarded the Nobel Prize for literature in 1913.
56. Nehru, *Glimpses of World History*, 767.
57. Zaidi and Zaidi, eds., *Encyclopedia INC*, 12:160.

58. Quoted in Brecher, *Israel, the Korean War, and China: Images, Decisions, and Consequences*, 39.
59. Brecher, "Israel and China," 219.
60. For a detailed discussion on the Latin American role, see Glick, *Latin America and the Palestine Problem.*
61. At that time, Sharett was out of office and was traveling to the continent in his personal capacity. For a recent discussion on the India leg of the tour and his meeting with Prime Minister Nehru, see Caplan, "The 1956 Sinai Campaign Viewed from Asia."
62. For a most authoritative discussion on the British promise, see Stein, *The Balfour Declaration.*
63. During World War II, a large number of Jewish refugees fled to India. During the postwar period, there refugees entered from Iraq and Afghanistan. Nevertheless, the number of Jews in India did not exceed sixty thousand.
64. The only exception being the anti-Jewish violence in Goa along the western coast during the sixteenth century. This happened when Goa was under Portuguese occupation and was a fallout of the Spanish Inquisition.
65. Phrase used in Mudiam, *India and the Middle East*, 143.
66. Among others, see Gordon, "Indian Nationalist Ideas About Palestine and Israel," 221–222.
67. Brecher, "Israel and China," 222. According to Philip Holden, "the British did not ban Nehru's autobiography in India, but they did proscribe the Hebrew translation in Palestine, fearful of the model it might provide for a very different nationalism." Holden, "Other Modernities: National Autobiography and Globalization," 90. See also Nehru to Indira Gandhi (August 12, 1944), in Nehru, *Selected Works of Jawaharlal Nehru, Series I*, 13:459–461.
68. Stein, *The Balfour Declaration*, 496–497.
69. Such trends continue still today. Many Muslim leaders see Israel as a threat not just to the Palestinians in the occupied territories but to the wider Islamic world. A dated but accurate picture of this conspiracy-centric attitude toward Israel can be found in Hamid, *The Unholy Alliance.*
70. The delegation consisted of Jamal al-Husseini (secretary of the Arab Executive headed by the grand mufti himself), Muhammad Murad (the mufti of Haifa), and Ibrahim al-Ansari (one of the sheikhs of al-Aqsa).
71. Porath, "Al-Hajj Amin al-Husayni, Mufti of Jerusalem," 154.
72. Nearly seventy years later, India's defense minister Pranab Mukherjee recalled the mufti connection: "Commitment to the Palestinian cause has been a bedrock of our foreign policy even before we gained independence. In a cable sent to Mufti of Jerusalem on 4th Sept 1937, Pandit Jawaharlal Nehru, who became our first Prime Minister after independence, had affirmed, 'The Indian National Congress sends you greetings and assurance of full solidarity in the struggle for Palestine Independence.'" Mukherjee's inaugural speech (January 30, 2006), at the Eighth Asian Security Conference organized by IDSA. Available online at http://www.idsa.in/speeches_at_idsa/8ASCInaugural.htm.

73. Kupferschmidt, "The General Muslim Congress of 1931 in Jerusalem," 129.
74. Ibid.
75. For background discussion of the conference, see Gibb, "The Islamic Congress at Jerusalem in December 1931"; and Kramer, *Islam Assembled*, 123–141.
76. Kupferschmidt, "The General Muslim Congress of 1931 in Jerusalem," 123.
77. Similarly, the Congress Party commemorated August 26, 1938, as Palestine Day and held meetings and rallies in different parts of the country. Heptulla, *Indo-West Asian Relations*, 153.
78. Jansen, *Zionism, Israel, and Arab Nationalism*, 169–181; Shimoni, *Satyagraha and the Jews.*
79. Jansen, *Afro-Asia and Non-Alignment*, 30.
80. Shimoni, *Satyagraha and the Jews*, 27–28.
81. Nehru to Olsvanger (February 2, 1938; May 5, 1947; June 10, 1954; October 16, 1956; March 23, 1958), CZA, K 11–81/3.
82. Weizmann to Nehru (June 27, 1938; September 13, 1938; November 15, 1947; November 27, 1947). In Weizmann, *Letters and Papers of Chaim Weizmann*, 18:206, 18:458–459, 23:31–32, 23:42–43.
83. She was a leading INC leader and a renowned poet.
84. Once considered a rival to Jawaharlal Nehru, he served as India's first home minister until his death in 1950.
85. Ambedkar was the leader of India's oppressed "untouchables" or *Dalit* community and played a key role in the drafting of the Indian Constitution.
86. A senior INC leader from the northern state of Uttar Pradesh.
87. A close confidant of Mahatma Gandhi.
88. As early as in 1916, she addressed a Bene-Israel Mitra Mandal meeting in Bombay. *India and Israel* (Bombay) 4, no. 4 (October 1951): 31.
89. *The Jewish Advocate* (Bombay) (October 1941): 9; *The Jewish Advocate* (Bombay) (November 1941): 9.
90. Olsvanger to Tagore (October 7, 1936) and A. K. Chanda, secretary to Tagore, to Olsvanger (October 23, 1936), CZA, S25/3583.
91. At the time of his death in 1940, Andrews was reportedly preparing to go to Palestine. Olga Feinberg to Epstein (June 8, 1940), CZA, S25/3591.
92. Epstein to the Jewish Agency (April 4, 1946), CZA, S25/3158. The scholar-philosopher was elected India's second president in 1962.
93. For details of his activities in India, see CZA, S25/3583.
94. For details, see CZA, S25/3586 and S25/3591.
95. Bhargava, ed., *India and West Asia*, 93.
96. Olsvanger to Ghaffar Khan (September 29, 1936), CZA, S25/3583.
97. Olsvanger to Iqbal (October 1, 1936) and Iqbal's reply (October 14, 1936), CZA, S25/3583.
98. Kallenbach to Weizmann (July 4, 1937), CZA, Z4/17342.
99. Olsvanger to M. Irfan (October 3, 1936), CZA, S25/3583.
100. Note of Richard Freund (December 20, 1937), CZA, S25/3586.
101. Weizmann to Vera Weizmann (June 18, 1909), in Weizmann, *Letters and Papers of Chaim Weizmann*, 5:135–136.

102. Malviya to Olsvanger (October 17, 1936), CZA, S25/3583.
103. Guha to Olsvanger (November 2, 1936), CZA, S25/3583.
104. For a detailed account of the contacts established during this conference, see CZA, S25/7485.
105. F. H. Kisch to Ms. May (August 23, 1931), CZA, S25/5689. Similar contacts were established with P. K. Dutt, the social secretary to the Indian Round Table Conference in 1931. Note of December 3, 1931, CZA, S25/5689. See also *The Jewish Advocate*, (Bombay) 9, no. 6 (July 1, 1938): 4.
106. Shanmukham Chetty to Olsvanger (October 30, 1936), CZA, S25/3583.
107. Revenue Minister of Bikaner to Moshe Shertok (January 29, 1938), and Shertok's reply (March 14, 1938), CZA, S25/7494.
108. Olsvanger to Selig Brodetsky (December 2, 1937), CZA, S25/3588.
109. Gershon Agronsky made this observation following his April 1930 visit to Bombay. Shimoni, *Satyagraha and the Jews*, 27–28.
110. Olsvanger to Arthur Lourie (September 15, 1939), CZA, Z4/15623.
111. K. M. Panikkar's memorandum on Hindu-Zionist relations (April 8, 1947), CZA, S25/9029.
112. Report of the Inter-Asian Conference (April 17, 1947), CZA, S25/7485.
113. Eytan's note (March 3, 1948), CZA, S25/9029. Emphasis added.
114. Brecher, *Israel, the Korean War, and China*, 39.
115. According to Eytan, he and Golda Meir were planning to visit India in September 1947. Eytan's note (March 3, 1948), CZA, S25/9029.
116. Moreover, by that time, David Ben-Gurion had overshadowed the architect of the Balfour Declaration.

4. The Islamic Prism: The INC Versus the Muslim League

The epigraph to this chapter is taken from Panikkar, "A Memorandum on Hindu-Zionist Relations" (April 8, 1947), CZA, S25/9029.

1. See Neimeijer, *The Khilafat Movement in India, 1919–1924*; and Minault, *The Khilafat Movement*.
2. Kumar, ed., *The Background of India's Foreign Policy*, 6.
3. Though the caliph is a Sunni institution, even Indian Shias took an active part in the Khilafat struggle. Hasan, *Nationalism and Communal Politics in India, 1885–1930*, 138.
4. Spurred by the British promise of an independent Arab kingdom, the Arabs led a revolt against the Ottoman Empire under the leadership of Sharif Hussein of Mecca.
5. Even if Hindus were seen in India as "People of the Book," or *Dhimmi*, they still remain nonbelievers.
6. For the complete text of Mohammed Ali's presidential address to the Cocanada (now Kakinada) session, see Zaidi and Zaidi, eds., *Encyclopedia INC*, 8:184–309.

7. Resolution adopted at the Amritsar session of the INC. Ibid., 7:531.
8. Ibid., 7:581–582.
9. Ibid., 8:415–416.
10. *Young India* (April 6, 1921), in Gandhi, *The Collected Works of Gandhi*, 19:530.
11. Gandhi, *The Collected Works of Gandhi*, 19:471.
12. Resolution adopted at the Lucknow session of the INC. Zaidi and Zaidi, eds., *Encyclopedia INC*, 8:478.
13. Resolution adopted at the Gaya session of the INC. Ibid., 8:542.
14. Resolution adopted at the Amritsar session of the INC. Ibid., 8:613. This was also the last Congress Party resolution on the Khilafat issue.
15. For a sympathetic treatment of the issue, see Lewis, *The Jews of Islam*.
16. Nanda, *Gandhi*, 373.
17. Chaudhuri, *Thy Hand, Great Anarch, 1921–1952*, 39. Likewise, Nanda, *Gandhi and His Critics*, 82, admitted that the Mahatma's hope that "the Hindus' spontaneous and altruistic gesture in supporting the cause of the Khilafat would permanently win the gratitude of the Muslim community was not to be realized."
18. Resolution adopted at the tenth session of the Muslim League in Calcutta, December 1917–January 1918. Pirzada, ed., *Foundations of Pakistan*, 1:442.
19. Ibid., 2:584.
20. Ibid.
21. Presidential address of A. K. Fazlul Haque at the eleventh Muslim League session in Delhi, December 1918. Ibid., 1:497–498. Emphasis added.
22. Resolution adopted at the twelfth Muslim League session at Amritsar, December 1919. Ibid., 1:537.
23. Presidential address of Maulana Hasrat Mohani at the fourteenth Muslim League session in Ahmedabad, December 1921. Ibid., 1:662.
24. Presidential address of Hafiz Hidayat Husain at the twenty-third Muslim League session in Delhi, November 1933. Ibid., 2:223.
25. Given his Westernized lifestyle, Jinnah was not an ideal Muslim, let alone one to be speaking on behalf of the worldwide Muslim population. Describing his complex personality, Rajmohan Gandhi observes: "He seemed on the way to leading India; he founded Pakistan instead. For much of his life he championed Hindu-Muslim unity; later he demanded, obtained, and, for a year, ran a separate Muslim homeland. Neither Sunni nor mainstream Shiite, his family belonged to the small Khoja or Ismaili community led by the Aga Khan; yet Mohammed Ali Jinnah was in the end the leader of India's Muslims. Anglicized and aloof in manner, incapable of oratory in an Indian tongue, keeping his distance from mosques, opposed to the mixing of religion and politics, he yet became inseparable, in that final phase, from the cry of Islam in danger." Gandhi, *Eight Lives*, 123.
26. Presidential address of M. A. Jinnah at the twenty-fifth Muslim League session in Lucknow, October 1937. Pirzada, ed., *Foundations of Pakistan*, 2:272.
27. For the text of the resolution adopted at the Lucknow session of the Muslim League in October 1937, see ibid., 2:277–278.

28. Presidential address of M. A. Jinnah at the twenty-sixth Muslim League session in Patna, December 1938. Ibid., 2:307.
29. For the text of the resolution adopted at the Patna session of the Muslim League in December 1937, see ibid., 2:315–316.
30. For a brief summary of the deliberations, see ibid., 2:316–318.
31. Ibid. Emphasis added.
32. For the text of the resolution adopted at the Lahore session of the League in March 1940, see ibid., 2:346.
33. For the text of the resolution adopted at the Delhi session of the Muslim League in April 1943, see ibid., 2:439–440. Jinnah himself proposed this resolution, which was adopted unanimously.
34. For the text of the resolution adopted at the Karachi session of the League in December 1943, see ibid., 2:489–490.
35. For the text of the resolution adopted at the Delhi council meeting on April 10, 1946, see ibid., 2:525.
36. For the text of the resolution adopted at the Karachi council meeting in December 1947, see ibid., 2:574–575.
37. Shaikh, "Muslims and Political Representation in Colonial India."
38. He had earlier served as president in 1923 and remains the youngest person to hold the leadership of the party.
39. Heptulla, *Indo-West Asian Relations*, 152.
40. Gopal, *Jawaharlal Nehru*, 1:232–233; Mudiam, *India and the Middle East*, 144.
41. While Muslim-majority areas of Bengal province became East Pakistan, the Muslim majority areas in the west became West Pakistan. This geographic anomaly of a large Indian territory between East and West Pakistan continued until 1971, when East Pakistan became the independent state Bangladesh.
42. Burke, *Pakistan's Foreign Policy*, 66.
43. Stein, *The Balfour Declaration*, 496–497.
44. Later that year, Shaukat Ali also met Stein and Sokolov in London.
45. There are suggestions that Shaukat Ali's "attitude towards Zionism seems to have been rather tolerant, in so far as he openly supported a solution without violent means for the outstanding questions in Palestine." Kupferschmidt, "The General Muslim Congress of 1931 in Jerusalem," 131.
46. Note of the interview by Selig Brodetsky (October 15, 1931), CZA, S25/3535.
47. Panikkar, *In Two Chinas*, 12.
48. Bergmann and Shimoni, "Report on the Inter-Asian Conference."
49. For a copy of the memorandum, see CZA, S25/9029. In the following quotations from the memorandum, the emphasis is in the original.
50. Interestingly, this "follow the lead" became the Indian position at the first special session of the UN General Assembly that met shortly after Panikkar's memorandum.
51. Panikkar, *In Two Chinas*, 12.
52. This, however, did not prevent Panikkar from meeting and interacting with Israeli officials. He lamented India's belated recognition and had a day-long

rendezvous with his old friend Eliyahu Elath in Basil Liddell Hart's farmhouse in 1953.

5. India, UNSCOP, and the Partition of Palestine

The epigraph to this chapter is taken from a letter from Vijayalakshmi Pandit to Bajpai (October 8, 1947), NAI, F-46 (1)-AWT/47.

1. India, *Constituent Assembly Debates*, session II (December 4, 1947), 1:1261. Emphasis added.
2. Among others, see India, *India and Palestine*; Mehrish, "Recognition of the Palestine Liberation Organization (PLO): An Appraisal of India's Policy"; and Agwani, "The Great Powers and the Partition of Palestine."
3. For example, see Khalidi, "Revisiting the UNGA Partition Resolution." The notable exception is the recent work by Ginat, "India and the Palestine Question."
4. For a discussion of the events leading up to this move, see Haron, "The British Decision to Give the Palestine Question to the United Nations"; and Jasse, "Great Britain and Palestine Towards the United Nations."
5. *UNSCOP Report*, 2:1.
6. Ministry of External Affairs telegram to Asaf Ali (April 24, 1947), NAI, F-2(16)-UNO-I/47.
7. Note by P. A. Menon (May 13, 1947), NAI, F-2(16)-UNO-I/47.
8. There are others who argued differently. For example, Prithvi Ram Mudiam, *India and the Middle East*, 145, maintained that Asaf Ali "adopted a balanced and conciliatory approach to the Palestinian question."
9. *UN General Assembly, First Special Session*, A/BUR/P.V./32 (May 2, 1947), 37.
10. Ibid., A/BUR/P.V./30 (April 30, 1947), 12.
11. On April 30, the General Committee overwhelmingly rejected the Egyptian proposal.
12. On May 13, the General Assembly rejected the proposal by fifteen to twenty-six votes, with twelve abstentions and two absentees.
13. For the details concerning the circumstances under which the Arab Higher Committee withdrew and then was persuaded to depose before the committee, see Robinson, *Palestine and the United Nations*, 130–137.
14. *UN General Assembly, First Special Session*, A/C.1/P.V.48 (May 7, 1948), 48.
15. For the full text of the statement, see *UN General Assembly*, A/AC.14/SR.11 (October 11, 1947).
16. Likewise, the Indian delegate unsuccessfully opposed a decision by the UNSCOP to visit the DP camps in Europe prior to the preparation of the final report. Abdur Rahman to Jawaharlal Nehru (July 15, 1947), NAI, F-2(16)-UNO-I/47.
17. *UN General Assembly, First Special Session*, A/C.1/P.V.51 (May 8, 1947), 57–62; Garcia-Granados, *The Birth of Israel*, 6.
18. *UN General Assembly*, A/BUR/P.V.30 (April 30, 1947), 2–10.

19. "Congress Betrays Arabs," editorial in *The Dawn* (May 5, 1947).
20. He also acted as the agency's liaison to the Special Session as well as to the UNSCOP and subsequently became Israel's first envoy to the United States.
21. Eliahu Epstein to P. S. Gourgey (January 19, 1948), CZA, Z-6/60. Emphasis added.
22. "Memorandum on India Before the United Nations, 1950" (September 16, 1950), ISA, 2413/28. Emphasis added. Incidentally, at that time Das was a member of the Indian delegation to the UN session.
23. Jawaharlal Nehru to Asaf Ali (May 1, 1947), in Nehru, *Selected Works of Jawaharlal Nehru, Series II,* 2:494. Emphasis added.
24. Jawaharlal Nehru to Asaf Ali (May 14, 1947), in ibid., 2:497. Emphasis added.
25. Ibid. Notes.
26. Note by P. A. Menon (May 13, 1947), NAI, F-2(16)-UNO-I/47. Emphasis added. He added that Asaf Ali's proposal for "the establishment without delay of Independent State of Palestine" went "beyond what was originally contemplated" and hence "committed the Government of India to a view of substance." Initially, the draft read that Asaf Ali committed the government "to a view of considerable substance." While signing the note, Menon struck off the word "considerable."
27. Ministry of External Affairs note (April 9, 1947), NAI, F-2(16)-UNO-I/47.
28. Note by H. Weightman (April 10, 1947), NAI, F-2(16)-UNO-I/47.
29. Ministry of External Affairs to Asaf Ali (April 18, 1947), NAI, F-2(16)-UNO-I/47.
30. They were Canada, Czechoslovakia, Iran, the Netherlands, Peru, Sweden, and Uruguay.
31. Guatemala and Yugoslavia.
32. Note by P. A. Menon (May 13, 1947), NAI, F-2(16)-UNO-I/47.
33. Asaf Ali to the Ministry of External Affairs (May 12, 1947), NAI, F.46(1)-AWT/47. Emphasis added.
34. In a detailed report, he remarked: "The feeling that India was definitely for Arab, led the US Delegation to omit India from their original proposal regarding the constitution of the Special Committee." Report by Asaf Ali on the Special Session to Secretary, Ministry of External Affairs (June 4, 1947), NAI, F.2(21)-UNO-I/47.
35. It adopted a resolution to form an eleven-member Committee that would not include the five big powers by thirteen votes to eleven. As many as twenty-nine countries abstained.
36. Asaf Ali to the Ministry of External Affairs (May 14, 1947), NAI, F.2(16)-UNO-I/47. Emphasis added.
37. Ibid.
38. H. C. Beaumont to S. E. Abbot (May 22, 1947), NAI, F-2(6)-UNO-I/47. Emphasis added.
39. Abdur Rahman to Emil Sandstorm (July 2, 1947), UN General Assembly, A/AC.13/35 (July 14, 1947), 1–2.

40. Abdur Rahman to Jawaharlal Nehru (July 15, 1947), NAI, F-2(16)-UNO-I/47. Rahman added: "For this reason, he does not seem to be much in favor with strong Arab nationalists." Even though Rahman met Jamal Husseini, the vice president of the Arab Higher Committee, in Jerusalem, "political matters" did not figure in their deliberations.
41. For the text of Abdur Rahman's cross examination, see *The Jewish Plan for Palestine: Memorandum and Statements Presented by the Jewish Agency for Palestine to the United Nations Special Committee on Palestine,* 367–380, 392–394, 469–473, 549–553. Rahman, for example, described David Ben-Gurion as an "extremist and aggressive demagogue." Abdur Rahman to Jawaharlal Nehru (July 15, 1947), NAI, F-2(16)-UNO-I/47.
42. Asaf Ali to Foreign Office (May 14, 1947), NAI, F-2(16)-UNO-I/47. Emphasis added.
43. Jawaharlal Nehru to Abdur Rahman (May 24, 1947), in Nehru, *Selected Works of Jawaharlal Nehru, Series II,* 2:474–475.
44. Zaidi and Zaidi, eds., *Encyclopedia INC,* 11:497.
45. Jawaharlal Nehru to Abdur Rahman (May 24, 1947), in Nehru, *Selected Works of Jawaharlal Nehru, Series II,* 2:474–475. Emphasis added.
46. Garcia-Granados, *The Birth of Israel,* 9.
47. Abdur Rahman to Jawaharlal Nehru (June 25, 1947), NAI, F-2(16)-UNO-I/47. Emphasis added.
48. Jawaharlal Nehru to Abdur Rahman (July 10, 1947), NAI, F-2(16)-UNO-I/47.
49. Abdur Rahman to Jawaharlal Nehru (August 20, 1947). Ibid. See also Rahman to Nehru (June 25, 1947), NAI, F-2(16)-UNO-I/47.
50. Official summary of Abdur Rahman's reports (September 10, 1947), NAI, F-2(5)-UNO-I/47.
51. Abdur Rahman to the Ministry of External Affairs (August 20, 1947), NAI, F-2(16)-UNO-I/47.
52. Ministry of External Affairs to Abdur Rahman (August 23, 1947). Ibid. This was perhaps a reminder, and the telegram was sent in Nehru's name. In a related development, Rahman was also instructed to withdraw the official memorandum that he had earlier prepared.
53. Prior to his departure for Palestine, Abdur Rahman met Azzam Pasha in New York. The secretary general of the Arab League told him that it would help the Arab cause if the committee were unable to present its report to the General Assembly by September 1, "because then the question would not come up before the United Nations for a fairly long time, during which period he expected things to change materially in favor of the Arabs." Abdur Rahman to Jawaharlal Nehru (June 25, 1947), NAI, F-2(16)-UNO-I/47.
54. For the complete text, see *UNSCOP Report,* 1:42–46. For the dissenting notes of Guatemala and Uruguay, see ibid., 2:23–24, 2:48–49.
55. Ibid., 1:47.
56. For the complete text, see ibid., 1:47–58.
57. Ministry of External Affairs telegram to Asaf Ali (April 23, 1947), NAI, F.2(16)-UNO-I/47.

58. *UNSCOP Report,* 1:59.
59. While expressing his sympathy for the "untold misery" of the Jews, Abdur Rahman passionately argued: "The duty of finding suitable places for these [displaced] persons rests on the whole of the world and not only on Palestine." Ibid., 2:75. On another occasion, he wrote: "While the problem of Jewish immigration is . . . closely related to the solution of the Palestine question, it cannot be contemplated that Palestine is to be considered in any sense as a means of solving the problem of world Jewry." Ibid., 1:64.
60. The population distribution of the partition plan is misleading. According to the plan, the Jewish state would include 498,000 Jews and 407,000 Arabs. However, it would also include about "90,000 Bedouins, cultivators and stock owners who seek grazing further afield in dry seasons." Since this additional population was not Jewish, at the time of partition the proposed Jewish state would consist of 498,000 Jews and 497,000 Arabs. It was only after the Arab-Israeli war of 1948 and the subsequent emigration of Arabs and immigration of Jews that Israel acquired Jewish demographic predominance.
61. Although Tel Aviv was part of the proposed Jewish state, there was no corresponding Arab city that could have become the capital of the Arab states. Having made Jerusalem an international city, the majority plan did not identify any city as the possible Arab capital.
62. This was not the first time the question of "dual loyalty" was raised to criticize the Zionist endeavors in Palestine. Prior to the Balfour Declaration, opponents of the move, including a section of the Anglo Jewry, feared that special treatment of the Jews in Palestine would question the loyalty of the Jews in the Diaspora and undermine their hard-earned equality in Europe.
63. *Report of Anglo-American Committee of Inquiry Regarding the Problems of European Jewry and Palestine,* 43.
64. For instance, Loy W. Henderson, the director of the Near East in the State Department, drew attention to this problem. His objections were overruled by the electoral considerations of President Harry S. Truman. For the text of his assessment, see Wilson, *Decision on Palestine,* 117–121.
65. While the Congress Party never expressed its formal opposition to the Declaration, it was a constant theme in Muslim League circles. Mahatma Gandhi, however, was critical of the Balfour position. In his confidential note to Kallenbach in 1937, he observed: "Neither the Mandate nor the Balfour Declaration can . . . be used in support of sustaining Jewish immigration into Palestine in the teeth of Arab opposition." In "Statement Given by Mahatma Gandhi to Kallenbach on Zionism in July 1937," CZA, S25/3587.
66. Speaking at the Special Session, Asaf Ali argued that the language of the Mandate was inconsistent with the spirit of article 22 of the League of Nations charter. Therefore "it was up to the people of Palestine to go up to the International Court of Justice . . . and lodge an appeal against it and get it reversed. Apparently they did not do it." *UN General Assembly, First Special Session,* A/BUT/P.V.30 (April 30, 1947), 11.
67. *UNSCOP Report,* 2:38.

68. For a recent discussion, see Ben-Dror, "The Arab Struggle Against Partition," 259–293.
69. *UNSCOP Report*, 1:13. Emphasis added.
70. Abdur Rahman to Jawaharlal Nehru (July 15, 1947), NAI, F-2(16)-UNO-I/47.
71. The UNSCOP recorded: "In times of crisis, as in 1936–38 . . . pressure has taken the form of intimidation and assassination. At the present time, nonconformity regarding any important question on which the Arab Higher Committee has pronounced a policy is represented as disloyalty to the Arab nation. . . . In the absence of an elective body to represent divergence of interests, [the Arab community] therefore shows a higher degree of centralization in its political life." *UNSCOP Report*, 1:25–26.
72. As a former U.S. State Department official described: "So well organized, in fact, was the *Yishuv* that all of us who followed the Palestine scene knew, long before the Jewish state came into being, that if the Jews were to secure their state, Weizmann would be the president, Ben-Gurion the prime minister, Shertok the foreign minister, [Eliezer] Kaplan the finance minister, and so on; and this is what came to pass." Wilson, *Decision on Palestine*, 33.
73. *UNSCOP Report*, 1:58. Emphasis added.
74. Ibid., 2:45.
75. Ibid., 2:42, 2:45.
76. For a historical discussion, see Kumaraswamy, "The Strangely Parallel Careers of Israel and Pakistan."
77. Nehru, *Selected Works of Jawaharlal Nehru, Series II*, 1:572n.
78. Burke, *Pakistan's Foreign Policy*, 66.
79. The members were Canada, Czechoslovakia, Guatemala, Poland, South Africa, the Soviet Union, the United States, Uruguay, and Venezuela.
80. The members were Afghanistan, Colombia, Egypt, Iraq, Lebanon, Pakistan, Saudi Arabia, Syria, and Yemen. The only non-Islamic member, Colombia, subsequently withdrew from the subcommittee. Horowitz, *State in the Making*, 262.
81. Citing this reason, Yugoslavia, one of the signatories to the federal plan, abstained during the final vote on the partition plan. Garcia-Granados, *The Birth of Israel*, 104. Moreover, on May 19, 1948, it became one of the first states to recognize Israel.
82. Vijayalakshmi Pandit to Bajpai (October 8, 1947), NAI, F-46 (1)-AWT/47.
83. It was rejected by twelve votes in favor to twenty-nine votes against, with fourteen abstentions.
84. Vijayalakshmi Pandit's cable to Bajpai (November 27, 1947), NAI, F-46(1)-AWT/47.
85. On November 28, Mrs. Pandit conceded that, afraid of the UN approval of the partition plan, "Arab spokesman for the first time showed anxiety for [a] compromise solution." Pandit, New York, to Bajpai, New Delhi (November 28, 1947). Ibid.
86. India, *Constituent Assembly Debates*, vol. 1, session II (December 4, 1947), col. 1261. Emphasis added.

87. Note by Jawaharlal Nehru (April 4, 1948), NAI, F-2(5)-UNO-I/48.
88. Ibid.
89. B. N. Rau to Jawaharlal Nehru (April 5, 1948). Ibid.
90. Ibid.
91. B. N. Rau, "Outline of Plan for Palestine" (November 24, 1947). Ibid.
92. Ministry of External Affairs, New Delhi, to Indian Delegation, New York (May 7, 1948). Ibid.
93. In instructing its UN delegation, New Delhi maintained: "At this stage we can only give you the general idea which is that partition should be avoided and at the same time largest measure of autonomy be given to the Jewish and Arab parts." Iyengar to Bajpai (April 6, 1948). Ibid. Likewise, a few weeks later India reiterated its opposition to partition. Indian Delegation, New York, to Ministry of External Affairs, New Delhi (April 23, 1948). Ibid.

6. Recognition Without Relations

The epigraph to this chapter is taken from Professor M. S. Agwani's inaugural remarks at a 1993 conference organized by Jawaharlal Nehru University, in Singh, ed., *Postwar Gulf*, 3.

1. Misra, *India's Policy of Recognition of States and Governments*; Mehrish, *India's Recognition Policy Towards New Nations*.
2. *Debates CA* (August 20, 1948), cols. 380–381. Emphasis added.
3. Mudiam, *India and the Middle East*, 149.
4. Nehru, *Letters to Chief Ministers*, 1:127–128.
5. ISA, 2424/19. Because of its legal implications, India did not even acknowledge Sharett's cable. External Affairs Ministry note (October 4, 1948), NAI, F.46 (21)-AWT/48.
6. The telegram from Moshe Shertok to Nehru can be found in NAI, F-11(8)-UNO-I/48.
7. Charge d' affairs to Foreign Office, New Delhi (May 19, 1948), NAI, F-11(8)-UNO-I/48.
8. Note prepared by UN Branch (May 21, 1948), NAI, F-11(8)-UNO-I/48. Emphasis added.
9. Embassy of India in Prague to Foreign Office (April 12, 1948), NAI, F-13(95)-1A/49.
10. Foreign Office to Embassy in Prague (May 21, 1948), NAI, F-13(95)-1A/49.
11. K. P. S. Menon to Indian missions abroad (May 28, 1948), NAI, F-13(95)-1A/49. See also official note (July 8, 1950), NAI, F-22(22)-AWT/50.
12. Nehru, *Letters to Chief Ministers*, 1:128.
13. Note (October 4, 1948), NAI, F-46(21)-AWT/48.
14. S. N. Haksar to al-Husseini (March 19, 1949), NAI, F-32(6)-1A/49. Not surprisingly given the prevailing political situation in the region, the letter was addressed to "Grand Mufti of Jerusalem, Cairo."

15. *Debates CA* (August 20, 1948), cols. 380–381.
16. Nehru, *Letters to Chief Ministers*, 1:275.
17. *Debates CA* (March 9, 1949), col. 1400.
18. Israel had originally applied for membership on November 29, 1948, and in its meeting held on December 17, the UN Security Council rejected the application by five in favor, one against, and five abstentions. On February 24, 1949, a day it signed the Armistice Agreement with Egypt, Israel applied for a second time. It was approved by the UN Security Council in early March 1949 and was admitted on May 11, 1949. *Israel and the United Nations*, 59–60.
19. The Indian vote was attributed to the Arab factor, and a cable sent from the Indian Embassy in Brussels disclosed that the Arab countries conveyed their satisfaction and happiness at India's vote against Israel's admission to the United Nations. Embassy to Foreign Office (May 20, 1949), NAI, F-32(6)-1A/49.
20. Nehru, *Letters to Chief Ministers*, 1:363.
21. E. Epstein to M. Shertok and A. Eban (September 28, 1948), *Israel Documents*, 1:653.
22. E. Elath to Ministry of Foreign Affairs (May 12, 1949). *Israel Documents, Companion*, 4:17.
23. Aide's memoir of the conversation between Abba Eban and Rau (June 23, 1949), *Israel Documents*, 4:158–159.
24. E. Elath to M. Sharett (September 30, 1949), ISA, 2181/6.
25. E. Elath to M. Sharett (October 14, 1949), *Israel Documents*, 4:547–548.
26. *Debates CA* (December 6, 1949), cols. 233–234.
27. For the original invitation, see ISA, 71/14.
28. C. Weizmann to Nehru (November 15, 1947), in Weizman, *Letters and Papers of Chaim Weizmann, Series A*, 23:31–32.
29. Both were members of the Indian delegation to the 1947 UN General Assembly session.
30. For Weizmann's letter to Nehru (December 16, 1947), see Weizman, *Letters and Papers of Chaim Weizmann, Series A*, 62; to B. N. Rau (May 23, 1948), see ibid., 126–127; to Churchill (August 6, 1948), see ibid., 201–203; to H. Z. Cynowitz (March 4, 1949), see ibid., 261–262.
31. K. L. Panjabi to H. Z. Cynowitz (March 26, 1949), ISA, 2555/5. Emphasis added.
32. Minutes of the meeting between Y. H. Levin and H. Evatt on September 8, 1949. *Israel Documents*, 4:447.
33. Gopal, *Jawaharlal Nehru*, 3:117.
34. *Debates PP* (February 27, 1950), cols. 495–496.
35. Personal conversations with Walter Eytan in Jerusalem in September 1988.
36. Official English summary of Eytan's communiqué to Israeli missions abroad (June 9, 1950), *Israel Documents, Companion*, 5:145.
37. Kumaraswamy, "South Asia and People's Republic of China-Israeli Diplomatic Relations," 131–152.
38. ISA, 71/14b.

39. *Jerusalem Post* (September 18, 1950).
40. Even if the new state was recognized, as von Glahn, *Law Among Nations*, 95–96, observed, such recognition "automatically involves recognition of the Government of that State, for no one could envision recognition of the whole unit without inclusion of its operating agency, its government."
41. Parakatil, *India and the United Nations Peace Keeping Operations*, 75. The timing of such an interpretation was significant, as the mid-1970s witnessed the height of Israel's international isolation.
42. Misra, *India's Policy of Recognition*, 192. The September 1950 statement was silent on the legal status.
43. Mehrish, *India's Recognition Policy*, 80.
44. *Debates LS*, series VI, vol. 6 (July 26, 1971), 116.
45. Walter Eytan's "New Delhi Diary," ISA, 2383/21.
46. India's recognition of the state of Palestine is a notable exception. But this should be seen in the context of traditional Indian support for the Palestinian cause and its recognition of the Palestine Liberation Organization (PLO) in 1975 as "the sole and legitimate representative" of the Palestinians.
47. E. Elath to M. Sharett (October 14, 1949), *Israel Documents*, 4:548.
48. Walter Eytan to Abba Eban (November 21, 1949), *Israel Documents*, 4:637.
49. Gopal, *Jawaharlal Nehru*, 2:169. Emphasis added.
50. Nehru's letter dated October 1, 1950. Nehru, *Letters to Chief Ministers*, 2:217. Emphasis added.
51. Official translation of ambassador's interview, which appeared in the September 21, 1950, issue of *Al Misri* (Cairo). NAI, F.22 (25)-AWT/50.
52. Israel signed the armistice agreements with Egypt (February 24, 1949), Lebanon (March 23, 1949), Jordan (April 3, 1949), and Syria (July 20, 1949), while Iraq and Saudi Arabia expressed their support for any Arab-Israeli armistice agreement.
53. This note of February 27, 1950, was prepared by the Ministry of External Affairs, anticipating supplementary questions on Israel in parliament. NAI, F.23 (2)-AWT/50.
54. Mehrish, *India's Recognition Policy*, 106–107.
55. India's refusal to endorse a separate Tamil homeland in Sri Lanka has inhibited the Tamil militant groups, especially the Liberation Tigers of Tamil Eelam (LTTE), from pursuing the option of a Unilateral Declaration of Independence (UDI).
56. Such conditions were absent in the case of the APG declared on September 22, 1948. Hence, despite supporting the Arabs in the past, India did not consider its request for recognition.
57. Bialer, "The Iranian Connections in Israel's Foreign Policy, 1948–1951."
58. On March 29, 1949.
59. On January 12, 1950, Israel recognized Indonesia, and in response Indonesian Prime Minister and Foreign Minister Muhammad Hatta sent a formal note to Moshe Sharett thanking him for the recognition. *Israel Documents*, 5:95. It is, however, very doubtful that this act alone constitutes

recognition or that the government of India was aware of this development at that time.

60. *Debates LS*, series I, vol. 9, part II (November 20, 1956), col. 594. Interestingly, this statement was made following the Suez war, which resulted in Nehru formally ruling out relations with Israel.
61. Brecher, *India and World Politics*, 78–79.
62. The resolution 273 (III) adopted by the UN General Assembly on May 11, 1949, explicitly refers to "its resolutions of 29 November 1947 and 11 December 1948 and taking note of the declarations and explanations made by the representatives of the Government of Israel before the *Ad Hoc* Political Committee in respect of the implementation of the said resolutions."
63. The Chinese angle came full circle in January 1992, when New Delhi followed Beijing's example of normalizing ties with Israel. For a discussion see Kumaraswamy, "South Asia and People's Republic of China-Israeli Diplomatic Relations."
64. In the Chinese case, the prime issue was of who represented China. Regarding Israel, the issue was not the nature of the government but the very existence of the state.
65. *Debates CA* (November 28, 1949), col. 20.
66. Misra, *India's Policy of Recognition*, 57–58.
67. *The Hindu* (Madras) (September 18, 1950).
68. *Debates CA* (August 20, 1948), 381.
69. See *Debates CA* (March 4, 1949; March 9, 1949; November 28, 1949; December 6, 1949) and *Debates PP* (February 27, 1950; March 17, 1950; June 11, 1950; August 4, 1950).
70. For the role played by Prof. Taraknath Das of New York University in securing India's recognition, see Jerome Unger to Nahum Goldman (October 9, 1950), CZA, Z6/372.
71. E. Elath to M. Sharett (October 14, 1949), *Israel Documents*, 4:548.
72. Weizmann's letters to Nehru (November 15, 1947; November 27, 1947; December 16, 1947) and to B. N. Rau (May 23, 1948). Weizman, *Letters and Papers of Chaim Weizmann, Series A*, vol. 23. It should, however, be remembered that until that time none of the leading Zionist leaders had established any personal contacts with the Indian nationalists.
73. CZA, K-11, 81/3.
74. In his reply, Nehru wrote, *inter alia*: "Where rights come into conflict it is not an easy matter to decide. . . . I confess that I have great deal of sympathy for the Jews, I feel sympathy for the Arabs also in this predicament. . . . I would like to do all in my power to help the Jewish people in their distress in so far as I can do without injuring other people." Nehru to Einstein (July 11, 1947). For the complete text of the letter, see Nehru, *Selected Works of Jawaharlal Nehru, Series II*, 3:393–396.
75. Singh, "India and the Crisis," 75.
76. Gopal, *Jawaharlal Nehru*, 2:169.
77. Cited in ibid.

78. Quoted in Schechtman, *The Mufti and the Fuehrer*, 234.
79. For a detailed discussion of the All-Palestine Government, see Shlaim, "The Rise and Fall of the All-Palestine Government in Gaza."
80. Ahmed Hilmi Pasha, Cairo, to Foreign Minister, New Delhi (September 30, 1948), NAI, F.46(21)-AWT/48.
81. Official note (October 4, 1948), NAI F.46(21)-AWT/48. Indeed, for the same reason, India did not acknowledge Shertok's May 1948 cable to Nehru for recognition.
82. Suggestions that Pakistan had recognized the Jordanian annexation has been challenged by Silverburg, "Pakistan and the West Bank."
83. Note by J. S. Mehta (October 4, 1948), NAI, F.46(21)-AWT/48.
84. Schechtman, "India and Israel," 52.
85. He presided over the World Ulema Conference held in Karachi in February 1952, and in May he led a Palestinian delegation that visited Pakistan. Jbara, *Palestinian Leader Hajj Amin al-Husayni*, 190.
86. For example, see India, *India and Palestine*; Agwani, "The Palestine Conflict in Asian Perspective," 456; Mehrish, *India's Recognition Policy*, 80; Parakatil, *India and the United Nations Peace Keeping Operations*, 75; Singh, "India and the Crisis," 75.
87. *Debates LS*, series I, vol. 9, part II (November 20, 1956), cols. 594–595.
88. This note was prepared when the Tel Aviv public notary Victor Grunwald made an initial offer in September 1950 to act as India's honorary consul in Israel. NAI, F.22 (31)-AWT/50.
89. Eytan, *The First Ten Years*, 130. Citing notes of Nehru's conversation with Eytan, Gopal, *Jawaharlal Nehru*, 2:70, concurs with this assessment.
90. Gopal, *Jawaharlal Nehru*, 2:170.
91. K. P. S. Menon to Walter Eytan (October 23, 1952), ISA, 2554/12.
92. *The Times* (London) (November 13, 1959), in Mudiam, *India and the Middle East*, 160.
93. Note for supplementaries, NAI, F.23(7)-AWT/50. The main question was raised in the parliament on December 11, 1950. However, no supplementary questions were asked.
94. Brecher, *India and World Politics*, 79.
95. India, *MEA Report 1948–1949*, 1–2.
96. Ibid. (1949–1950), 2.
97. Ibid. (1950–1951), 1.
98. For a similar statement on concurrent accreditation see ibid. (1950–1951), 4; ibid. (1951–1952), 2, 3, 4, 10, 12; and ibid. (1962–1963), 2.
99. Ya'acov Shimoni to F. W. Pollack (December 16, 1951), ISA, 2554/12.
100. *Debates PP* (December 11, 1950), col. 793.
101. India, *MEA Report 1951–1952*, 10. Emphasis added.
102. *Debates LS*, series I, vol. 9, part II (November 20, 1956), col. 595.
103. Jawaharlal Nehru, *India's Foreign Policy*, 414–415.
104. *ISA Documents, Companion*, 14:738.
105. *Debates LS*, series III, vol. 20 (September 9, 1963), 5019.

106. *Foreign Affairs Record* (New Delhi) 15, no. 5 (May 1969): 110.
107. Agwani, "India and the Arab World," 75. See also India, *India and Palestine*, 31.
108. *Foreign Affairs Record* (New Delhi) 15, no. 5 (May 1969): 110.
109. In 1981, President Zia ul-Haq observed: "Pakistan is like Israel, an ideological state. Take out the Judaism from Israel and it will fall like a house of cards. Take Islam out of Pakistan and make it a secular state; it would collapse." *The Economist* (December 12, 1981).
110. India's endorsement of the NAM consensus on Palestine could be cited as the prime example.
111. Rafael, *Destination Peace*, 89.
112. Brecher, *India and World Politics*, 79.
113. Personal interview with Morarji Desai on October 22, 1987, in Mumbai. When he was prime minister, Israel's foreign minister Moshe Dayan paid an incognito visit to India. See also Agwani, *Contemporary West Asia*, 253.
114. Quoted in Mudiam, *India and the Middle East*, 161.
115. Quoted in Brecher, "Israel and China," 223.
116. David Ben-Gurion, Jerusalem, to Jawaharlal Nehru (July 28, 1960), *Israel Documents*, 14:686–687.
117. Jawaharlal Nehru, New Delhi, to David Ben-Gurion (August 9, 1960), *Israel Documents*, 14:689.
118. Nehru, *Letters to Chief Ministers*, 5:361.
119. In September 1947, for example, the government was confronted with the question of the prolonged stay of Jewish refugees from Afghanistan. Nehru to Vallabhbhai Patel (September 27, 1947), in Nehru, *Selected Works of Jawaharlal Nehru, Second Series*, 4:639–640.
120. Moreover, between 1949 and 1960, about five thousand Bene-Israeli and Iraqi Jews emigrated to Israel from India. *Israel Year Book* (1961), 378.
121. K. L. Panjabi to H. Z. Cynowitz (March 26, 1949), ISA, 2555/5.
122. Cable to Government of India (December 28, 1950), ISA, 2554/12.
123. The formal designation for ambassadors among members of the British Commonwealth.
124. Kidron to V. K. Krishna Menon (May 24, 1950), ISA, 2554/12.
125. Ya'acov Shimoni to F. W. Pollack (November 6, 1950), ISA, 2554/12.
126. Kidron to V. K. Krishna Menon (November 27, 1950), ISA, 2554/12.
127. Ya'acov Shimoni to F. W. Pollack (January 15, 1951), ISA, 2554/12.
128. Ibid.
129. Leilamani Naidu to F. W. Pollack (March 8, 1951), ISA, 2554/12.
130. Ya'acov Shimoni to F. W. Pollack (March 4, 1951), ISA, 2554/12.
131. ISA, 2554/12.
132. F. W. Pollack to Ya'acov Shimoni (June 15, 1951), ISA, 2554/12.
133. Ya'acov Shimoni to F. W. Pollack (June 25, 1951), ISA, 2554/12.
134. Ya'acov Shimoni to F. W. Pollack (July 29, 1951), ISA, 2554/12.
135. Personal interviews in July and August 1988 in Jerusalem with Israeli consuls who served in Bombay.

136. A copy of the Indian notification can be found in ISA, 2554/12.
137. Note from the Ministry of External Affairs to Pollack (August 31, 1951), ISA, 2554/12.
138. Bhansali to Pollack (January 30, 1953), ISA, 2554/12.
139. M. Michael (Bombay) to Asia and Africa Division, Jerusalem (February 19, 1960), summary, *Israel Documents, Companion*, 14:356. Emphasis added.
140. M. Michael to Minister of Foreign Affairs (October 25, 1960), summary, *Israel Documents, Companion*, 14:386.
141. *Debates RS*, vol. 47 (May 5, 1964), col. 1777.
142. *Debates LS*, series 3, vol. 31 (May 4, 1964), 14014.
143. Personal interviews with Reuven Dafni, who served in Bombay from 1965 to 1969, and the wife of Avshalom Caspi, who served from 1956 to 1959.
144. Brecher, *The Foreign Policy Systems of Israel*, 386–387; Medzini, "Reflections on Israel's Asian Policy," 203.
145. Gopal, *Jawaharlal Nehru*, 2:170.
146. Shimoni to Pollack (December 16, 1951), ISA, 2554/12.
147. Ibid.
148. Cited in Shimoni to Pollack (December 23, 1951), ISA, 2554/12.
149. Unless otherwise stated, the entire account of the activities of Eytan is based on his "New Delhi Diary," ISA, 2383/21.
150. Accordingly, Eytan sent a detailed reply indicating that it would be advisable to buy rather than rent a house in Israel. Eytan to Avtar Singh (March 20, 1952), ISA, 2554/12.
151. M. Pragai to Walter Eytan (March 10, 1953), *Israel Documents, Companion* (1953), 8:116. The meeting took place between Pragai and Avtar Singh, with whom Eytan met in New Delhi. Singh had then moved to New York as the first secretary in the Indian mission.
152. Panikkar's relations with the Zionists could be traced as far back as 1937. Panikkar to Elath (July 1937), CZA, S25/10228. Similarly, C. S. Jha had met with Abba Eban and others during the Lake Success Conference in December 1946. Sasson to Divon (November 14, 1950), ISA, 2413/28. Rao was one of the organizers of the Asian Relations Conference in New Delhi in March–April 1947, which was attended by a ten-member Jewish delegation from Palestine.
153. For example, the Indian High Commission in London was used as a conduit for its proposal to appoint a Trade Commission to India.
154. Alluding to past meetings in Ankara, a senior Israeli diplomat observed in April 1954: "To the extent that politics depend on personnel connections, Mr. Jha's occupation of a responsible post in New Delhi is bound to have a beneficent influence on Indo-Israeli relations." Meroz to MAAR (April 20, 1954), ISA, 2413/29.
155. For a first-person account of this meeting, see E. Sasson to S. Divon (July 1, 1951), ISA, 2413/29.
156. Menon to Eytan (October 23, 1952), ISA, 2554/12.
157. Elath wrote a twelve-page report on this day-long meeting. On the nature of the meeting, Elath remarked: "I had heard from several mutual friends that

he [Panikkar] had been asking after me and looking for a chance of meeting me again privately, since his official position as Indian Ambassador to Egypt and some other Arab countries . . . now makes it impossible for him to meet me in public." Elath to Eytan (September 8, 1953), ISA, 2413/29.

158. Sasson to Divon (June 22, 1951), ISA, 2413/29.
159. Mudiam, *India and the Middle East*, 166.
160. Six years later, another six-member delegation went to Israel to study the working of the cooperative system. *Debates LS*, series 2, vol. 43 (April 21, 1960), 12917–12920.
161. Ben-Gurion to Nehru (July 28, 1960) in Aynor, *The Role of the Israeli Labor Movement in Establishing Relations with States in Africa and Asia*, 44.
162. Personal diaries of Ya'acov Shimoni.
163. Menon to Eytan (September 14, 1954), ISA, 2413/29.
164. For example, the Israeli consul in Bombay hosted a dinner in January 1974 in honor of the four-member Israeli delegation. Among others, the noted physicist M. G. K. Menon was present. *News From Israel* (Bombay) 21, no. 3 (February 1, 1972): 7.
165. For example, see ibid., 12.
166. For a detailed assessment, see Caplan, "The 1956 Sinai Campaign Viewed from Asia."
167. Rafael, *Destination Peace*, 89.
168. For the minutes of this meeting, see CZA, Z6/2344.
169. Official note (August 4, 1953), in India, Ministry of External Affairs, *Protocol Hand Book*, 193–194.
170. Nehru's press interviews on September 26, 1946. In Nehru, *Selected Works of Jawaharlal Nehru, Series II*, 1:501.
171. Personal interview with Ya'acov Shimoni in Jerusalem in September 1988.
172. Personal interviews with former Israeli diplomats. The exact date is not available. This most likely had happened in the late 1950s or early 1960s, yet the suggestions were frequently raised during the tenure of Shastri, Indira Gandhi, and Morarji Desai.
173. Rafael, *Destination Peace*, 87.
174. For a detailed study, see Nachmani, *Israel, Turkey, and Greece*, 50–55.

7. Domestic Politics

The epigraph to this chapter is taken from Wilson, *Decision on Palestine*, 58. Truman made this statement in November 1945. Emphasis added.

1. Appadorai, *Domestic Roots of India's Foreign Policy*, 119–169.
2. The overwhelmingly religious or nonsecular character of most of the countries of the Middle East, however, rarely evoke interest, let alone criticism, in India.
3. Nehru, *Glimpses of World History*.

4. Quoted in Jansen, *Zionism, Israel, and Asian Nationalism*, 302. Emphasis added.
5. India, *MEA Report 1964–1965*, 58–59.
6. *Foreign Affairs Report* 15, no. 5 (May 1969): 110.
7. *Debates RS*, vol. 71 (March 26, 1970), col. 28.
8. Heptulla, *Indo-West Asian Relations*, 152. Emphasis added.
9. Agwani, "India and the Islamic World," 6.
10. Varadarajan, "When Jaswant Took Indian Politics to Foreign Shores."
11. Pradhan "Changing Dynamics of India's West Asia Policy," 1.
12. Ibid., 86. Emphasis added.
13. Ibid. Emphasis added.
14. National Commission on Minorities. Available online at http://ncm.nic.in/minority_population.pdf.
15. Heptulla, *Indo-West Asian Relations*, 163.
16. Eytan, "New Delhi Diary," ISA, 2383/21; E. Elath to M. Sharett (October 14, 1949), *Israel Documents*, 4:547–548.
17. Navari, "Arnold Toynbee (1889–1975): Prophecy and Civilization," 292. For Toynbee's later argument disapproving of the divine rights of Jews, Christians, and Muslims, see Toynbee, "Jewish Rights in Palestine."
18. India, Ministry of External Affairs, *India and Palestine*, 22–23, 51.
19. "Congress Betrays Arabs," editorial, *The Dawn* (May 5, 1947).
20. H. C. Beaumont to S. E. Abbot (May 22, 1947), NAI, F-2(6)-UNO-I/47. Emphasis added.
21. Brecher, *The New States of Asia*, 130.
22. In subsequent years, Pakistan assumed that stance and argued that it should be considered the true voice of Muslims of the subcontinent, including the Indian Muslims.
23. Gandhi, *Understanding the Muslim Mind*, 219.
24. Maulana Azad was India's minister for education from August 15, 1947, until his death on February 22, 1958.
25. Heptulla, *Indo-West Asian Relations*, 166.
26. Nehru's note to Secretary, Commonwealth Relations (March 23, 1948), in Nehru, *Selected Works of Jawaharlal Nehru, Series II*, 5:548.
27. Mathai, *Reminiscences of the Nehru Age*, 221.
28. Agwani, "Ingredients of India's Arab Policy," 12.
29. I am grateful to Professor K. R. Singh for highlighting this nuanced difference.
30. E. Sasson to S. Divon (July 1, 1951), ISA, 2413/29.
31. Brecher, *Nehru*, 571–572.
32. Brecher, *The New States of Asia*, 130.
33. Brecher, *Nehru*, 564–565.
34. Gopal, *Jawaharlal Nehru*, 2:170.
35. Copy of the report from Special Branch Inspector, Patna (July 14, 1948), NAI, F-46(22)-AWT/48.

36. Surjeet Singh, Director of Monitoring Service, Simla, to Secretary Ministry of External Affairs (July 13, 1948), NAI, F-19(119)-1A/48.
37. *Debates CA* (August 9, 1948), 28.
38. *Debates CA* (August 20, 1948), 381.
39. Gopal, *Jawaharlal Nehru*, 2:169.
40. Ibid., 2:169–170. Emphasis added.
41. E. Elath to M. Sharett (October 14, 1949), *Israel Documents*, 4:547–548.
42. Eytan, "New Delhi Diary," ISA, 2383/21.
43. This note, dated February 27, 1950, was prepared anticipating supplementary questions on Israel in parliament. NAI, F.23 (2)-AWT/50.
44. The issue was sorted out when Jordan agreed to provide temporary travel documents that were recognized by Riyadh.
45. Agwani, *Contemporary West Asia*, 230.
46. Desai, *The Story of My Life*, 2:257.
47. Dayan, *Breakthrough*, 29.
48. *The Hindustan Times* (May 24, 1980). See also Gandhi, *The Morarji Papers*, 235–236.
49. *Janata* (New Delhi) 33 (November 5, 1978): 19. Jagjivan Ram expressed his "shock" when Dayan's visit was disclosed in May 1980.
50. M. L. Sondhi, quoted in Malik and Singh, *Hindu Nationalists in India*, 125.
51. Ibid.
52. Dixit, *My South Block Years*, 311.
53. Pasha, *India and OIC*, 52–53.
54. Interestingly, on August 24, 2000, weeks after the visit, a lawmaker asked "whether the hon'ble Prime Minister has made a statement during his visit to Israel that diplomatic relations between India and Israel were delayed because of Muslim vote-bank in India." Since it was the foreign minister who visited and made these remarks, the government responded, saying: "Do not arise as Prime Minister did not visit Israel." Debates RS, unstarred question (August 24, 2000).
55. Varadarajan, "When Jaswant Took Indian Politics to Foreign Shores."
56. Noorani, "Palestine and Israel." Interestingly, in 1969 Noorani had lambasted Indira Gandhi's government over the Rabat episode.
57. Press conference of Prime Minister Dr. Manmohan Singh, New York (September 16, 2005), Ministry of External Affairs (New Delhi). Available online at http://meaindia.nic.in/pressbriefing/2005/09/16pb01.htm. Similar arguments were put forth by National Security Advisor M. K. Narayanan when he announced the brief stopover visit by the Iranian president, Mahmoud Ahmedinejad, in April 2008.
58. Heptulla, *Indo-West Asian Relations*, 160–161.
59. Bagchi, "Shalom," 18.
60. *Statesman* (Calcutta) (February 28, 1992).
61. For a brief discussion on Sharon's visit see Cucciniello and Mitra, "India and Israel Move Closer Together."
62. Pasha, *India and OIC*, 42.

63. Interview to *Sunday Observer* (Bombay) (June 27, 1982).
64. Rafael, *Destination Peace*, 88–90.
65. Bhagat, "The Drama and Trauma of Gaza." See also *The Hindu* (March 29, 2006; June 7, 2005).
66. Menon, "U.S. Politics Impinges on West Asian Situation."
67. Quoted in Teslik, *Congress, the Executive Branch, and the Special Interests*, 36.
68. *Debates CA*, first session, part II (December 4, 1947), 1258.
69. *Debates CA* (August 20, 1948), 381; *Debates CA* (March 4, 1949), 1256; *Debates CA* (March 9, 1949), 1400–1401; *Debates CA* (November 28, 1949), 20; *Debates CA* (December 6, 1939), 233–234. *Debates PP* (February 27, 1950), 495; *Debates PP* (March 17, 1950), 1730–1731; *Debates PP* (June 11, 1950), 1270; *Debates PP* (August 4, 1950), 216–217.
70. Such amendments moved in the Lok Sabha include those proposed by Premjibhai R. Assar (April 9, 1958), M. B. Thakor (March 1959), Assar (March 16, 1959), S. Dwivedy (March 16, 1960), Assar (March 16, 1960), A. B. Vajpayee (August 31, 1960), Aurobindo Ghosh (April 3, 1961), P. Vishwambharam (April 3, 1969), Bal Raj Madhok (April 3, 1969), Digvijai Nath (April 3, 1969), B. S. Sharma (April 7, 1970), Piloo Mody (April 7, 1970), R. K. Amin (April 23, 1973), and Ram Jethmalani (April 17, 1978). In the Rajya Sabha, such motions included those proposed by V. M. Chordia (November 22, 1966) and V. D. Mani (June 23, 1967).
71. Agwani, *Contemporary West Asia*, 220–221.
72. Among others, see *Report of the Eighth National Conference of the Socialist Party*, 11–12, 219; Gordon, "Indian-Israeli Relations: Perspective and Promise," 28; and M. S. Gokhale, Secretary Foreign Relations committee PSP to Mapai (September 3, 1952); and Prem Bhatin, PSP to Barkatt, Director Political Department of Histadrut (November 20, 1958), both in Aynor et al., *The Role of the Israeli Labor Movement in Establishing Relations with States in Africa and Asia*, 20, 43–44.
73. Among others, see *Janata* (September 5, 1954; July 7, 1957; June 25, 1961; July 9, 1967; October 8, 1967).
74. Heptulla, *Indo-West Asian Relations*, 146.
75. Bharatiya Jana Sangh, *Party Documents*, 1:49.
76. *Debates LS*, series 1, vol. 10 (December 23, 1953), col. 2992. For a broader discussion of Jan Sangh policy, see Kishore, *Jana Sangh and India's Foreign Policy*, 128–131.
77. Bharatiya Jana Sangh, *Party Documents*, 3:34–35.
78. Ibid., 3:137.
79. Quoted in Schechtman, "India and Israel," 53.
80. Jansen, *Zionism, Israel, and Asian Nationalism*, 305–307.
81. Agwani, *Contemporary West Asia*, 221.
82. Karat, "The Bush-Sharon Axis of Evil." See also Karat's interview in *Frontline* 20, no. 5 (March 1–14, 2003). Available online at http://www.frontlineonnet.com/fl2005/stories/20030314007001600.htm.
83. Pasha, *India and OIC*, 44.

84. Jafferlot, "The Idea Exchange."
85. Vanaik, "Making India Strong: The BJP-led Government's Foreign Policy Perspectives," 333n.
86. "Aggression by Israel Condemned," *People's Democracy* 30, no. 30 (July 23, 2007).

8. International Factors

1. Aide-memoire of conversation (of Abba Eban) with B. N. Rau (June 23, 1949), ISA, 71/14.
2. For the complete text of the memorandum, dated March 1, 1952, see ISA, 2554/12.
3. Eytan to Shiloah (August 11, 1949), ISA, 2441/2.
4. Jansen, *Zionism, Israel, and Asian Nationalism*, 181. Emphasis added.
5. Jansen, *Afro-Asia and Non-Alignment*, 29–33; Zaidi and Zaidi, eds., *Encyclopedia INC*, 11:478, 12:156; Quraishi, *Liberal Nationalism of Egypt*, 45, 129–130; Nehru, *A Bunch of Old Letters*, 284–286; Musa, *The Education of Salama Musa*, 138; Agwani, "India and the Arab World, 1947–1964," 54; Singh, "India and WANA," 625.
6. Among others, see the writings of Jansen, Agwani, Heptulla, and Mudiam.
7. India, *Documents of the Gatherings of Nonaligned Countries, 1961–1979*, 5.
8. During the prolonged Iran-Iraq war, for example, opposition from a handful of its members prevented the NAM from declaring Iraq the aggressor.
9. Castigating Pakistan for overplaying its Islamic credentials, King Farouq of Egypt is reported to have observed: "Don't you know that Islam was born on 14 August 1947 [date of Pakistan's independence]?" Burke, *Mainsprings of Indian and Pakistani Foreign Policies*, 133.
10. Summary by Eliyahu Elath on his meeting with Pandit (May 12, 1949). *Israel Documents, Companion*, 4:17.
11. Brecher, *The New States of Asia*, 130.
12. Rafael, *Destination Peace*, 89.
13. Among others, see Agwani, "India and the Arab World, 1947–1964," 61; Banerjee, "India and West Asia: Changing Images Reflect Shifts in Regional Balance of Power," 28, 30; Singh, "India and the Crisis," 75; Singh, "India and WANA," 18; and Jain, "Disillusionment with the Arabs: A Shift in Indian Opinion," 437.
14. They were Egypt, Iraq, Lebanon, Saudi Arabia, Syria, and Yemen.
15. It is essential to remember that even the Hindu-nationalist Bharatiya Janata Party (BJP), which assumed office following the 1998 parliamentary elections, is not committed to making India a religious state like Pakistan. Despite all signs of extremism, the BJP, unlike its Pakistani counterparts, does not seek to mold the legislature or judiciary in conformity with Hindu religious laws.
16. Hamid, *The Unholy Alliance*, 15. For similar arguments, see Jaffer, "Brahminic-Talmudist Alliance."

17. For a detailed discussion, see Kramer, *Islam Assembled.*
18. Shukat Ali, for example, was a moving spirit behind the Jerusalem conference of 1931.
19. Bahadur, "Pakistan as a Factor in Indo-OIC Relations," 21.
20. For details, see Pirzada, "Pakistan and the OIC," 14–38.
21. A Pakistani military unit headed by Brigadier (later General and President) Zia ul-Haq was training the Jordanian army during the Black September massacre of the Palestinians in 1970. A few years later, Zia was honored by King Hussein for his "services" to the Hashemite Kingdom. Ali, *Can Pakistan Survive? Death of a State*, 224n; and Shah, *The Foreign Policy of Pakistan*, 27.
22. Eliahu Elath to Walter Eytan (September 8, 1953), ISA, 2413/29.
23. Eliahu Sasson to S. Divon (December 28, 1950), ISA, 53/6b. Emphasis added.
24. Brecher, *India and World Politics*, 79.
25. For a detailed discussion, see Abidi, "India's Policy Towards Muslim States."
26. Agwani, "India and the Islamic World," 6.
27. Jansen, *Militant Islam*, 96.
28. India, *MEA Report 1948–1949*, 4.
29. Marwah, "India's Relations with West Asian, North African Countries," 22.
30. Heikal, *The Cairo Document*, 277–299.
31. Ibid., 280.
32. Akbar, *Nehru*, 497.
33. Brecher, *India and World Politics*, 67–68, 77.
34. Despite its initial opposition to the French undertaking this venture, the shortened route became vital for British interests in India. In the very first year of its operation, British shipping accounted for as much as 71 percent of the total cargo handled by the Suez Canal. This preeminence continued until after World War II, and the gradual decline coincided with waning power of the British Empire. The British share was 62.59 percent in 1946, 47.23 in 1947, 37.63 in 1948, 32.11 in 1954, and 28.33 in 1955. For complete figures between 1869 and 1955, see Farnie, *East and West of Suez*, 751–752.
35. Agwani, *Contemporary West Asia*, 216.
36. *Debates LS*, series 2, vol. 41 (March 31, 1960), 8909; series 3, vol. 3 (May 16, 1962), 4617.
37. Srivastava, "India-Israel Relations," 257–258.
38. Driven by the need to evacuate thousands of Indians who were stranded in Kuwait following the Iraqi invasion, India sided with Saddam Hussein and even closed its embassy in Kuwait within days after the invasion. It was only after the successful airlifting of about 150,000 Indians was completed in October 1990 that India became more critical of Iraq. For a discussion see Jayaramu, "India and the Gulf Crisis: Pro-Iraq or Pro-India."
39. International Energy Agency, *World Energy Outlook, 2005*, 254.
40. Until the Kuwait crisis and subsequent UN sanctions, Iraq was India's principal oil supplier.
41. For a recent discussion, see Feiler, *From Boycott to Economic Cooperation.*

42. *Israel and the United Nations*, 166.
43. Quoted in Kimche, "The Arab Boycott of Israel," 6.
44. Israel joined the West European and Others Group in 2000 and thus became eligible to contest elections to UN Security Council.
45. The Arab boycott has been studied extensively and some of the notable works include: Sarna, *Boycott and Blacklist*; Teslik, *Congress, the Executive Branch, and the Special Interests*; Chill, *The Arab Boycott of Israel*; and Prittie and Nelson, *The Economic War Against the Jews*. The Arab points of view are available in Iskandar, *The Arab Boycott of Israel*; and Meo et al., *The Arab Boycott of Israel*.
46. Mandel, *The Arabs and Zionism Before World War I*, 81.
47. Prittie and Nelson, *The Economic War Against the Jews*, 142; Sarna, *Boycott and Blacklist*, 185.
48. M. R. Baveja, Cairo, to Ministry of Commerce, New Delhi (April 21, 1948), and Foreign Office to Embassy, Cairo (April 19, 1949), NAI, F-13(70)-1A/49.
49. *Debates PP*, vol. 6, part 1 (February 20, 1951), 1580; *Debates RS*, vol. 40 (August 13, 1962), cols. 1319–1320.
50. Sarna, *Boycott and Blacklist*, 185.
51. FICCI, *Report of the Indian Delegation to West Asian Countries*, 27. Emphasis added. Arab countries often used the expression "Israeli" as a synonym for "Zionist" or "Jew."
52. Ibid.
53. India, *Documents of the Gatherings of Nonaligned Countries, 1961–1979*, 94.
54. Ibid., 111. Chapter 7 deals with the powers of the Security Council in dealing with "threats to the peace, breaches of peace and acts of aggression" and empowers the council to impose and enforce punitive measures against states violating its recommendations.
55. India, Ministry of External Affairs, http://meaindia.nic.in/foreignrelation/palestine.pdf, p. 6.; and Pradhan, "Changing Dynamics of India's West Asia Policy," 10.
56. Korey, "India and Israel," 8. It is rather surprising that none of the Indian writers have mentioned this reported visit.
57. *Debates LS*, series 4, vol. 33 (November 19, 1969), 36–37; vol. 34 (December 3, 1969); and vol. 37 (March 4, 1970), 166–167.
58. *Debates RS*, vol. 73 (August 26, 1970), col. 123.
59. India, *MEA Report 1969–1970*, 56.
60. *Debates RS*, vol. 71 (March 26, 1970), col. 28.
61. India, *Documents of the Gatherings of Nonaligned Countries, 1961–1979*, 32.
62. Ibid., 138.
63. Ibid., 186.
64. *Debates LS*, series 4, vol. 40 (April 22, 1970), 230.
65. *International Documents on Palestine 1973*, 525.
66. *Debates RS*, vol. 90 (November 22, 1974), col. 47.
67. *Hindustan Times* (December 23, 1974).
68. *Asian Recorder* 21 (March 5–11, 1975): 12475. Until then, the Arab League office in New Delhi was looking after the interests of the PLO.

69. *International Documents on Palestine, 1975*, 372.
70. For example, see *MEA Report 1975–1976*, 75.
71. Statement of Foreign Minister P. V. Narasimha Rao, *Debates LS*, 7:3 (March 26, 1980), 313–314.
72. *Hindustan Times* (April 12, 1981).
73. India has consistently supported "the right of the refugees to have an unfettered choice either to return to their homeland or to compensation. . . . India appreciated the aspirations of the Palestine refugees to return to their homes. India also took the position that the UN was responsible for the partitioning of the country and that the rights of the refugees to choose between repatriation and compensation which had been clearly recognized in Resolution 194, should be respected." India, *India and Palestine*, 51.
74. Ibid. It should be noted that India, especially during Nehru's time, relied heavily on the authority of the Western historian Arnold Toynbee, known for his anti-Jewish sentiments and writings, to repudiate these claims.
75. India, *India and Palestine*, 31.
76. Statement of the official spokesperson reported in *The Hindu* (September 18, 1950).
77. India, *India and Palestine*, 31.
78. For a detailed and pioneering study, see Harkabi, *The Palestinian Covenant and Its Meaning*.
79. *Asian Recorder* 18 (September 30–October 6, 1972): 11016.
80. When three Western diplomats were killed in Khartoum in March 1973, India characterized it as a "condemnable act of lawlessness." *MEA Report 1972–1973*, 33.
81. *Debates RS*, vol. 71 (March 26, 1970), col. 27. Despite this, India could not prevent its territories from being used for Palestinian acts of violence. According to a study during 1970 and 1984, as many as ten Palestinian acts of terrorism either originated from or happened in India. They were 1970 (1), 1971 (3), 1974 (1), 1976 (1), 1982 (2), 1983 (1), and 1984 (1). Merari and Elad, *The International Dimensions of Palestinian Terrorism*, 119, 130–142.
82. India, *Documents of the Gatherings of Nonaligned Countries, 1961–1979*, 203. Emphasis added. However, Israel had different understanding of Idi Amin's "humanitarian efforts" and thus acted differently.

9. Nehru and the Era of Deterioration, 1947–1964

The epigraph to this chapter is taken from Panikkar, *A Memorandum on Hindu-Zionist Relations* (April 4, 1947), CZA, S25/7486.

1. Edwards, "Illusions and Reality in Indian Foreign Policy," 49.
2. Nehru, however, had deputies to assist him. They were A. K. Chanda (August 12, 1952, to May 1, 1957), Syed Mahmud (December 7, 1954 to April 17,

1957), and Lakshmi Menon (April 17, 1957, to April 10, 1962, and April 16, 1962, to May 27, 1964).

3. They are Jawaharlal Nehru (1947–1964), Lal Bahadur Sastri (1964–1966), Indira Gandhi (1966–1977), Morarji Desai (1977–1979), Charan Singh (1979–1980), Indira Gandhi (1980–1984), Rajiv Gandhi (1984–1989), V. P. Singh (1989–1990), Chandra Shekhar (1990–1991), and P. V. Narasimha Rao (1991–1996). Subsequently, India had the following prime ministers: Atal Behari Vajpayee (1996), Deva Gowda (1996–1997), I. K. Gujral (1997–1998), A. B. Vajpayee (1998–2004), and Manmohan Singh (2004–).
4. Gopal, *Jawaharlal Nehru*, 1:344. The Jewish delegation, however, felt "most of the real problems have either not been touched at all, or were touched on slightly and casually and immediately hushed up." "Report of the Inter-Asian Conference" (April 17, 1947), CZA, S 25/7485, p. 2.
5. The delegation also included the Sanskrit scholar Immanuel Olsvanger, who came to India in 1936 as the official emissary of the Jewish Agency, and Ya'acov Shimoni, who later on joined the foreign ministry and shaped Israel's Asia policy.
6. "Report of the Inter-Asian Conference" (April 17, 1947), CZA, S 25/7485, p. 4.
7. For example, Nehru's biographer refers to delegates from the "Hebrew University." Gopal, *Jawaharlal Nehru*, 1:344.
8. "Report of the Inter-Asian Conference," CZA, S 25/7485, p. 4. Emphasis in the original. In his speech over All-India Radio, Shimoni repeatedly referred to "our country." For the transcript of Shimoni's speech, see *Asian Relations Conference: Publicity Section* (March 1947), CZA, S25/7485.
9. Jansen, *Afro-Asia and Non-Alignment*, 45.
10. Kochan, "Israel in the Third World Forums," 248.
11. "Report of the Inter-Asian Conference" (April 17, 1947), CZA, S 25/7485, p. 1.
12. Jansen, *Zionism, Israel, and Asian Nationalism*, 191.
13. For example, see Kochan, "Israel in the Third World Forums," 248.
14. "Report of the Inter-Asian Conference" (April 17, 1947), CZA, S 25/7485, p. 4.
15. Ibid.
16. For the complete text of Bergmann's speech, see *Asian Relations: Report of the Proceedings and Documents of the First Asian Relations Conference, New Delhi, March–April 1947*.
17. For the transcript of Shimoni's speech, see *Asian Relations Conference: Publicity Section* (March 1947), CZA, S25/7485.
18. According to Shimoni, Nehru was not present when Bergmann spoke. "Report of the Inter-Asian Conference," CZA, S 25/7485, p. 8. However, it is not clear if this was deliberate or due to Nehru's other responsibilities.
19. Jansen, *Zionism, Israel, and Asian Nationalism*, 192. See also Appadorai, "The Asian Relations Conference in Perspective," 281–282.
20. "Report of the Inter-Asian Conference," CZA, S 25/7485, p. 8.
21. Ibid.
22. Nehru, *Selected Works of Jawaharlal Nehru, Series II*, 2:511.

23. Ibid.
24. "Report of the Inter-Asian Conference," CZA, S 25/7485, p. 6. This position, however, was not shared by some members of the delegation, who "ascribed it to our being too sensitive."
25. Ibid., 9.
26. He played a key role in the initial contacts between Israel and the People's Republic of China. However, these contacts did not blossom into full diplomatic ties.
27. Held at Nehru's residence, only his sister Vijayalakshmi Pandit and daughter Indira Gandhi were present.
28. "Report of the Inter-Asian Conference," CZA, S 25/7485, p. 6.
29. Ibid., 7.
30. Panikkar, "A Memorandum on Hindu-Zionist Relations."
31. "Report of the Inter-Asian Conference," CZA, S 25/7485, pp. 8–9; Alfred Bonne, "Supplementary Notes to the Report of the Delegation on the Inter-Asian Conference in New Delhi" (April 30, 1947), CZA, S25/7485.
32. Jansen, *Afro-Asia and Non-Alignment*, 71.
33. *The Zionist Review*, quoted in Jansen, *Zionism, Israel, and Asian Nationalism*, 194.
34. Agwani, *Contemporary West Asia*, 154.
35. Gopal, *Jawaharlal Nehru*, 2:169.
36. Cited in Agwani, "The Palestine Conflict in Asian Perspective," 456. Interestingly, a couple of decades later, India was instrumental in the formation of Bangladesh, whose independence was achieved by an India-backed war rather than through negotiations with Pakistan. Moreover, while an act of war can be unilateral, peace always demands the cooperation of two parties, something that the Arabs were not prepared to offer in 1948.
37. Shiva Rao's D. O. letter (April 30, 1949), NAI, F-32(6)-1A/49.
38. L. Panjabi to H. Z. Cynowitz (March 26, 1949), ISA, 2555/5.
39. Advisory Opinion (May 28, 1948), ICJ, Reports of Judgment, Advisory Opinion and Orders, 65.
40. Quoted in Appleton, *The Eternal Triangle*, 19.
41. *Israel and the United Nations*, 50.
42. Appleton, *The Eternal Triangle*, 26.
43. For this statement and for a detailed discussion, see Ramakrishna Reddy, *India's Policy in the United Nations*, 18–22.
44. This is often referred to as Israel's "missed opportunity." For a background discussion, see Shichor, "Hide-and-Seek: Sino-Israeli Relations in Perspective."
45. The following discussion is based on Jansen, *Afro-Asia and Non-Alignment*, 143–168.
46. Jansen, *Zionism, Israel, and Asian Nationalism*, 251.
47. For example, see the speech of Pakistan's foreign minister, Muhammad Zafrullah Khan, "Thanksgiving Day at Lake Success, New York, 27 November 1949," in Khalidi, ed., *From Heaven to Conquest*, 709–722.

48. Joint communiqué by the prime ministers of Burma, Ceylon, India, Indonesia, and Pakistan, Colombo, 1954. In Jansen, *Afro-Asia and Non-Alignment*, 414.
49. UN Resolution 194, adopted on December 11, 1948, was not as unequivocal and categorical on the Palestinian refugees as commonly believed, interpreted, and presented. It declared that "the refugees wishing to return to their homes and live at peace with their neighbors should be permitted to do so at the earliest practicable date, and that compensation should be paid for the property of those choosing not to return."
50. Jansen, *Afro-Asia and Non-Alignment*, 164.
51. Initially, Nehru was not favorable to the idea. Gopal, *Jawaharlal Nehru*, 2:232.
52. For the complete text of the joint communiqué issued on December 29, 1954, see India, *MEA Report 1954–1955*, 55–58.
53. Behbehani, *China's Foreign Policy in the Arab World, 1955–75*, 4.
54. They were Egypt, Iraq, Jordan, Lebanon, Libya, Sudan, Syria, and Yemen.
55. Also excluded were apartheid South Africa and the breakaway Taiwanese republic, which was still a member of the United Nations as well as the Security Council. Questioning the logic of the invitation, Michael Brecher observed: "the Gold Coast was invited even though it was two years away from independence, as was Ghana. As if to underline the inconsistency, both North and South Vietnam were invited, but the two Koreas were not." Brecher, *The New States of Asia*, 133.
56. In addition to eight Arab countries, Afghanistan, Iran, Pakistan, and Turkey attended the Bandung Conference.
57. Jansen, *Afro-Asia and Non-Alignment*, 174–175.
58. Ibid., 175.
59. *Israel and the United Nations*, 166.
60. Quoted in Feiler, *From Boycott to Economic Cooperation*, 30.
61. Quoted in Kochan, "Israel in Third World Forums," 251. Emphasis added.
62. Gopal, *Jawaharlal Nehru*, 2:232.
63. In his assessment, "For us to be told . . . that the United States and the United Kingdom will not like the inclusion of China in the Afro-Asian conference is not very helpful. In fact, it is somewhat irritating. There are many things that the United States and the United Kingdom have done which we do not like at all." In Gopal, *Jawaharlal Nehru*, 2:233.
64. Brecher, *The New States of Asia*, 210–211.
65. Brecher, *India and World Politics*, 52.
66. Ibid., 79.
67. Ibid., 60.
68. Jansen, *Zionism, Israel, and Asian Nationalism*, 259.
69. Cited in ibid., 260.
70. Brecher, *India and World Politics*, 79.
71. Cited in Jansen, *Zionism, Israel, and Asian Nationalism*, 260.
72. Jansen identified them as Ceylon, Formosa, the Philippines, and Burma in 1949; India and Thailand in 1950; and Japan in 1952. Jansen, *Zionism, Israel,*

and Asian Nationalism, 203–204. The full-fledged Israeli consulate in India became operational only 1953.

73. Menon also referred to an incident when the Lebanese ambassador to India walked out of an official Indian party in October 1964 because of the presence of an Indian professor who was a member of the Indo-Israel Cultural Society. Brecher, *India and World Politics*, 79.
74. Brecher, *India and World Politics*, 80.
75. David Ben-Gurion's statement of January 5, 1957, quoted in *New Outlook* (Tel Aviv) 1, no. 3 (September 1957): 21. This was a radical change in Israel's stand. On the eve of the Suez crisis, Nehru received "an informal message . . . from the Prime Minister of Israel to the effect that Israel had made a mistake in leaning on the Western Powers and the Israelis now realized more than ever that they were of Asia and must look to Asia." Gopal, *Jawaharlal Nehru*, 2:277. Gopal did not identify the person, but perhaps he was referring to Moshe Sharett, the former Israeli prime minister who had met Nehru in New Delhi on October 30, 1956.
76. Some of the best documentary works on the crisis include Eayrs, ed., *The Commonwealth and Suez*; U.S. State Department, *The Suez Canal Problem*; and India, Lok Sabha Secretariat, *Suez Canal: Nationalization and After*. On the legal aspects, see Lapidoth, *Freedom of Navigation with Special Reference to International Waterways in the Middle East*; Obeita, *The International Status of the Suez Canal*; and, on India, see Mohan, "India, Pakistan, Suez, and the Commonwealth."
77. For the complete text of Menon's statement at the London Conference, see U.S. State Department, *The Suez Canal Problem*, 159–178.
78. For Nehru's statement in the parliament, *Debates LS*, series 1, vol. 7, part 2 (August 8, 1956), cols. 2536–2544.
79. Ibid.
80. U.S. State Department, *The Suez Canal Problem*, 174–175.
81. For the full text, see http://domino.un.org/UNISPAL.NSF/181c4bf00c44e5fd85256cef0073c426/38a514ea8dc0d345852560c20072ecb6.
82. *Foreign Affairs Record* 2, no. 10 (October 1956): 150.
83. Jawaharlal Nehru to Anthony Eden (November 1, 1956), cited in Gopal, *Jawaharlal Nehru*, 2:286.
84. *The Hindu* (November 2, 1956).
85. For a detailed discussion, see Gopal, *Jawaharlal Nehru*, 2:291–299.
86. Eden, *Full Circle*, 545; Gopal, *Jawaharlal Nehru*, 2:291.
87. Gopal, *Jawaharlal Nehru*, 2:292.
88. *Debates LS*, series 1, vol. 9, part 2 (November 20, 1956), col. 592. For a similar statement, see *Debates LS*, series 2, vol. 3 (July 23, 1957), 4832.
89. "My anger was the greater because the invasion [the Suez crisis] diverted attention from Hungary and I felt that if the world's attention could be concentrated on Hungary, the Soviet Union might decide not to crush the revolt." Reid, *Envoy to Nehru*, 150.

90. Quoted in Selak, "A Consideration of the Legal Status of the Gulf of Aqaba," 2:711.
91. They are Egypt (100 miles), Saudi Arabia (100 miles), Israel (6.5 miles), and Jordan (3.5 miles).
92. Selak, "A Consideration of the Legal Status of the Gulf of Aqaba," 2:711.
93. At its northern end, where all four states are contiguous, the breadth of the gulf is just three miles. The territorial zones claimed are six nautical miles each for Egypt, Israel, and Saudi Arabia, and three nautical miles for Jordan. Bloomfield, *Egypt, Israel, and the Gulf of Aqaba in International Law*, 2.
94. *Debates LS*, series 1, vol. 9, part 2 (November 20, 1956), cols. 594–595.
95. Gopal, *Jawaharlal Nehru*, 2:290.
96. Heikal, *The Cairo Documents*, 294.
97. *The Jerusalem Post* (October 29, 1962).
98. Maxwell, *India's China War*, 385; Heikal, *The Cairo Documents*, 297; Mudiam, *India and the Middle East*, 161–162. This event subsequently got Israel into trouble with China, as Chairman Mao began using this arms supply to justify and impede Sino-Israeli ties.
99. Heikal, *The Cairo Documents*, 297–298. See also Heptulla, *Indo-West Asian Relations*, 191.
100. India, *MEA Report 1963–1964*, 45–48. In the words of Gopal, "India was now prepared to obtain arms from any source. Even with Israel there were talks, which had soon to be ended because of Nasser's opposition." As in the case of Maulana Azad's role regarding nonrelations with Israel, once again Gopal relied on an external source to make this argument, namely Heikal. Gopal, *Jawaharlal Nehru*, 3:224.
101. For example, see Agwani, "India and West Asia," 169–171.

10. The Years of Hardened Hostility, 1964–1984

The epigraph to this chapter is taken from Agwani, *Contemporary West Asia*, 253.

1. India, *Documents of the Gatherings of Nonaligned Countries, 1961–1979*, 21.
2. Korey, "India and Israel," 8.
3. *Debates LS*, series 3, vol. 44 (August 23, 1965), 1194–1195.
4. *MEA Report 1965–1966*, 36–37; *MEA Report 1966–1967*, 31; *Debates RS*, vol. 54 (November 22, 1965), col. 2127.
5. *Debates RS*, vol. 54 (November 22, 1965), col. 2127.
6. Personal interviews with Reuven Dafni, who served as Israeli consul during this period, in Jerusalem, 1992. Details, however, are not available.
7. For a background discussion on the bilateral relations, see Kozichi, "Nepal and Israel."

8. Though the Congress Party was in power, the communists had significant influence in the state of West Bengal, which later on became the bastion of the Indian Left.
9. *Debates RS*, vol. 55 (March 25, 1966), col. 4546–4547.
10. *Debates RS*, vol. 56 (May 3, 1966), col. 23.
11. Under a bilateral treaty signed in July 1950, India enjoyed considerable influence and leeway in Nepalese foreign policy, and thus the row could also be interpreted as a discourtesy to the Himalayan kingdom.
12. For the complete text, see *Debates LS*, series 4, vol. 3 (May 5, 1967), 871–876.
13. *Debates LS*, series 2, vol. 18 (August 14, 1958), 869–880.
14. In a letter dated November 6, 1956, to the UN Secretary General, India's ambassador, Arthur Lall, declared, "it is understood the Force [that is, UNEF] may have to function through Egyptian territory. Therefore, there must be Egyptian consent for its establishment." Eayrs, *The Commonwealth and Suez*, 360. For a similar statement, see *Debates RS*, vol. 30 (August 11, 1960), col. 619.
15. Chagla, *Roses in December*, 425.
16. For the text of the June 5 opposition appeal to the prime minister, see *Debates LS*, series 4, vol. 4 (June 6, 1967), 3296.
17. *Debates LS*, series 4, vol. 4 (June 6, 1967), 3315. However, for an equally forceful but opposite argument made by Indira Gandhi, who advised caution on the Czech crisis, see *Debates LS*, series 4, vol. 20 (August 22, 1968), 459–462.
18. *Debates LS*, series 4, vol. 7 (July 18, 1967), 12702.
19. A detailed account of the diplomatic efforts leading up to the adoption of Security Council Resolution 242 can be found in Bailey, *The Making of Resolution 242*.
20. *Debates LS*, series 4 (June 6, 1967), 3316.
21. For the text of the AICC resolution, see Zaidi and Zaidi, eds., *Encyclopedia INC*, 19:356–357.
22. During this period, there was a threat of early elections to the Lok Sabha. Kozichi, "Indian Policy Towards the Middle East," 786.
23. Chagla, *Roses in December*, 426.
24. Bhargava, *India and West Asia*.
25. Jha, *From Bandung to Tashkent*, 308–309.
26. Baxter, *The Jana Sangh*, 306. Emphasis added.
27. At the time of the war, UNEF had about eight thousand soldiers from Brazil, Canada, Colombia, Denmark, Finland, India, Indonesia, Norway, Sweden, and Yugoslavia. Rikhye, *The Sinai Blunder*, 2.
28. Ibid., 151.
29. *Times of India* (June 7, 1967).
30. Singh, "India and the Crisis," 79.
31. Rikhye, *The Sinai Blunder*, 151.
32. Ibid., 150.
33. Ibid., 152.
34. Ibid.

35. Ibid.
36. Ibid., 154.
37. Ibid., 155.
38. Frisch, “Has the Israeli-Palestinian Conflict Become Islamic?” 393.
39. *Debates LS*, 4:32 (August 28, 1969), 251–252.
40. *Debates RS*, 59 (August 28, 1969), col. 5919.
41. *Patriot* (August 27, 1969).
42. *Times of India* (August 29, 1969).
43. *The Hindu* (Chennai) (September 10, 1969).
44. *National Herald* (New Delhi) (August 30, 1969).
45. Ibid.
46. *Annual Report of the Security Council*, 1969, reproduced in *Palestine Documents* (1970), 475. Emphasis added.
47. A detailed and dispassionate discussion of the OIC can be found in Baba, *Organisation of Islamic Conference*.
48. Singh, “Oral History: India at the Rabat Islamic Summit (1969),” 106. Some have wrongly argued that since “Zakir Hussein (1977–1969) was then President of India, an official delegation was invited to attend.” Mansingh, *India's Search for Power*, 211. Hussein had passed away in May, and on August 24, V. V. Giri took over as the new president of India.
49. Baba, *Organisation of Islamic Conference*, 65.
50. Noorani, “Rabat: Religion and Diplomacy.”
51. Soz, “The OIC and Indian Muslims,” 125.
52. Mansingh, *India's Search for Power*, 212.
53. Dixit, *My South Block Years*, 300–301. See also Agwani, *Contemporary West Asia*, 240.
54. *Debates LS*, 4:33 (November 17, 1969), 430.
55. *Debates RS*, 70 (November 21, 1969), col.810. In his personal recollections more than thirty years later, India's ambassador in Rabat at that time, Gurbachan Singh, did not admit the existence of a written invitation. See his “Oral History,” 105–120.
56. Quoted in Noorani, “Rabat: Religion and Diplomacy.”
57. *Debates LS*, 4:33 (November 18, 1969), 135, 146.
58. Quoted in Noorani, “Rabat: Religion and Diplomacy.”
59. For a statement by Foreign Minister Dinesh Singh, see *Debates LS*, 3:38 (February 22, 1965), 651.
60. Quoted in Bahadur, “Pakistan as a Factor in Indo-OIC Relations,” 21. This was not the first occasion when the subcontinent cast a shadow over international Muslim gatherings. As early as in 1926, the Mecca conference was dominated over the usage of Urdu. While the Arab participants declared Arabic, the language of the Qur'an, as the pan-Islamic one, non-Arab participants primarily from India insisted on speaking in Urdu or English. The same conflict occurred in 1931, when the mufti hosted the General Muslim Congress in 1931. Kupferschmidt, “The General Muslim Congress of 1931 in Jerusalem,” 126–127.

61. Pasha, *India and OIC*, vi.
62. India, *MEA Report 1971–1972*, 42–43; *MEA Report 1972–1973*, 34. *Debates RS*, vol. 77 (August 14, 1972), col. 32. For a detailed discussion on the Middle East response, see Singh, "Subcontinent and WANA countries," 101–116.
63. India, *MEA Report 1971–1972*, 45–50; *Debates RS*, vol. 77 (July 21, 1971), cols. 1–8.
64. *Debates RS*, vol. 75 (March 31, 1971), cols. 123–124; *Debates RS*, vol. 77 (July 28, 1971), col. 8; *Debates RS*, vol. 77 (August 4, 1971), col. 68.
65. *Debates LS*, series 5, vol. 14 (April 26, 1972), 227.
66. *Debates RS*, vol. 76 (November 30, 1973), col. 92; and India, *MEA Report 1973–1974*, 45.
67. *Debates RS*, vol. 76 (December 12, 1973), cols. 256–257.
68. For a detailed discussion on the resolution, see Lewis, "The Anti-Zionist Resolution."
69. India, *MEA Report 1975–1976*, 76.
70. *ADL International Report: India's Campaign Against Israel.*
71. Until the Congress split in the late 1960s, he was a prominent leader of the party and served as deputy prime minister under Indira Gandhi.
72. India, *MEA Report 1977–1978*, 12. See also Gangal, "Trends in India's Foreign Policy," 50–51.
73. India, *MEA Report 1977–1978*, v.
74. For the text of the resolution adopted at Khartoum Arab League summit meeting on September 1, 1967, see http://www.mfa.gov.il/MFA.
75. *Debates LS*, series 6, vol. 19 (November 23, 1978), 21; *Debates RS*, vol. 109 (May 16, 1979), col. 343; and India, *MEA Report 1979–1980*, 18. The last, however, was prepared after Indira Gandhi became prime minister in January 1980.
76. *Times of India* (New Delhi) (October 1, 1978).
77. Indeed, this happened when India was ruled by a minority government headed by Charan Singh and Egypt was allowed to participate in the NAM Havana summit.
78. Egypt is a founding member of both these organizations.
79. Dayan, *Breakthrough*, 26.
80. Desai's press conference in Bombay on May 16, 1980, *Indian Express* (New Delhi) (May 17, 1980). Personal interview with Desai in Bombay (October 22, 1987).
81. *Times of India* (New Delhi) (May 22, 1980).
82. *Debates LS*, series 7, vol. 4 (June 12, 1980), 12.
83. "Dayan Visit Tarnished India's Image, Says Narasimha Rao," *Hindustan Times* (June 13, 1980).
84. There was also a fundamental transformation in Israel. Just as the Congress Party lost power, in June 1977 the Likud party defeated the Labor Party, which had been in power since the establishment of Israel.
85. Dayan, *Breakthrough*, 28–29; Personal interview with Desai in Bombay (October 22, 1987).

86. Dayan, *Breakthrough*, 29. Desai, however, denied ever having made such statements. Personal interview with Desai in Bombay (October 22, 1987). Similarly, Desai's secret meeting with Foreign Minister R. S. Botha of apartheid-ruled South Africa in Frankfurt in June 1979 led to a huge uproar in India.
87. Statements of Foreign Minister Rao, *Debates LS*, series 7, vol. 4 (June 12, 1980), 16, 173–174.
88. Rikhye, "Dayan, Desai, and South Africa."
89. Reddy, "Dayan Paid Secret Visit During Janata Rule: PM," *The Hindu* (May 11, 1980).
90. "Dayan Visit Tarnished India's Image, Says Narasimha Rao," *Hindustan Times* (June 13, 1980).
91. *Patriot* (June 13, 1980); *Statesman* (June 13, 1980).
92. *The Hindustan Times* (June 9, 1980).
93. Bahbah, "Israel's Private Arms Network," 10; and Shichor, "Israel's Military Transfer to China and Taiwan," 73–74.
94. Rikhye, "Dayan, Desai, and South Africa."
95. Weizmann met Desai in London prior to Dayan's visit. Personal interview with Desai in Bombay (October 22, 1987). Desai's principal secretary, V. Shankar, visited Israel in June 1979.
96. Taiwan and apartheid-ruled South Africa were the other two countries where Indian passports were declared not valid.
97. *Tribune* (Chandigarh) (November 10, 1979).
98. For details, see Bhambhri, "Lok Sabha Elections, January 1980."
99. *Janata* (New Delhi) 33 (November 5, 1978): 19. He expressed his "shock" when Dayan's visit was disclosed in May 1980.
100. *The Hindustan Times* (May 24, 1980). See also Gandhi, *The Morarji Papers*, 235–236.
101. *Sunday Observer* (Bombay) (June 27, 1982).
102. Periodic tit-for-tat expulsions of Indian and Pakistan diplomats are an exception.
103. Personal conversations with Israeli diplomats in Jerusalem in July and August 1988.
104. Avimor, ed., *Relations Between Israel and Asian and African States*, 382.
105. Kumaraswamy, "India, Israel, and the Davis Cup Tie 1987."

11. Prelude to Normalization

The epigraph to this chapter is taken from N. R. Mohanty, "Jewish Leader Finds Rao Pragmatic," *Times of India* (November 23, 1991).

1. Ever since his elevation to general secretary of the ruling Congress Party in 1981, he was groomed as a successor to Indira Gandhi.
2. While Rajiv accompanied his mother during foreign tours, his exposure to international diplomacy was limited. This was in contrast to the experiences

of his mother, Indira. During Nehru's seventeen-year tenure as prime minister, his daughter often accompanied him on foreign tours and took part in many meetings with foreign dignitaries. For example, she was present during the lunch Nehru gave to the Israeli diplomat Walter Eytan in February 1952.

3. For a detailed discussion of his term as prime minister, see Sengupta, *Rajiv Gandhi.*
4. Kumaraswamy, "The Star and the Dragon." For a detailed discussion on Sino-Saudi ties, see Shichor, *East Wind Over Arabia.*
5. *ADL International Report: India's Campaign Against Israel.*
6. *The Hindu* (Madras) (December 30, 1988).
7. Khergamvala, "Covert Contact with Israel," *The Hindu* (January 18, 1989). He also highlights internal opposition within India regarding Israel.
8. "Leak to Media by Jewish Leader Aborts Improvement of India-Israel Status," *Middle East Times* (July 23–29, 1988); Joseph, "Solarz Gushes Over Thaw in Indo-Israeli Ties," *Pioneer* (January 31, 1992).
9. "Jewish Leaders and Solarz Meet Gandhi," *India Abroad* (June 17, 1988); Akbar, "New York Diary," *Telegraph* (Calcutta) (June 12, 1988).
10. *Ha'aretz* (July 15, 1988), in *FBIS-NES* (July 19, 1988): 45; *India Today* (September 30, 1988): 155.
11. Interestingly, exactly three years later, as prime minister, Rao normalized relations, and Singh became India's first ambassador to Israel.
12. Hordes, "Is India Rethinking Its Policy on Israel?" 3–5.
13. Khergamvala, "Covert Contact with Israel."
14. For details of this attack, see Perlmutter, Handel, and Bar-Joseph, *Two Minutes Over Baghdad.*
15. *Israeli Foreign Affairs* (April 1987): 4.
16. See the text of Pollard's August 1986 memo to the court, in Henderson, *Pollard,* 51–78; *Indian Express* (March 28, 1988); Blitzer, *Territory of Lies,* 168–169; and *Israeli Foreign Affairs* (April 1987): 1.
17. *Sunday Observer* (New Delhi) (January 17, 1988). Emphasis added.
18. For the text of his speech, see *Indian Express* (October 14–15, 1985).
19. *The Islamic Bomb,* written by Steve Weissman and Herbert Krosney (1981), propagated this idea and was quickly picked up by others.
20. However, a formal agreement to this effect was signed on December 31, 1988, and came into force in January 1993, nearly two years after Gandhi's assassination.
21. For a detailed discussion, see Kumaraswamy, "India, Israel, and the Davis Cup Tie 1987."
22. For a first-person account, see Dayan, *Breakthrough,* 26–29.
23. India eventually lost to Sweden in the finals. India previously had reached the Davis Cup finals in 1974. By refusing to play against the apartheid regime, it forfeited the match to South Africa, which was awarded the title.
24. The following year, however, India refused to play the relegation match, thereby underscoring the limitations of sanctions.

25. Waggonner, *The So-Called New Era of Ping-Pong Diplomacy with Communist China.*
26. *The Hindu* (March 28, 1987).
27. The onset of the intifada later that year, however, considerably undermined some of this goodwill toward Israel.
28. For example, in 2007 an Israeli journalist working for the Yediot *Ahoronot* newspaper visited Syria and reported on the Israeli airstrike on a suspected nuclear plant, in Deir er Zor in eastern Syria.
29. Personal conversations with Israeli diplomats in Jerusalem in August 1988.
30. Personal conversation with Jewish leaders in New Delhi in May 1988.
31. *India Today* (New Delhi) (October 31, 1989): 163.
32. Ibid.
33. A full-page advertisement in the *Jerusalem Post* (May 23, 1991). See also "'Little India' Thrives Amid Diamond Industry," *Jerusalem Post* (May 24, 1991).
34. Quoted in Ward, *India's Pro-Arab Policy*, 123.
35. Ibid., 124.
36. An editorial in the *Jerusalem Post* (March 27, 1988) called it the "Indian rope trick." My sincere thanks to the late Walter Eytan for bringing this editorial to my notice.
37. This is true for the pro-Arab stance in the United States.
38. Due to the violent situation, elections were postponed in the state of Punjab.
39. It was therefore not surprising that Singh was one of the handful of leaders to criticize Prime Minister Narasimha Rao's decision to establish diplomatic relations with Israel.
40. This happened in the middle of the Lok Sabha elections. The award was formally presented to Arafat in March 1990 by Gandhi's successor, V. P. Singh.
41. For a background discussion, see Somaratna, "Renewal of Ties Between Sri Lanka and Israel; and Somaratna, "Sri Lanka's Relations with Israel."
42. Some even argued that India was compelled to intervene in Sri Lanka because of Colombo's "security connections" with Israel. Dixit, *Assignment Colombo*, 327.
43. For the full text of the accord, see ibid., 355–361.
44. "Now in Fiji," *Israeli Foreign Affairs* (November 1987): 1, 7; *Ha'aretz* (November 13, 1986) in *FBIS-MEA* (November 14, 1986): I/3–4; "Israelis in Fiji," *Israeli Foreign Affairs* (August 1988): 1, 4.
45. Interaction with a senior Indian diplomat who served in Fiji during that period in 1991.
46. Among others, see Iqbal Masud, "Strange Bedfellows," *Indian Express* (April 20, 1986); Girilal Jain, "An Israel-Pak Alliance," *Times of India* (May 1, 1987); and Lawrence Lifschutz, "Pakistan Was Iran-Contra's Secret Back Door," *Times of India* (November 24, 1991).
47. Fighting for a separate Tamil homeland in Sri Lanka, the LTTE is declared as terrorist organization by a number of countries, including India and the United States, and is proscribed from operating.
48. Ganguly, "India's Foreign Policy Grows Up," 43.

49. Interestingly, in late 1988, Hadass's scheduled visit to India through Bangkok was canceled due to premature media leaks.
50. Pradhan, "India's Policy Towards the PLO," 71–72; Pradhan, "Seeking Clarity in Arafat's Message," 30–31; and Pradhan, "Changing Dynamics of India's West Asia Policy," 17.

12. Normalization and After

1. Normally, such announcements are made by a junior official in charge of the External Publicity Division, who also functions as the official spokesperson of the ministry.
2. More than a decade later, Prime Minister Manmohan Singh, who was the finance minister during this period, recollected those times. "When I became finance minister [in 1991] India was in the midst of the worst possible crisis. Our foreign exchange reserves had literally exhausted. Even to raise a small loan of $500 million, we had to physically send India's gold reserves to the vaults of the Bank of England." Interview of PM on the Charlie Rose Show (September 21, 2004). Available online at http://pmindia.nic.in/visits/content.asp?id=22.
3. Israeli diplomat Moshe Yegar, who was heading the Asian desk when India recognized Israel. Personal conversation in Jerusalem on August 18, 1997.
4. For example, see Gupta, *The Diaspora's Political Efforts in the United States.*
5. Shichor, "Hide and Seek." See also Kumaraswamy, "China and Israel."
6. For background discussions, see, among others, Abed, "The Palestinians and the Gulf Crisis"; and Adnoni, "The PLO at Crossroads."
7. Under intense U.S. pressure Saudi Arabia modified its stance; until his death in November 2004, Kuwait refused to host the Palestinian leader. The brief reconciliation efforts by the Palestinian leader Faisal al-Husseini in May 2001 ended in a tragedy when he was confronted by Kuwait lawmakers over his presence in Kuwait. Later that night, Husseini died of a heart attack.
8. However, some conservative critics argued that normalization "was not a precondition" for India's association with the peace process. Pradhan, "India's Policy Towards the PLO," 73.
9. Kumaraswamy, "South Asia and Sino-Israeli Diplomatic Relations."
10. Inbar, "The Indian-Israeli Entente," 90.
11. A detailed and provocative discussion can be found in Swamy, "The Secret Friendship Between India and Israel."
12. Joshi, "Changing Equations," 113. According to a former official of the R&AW, shortly after its formation in September 1968, the external-intelligence agency, "with the approval of [Prime Minister] Indira Gandhi, had set up a secret liaison relationship with Mossad." Raman, *The Kaoboys of R&AW*, 127.
13. Raman, *The Kaoboys of R&AW*, 127. Interestingly, this happened just over a year after the June war, when India was vociferously critical of Israel even before the commencement of hostilities.

14. The most senior career diplomat in the Ministry of Foreign Affairs and the equivalent of the permanent undersecretary in the U.S. State Department.
15. J. N. Dixit's interview to *The Week* (February 9, 1992): 37.
16. For example, during the June 1967 war, some opposition members of parliament cried that India was acting like "the fourteenth Arab state."
17. Pradhan, "India's Policy Towards the PLO," 69.
18. Shukla, "Talking Too Much," 40.
19. Pradhan, "India's Policy Towards the PLO," 73. See also Dasgupta, "Betrayal of India's Israel Policy."
20. He was referring to the INC meeting in the southern city of Tirupati in April 1992. Aiyar, "*Chutzpah.*" See also Rubinoff, "Normalization of India-Israel relations."
21. Aiyar, "Panchayati Raj in the Gaza Strip." See also Aiyar, "The Moral Dimension."
22. Agwani, "Inaugural Remarks," 3.
23. Dixit, *My South Block Years*, 311. Interestingly, Arjun Singh subsequently became one of the senior Indian leaders to make an official visit to Israel.
24. Pasha, *India and OIC*, 52–53.
25. Pradhan, "India's Policy Towards the PLO," 81.
26. "Diplomatic Ties with Israel," *Statesman* (New Delhi) (January 31, 1992).
27. Days after the Iraqi invasion, India closed its embassy in Kuwait.
28. Pasha, *India and OIC*, 42. Emphasis added. This is a typical Indian euphemism; at *home* refers to Indian Muslims and *abroad* denotes Arabs.
29. Agwani, *Contemporary West Asia*, 253–254.
30. The absence of relations with Israel since June 1967 prevented the Soviet Union from mediating in the Arab-Israeli conflict.
31. For example, see Dasgupta, "Betrayal of India's Israel Policy," 767–772.
32. At Khartoum, the Arab League enunciated a policy of "no recognition, no negotiation, and no peace" with Israel.
33. Conscious of the Middle Eastern predicaments, India often expressed its willingness to mediate "should both parties so desire."
34. Subsequently, domestic compulsions, especially pressures from the left, resulted in India becoming less vocal regarding civilian deaths in Israel. Hence on July 31, 2006, the Lok Sabha unanimously adopted a partisan resolution on the Lebanese crisis. See http://meaindia.nic.in/pressrelease/2006/07/31pr02.htm.
35. Interestingly, the position was articulated by the communist leader Sitaram Yechuri, who was part of the official delegation to the UN General Assembly. See "Concern Over Israeli Violations of Palestinian Rights," *People's Democracy* (November 20, 2005).
36. In the wake of the publication of the MacDonald White Paper in 1939 that distanced the British government from the Balfour Declaration, the *yishuv* leadership evolved a policy in Mandate Palestine that could be summarized as follows: "To fight the War as if there is no White Paper and to fight the White Paper as if there is no War."

37. Kumaraswamy, "Indo-Israeli Military Ties Enter Next Stage."
38. Among others, see Ghosh, "The Dubious New Alliance"; Cherian, "A Breach of Trust"; and "Firm Up Support to Palestine," editorial, *The Hindu* (May 26, 2005).
39. In November 1995, Finance Minister Manmohan Singh represented India at Rabin's funeral.
40. In his previous role as scientific adviser to the defense minister, Kalam had visited Israel in 1996. Some suggest that he visited Israel just prior to the May 1998 nuclear tests.
41. The final decision was further delayed by bureaucratic procrastination; the first attaché did not arrive until early 1997.
42. For example, during their official visits to Israel in the summer of 2000, both Home Minister L. K. Advani and Foreign Minister Jaswant Singh met Arafat. Israel, which opposed similar moves by other foreign leaders, was accommodating of the Indian requests.
43. During his meeting with the Israeli diplomat Gideon Rafael in New Delhi in 1961, Nehru "paid a few friendly compliments to Israel's technological and scientific progress and its impressive work of technical assistance. He agreed that India and Israel should intensify their cooperation in these fields, commending the success of Israel's experts in the development of water resources in the [Rajasthan] desert." Rafael, *Destination Peace*, 90.
44. Pasha, *India and OIC*, 44.
45. According to Rubinoff, "Normalization of India-Israel Relations," 487, normalization was Rao's symbolic gesture "to distinguish its foreign policy from previous administrations."
46. Dixit, *My South Block Years*; Aiyar, "*Chutzpah*."
47. *India Today* (June 26, 2000).
48. His team included Home Secretary Kamal Pande, Central Bureau of Intelligence (CBI) Chief B. K. Raghavan, Intelligence Bureau (IB) Director Shyamal Dutta, Border Security Force (BSF) Director-General E. N. Rammohan, and Joint Secretary (Home) Vinay Kumar.
49. Karat, "The Bush-Sharon Axis of Evil."
50. Among others, see Cherian, "India's Changing Stand"; and Cherian, "A Breach of Trust."
51. Srinivasan, "India-Israel Tango Gains Pace."
52. For a dated discussion, see Kumaraswamy, *India and Israel*.
53. Lavoy, "India in 2006," 120.
54. Withington, "Israel and India Partner Up," 18–19.
55. *The Hindu* (August 16, 2001).
56. "Nod for Missile Venture with Israel," *The Hindu* (July 13, 2007).
57. *Rajya Sabha*, Unstarred Questions 4481 (May 16, 2007), http://164.100.24.219/rsq/quest.asp?qref=126094.
58. For example, see Inbar, *The Israeli-Turkish Entente*, 40.
59. For an illuminating overall discussion, see Mohan, *Crossing the Rubicon*. On the nuclear question, see Mohan, *Impossible Allies*.

60. For a background discussion on the post–weapons test Indo-U.S. rapprochement, see Talbott, *Engaging India*.
61. Kumaraswamy, "At What Cost Israel-China Ties?"; Kumaraswamy, "Israel-China Relations and the Phalcon Controversy."
62. Within days after its nuclear tests, there were fears that Israel would follow the American lead and suspend all military-related deals. Its dependence upon Washington for political support, economic largess, and strategic commitments circumscribe Israel's ability to pursue an independent arms-export policy. It even cancelled the visit of Chief of Staff Lieutenant General Amnon-Lipkin Shahak, slated for later that month. Gradually, Israel became more understanding of India's compulsion to go nuclear and refrained from joining the international chorus against New Delhi. Within a year, Israel proved to be a reliable friend when it quickly responded to Indian demands for small arms and ammunition during the Kargil war. See Menon and Pandey, "Axis of Democracy?"
63. Ministry of External Affairs, http://meaindia.nic.in/speech/2003/05/08spc01.htm.
64. See Inbar, "The Indian-Israeli Entente," 89–104; and Berman, "Israel, India, and Turkey."
65. It was only in December 2008 that the 1997 Nehru award was formally received by President Mubarak during his state visit to India.
66. Mohan, "India and the Islamic World."
67. This was only superseded by the visit of U.S. President George W. Bush in March 2006, when the leftist parties, for four years part of the ruling coalition, spearheaded massive protests all over India.
68. Surjeet, "Hamas Leader's Assassination."
69. Unlike the decision of Prime Minister Indira Gandhi in 1982 to expel the Israeli consul, this time the government resolved its displeasure quietly, and thus the issue never generated any debate in India. Writing a year later, one commentator observed: "The Palestinian envoy to India, Khalid Sheikh, one of the longest-serving diplomats, was virtually declared *persona non grata* by the NDA government. He was recalled by Arafat under pressure from New Delhi." Cherian, "A Breach of Trust." See also "Israeli Pressure Caused Envoy's Exit, Says NGO," *Khaleej Times* (February 10, 2003).
70. President Abdul Kalam's address to the joint session of Parliament (June 7, 2004), Office of the President of India, New Delhi.
71. Cherian, "A Breach of Trust."

13. Conclusion

1. Quoted in Sudarshan, "Sharon's Stones on Our Heart."

Bibliography

For reasons of brevity and uniformity, abbreviations are used in certain primary sources and the respective abbreviated forms are given in parenthesis. Archival materials are cited as follows:

- Central Zionist Archives, Jerusalem: CZA
- Israel State Archives, Jerusalem: ISA
- National Archives of India, New Delhi: NAI

Primary Materials

Official documents, archival materials, party documents, and autobiographical works.

ADL International Report: India's Campaign Against Israel. New York: Anti-Defamation League of Bnái Brith, 1987.

Asian Relations: Report of the Proceedings and Documents of the First Asian Relations Conference, New Delhi, March–April 1947. New Delhi: Asian Relations Organization, 1948.

Avimor, Shimon, ed. *Relations Between Israel and Asian and African States: A Guide to Selected Documentation.* No. 6, *India.* Jerusalem: Harry S. Truman Research Institute for the Advancement of Peace, 1991.

Aynor, H. S., et al. *Role of the Israeli Labor Movement in Establishing Relations with States of Africa and Asia: Documents, 1948–1975*. Jerusalem: Harry S. Truman Institute for the Advancement of Peace, 1989.

Ben-Gurion Looks Back, In Talks with Moshe Pearlman. London: Weidenfeld & Nicolson, 1965.

Bharatiya Jana Sangh Party Documents, 1951–1972. 5 vols. New Delhi: BJS, 1973.

Buber, Martin, and Judah Magnes. *Two Letters to Gandhi*. Jerusalem: The Bund, 1939.

Chagla, M. C. *Roses in December: An Autobiography*. Bombay: Bharatiya Vidya Bhavan, 1973.

Congress Marches Ahead, January 1996–December 1997. New Delhi: All-India Congress Committee, 1998.

Dayan, Moshe. *Breakthrough: A Personal Account of the Egypt-Israel Peace Negotiations*. London: Weidenfeld & Nicholson, 1981.

Desai, Morarji. *The Story of My Life*. Madras: MacMillian, 1974.

Dixit, J. N. *Assignment Colombo*. New Delhi: Konark, 1998.

——. *My South Block Years: Memoirs of a Foreign Secretary*. New Delhi: UBS, 1996.

Eytan, Walter. *The First Ten Years: A Diplomatic History of Israel*. New York: Simon & Schuster, 1958.

FICCI. *Report of the Indian Delegation to West Asian Countries*. New Delhi, 1975.

Fischer, Louis. *A Week with Gandhi*. New York: Duell, Sloan & Pearce, 1944.

Gandhi, Mohandas Karamchand. *The Collected Works of Mahatma Gandhi*. 90 vols. New Delhi: Publications Division, 1958ff.

Garcia-Granados, Jorge. *The Birth of Israel: The Drama as I Saw It*. New York: Knopf, 1949.

India. [*MEA Report*]. *Annual Report of the Ministry of External Affairs*, 1947–.

——. [*Debates CA*]. *Constituent Assembly Debates*, 1947–1949.

——. [*Debates LS*]. *Debates of India*, 1952–. New Delhi: Lok Sabha Secretariat.

——. [*NAM Documents*]. *Documents of the Gatherings of Non-Aligned Countries, 1961–1979*. New Delhi: Ministry of External Affairs, 1981.

——. *Foreign Policy of India: Texts of Documents, 1947–1964*. New Delhi: Lok Sabha Secretariat, 1966.

——. *India and Palestine: Evolution of a Policy*. New Delhi: Ministry of External Affairs, n.d.

——. *Legislative Assembly Debates, Official Report, Fifth Legislative Assembly*. February 1939.

——. *Monthly Statistics of Foreign Trade of India*. Calcutta: Department of Commercial Intelligence and Statistics, n.d.

——. *Protocol Hand Book*. New Delhi: Ministry of External Affairs, 1965.

——. [*Debates PP*]. *Provisional Parliament Debates*, 1950–1952.

——. [*Debates RS*]. *Rajya Sabha Debates*, 1952–.

——. *Report of Indian Industrialists' Goodwill Delegation to West Asian Countries*. New Delhi: Directorate of Commercial Publicity, n.d.

——. *Suez Canal: A Documentary Study*. New Delhi: Lok Sabha Secretariat, 1956.

——. *Suez Canal: Nationalization and After (July 19–September 13, 1956)*. New Delhi: Lok Sabha Secretariat, 1956.

Israel State Archives and Central Zionist Archives. [*Israel Documents*]. *Documents of the Foreign Policy of the State of Israel*. Jerusalem: Israel Government Press, 1981–.

——. *Political and Diplomatic Documents, December 1947–May 1948*. Jerusalem: Israel Government Press, 1980.

——. *The Suez Canal and the Freedom of the Seas*. Jerusalem: Ministry of Foreign Affairs, 1959.

Jha, C. S. *From Bandung to Tashkent: Glimpses of India's Foreign Policy*. Madras, 1983.

Khalil, Muhammad, ed. *The Arab States and the Arab League: A Documentary Record*. 2 vols. Beirut: Khayats, 1962.

Mathai, M. O. *Reminiscences of the Nehru Age*. New Delhi, 1978.

Meir, Golda. *My Life*. London, 1975.

Nehru, Jawaharlal. *A Bunch of Old Letters*. Bombay: Asia Publishing House, 1958.

——. *Discovery of India*. New Delhi: Jawaharlal Nehru Memorial Fund, 1985.

——. *Eighteen Months in India, 1936–37*. Allahabad, 1938.

——. *Glimpses of World History*. New Delhi: Jawaharlal Nehru Memorial Fund, 1987.

——. *India's Foreign Policy*. New Delhi: Ministry of Information and Broadcasting, 1983.

——. *Letters to Chief Ministers, 1947–1964*. Edited by G. Parthasarathy. New Delhi: Oxford, 1985ff.

——. *Selected Works of Jawaharlal Nehru, Series I*. Edited by S. Gopal. New Delhi: Orient Longman, 1972ff.

——. *Selected Works of Jawaharlal Nehru, Series II*. New Delhi: Jawaharlal Nehru Memorial Fund, 1984ff.

Panikkar, K. M. *In Two Chinas: Memoirs of a Diplomat*. London, 1955.

Pirzada, S. S., ed. *Foundations of Pakistan: All-India Muslim League Documents, 1906–1947*. 2 vols. Karachi: National Publishing House, 1970.

Rafael, Gideon. *Destination Peace: Three Decades of Israeli Foreign Policy—A Personal Memoir*. London: Weidenfeld & Nicholson, 1981.

Reid, Escort. *Envoy to Nehru*. New Delhi: Oxford University Press, 1981.

Report of the Eighth National Conference of the Socialist Party. Bombay, 1950.

Rikhye, Inder Jit. *The Sinai Blunder: Withdrawal of the United Nations Emergency Force Leading to the Six-Day War of June 1967*. New Delhi: Oxford University Press, 1978.

Singh, Gurbachan. "Oral History: India at the Rabat Islamic Summit, 1969." *Indian Foreign Affairs Journal* (New Delhi) 1, no. 2 (April 2006): 105–120.

The Jewish Plan for Palestine: Memorandum and Statements Presented by the Jewish Agency for Palestine to the United Nations Special Committee on Palestine. Jerusalem, 1947.

United Nations. *The Economic Effects of the Closure of the Suez Canal: Study by the Secretariat of UNCTAD*. New York, 1973.

United Nations. *United Nations Special Committee on Palestine: Report to the General Assembly*. 5 vols. New York, 1947.

U.S. State Department. *The Suez Canal Problem, July 26–September 22, 1956*. Washington, 1956.

——. "U.S. Policy of Nonrecognition of Communist China, 1958." *The Department of State Bulletin* 39, no. 1002 (September 8, 1956): 385–390.

Weizmann, Chaim. *Letters and Papers of Chaim Weizmann*. Jerusalem: Israel Universities Press, 1971–.

Zaidi, A. G., and S. G. Zaidi, ed. [*Encyclopedia INC*]. *The Encyclopedia of Indian National Congress*. 25 vols. New Delhi, 1977–.

Secondary Materials

Aaron, Sushil J. *Straddling Faultlines: India's Foreign Policy Towards the Greater Middle East*. CSH Occasional Paper 7. New Delhi: Centre de Sciences Humaines, 2003.

Abed, George T. "The Palestinians and the Gulf Crisis." *Journal of Palestine Studies* 20, no.1 (Winter 1991): 29–42.

Abidi, A. H. H. "India's Policy Towards Muslim States: Approach and Problems." *Problems of Non-Alignment* (New Delhi) 2, no. 2 (June–August 1984): 145–156.

Adnoni, Lamis. "The PLO at Crossroads." *Journal of Palestine Studies* 21, no. 1 (Autumn 1991): 54–65.

Agwani, M. S. *Contemporary West Asia*. New Delhi: Har-Anand, 1995.

——. "The Great Powers and the Partition of Palestine." In *Studies in Politics: National and International*, ed. M. S. Rajan, 348–368. New Delhi: Vikas, 1971.

——. "Inaugural Remarks." In *Postwar Gulf: Implications for India*, ed. K. R. Singh. New Delhi: Lancer, 1993.

——. "India and Palestine." *Man and Development* (Chandigarh), 5. no. 3 (September 1993): 31–37.

——. "India and the Arab World." In *Indian Foreign Policy: The Nehru Years*, ed. B. R. Nanda, 60–70. New Delhi: Vikas, 1976.

——. "India and the Islamic World." In *India and the Islamic World*, ed. Riyaz Punjabi and A. K. Pasha. New Delhi: Radiant, 1998.

——. "India and West Asia." *International Studies* (New Delhi) 5, no. 1 (July–October 1963): 169–171.

——. "Ingredients of India's Arab Policy." *Indian and Foreign Affairs* (New Delhi) 10, no. 12 (April 1, 1973): 12ff.

——. "The Palestine Conflict in Asian Perspective." In *The Transformation of Palestine*, ed. Ibrahim Abu-Lughod, 443–462. Evanston, Ill.: Northwestern University Press, 1971.

——, ed. *Politics in the Gulf*. New Delhi: Vikas, 1978.

——, ed. *The West Asian Crisis, 1967*. Meerut: Meenakshi Prakashan, 1968.

Aiyar, Mani Shankar. "*Chutzpah*." *Sunday* (Calcutta) (June 6, 1993): 14–17.

——. "The Moral Dimension: Kashmir, Palestine, and Bosnia—The Interconnection." *Sunday* (Calcutta) (September 10, 1995): 16–18.

——. "Panchayati Raj in the Gaza Strip." *Sunday* (Calcutta) (September 25, 1993): 16–18.

Akbar, M. J. *Nehru: The Making of India.* London, 1988.

Ali, Tariq. *Can Pakistan Survive? Death of a State.* London, 1983.

Appadorai, A. *Domestic Roots of India's Foreign Policy, 1947–1972.* New Delhi: Oxford University Press, 1981.

——. "The Asian Relations Conference in Perspective." *International Studies* (New Delhi) 16, no. 3 (July–September 1979).

——. "The Bandung Conference." *India Quarterly* (New Delhi) 11, no. 3 (July–September 1955).

Appleton, Shelton. *The Eternal Triangle? Communist China, the United States, and the United Nations.* East Lansing, Mich., 1961.

Baba, Noor Ahmad. *Organisation of Islamic Conference: Theory and Practice of Pan-Islamic Cooperation.* New Delhi, 1994.

Bagchi, Rajiv. "Shalom." *Sunday* (Calcutta) 20, no. 36 (September 5, 1993).

Bahadur, Kalim. "Pakistan as a Factor in Indo-OIC Relations." In *India and the Islamic World,* ed. Riyaz Punjabi and A. K. Pasha. New Delhi: Radiant, 1998.

Bahbah, Bishara A. "Israel's Private Arms Network." *MERIP Middle East Report* 144 (January–February 1987).

Bailey, Sydney D. *The Making of Resolution 242.* Dordrecht: Martinus Nijhoff, 1985.

Bakshi, S. R. *Gandhi and Khilafat.* New Delhi: Gitanjali Publishing House, 1985.

Bandyopadhyaya, J. *The Making of India's Foreign Policy: Determinants, Institutions, Processes, and Personalities.* New Delhi: Allied, 1984.

Banerjee, A. K. "India and West Asia: Changing Images Reflect Shifts in Regional Balance of Power." *Round Table* 305 (1988): 26–38.

Baxter, Craig. *The Jana Sangh: A Biography of an Indian Political Party.* Bombay: Oxford University Press, 1969.

Behbehani, Hashim S. H. *China's Foreign Policy in the Arab World, 1955–1975: Three Case Studies.* London, 1981.

Ben-David, Yohanan. *Indo-Judaic Studies: Some Papers.* New Delhi: Northern Book Centre, 2002.

Ben-Dror, Elad. "The Arab Struggle Against Partition: The International Arena of Summer 1947." *Middle Eastern Studies* 43, no. 2 (March 2007): 259–293.

Bergmann, S. H., and Ya'acov Shimoni. "Report on the Inter-Asian Conference, April 17, 1947." CZA, S25/7485.

Berman, Ilan. "Israel, India, and Turkey: Triple Entente?" *Middle East Quarterly* 9, no. 4 (Fall 2002): 33–40.

Bhadur, Kalim. "Pakistan as a Factor in Indo-OIC Relations." In *India and the Islamic World,* ed. Riyaz Punjabi and A. K. Pasha, 19–26. New Delhi: Radiant, 1998.

Bhagat, Rasheeda. "The Drama and Trauma of Gaza." *Business Line* (Chennai) (August 25, 2005).

Bhambhri, C. P. "Lok Sabha Elections, January 1980: Ideas on Foreign Policy in the Election Manifestos." *International Studies* 19, no. 2 (April–June 1980): 243–252.

Bhargava, G. S., ed. *India and West Asia: A Survey of Public Opinion*. New Delhi: Popular Book Service, 1967.

Bialer, Uri. "The Iranian Connections in Israel's Foreign Policy, 1948–1951." *Middle East Journal* 39, no. 2 (Spring 1985): 292–315.

Bishku, Michael B. "Personalities and Perceptions: Political and Economic Factors Which Led to India's Involvement in the Suez Crisis of 1956." *Journal of South Asian and Middle Eastern Studies* 10, no. 4 (Summer 1987): 17–33.

Blitzer, Wolf. *Territory of Lies*. New York, 1988.

Bloomfield, Louis H. *Egypt, Israel, and the Gulf of Aqaba in International Law*. Toronto, 1957.

Brecher, Michael. *Decisions in Israel's Foreign Policy*. New Haven, Conn.: Yale University Press, 1975.

——. *Foreign Policy Systems of Israel: Setting, Images, Processes*. London: Oxford University Press, 1972.

——. *India and World Politics: Krishna Menon's View of the World*. London, 1968.

——. *Israel, the Korean War, and China: Images, Decisions, and Consequences*. Jerusalem: Institute of Asian and African Studies, 1974.

——. *Nehru: A Political Biography*. London: Oxford University Press, 1959.

——. *The New State of Asia: A Political Analysis*. London: Oxford University Press, 1968.

——. "Israel and China: A Historic 'Missed Opportunity.'" In *Israel in the Third World*, ed. Michael Curtis and Susan Aurelia Gitelson. New Brunswick, N.J.: Transaction Books, 1976.

Burke, S. M. *Mainsprings of Indian and Pakistani Foreign Policies*. Minneapolis, Minn., 1974.

——. *Pakistan's Foreign Policy: An Historical Analysis*. London, 1973.

Caplan, Neil. "The 1956 Sinai Campaign Viewed from Asia: Selections from Moshe Sharett's Diaries." *Israel Studies* 7, no.1 (Spring 2002): 81–103.

Chatterjee, Margaret. *Gandhi and His Jewish Friends*. Houndsmills: Macmillan, 1992.

Chaudhuri, Nirad C. *Thy Hand, Great Anarch, 1921–1952*. London, 1987.

Cherian, John. "A Breach of Trust." *Frontline* (Chennai) (December 4–17, 2004). http://www.frontlineonnet.com/fl2125/stories/20041217000405900.htm.

——. "India's Changing stand", *Frontline* (Chennai) (October 28–November 10, 2000). http://www.frontlineonnet.com/fl1722/17220140.htm.

Chill, Dan S. *The Arab Boycott of Israel: Economic Aggression and World Reaction*. New York, 1976.

Cucciniello, Armand, and Pramit Mitra. "India and Israel Move Closer Together." *South Asia Monitor* (CSIS) 63 (October 1, 2003).

Curtis, Michael, and Susan Aurelia Gitelson, eds. *Israel in the Third World*. New Brunswick, N.J.: Transaction Books, 1976.

Dasgupta, Punyapriya. "Betrayal of India's Israel Policy." *Economic and Political Weekly* (Bombay) 27, no. 15–16 (April 11–18, 1992): 767–772.

Dastur, Aloo J. "India and the West Asian Crisis." *United Asia* 2, no. 1 (January–February 1968).

Decalo, Samuel. "Israel's Foreign Policy and the Third World." *Orbis* 11, no. 3 (Fall 1967): 724–745.

Desch, Michael. "The Myth of Abandonment: The Use and Abuse of the Holocaust Analogy." *Security Studies* 15, no. 1: 106–145.

Dewan, Manorama. *Arabs and Israel: An Indian Interpretation of the Palestine Problem*. New Delhi: Afro-Asian Publications, 1966.

Eayrs, James, ed. *The Commonwealth and Suez: A Documentary Survey*. London: Oxford University Press, 1964.

Eden, Anthony. *Full Circle*. London, 1958.

Edwards, Michael. "Illusions and Reality in Indian Foreign Policy." *International Affairs* 41 (January 1965).

Farnie, Douglas Antony. *East and West of Suez: The Suez Canal History, 1854–1956*. Oxford: Oxford University Press, 1969.

Feiler, Gil. *From Boycott to Economic Cooperation: The Political Economy of the Arab Boycott of Israel*. London: Frank Cass, 1998.

Fischer, Louis. *Gandhi and Stalin: Two Signs at the World's Crossroads*. Delhi: Rajkamal Publications, 1947.

Frisch, Hillel. "Has the Israeli-Palestinian Conflict Become Islamic? Fatah, Islam, and the al-Aqsa Martyrs Brigade." *Terrorism and Political Violence* 17, no. 2 (June 2005).

Gandhi, Arun. *The Morarji Papers: Fall of the Janata Government*. New Delhi, 1983.

Gandhi, Rajmohan. *Eight Lives: A Study of the Hindu-Muslim Encounter*. Albany, N.Y., 1986.

——. *Understanding the Muslim Mind*. New Delhi, 1987.

Gangal, S. C. "Trends in India's Foreign Policy." In *Janata's Foreign Policy*, ed. K. P. Misra. New Delhi, 1979.

Ganguly, Sumit. "India's Foreign Policy Grows Up." *World Policy Journal* 20, no. 4 (Winter 2003–2004).

Ghosh, Jayati. "The Dubious New Alliance." *Frontline* (Chennai) (June 7–20, 2003). http://www.frontlineonnet.com/fl2012/stories/20030620005411900.htm.

Gibb, H. A. R. "The Islamic Congress at Jerusalem in December 1931." In *Survey of International Affairs, 1934*, 99–109. London: Oxford University Press, 1935.

Ginat, Rami. "India and the Palestine Question: The Emergence of the Afro-Asian Bloc and India's Quest for Hegemony in the Postcolonial Third World." *Middle Eastern Studies* 40, no. 6 (November–December 2004): 189–218.

von Glahn, Gerhard. *Law Among Nations: An Introduction to Public International Law*. London, 1970.

Glick, Edward B. *Latin America and the Palestine Problem*. New York, 1958.

Glucklich, Ariel. "Brahmins and Pharisees: The Roots of India's Anti-Zionism." *Midstream* 34, no. 1 (January 1988): 12–15.

Gopal, S. *Jawaharlal Nehru: A Biography.* 3 vols. New Delhi: Oxford University Press, 1979–.

Gordon, Leonard A. "Indian Nationalist Ideas About Palestine and Israel." *Jewish Social Studies* 37, no. 3–4 (Summer–Fall 1975): 221–222.

Gordon, Murray. "Indian-Israeli Relations: Perspective and Promise." *Midstream* 20, no. 9 (November 1971).

Goyal, D. R. and S. Bhutani. *Non-Alignment and the Palestine Question.* New Delhi: League of Arab States Mission, 1985.

Gupta, Amit. *The Diaspora's Political Efforts in the United States.* ORF Occasional Paper. New Delhi, September 2004. http://www.observerindia.com/cms/export/orfonline/modules/occasionalpaper/attachments/op040918_1163398084234.pdf.

Gupta, Sisir. "Moslems in Indian Politics, 1947–60." *India Quarterly* 18, no. 4 (October–December 1962): 355–381.

Hamid, Muhammad. *The Unholy Alliance: Indo-Israel Collaboration Against the Muslim World.* Lahore: Islamic Book Center, 1978.

Harkabi, Yehoshafat. *The Palestinian Covenant and Its Meaning.* London, 1979.

Haron, Miriam Joyce. "The British Decision to Give the Palestine Question to the United Nations." *Middle Eastern Studies* 17, no. 2 (April 1981): 241–248.

Hasan, Mushirul. *Nationalism and Communal Politics in India, 1885–1930.* New Delhi: Manohar, 1994.

——. "To Arafat, in Anguish." *The Hindu* (April 9, 2002).

Hathaway, Robert M., C. Christine Fair, Jalil Roshaandel, Sunil Dasgupta, and P. R. Kumaraswamy. "The 'Strategic Partnership' Between India and Iran." Special Report 120. Asia Program, Woodrow Wilson Center, Washington. April 2004.

Heikal, Mohammed H. *The Cairo Documents: The Inside Story of Nasser and His Relationship with World Leaders, Rebels, and Statesmen.* New York: Doubleday, 1973.

Heimsath, Charles H., and Surjit Mansingh. *A Diplomatic History of Modern India.* New Delhi: Allied, 1971, 1981.

Henderson, Bernard R. *Pollard: The Spy's Story.* New York: Alpha, 1988.

Heptulla, Najma. *Indo-West Asian Relations: The Nehru Era.* New Delhi: Allied, 1991.

Holden, Philip. "Other Modernities: National Autobiography and Globalization." *Biography* 28, no. 1.

Hordes, Jesse N. "Is India Rethinking Its Policy on Israel?" *ADL Bulletin* 46, no. 4 (April 1989): 3–5.

Horowitz, David. *State in the Making.* Trans. Julian Meltzer. New York, 1953.

Inbar, Efraim. *The Israeli-Turkish Entente.* London: King's College, 2001.

——. "The Indian-Israeli Entente." *Orbis* 48, no. 1 (Winter 2004): 89–104.

International Documents on Palestine 1973. Beirut, 1976.

International Energy Agency. *World Energy Outlook, 2005: Middle East and North Africa Insights.* Paris: International Energy Agency.

Iskandar, Marwan. *The Arab Boycott of Israel.* Beirut, 1966.

Israel and the United Nations: Report of a Study Group Set up by the Hebrew University of Jerusalem. New York: Manhattan Publishing Co., 1956.

Jaffer, Ghani. "Brahminic-Talmudist Alliance." *Regional Studies* (Islamabad) 20, no. 2 (Spring 2002): 3–65.

Jaffrelot, Christopher. *The Hindu Nationalist Movement in India.* New York, 1996.

——. "The Idea Exchange." *Indian Express* (April 22, 2007).

Jain, Girilal. "Disillusionment with the Arabs: A Shift in Indian Opinion." *Round Table* 228 (October 1967): 433–438.

Jansen, G. H. *Afro-Asia and Non-Alignment.* London: Faber and Faber, 1966.

——. *Militant Islam.* London, 1980.

——. *Zionism, Israel, and Asian Nationalism.* Beirut: Institute for Palestine Studies, 1971.

Japheth, M. D., and P. K. Rajiv. *The Arab-Israeli Conflict: An Indian Point of View.* Bombay: Pearl Publications, 1967.

Jasse, Richard L. "Great Britain and Palestine Towards the United Nations." *Middle Eastern Studies* 30, no. 3 (July 1994): 558–578.

Jayaramu, P. S. "India and the Gulf Crisis: Pro-Iraq or Pro-India." In *The Gulf in Turmoil: A Global Response,* ed. A. K. Pasha, 148–162. New Delhi, 1992.

Jbara, Taysir. *Palestinian Leader Hajj Amin al-Husayni: Mufti of Jerusalem.* Princeton, N.J., 1968.

Joshi, Manoj. "Changing Equations: The Coming Together of India and Israel." *Frontline* (Chennai) (June 4, 1993).

Prakash Karat, "The Bush-Sharon axis of evil", *People's Democracy,* vol.26, no.18, 12 May 2002.

Khalidi, Walid, ed. *From Heaven to Conquest: Readings in Zionism and the Palestine Problem Until 1948.* Beirut, 1971.

——. "Revisiting the UNGA Partition Resolution." *Journal of Palestine Studies* 27, no. 1 (Autumn 1997): 5–21.

Kimche, Jon. "The Arab Boycott of Israel: New Aspects." *Midstream* 10, no. 3 (September 1964).

Kishore, Mohammed Ali. *Jana Sangh and India's Foreign Policy.* New Delhi: Associated Publishing House, 1969.

Kochan, Ran. "Israel in Third World Forums." In *Israel in the Third World,* ed. Michael Curtis and Susan A. Gitelson, 247–269. New Brunswick, N.J.: Transaction Books, 1976.

Korey, William. "India and Israel: Unmasking a Neutral." *New Leader* 50, no. 15 (July 17, 1967): 6–9.

Kozichi, Richard J. "Indian Policy Towards the Middle East." *Orbis* 11, no. 3 (Fall 1967): 786–797.

——. "Nepal and Israel: Uniqueness in Asian Relations." *Asian Survey* 9, no. 5 (May 1969): 331–342.

Kramer, Martin. *Islam Assembled: The Advent of Muslim Congresses.* New York: Columbia University Press, 1986.

Kumaraswamy, P. R. *Beyond the Veil: Israel-Pakistan Relations.* Memorandum 55. Tel Aviv: Jaffee Center for Strategic Studies, 2000.

——. *The Friendship with Israel: India Squares the Circle*. Singapore: Middle East Institute, 2009.

——. *India and Israel: Evolving Strategic Partnership*. Security and Policy Studies 40. Ramat Gan: BESA Centre for Strategic Studies, 1998.

——. *Israel's New Arch of Friendship: India, Russia, and Turkey*. Dubai: Gulf Research Center, 2005.

——. "At What Cost Israel-China Ties?" *Middle East Quarterly* 13, no. 2 (Spring 2006): 37–44.

——. "China and Israel: Normalization and after." *China Report* (New Delhi) 34, no. 3–4 (July–December 1998): 265–286.

——. "India and Israel: Emerging Partnership." In *India as an Emerging Power*, ed. Sumit Ganguly, 192–206. London: Frank Cass, 2002.

——. "India and Israel: Prelude to Normalization." *Journal of South Asian and Middle Eastern Studies* 19, no. 2 (Winter 1995): 53–73.

——. "India and Israel: The Diplomatic History." In *Indo-Judaic Studies in the Twenty-First Century: A View from the Margin*, ed. Nathan Katz et al., 212–224. New York: Palgrave Macmillan, 2007.

——. "India and the Holocaust: Perceptions of the Indian National Congress." *Journal of Indo-Judaic Studies* 3 (April 2000): 117–125.

——. "India, Israel, and the Davis Cup Tie, 1987." *Journal of Indo-Judaic Studies* 5 (June 2002): 29–39.

——. "India's Recognition of Israel, September 1950." *Middle Eastern Studies* 31, no. 1 (January 1995): 124–138.

——. "Indo-Israeli Military Ties Enter Next Stage." *Security Watch* (Zurich) (August 3, 2007).

——. "Israel and Pakistan: Public Rhetoric Versus Political Pragmatism." *Israel Affairs* 12, no. 1 (January 2006): 123–135.

——. "Israel-China Relations and the Phalcon Controversy." *Middle East Policy* 12, no. 2 (Summer 2005): 93–103.

——. "Israel-India Relations: Seeking Balance and Realism." In *Israel in the International Arena*, ed. Efraim Karsh, 254–272. London: Frank Cass, 2003.

——. "Mahatma Gandhi and the Jewish National Home: An Assessment." *Asian and African Studies* (Haifa) 26, no. 1 (March 1992): 1–13.

——. "Sardar K. M. Panikkar and India-Israel Relations." *International Studies* (New Delhi) 32, no. 3 (July 1995): 327–337.

——. "South Asia and Sino-Israeli Diplomatic Relations." In *China and Israel, 1948–1998: A Fifty-Year Retrospective*, ed. Jonathan Goldstein, 131–152. Westport, Conn.: Praeger, 1999.

——. "The Star and the Dragon: An Overview of Israeli-PRC Military Relations." *Issues and Studies* (Taipei) 30, no. 4 (April 1994): 36–55.

——. "The Strangely Parallel Careers of Israel and Pakistan." *Middle East Quarterly* 4, no. 2 (June 1997): 31–39.

Kupferschmidt, Uri M. "The General Muslim Congress of 1931 in Jerusalem." *Asian and African Studies* (Haifa) 12, no. 1 (March 1978): 123–162.

Lal, Nand. "India and the Withdrawal of the UN Emergency Force, 1967." *International Studies* 13, no. 3 (April–June 1974): 309–323.

Lapidoth, Ruth. *Freedom of Navigation with Special Reference to International Waterways in the Middle East.* Jerusalem, 1975.

Lavoy, Peter R. "India in 2006: A New Emphasis on Engagement." *Asian Survey* 47, no. 1 (January–February 2007).

Lewis, Bernard. *The Jews of Islam.* Princeton, N.J.: Princeton University Press, 1987.

——. "The Anti-Zionist Resolution." *Foreign Affairs* 55, no. 1 (October 1976): 54–64.

Malik, Yogendra K., and V. B. Singh. *Hindu Nationalists in India: The Rise of the Bharatiya Janata Party.* New Delhi: Vistaar, 1994.

Mandel, Neville J. *The Arabs and Zionism Before World War I.* Berkeley, Calif., 1980.

Mansingh, Surjit. *India's Search for Power: Indira Gandhi's Foreign Policy, 1966–1982.* New Delhi: Sage, 1984.

Marwah, Onkar S. "India's Relations with West Asian, North African Countries." *Middle East Information Series* 22 (February 1973): 21–27.

Maxwell, Neville. *India's China War.* Bombay, 1970.

Medzini, Meron. "Reflections on Israel's Asian policy." In *Israel in the Third World*, ed. Michael Curtis and Susan Aurelia Gitelson, 200–211. New Brunswick, N.J.: Transaction, 1976. Originally published in *Midstream* 18, no. 6 (June–July 1972): 25–35.

Mehrish, B. N. *India's Recognition Policy Towards New Nations.* New Delhi: Oriental Publishers, 1972.

——. "Recognition of the Palestine Liberation Organization (PLO): An Appraisal of India's Policy." *Indian Journal of Political Science* (Chandigarh) 36, no. 2 (April–June 1975): 137–160.

Menon, Kesava. "U.S. Politics Impinges on West Asian Situation." *The Hindu* (August 9, 2000).

Menon, Rajan, and Swati Pandey. "Axis of Democracy? The Uncertain Future of Israeli-Indian Relations." *National Interest* (Summer 2005). http://findarticles.com/p/articles/mi_m2751/is_80/ai_n15696639/print.

Meo, Leila, et al. *The Arab Boycott of Israel.* Shrewsbury, Mass., 1976.

Merari, Ariel, and Ahlomi Elad. *The International Dimensions of Palestinian Terrorism.* Jerusalem, 1986.

Minault, Gail. *The Khilafat Movement: Religious Symbolism and Political Mobilization in India.* New Delhi: Oxford University Press, 1999.

Mishra, K. P. *India's Policy of Recognition of States and Governments.* Bombay: Allied, 1966.

——. "India and the Status of Aqaba and Tiran." *International Problems* (Tel Aviv) 13, no. 1–2 (January 1974): 283–290.

Mohan, C. Raja. *Crossing the Rubicon: The Shaping of India's New Foreign Policy.* New Delhi, 2003.

——. *Impossible Allies: Nuclear India, the United States, and the Global Order.* New Delhi, 2006.

——. "India and the Islamic World." *The Hindu* (April 12, 2001). http://www.hinduonnet.com/2001/04/12/stories/05122523.htm.

Mohan, Jitendra. "India, Pakistan, Suez, and the Commonwealth." *International Journal* 15, no. 3 (Summer 1960): 185–199.

Mohanty, N. R. "Jewish Leader Finds Rao Pragmatic." *Times of India* (November 23, 1991).

Mudiam, Prithvi Ram. *India and the Middle East.* London, British Academy Press, 1994.

Musa, Salama. *The Education of Salama Musa.* Trans. L. O. Schuman. Leiden, 1961.

Nachmani, Amikam. *Israel, Turkey, and Greece: Uneasy Relations in the East Mediterranean.* London, 1987.

Nanda, B. R. *Gandhi: Pan-Islamism, Imperialism and Nationalism in India.* Bombay: Oxford University Press, 1989.

Navari, Cornelia. "Arnold Toynbee (1889–1975): Prophecy and Civilization." *Review of International Studies* 26 (2000).

Neimeijer, A. C. *The Khilafat Movement in India, 1919–1924.* The Hague: Martinus Nijhoff, 1972.

Noorani, A. G. "Palestine and Israel." *Frontline* (Chennai) 18, no. 14 (July 7–20, 2001). http://www.frontlineonnet.com/fl1814/18140760.htm.

——. "Rabat: Religion and Diplomacy." *Indian Express* (December 4, 1969).

Nuri, Maqsudul Hasan. "The Indo-Israeli Nexus." *Regional Studies* (Islamabad) 12, no. 3 (Summer 1994): 3–54.

Obeita, Joseph A. *The International Status of the Suez Canal.* The Hague, 1960.

Padmanabhan, L. K. "India, Israel, and the Arab World." *International Problems* 14, no. 1–2 (February 1975): 11–14.

Palestine: A Symposium (New Delhi: League of Arab States Mission, 1969).

Parakatil, Francis. *India and the United Nations Peace Keeping Operations.* New Delhi, 1975.

Pasha, A. K. *India and OIC: Strategy and Diplomacy.* New Delhi: Centre for Peace Studies, n.d.

Perlmutter, Amos, Michael I. Handel, and Uri Bar-Joseph. *Two Minutes Over Baghdad.* London, 1982.

Pirzada, S. S. "Pakistan and the OIC." *Pakistan Horizon* 40, no. 2 (1987): 14–38.

Porath, Yehoshua. "Al-Hajj Amin al-Husayni, Mufti of Jerusalem: His Rise to Power and the Consolidation of His Position." *Asian and African Studies* (Haifa) 7 (1971).

Pradhan, Bansidhar. "Changing Dynamics of India's West Asia Policy." *International Studies* (New Delhi) 41, no. 1 (January–March 2004): 1–88.

——. "India's Policy Towards the PLO." In *India and the Islamic World,* ed. Riyaz Punjabi and A. K. Pasha, 65–83. New Delhi: Radiant, 1998.

——. "Seeking Clarity in Arafat's Message." *Link* 34, no. 25 (February 2, 1992).

Prittie, Terence, and Walter Henry Nelson. *The Economic War Against the Jews.* London, 1977.

Qureshi, Khalil. "Indo-Israeli Tie Against Muslims." *Frontier Post* (May 5, 1992).
Quraishi, Z. M. *Liberal Nationalism of Egypt: Rise and Fall of the Wafd Party*. Allahabad, 1967.
Raman, B. *The Kaoboys of R&AW: Down Memory Lane*. New Delhi, 2007.
Ramana Murti, V. V. "Buber's Dialogue and Gandhi's Satyagraha." *Journal of History of Ideas* 29, no. 4 (October–December 1968).
Reddy, T. Ramakrishna. *India's Policy in the United Nations*. Rutherford, 1996.
Rikhye, Inder Jit. "Dayan, Desai, and South Africa." *Tribune* (Chandigarh) (May 27, 1980).
Robinson, Jacob. *Palestine and the United Nations: Prelude to Solution*. Washington: Pubic Affairs Press, 1947.
Rose, Norman Anthony. *The Gentile Zionists: A Study of Anglo-Zionist Diplomacy, 1929–1939*. London, 1973.
Rubinoff, Arthur G. "Normalisation of India-Israel Relations: Stillborn for Forty Years." *Asian Survey* 35, no. 5 (May 1995): 487–505.
Sareen, Tilak Raj. "Indian Responses to the Holocaust." In *Jewish Exile in India, 1933–1945*, ed. Anil Bhatti and Johannes H. Voigt. New Delhi: Manohar, 1999.
Sarna, Aaron J. *Boycott and Blacklist: A History of Arab Economic Warfare Against Israel*. Totowa, N.J., 1986.
Schechtman, Joseph B. *The Mufti and the Fuehrer: The Rise and Fall of Hajj Amin el-Hussein*. New York, 1965.
——. "India and Israel." *Midstream* 12, no. 7 (August–September 1966): 48–61.
Selak, Charles B. "A Consideration of the Legal Status of the Gulf of Aqaba." In *The Arab-Israeli Conflict*, ed. John Norton Moore. Princeton, N.J.: Princeton University Press, 1972.
Sengupta, Bhabani. *Rajiv Gandhi: A Political Study*. New Delhi, 1989.
Shah, Mehtab Ali. *The Foreign Policy of Pakistan: Ethnic Impacts on Diplomacy, 1971–1994*. London, 1997.
Shaikh, Farzana. "Muslims and Political Representation in Colonial India: The Making of Pakistan." *Modern Asian Studies* (July 1986).
Shichor, Yitzhak. *East Wind Over Arabia: Origins and Implications of the Sino-Saudi Missile Deal*. Berkeley, Calif., 1989.
——. "Hide-and-Seek: Sino-Israeli Relations in Perspective." *Israel Affairs* 1, no. 2 (Winter 1994): 16–35.
——. "Israel's Military Transfer to China and Taiwan." *Survival* 40, no. 1 (Spring 1998).
Shimoni, Gideon. *Gandhi, Satyagraha, and the Jews: A Formative Factor in India's Policy Towards Israel*. Jerusalem: Leonard Davis Institute for International Relations, 1977.
Shlaim, Avi. "The Rise and Fall of the All-Palestine Government in Gaza." *Journal of Palestine Studies* 20, no.1 (Autumn 1990): 37–53.
Shourie, Arun. *Only Fatherland*. New Delhi: South Asia Books, 1991.
Shukla, Rajiv. "Talking Too Much." *Sunday* (June 13, 1993).
Silverburg, Sanford R. "Pakistan and the West Bank: A Research Note." *Middle Eastern Studies* 19, no. 2 (1983): 261–263.

Singh, K. R. "India and the Crisis." In *The West Asian Crisis, 1967*, ed. M. S. Agwani. Meerut, India, 1968.

——. "India and WANA." *International Studies* 17, no. 2–4 (July–December 1978): 625–637.

——. "Subcontinent and WANA Countries." In *The Himalayan Subcontinent: Emerging Patterns*, ed. Dev Dutt, 101–116. New Delhi, 1972.

——, ed. *Postwar Gulf: Implications for India*. New Delhi: Lancer, 1993.

Singh, Surjit. "Indo-Israel Relations: A Study of Some Aspects of India's Foreign Policy." *Journal of Indian History* 57, no. 2–3 (August–December 1979): 387–399.

Somaratna, G. P. V. "Renewal of Ties Between Sri Lanka and Israel." *Jerusalem Journal of International Relations* 11, no. 1 (1989): 74–86.

——. "Sri Lanka's Relations with Israel." In *External Compulsions of South Asian Politics*, ed. Shelton U. Kodikara, 194–225. New Delhi: Sage, 1993.

Soz, Saifuddhin. "The OIC and Indian Muslims." In *India and the Islamic World*, ed. Riyaz Punjabi and A. K. Pasha. New Delhi: Radiant, 1998.

Srinivasan, G. "India-Israel Tango Gains Pace." *Business Line* (August 20, 2007).

Srivastava, R. K. "India-Israel Relations." *Indian Journal of Political Science* 31, no. 3 (July–September 1970): 238–264.

Stein, Leonard. *The Balfour Declaration*. London, 1961.

Student of West Asian Affairs. *India and Palestine: A Reply*. New Delhi: Society for Parliamentary Studies, n.d.

Sudarshan, V. "Sharon's Stones on Our Heart." *Outlook* (New Delhi) (September 15, 2003). http://www.outlookindia.com/fullprint.asp?choice=2&fodname=20030915&fname=Indo+Israel&sid=1.

Surjeet, Harkishan Singh. "Hamas Leader's Assassination." *People's Democracy* (March 28, 2004).

Swamy, Subramaniam. "The Secret Friendship Between India and Israel." *Sunday* (November 28, 1982): 18–24.

Syed, Ayub. *India and the Arab World*. New Delhi: Orient Publishers, 1965.

Talbott, Strobe. *Engaging India: Diplomacy, Democracy, and the Bomb*. Washington, 2004.

Teslik, Kennan Lee. *Congress, the Executive Branch, and the Special Interests: The American Response to the Arab Boycott of Israel*. Westport, Conn.,1982.

Toynbee, Arnold. "Jewish Rights in Palestine." *Jewish Quarterly Review* 52, no. 1 (July 1961): 1–11.

Vanaik, Achin. "Making India Strong: The BJP-led Government's Foreign Policy Perspectives." *South Asia* 25, no. 3 (2002).

Varadarajan, Siddharth. "When Jaswant Took Indian Politics to Foreign Shores." *The Hindu* (September 16, 2005).

Waggonner, Joe D. *The So-Called New Era of Ping-Pong Diplomacy with Communist China* (Washington: Government Printing Office, 1971).

Ward, Richard Edmund. *India's Pro-Arab Policy: A Study in Continuity*. Westport, Conn.: Praeger, 1992.

Wilson, Evan M. *Decision on Palestine: How the United States Came to Recognize Israel*. Stanford, Calif., 1979.

Withington, Thomas. "Israel and India Partner Up." *Bulletin of the Atomic Scientists* 57, no. 2 (January–February 2001): 18–19.

Wright, Theodore P., "Ethnic Groups' Pressures in Foreign Policy: Indian Muslims and American Jews." *Economic and Political Weekly* 17, no. 40 (October 1982): 1655–1660.

——. "Indian Muslims and Middle East." *Journal of South Asian and Middle Eastern Studies* 6, no. 1 (Fall 1982): 48–56.

Ye'or, Bat. *The Dhimmi: Jews and Christians Under Islam*. Cranbury, N.J.: Associated University Presses, 1985.

——. *Islam and Dhimmitude: Where Civilizations Collide*. Cranbury, N.J.: Associated University Presses, 2002.

Yegar, Moshe. "Israel in Asia." *Jerusalem Quarterly* 18 (Winter 1981): 15–28.

Zaidi, A. M. *Evolution of Muslim Political Thought in India*. Vol. 2: *Sectarian Nationalism and Khilafat*. New Delhi, 1975.

Zangwill, Israel. "The Return to Palestine." *New Liberal Review* 2 (1901).

Index